Preventing Bullying Among Children With Special Educational Needs

Sohni Siddiqui
Technische Universität Berlin, Germany

Mahwish Kamran
Iqra University, Karachi, Pakistan

Vice President of Editorial	Melissa Wagner
Managing Editor of Acquisitions	Mikaela Felty
Managing Editor of Book Development	Jocelynn Hessler
Production Manager	Mike Brehm
Cover Design	Phillip Shickler

Published in the United States of America by
IGI Global Scientific Publishing
701 East Chocolate Avenue
Hershey, PA, 17033, USA
Tel: 717-533-8845
Fax: 717-533-8661
E-mail: cust@igi-global.com
Website: https://www.igi-global.com

Copyright © 2025 by IGI Global Scientific Publishing. All rights reserved. No part of this publication may be reproduced, stored or distributed in any form or by any means, electronic or mechanical, including photocopying, without written permission from the publisher.
Product or company names used in this set are for identification purposes only. Inclusion of the names of the products or companies does not indicate a claim of ownership by IGI Global Scientific Publishing of the trademark or registered trademark.

Library of Congress Cataloging-in-Publication Data

Names: Siddiqui, Sohni, 1985- editor. | Kamran, Mahwish, 1979- editor.
Title: Preventing bullying among children with special educational needs /
   Edited by Sohni Siddiqui, Mahwish Kamran.
Description: Hershey, PA : IGI Global Scientific Publishing, [2025] |
   Includes bibliographical references and index. | Summary: "This book
   delves into the strategies employed by schools or institutions to
   address these regrettable instances of bullying involving children with
   special needs. It also explores the current global status of bullying
   and the interventions implemented to counteract such occurrences"--
   Provided by publisher.
Identifiers: LCCN 2024053195 (print) | LCCN 2024053196 (ebook) | ISBN
   9798369353158 (hardcover) | ISBN 9798369353165 (paperback) | ISBN
   9798369353172 (ebook)
Subjects: LCSH: Children with disabilities--Education. | Bullying in
   schools--Prevention. | Special education. | Inclusive education.
Classification: LCC LC4015 .P653 2025 (print) | LCC LC4015 (ebook) | DDC
   371.9--dc23/eng/20241214
LC record available at https://lccn.loc.gov/2024053195
LC ebook record available at https://lccn.loc.gov/2024053196
ISBN:979-8-3693-5315-8
eISBN:979-8-3693-5317-2

British Cataloguing in Publication Data
A Cataloguing in Publication record for this book is available from the British Library.

All work contributed to this book is new, previously-unpublished material.
The views expressed in this book are those of the authors, but not necessarily of the publisher.
This book contains information sourced from authentic and highly regarded references, with reasonable efforts made to ensure the reliability of the data and information presented. The authors, editors, and publisher believe the information in this book to be accurate and true as of the date of publication. Every effort has been made to trace and credit the copyright holders of all materials included. However, the authors, editors, and publisher cannot assume responsibility for the validity of all materials or the consequences of their use. Should any copyright material be found unacknowledged, please inform the publisher so that corrections may be made in future reprints.

Table of Contents

Preface xi

Chapter 1
Academic, Emotional, and Social Consequences of Bullying on Special
Needs Students 1
    Fareeha Syeda Ziyan, Centre of Inclusive Care, Pakistan
    Aisha Kadri, GEMS Winchester School, Dubai, UAE

Chapter 2
An Analysis of the Cultural and Social Dimensions of Bullying Among
Pakistani Children With Special Educational Needs 35
    Kefayat Ullah, Quaid-i-Azam University, Islamabad, Pakistan
    Sadia Saeed, Quaid-i-Azam University, Islamabad, Pakistan

Chapter 3
Bullying and Neurodiverse Adolescents: Mapping Review and Implications..... 65
    Victoria Maria Ribeiro Lembo, Pontifical Catholic University of
        Campinas, Brazil
    Tatiana de Cássia Nakano, Pontifical Catholic University of Campinas,
        Brazil
    Wanderlei Abadio de Oliveira, Pontifical Catholic University of
        Campinas, Brazil

Chapter 4
Bullying Faced by Children With Special Needs in Pakistan: Challenges,
Interventions, and Societal Implications for Educational Inclusion 93
    Afaf Manzoor, University of Education, Lahore, Pakistan
    Muhammad Usman Khalid, University of Education, Lahore, Pakistan
    Asifa Rashid, University of Education, Lahore, Pakistan

Chapter 5
Collaboration Between Parents, Children With Disabilities, and School
Personnel: A Key Component of School-Based Bullying Prevention 125
    Hannah Rapp, University at Buffalo, SUNY, USA
    Julianna Casella, University at Buffalo, SUNY, USA
    Amanda Nickerson, University at Buffalo, SUNY, USA

Chapter 6
Fostering Inclusion and Safety: A Case Study of Anti-Bullying Practices at
the Praxis Inclusive School 155
    Mahwish Kamran, Iqra University, Pakistan
    Sohni Siddiqui, Technische Universität Berlin, Germany

Chapter 7
Lifting the Veil: Exploring Bullying Towards Students With Special Needs in
Inclusive Settings 185
    Marie Gomez Goff, Southeastern Louisiana University, USA

Chapter 8
Peer Bullying of Inclusion Students: Understanding Prevention and
Intervention Strategies 215
    Sahin Cincioglu, Trakya University, Turkey

Chapter 9
Practical Interventions to Address Bullying and Support Students With
Special Educational Needs 249
    Afroditi Malisiova, Aristotle University of Thessaloniki, Greece
    Vasiliki Folia, Aristotle University of Thessaloniki, Greece

Chapter 10
Relations Among Perceived Peer Acceptance, Fear of Missing Out, and
Cyberbullying: A Comparative Study Between Elementary School Students
Without and With High Functioning ASD 279
    Thanos Touloupis, University of the Aegean, Greece
    Anastasia Alevriadou, Aristotle University of Thessaloniki, Greece
    Asimenia Papoulidi, University of West Attica, Greece

Compilation of References 303

About the Contributors 379

Index 385

Detailed Table of Contents

Preface xi

Chapter 1
Academic, Emotional, and Social Consequences of Bullying on Special
Needs Students 1
   Fareeha Syeda Ziyan, Centre of Inclusive Care, Pakistan
   Aisha Kadri, GEMS Winchester School, Dubai, UAE

This chapter explores the profound impact of bullying on students with SEN, highlighting both academic and social-emotional consequences. SEN students, particularly those with learning disabilities, face significantly higher rates of bullying compared to their neurotypical peers. This victimization leads to severe academic repercussions, including decreased concentration, lower grades, and reduced engagement in school activities. Socially and emotionally, bullying results in heightened levels of anxiety, depression, and social withdrawal, with long-term implications for mental health. A comprehensive literature review, as well as case studies, illustrate the detrimental effects of bullying on academic performance and social-emotional well-being of SEN students, emphasizing the urgent need for effective interventions and support strategies. By examining the interconnected nature of these consequences, this chapter highlights the necessity of comprehensive approaches and identifies relevant interventions to create safer, more inclusive educational environments for students with SEN.

Chapter 2
An Analysis of the Cultural and Social Dimensions of Bullying Among
Pakistani Children With Special Educational Needs 35
   Kefayat Ullah, Quaid-i-Azam University, Islamabad, Pakistan
   Sadia Saeed, Quaid-i-Azam University, Islamabad, Pakistan

In this study, we examined the social and cultural factors causing bullying of children with special needs, particularly in the socio-cultural context of Pakistan. Despite the global attention on bullying, there remains a significant gap in understanding how cultural norms, social stigmas, and community attitudes affect bullying among children with special needs in Pakistan. This study aims to fill this gap. The study analyzed multiple research studies including research papers, academic articles, books, reports, and policy analyses to examine the different dimensions of bullying of children with special needs in Pakistan. The study findings reveal that embedded cultural norms and social stigmas contribute significantly to the increasing cases of bullying. Community attitudes, lack of awareness, and inadequate anti-bullying policies further aggravate this issue. The insights gained from this study can inform policies that focus on culturally sensitive and inclusive anti-bullying strategies to provide friendlier and more conducive learning environment for all children.

Chapter 3
Bullying and Neurodiverse Adolescents: Mapping Review and Implications..... 65
    Victoria Maria Ribeiro Lembo, Pontifical Catholic University of
        Campinas, Brazil
    Tatiana de Cássia Nakano, Pontifical Catholic University of Campinas,
        Brazil
    Wanderlei Abadio de Oliveira, Pontifical Catholic University of
        Campinas, Brazil

This chapter aims to review the literature on bullying among adolescents with neurodiversity, to determine the prevalence and characteristics of such dynamics among this population. This is a mapping review, and the study search procedures were applied to three databases (SCOPUS, PubMed, and Web of Science). As a result of the entire analysis and selection process, 14 articles were included in the analytical corpus. The articles identified revealed the complexity of the variables and specificities involved in the relationships about bullying and neurodiversity. The findings reveal that students diagnosed with attention deficit hyperactivity disorder and autism spectrum disorder are more frequently involved in bullying situations compared to their neurotypical peers. The chapter, according to the authors, offers some implications for considering care practices in school psychology for neurodivergent adolescents.

Chapter 4
Bullying Faced by Children With Special Needs in Pakistan: Challenges, Interventions, and Societal Implications for Educational Inclusion 93
    Afaf Manzoor, University of Education, Lahore, Pakistan
    Muhammad Usman Khalid, University of Education, Lahore, Pakistan
    Asifa Rashid, University of Education, Lahore, Pakistan

The proposed book chapter aims to landscape the case of children with special needs in Pakistan who are victims of persistent bullying and are at high risk of being targeted for facing discrimination due to differences in their physical appearance, communication challenges and social interactions. Based on empirical research and theoretical frameworks, the book chapter consists of five sections; the first section will conceptualize the understanding about the bully and its type, the second section narrates the state of bullying in Pakistan and the challenges of children with special needs within the community and schools. The third section is based on the review of legislation to protect against bullying and support prevention. The fourth section shares the findings of a study conducted as part of this chapter to explore the perspectives of teachers on their knowledge and understanding of bullying and its impact on children with special needs. The final section of the chapter presents the recommendations.

Chapter 5
Collaboration Between Parents, Children With Disabilities, and School
Personnel: A Key Component of School-Based Bullying Prevention 125
    Hannah Rapp, University at Buffalo, SUNY, USA
    Julianna Casella, University at Buffalo, SUNY, USA
    Amanda Nickerson, University at Buffalo, SUNY, USA

School-aged children with disabilities face heightened rates of bullying victimization compared to their typically developing peers. This chapter emphasizes the important role that parents of children with disabilities play in bullying prevention and intervention. First, school-based interventions for reducing bullying victimization among children with disabilities, such as inclusion, social-emotional learning, and multi-component programming, are reviewed. Furthermore, this chapter reviews recommendations for how parents can engage in communication with their child regarding bullying and strategies to help children with disabilities develop skills for handling such situations. Guidelines are provided for parents who seek to report bullying incidents to school personnel. This chapter also outlines helpful responses to bullying by school personnel as perceived by parents of children with disabilities. Lastly, this chapter explores considerations for schools and parents when supporting children with disabilities who are both bullied and bully others.

Chapter 6
Fostering Inclusion and Safety: A Case Study of Anti-Bullying Practices at
the Praxis Inclusive School 155
    Mahwish Kamran, Iqra University, Pakistan
    Sohni Siddiqui, Technische Universität Berlin, Germany

While inclusive education is a cornerstone of contemporary civil rights movements, concerns persist among educators regarding the widespread placement of students with learning disabilities (LD) in mainstream classrooms. One of the most compelling reasons for this apprehension is the potential for increased bullying incidents in inclusive settings. This chapter delves into the experiences of bullying faced by children with LD in inclusive environments and explores strategies for fostering safe and secure classrooms. It further examines pedagogical practices that can equip teachers to effectively manage the learning needs of both students with LD and their typically developing peers. The chapter's primary objective is to present the findings from a case study conducted within an inclusive school in Pakistan. It analyzes how the pedagogical practices adopted by this specific school can be leveraged to promote the inclusion of children with LD by mitigating bullying and fostering greater educational equity.

Chapter 7
Lifting the Veil: Exploring Bullying Towards Students With Special Needs in
Inclusive Settings 185
    Marie Gomez Goff, Southeastern Louisiana University, USA

This chapter is about bullying towards students with special needs in inclusive educational settings. By examining the various forms of bullying that these students may encounter, including physical aggression, verbal abuse, social exclusion, cyber harassment, mistreatment by teachers and staff, and the intersectionality of discrimination, this segment aims to illuminate the complexities and challenges faced by this vulnerable population. The chapter also explores the prevalence, impact, and contributing factors of bullying, emphasizing the urgent need for targeted interventions and prevention strategies. By fostering a deeper understanding of the dynamics of bullying towards students with special needs, educators, policymakers, and stakeholders can work collaboratively to create safe, inclusive environments where every student is valued, respected, and supported in their academic and social development. This chapter underscores the importance of addressing bullying in inclusive educational settings as a critical step towards promoting empathy, inclusivity, and equity for all students with special needs.

Chapter 8
Peer Bullying of Inclusion Students: Understanding Prevention and
Intervention Strategies 215
    Sahin Cincioglu, Trakya University, Turkey

Students in inclusive education settings are at greater risk of being bullied because of their special needs. Bullying can manifest itself in harmful behaviors that negatively impact these students socially, emotionally, or physically. At the heart of peer bullying is a power imbalance, and research shows that students with special needs are more likely to be bullied than their peers without disabilities. To address this, a comprehensive strategy involving all stakeholders is essential to understand, prevent, and respond to bullying of students in inclusive settings. Recognizing the signs and effects of peer bullying on these students is critical. To effectively prevent bullying, schools must implement programs that promote tolerance and empathy and ensure a safe, inclusive environment for all students.

Chapter 9
Practical Interventions to Address Bullying and Support Students With
Special Educational Needs 249
    Afroditi Malisiova, Aristotle University of Thessaloniki, Greece
    Vasiliki Folia, Aristotle University of Thessaloniki, Greece

The number of bullying incidents in school environments worldwide has increased rapidly over the past few decades undermining and obstructing the creation of inclusive classrooms in which all students feel appreciated, respected, and welcome. Despite increased awareness and efforts of the stakeholders, including educators, psychologists, parents, and students to combat and mitigate bullying, it remains a persistent problem, constantly deteriorating and seeking victims among whom students with Special Educational Needs (SEN) constitute the majority. The present chapter, drawing upon a narrative literature review, will delve into the various forms and expressions of bullying toward all students while focusing on children with SEN since they are more frequently victimized. It aims to highlight the underlying causes and the far-reaching effects and to suggest effective solutions, strategies, and antibullying interventions to address this critical problem by underscoring the significance of school counseling in promoting respect, empathy, interaction, and collaboration among students.

Chapter 10
Relations Among Perceived Peer Acceptance, Fear of Missing Out, and
Cyberbullying: A Comparative Study Between Elementary School Students
Without and With High Functioning ASD 279
    Thanos Touloupis, University of the Aegean, Greece
    Anastasia Alevriadou, Aristotle University of Thessaloniki, Greece
    Asimenia Papoulidi, University of West Attica, Greece

The present chapter presents a study which investigated comparatively cyberbullying (as victims/bullies) between students without and with high functioning ASD. Also, the contributing role of perceived peer acceptance and FoMO was examined. Overall, 252 students without (53% boys) and 239 students with high functioning ASD (63% boys) of fifth and sixth grades of Greek elementary schools completed a related self-report scales. The results showed that both male and female students with high functioning ASD engage in cyberbullying (as victims/bullies) to a greater extent than their typically developing peers. Additionally, in the relationship between perceived peer acceptance and cyberbullying involvement FoMO proved a full mediator for typically developing students and a partial mediator for students with high functioning ASD. The findings imply the intensification of cyberbullying prevention actions in elementary education, especially for students with ASD, which could be enriched with experiential activities aimed at strengthening face to face peer relationships.

Compilation of References 303

About the Contributors 379

Index 385

Preface

Bullying remains a pervasive and deeply concerning issue in education systems worldwide, affecting students across various social, cultural, and developmental contexts. For children with special educational needs (SEN), the impact of bullying is often more profound, as they face unique vulnerabilities related to their learning, social, and emotional development. These students are frequently subjected to higher rates of bullying than their neurotypical peers, leading to significant academic, psychological, and social consequences. This issue is further compounded in inclusive education environments, where students with SEN are integrated into mainstream classrooms, often without adequate support structures to ensure their protection.

Preventing Bullying Among Children with Special Educational Needs offers a comprehensive examination of the nature, causes, and consequences of bullying experienced by SEN students. This volume delves into the cultural, social, and systemic factors that contribute to bullying and provides evidence-based interventions, strategies, and recommendations to foster safer, more inclusive educational environments. Through research-driven insights and practical solutions, this book serves as a crucial resource for educators, parents, policymakers, and researchers dedicated to promoting equity, empathy, and respect for all students.

The chapters in this book represent a wide range of perspectives and experiences from contributors around the world. Their collective efforts emphasize the need for a multi-stakeholder approach to address bullying, involving educators, parents, policymakers, and mental health professionals. From exploring the role of school-based interventions and collaboration with parents to examining case studies in specific cultural contexts like Pakistan, this book addresses bullying through a global and inclusive lens. Each chapter builds on the previous one, providing readers with a holistic understanding of the challenges faced by students with SEN and the systemic changes needed to create a more inclusive education system.

CHAPTER OVERVIEWS

Chapter 1: *Academic, Emotional, and Social Consequences of Bullying on Special Needs Students* examines the adverse academic, emotional, and social consequences of bullying for students with special needs. The chapter highlights the urgent need for schools to implement evidence-based interventions that support these students academically and emotionally.

Chapter 2: *An Analysis of the Cultural and Social Dimensions of Bullying Among Pakistani Children with Special Educational Needs* explores the role of cultural norms, social stigmas, and community attitudes in shaping the bullying experiences of SEN children in Pakistan. This chapter calls for culturally sensitive anti-bullying strategies and policy reforms to foster more inclusive learning environments.

Chapter 3: *Bullying and Neurodiverse Adolescents – Mapping Review and Implications* presents a mapping review of studies on bullying experienced by neurodiverse adolescents, including those with ADHD and Autism Spectrum Disorder (ASD). This chapter highlights the complexity of bullying among neurodivergent students and offers school psychology implications for better support and intervention.

Chapter 4: *Bullying Faced by Children with Special Needs in Pakistan: Challenges, Interventions, and Societal Implications for Educational Inclusion* addresses the specific challenges of bullying faced by children with SEN in Pakistan. It outlines key findings from a study on teachers' perspectives regarding bullying and offers policy recommendations to protect these vulnerable students.

Chapter 5: *Collaboration Between Parents, Children with Disabilities, and School Personnel: A Key Component of School-Based Bullying Prevention* emphasizes the critical role of parents in school-based bullying prevention. The chapter outlines strategies for parent-school collaboration, as well as communication techniques that support children with disabilities in addressing bullying incidents.

Chapter 6: *Fostering Inclusion and Safety – A Case Study of Anti-Bullying Practices at The Praxis Inclusive School* presents a case study from an inclusive school in Pakistan, examining how anti-bullying practices can be leveraged to create safer learning environments for children with learning disabilities (LD). This chapter explores how inclusive pedagogical practices can support both students with learning disabilities and their neurotypical peers.

Chapter 7: *Lifting the Veil: Exploring Bullying Towards Students with Special Needs in Inclusive Settings* explores the multifaceted nature of bullying towards SEN students in inclusive educational settings. The chapter identifies different forms of bullying, including physical aggression, verbal abuse, and cyber harassment, and provides recommendations for fostering safe, inclusive learning environments.

Chapter 8: *Peer Bullying of Inclusion Students: Understanding Prevention and Intervention Strategies* examines the unique bullying dynamics that affect students with special needs in inclusive educational environments. It underscores the critical role of empathy-building initiatives, tolerance-promoting activities, and school-wide anti-bullying campaigns.

Chapter 9: *Practical Interventions to Address Bullying and Support Students with Special Educational Needs* explores various school-based interventions and support mechanisms that can reduce bullying against SEN students. It highlights the importance of school counseling and multi-stakeholder collaboration to foster inclusive, bully-free learning spaces.

Chapter 10: *Relations Among Perceived Peer Acceptance, Fear of Missing Out, and Cyberbullying: A Comparative Study Between Elementary School Students Without and With High-Functioning ASD* focuses on the issue of cyberbullying experienced by students with high-functioning autism spectrum disorder (ASD). This chapter highlights the connection between peer acceptance, fear of missing out (FoMO), and bullying experiences, offering essential insights into how educators and parents can support students' social-emotional development in a digital context.

CONCLUSION

Bullying among children with special educational needs is a multifaceted challenge that requires a holistic approach to prevention and intervention. This book addresses this issue by offering a comprehensive exploration of the root causes, the social and cultural contexts in which bullying occurs, and the interventions that have proven to be effective in mitigating its impact. From collaborative strategies that involve parents, peers and educators to the development of inclusive school policies, the insights shared in this volume aim to empower all stakeholders to take a stand against bullying.

Through the experiences and perspectives presented in each chapter, it is clear that addressing bullying against SEN students requires more than reactive measures — it calls for proactive, systemic change. This change involves fostering inclusive educational environments, promoting empathy and understanding, and developing policies that protect the most vulnerable learners. Schools must ensure that their educational spaces are safe, nurturing, and inclusive for all students, regardless of their abilities or learning differences.

We hope that this book serves as a resource for educators, parents, researchers, and policymakers who seek to understand and confront the realities of bullying in special education. By applying the strategies and recommendations outlined in these chapters, readers can play an active role in promoting safe, inclusive, and empathetic learning environments for every child. Together, we can create a future where no child feels isolated, excluded, or fearful in their educational journey.

Sohni Siddiqui
Technische Universität Berlin, Germany

Mahwish Kamran
Iqra University, Karachi, Pakistan

Chapter 1
Academic, Emotional, and Social Consequences of Bullying on Special Needs Students

Fareeha Syeda Ziyan
https://orcid.org/0009-0009-5015-7683
Centre of Inclusive Care, Pakistan

Aisha Kadri
https://orcid.org/0009-0007-4231-5624
GEMS Winchester School, Dubai, UAE

ABSTRACT

This chapter explores the profound impact of bullying on students with SEN, highlighting both academic and social-emotional consequences. SEN students, particularly those with learning disabilities, face significantly higher rates of bullying compared to their neurotypical peers. This victimization leads to severe academic repercussions, including decreased concentration, lower grades, and reduced engagement in school activities. Socially and emotionally, bullying results in heightened levels of anxiety, depression, and social withdrawal, with long-term implications for mental health. A comprehensive literature review, as well as case studies, illustrate the detrimental effects of bullying on academic performance and social-emotional wellbeing of SEN students, emphasizing the urgent need for effective interventions and support strategies. By examining the interconnected nature of these consequences, this chapter highlights the necessity of comprehensive approaches and identifies relevant interventions to create safer, more inclusive educational environments for students with SEN.

DOI: 10.4018/979-8-3693-5315-8.ch001

INTRODUCTION

Bullying is a pervasive issue that affects students worldwide, transcending boundaries of age, ethnicity, and ability (González Contreras et al., 2021; Rose et al., 2017). However, its impact on students with special education needs (SEN) remains a critical area requiring deeper exploration. Despite increasing recognition of its prevalence in literature and pedagogical practice, there is a notable gap in understanding the specific challenges faced by SEN students in educational settings (Hartley et al., 2015). This chapter seeks to address this gap by examining the academic and emotional consequences of bullying on students with SEN, shedding light on the multifaceted nature of their experiences and the implications for their overall well-being.

Students with SEN, including those with learning disabilities, autism spectrum disorder (ASD), and other developmental disorders, are particularly vulnerable to bullying. Research consistently shows that these students are at a significantly higher risk of being targeted compared to their neurotypical peers (González-Calatayud et al., 2021). For instance, Blake et al. (2012) demonstrate that children with ASD are more likely to experience bullying due to their social communication difficulties and behavioral characteristics. Similarly, Rose et al. (2011) found that students with disabilities are frequently subjected to both verbal and physical bullying, further complicating their school experiences.

The academic repercussions for bullied SEN students are severe. Studies by Ralph (2018) and Rose et al. (2012) highlight that the stress and anxiety caused by bullying affects students' ability to concentrate and retain information, resulting in lower grades and reduced academic engagement. Hartley et al. (2015) and Iqbal et al. (2021) emphasize that bullying leads to decreased motivation and a general withdrawal from school activities, manifesting in lower participation in class and diminished effort on assignments.

Socially and emotionally, the impact of bullying on SEN students is equally profound. Victimization can lead to significant emotional distress, including anxiety, depression, and social withdrawal (Rowley et al., 2012; Zablotsky et al., 2014). These emotional consequences not only affect the students' current well-being but also have long-term implications for their mental health. Heyne et al. (2011) and Kearney and Albano (2004) discuss how the emotional distress from bullying can lead to Emotionally Based School Avoidance (EBSA), where students avoid school due to the emotional pain, further impacting their educational outcomes. Moreover, the long-term implications of such emotional distress are significant. Rose et al. (2011) discuss how chronic bullying can lead to persistent emotional and psychological issues, affecting the overall quality of life for SEN students. Addressing these emotional impacts is crucial for ensuring the mental well-being and academic success of SEN students (Norwich & Kelly, 2004; Rowley et al., 2012).

Given the heightened vulnerability of SEN students to bullying and its relentless academic and emotional repercussions, there is a pressing need to raise awareness in this domain in order to work towards effective interventions. This chapter will delve into the available literature on the academic and social-emotional consequences of bullying on SEN students, providing a comprehensive overview of the challenges they face, and discussing the implications for their overall well-being and development within educational settings. Additionally, case studies drawn from the authors' professional observations will be brought to the forefront of students with SEN experiencing academic and social-emotional consequences as a direct result of bullying. By examining these issues, the chapter aims to highlight the critical areas where support is needed, as well as identify relevant interventions to create a safer and more inclusive school environment for all students.

THE ACADEMIC CONSEQUENCES OF BULLYING ON STUDENTS WITH SEN

Bullying can have drastic effects on academic performance, attendance, and engagement among students with SEN (Cerda et al., 2018). This section explores how bullying impacts their educational outcomes – analyzing factors such as decreased motivation, avoidance of school-related activities, and disrupted learning environments will be analyzed to understand the extent of academic detriment experienced by students with SEN as a result of bullying.

Exacerbation of Existing Learning Difficulties

For students with SEN who already face significant learning challenges, bullying can exacerbate these difficulties. The stress and anxiety from being bullied can negatively impact cognitive functions such as memory, attention, and processing speed, making it harder for these students to keep up academically with their peers (Eilts & Koglin, 2022). In a study conducted in Germany, 65% of bullied SEN students reported difficulties in concentrating on their studies, with a significant number also experiencing issues with memory retention and information processing (ibid).

Bullying of special education students can intensify their existing educational challenges, further impeding their academic progress. Hartley et al. (2015) report that SEN students who are bullied show a marked decline in academic performance, with bullied students performing 20% worse on standardized tests compared to their non-bullied counterparts. This decline is attributed to the intensified stress and anxiety that bullying adds to their existing difficulties, creating an environment where learning becomes even more challenging. Table 1 highlights a case study where bullying directly causes the exacerbation of existing learning difficulties in a student with SEN.

Table 1. Case study 1

Case Study 1: Academic Consequences of Bullying on E., a Student with ADHD

Background

E. is a 7-year-old student in the second grade diagnosed with Attention-Deficit/Hyperactivity Disorder (ADHD). E. has been identified as having slow processing speed and executive functioning difficulties that affect his ability to keep up with classroom tasks and instructions.

Nature of the Bullying

E. has been subjected to both verbal and physical bullying by his peers. He is often taunted with names such as "slow boy" and physically pushed or shoved during physical education (P.E) lessons and recess. These bullying behaviors occur frequently and have negatively affected E.'s academic performance.

School Environment and Support

The school environment has not been supportive of E.'s needs. Teachers often fail to address the bullying incidents, and classroom practices further exacerbate E.'s difficulties. For example, teachers erase the board before E. has had a chance to copy down the notes, hindering his ability to complete assignments and participate in lessons.

Academic Consequences

The continuous bullying and lack of support have severely impacted E.'s academic performance, with the stress and anxiety of being bullied impairing E.'s cognitive functions, such as memory and attention, leading to a noticeable decline in his academic achievements (Eilts & Koglin, 2022). E.'s ADHD symptoms and slow processing speed have been observed to have increased by the bullying and lack of adequate support. Verbal taunts and physical aggression increase his anxiety and distractibility, further slowing his cognitive processing and reducing his ability to concentrate on schoolwork (Blake et al., 2012). Bullying intensifies the existing educational challenges that SEN students face, adding an extra layer of stress and anxiety, which undermines their ability to succeed academically (Hartley et al., 2015). This increased difficulty can lead to a sense of hopelessness and frustration, causing further disengagement from their educational journey. Consequently, bullied SEN students often experience a decline in academic involvement, making it challenging for them to achieve their full potential (Iqbal et al., 2021).

Conclusion

E.'s case highlights the serious academic consequences of bullying on students with SEN, particularly those with ADHD. The lack of support from the school has an increased negative impact on his learning difficulties, leading to a significant decline in academic performance. This case underscores the urgent need for effective interventions to support bullied SEN students and ensure that they receive the necessary accommodations and educational support to succeed academically.

Blake et al. (2012) emphasize that bullied SEN students frequently experience heightened levels of stress, which interferes with their ability to utilize the support resources provided to them. This stress impacts cognitive functions crucial for learning, such as concentration and memory, further widening the academic gap between them and their peers. This increased difficulty in keeping up academically can lead to a sense of hopelessness and frustration, further disengaging them from their educational journey. Iqbal et al. (2021) found that 70% of bullied SEN students expressed feelings of frustration and hopelessness regarding their academic capabilities, leading to further disengagement and withdrawal from school activities. This disengagement is detrimental as it prevents these students from fully benefiting from the educational opportunities available to them, ultimately impacting their long-term academic and career prospects.

Lower Grades

Several studies have documented a direct correlation between bullying and decreased academic achievement among students with SEN. For instance, Ralph (2018) found that SEN students who experience bullying often show a significant decline in their grades. The study indicates that approximately 70% of bullied SEN students reported a noticeable drop in their academic performance, highlighting the detrimental impact of bullying on their educational outcomes. Rose et al. (2012) also emphasize that the stress and anxiety induced by bullying affects victims' ability to concentrate and retain information, resulting in poorer academic outcomes. Their research revealed that bullied SEN students had an average GPA drop of 0.5 points compared to their non-bullied peers.

Moreover, González Contreras et al. (2021) indicate that the persistent exposure to bullying erodes the academic performance of SEN students by continuously distracting them from their educational activities. This study involved a survey of 945 students, showing that those who experienced frequent bullying had lower test scores and grades compared to those who were not bullied. The constant state of anxiety and fear hampers their cognitive abilities, making it difficult for them to process and retain information during lessons. This cumulative stress impairs learning abilities over time, leading to an average decline of 15% in academic performance over the course of a school year.

Blake et al. (2012) provide additional quantitative data, demonstrating that students with autism spectrum disorder (ASD) who are bullied are three times more likely to experience academic difficulties than their non-bullied counterparts. Their study, which included a sample of over 1,200 students, found that 60% of bullied ASD students reported failing at least one subject compared to 20% of non-bullied ASD students.

Reduced Academic Engagement

Bullying can lead to a lack of interest in school activities and reduced academic engagement among students with SEN. This disengagement manifests itself in a variety of ways, including reduced participation in class discussions, decreased effort on assignments, and a general withdrawal from school activities. A study by Hartley et al. (2015) found that bullied SEN students were 2.5 times more likely to avoid participating in classroom activities compared to their non-bullied peers. This reduced engagement is detrimental to their overall academic success, as it prevents them from fully benefiting from educational opportunities.

Additionally, bullying significantly diminishes students' intrinsic motivation to engage in academic tasks. Rose et al. (2012) emphasize that the ongoing stress and emotional drain from bullying make these students less likely to actively participate in their education. Their study found that 68% of bullied SEN students reported a lack of motivation to complete schoolwork, compared to 30% of their non-bullied counterparts. This decline in motivation is a critical factor contributing to reduced academic engagement.

The emotional distress caused by bullying is linked to decreased academic involvement, creating a cycle of disengagement that significantly impacts students' educational experiences and outcomes (Iqbal et al., 2021). Through qualitative interviews with SEN students, it was found that 75% of the participants expressed feelings of hopelessness and a lack of interest in school due to bullying (ibid). This emotional burden further fuels their disengagement from academic activities.

The decrease in engagement can be attributed to the psychological toll that bullying places on students. SEN students, already grappling with learning challenges, find it even more difficult to stay motivated and involved in school when they are constantly worried about being bullied. Rose et al. (2012) highlight that the emotional toll of bullying results in a significant decrease in school attendance and participation, with bullied students missing an average of 10 more days of school per year compared to their non-bullied peers. This reduced engagement is detrimental to their overall academic success, as it prevents them from taking full advantage of the educational opportunities available to them.

Heightened Risk of School Dropout

The adverse effects of bullying can be so severe that they lead some students with SEN to avoid school altogether. The fear and anxiety of facing bullies can result in increased absenteeism, and in extreme cases, lead to school dropout (González Contreras et al., 2021). Bullied SEN students were twice as likely to have higher absenteeism rates compared to their non-bullied peers (ibid). This chronic absenteeism due to fear and anxiety significantly disrupts the educational experience – another academic consequence.

The victimization experiences of children with autism spectrum disorder (ASD) significantly correlate with their desire to avoid the school environment, which can culminate in dropping out of school, as found in a study conducted by Rowley et al. (2012) with 150 children with ASD, presenting the findings that 60% of those who experienced bullying had considered dropping out of school due to the subsequent emotional toll. This avoidance behavior is particularly detrimental as it deprives these students of educational opportunities and the benefits of structured learning environments.

The risk of dropout is heightened by the persistent fear and anxiety that bullying instills in SEN students. Hartley et al. (2015) report that SEN students who are bullied are three times more likely to drop out of school compared to their non-bullied counterparts. The school environment, which should be a safe and supportive place for learning, becomes a source of stress and trauma, leading to chronic absenteeism as students try to avoid their bullies. This ultimately culminates in a complete withdrawal from school. Additionally, Heyne et al. (2011) found that 70% of SEN students with EBSA reported bullying as a primary factor for their school avoidance. This is not a new concept; earlier research by Kearney and Albano (2004) emphasized that the anxiety and depression resulting from bullying significantly contribute to school avoidance, which, if not addressed, could lead to long-term educational disengagement and dropout. Table 2 highlights a case study where the risk of a student with SEN's dropout from school was heightened due to bullying.

Table 2. Case study 2

Case Study 2: Academic Consequences of Bullying on A., a Student with Autism
Background
A. is a 14-year-old ninth-grade student who has been diagnosed with autism. She exhibits behaviors such as missing social cues and "stimming" behaviors like hand-flapping and hair-sniffing, which have made her a target for bullying.
Nature of Bullying
A. faces both verbal and physical bullying from her peers, which has escalated to cyberbullying. A WhatsApp group was created specifically to share memes mocking her, exacerbating her social isolation and anxiety. The bullying occurs both in-person and online, significantly impacting her well-being.
School Environment and Support
Despite the presence of a resource teacher, the support provided by the school has been insufficient in addressing the bullying A. is experiencing. The bullying extends beyond school boundaries, making it difficult for the school to manage and mitigate its impact. The cyberbullying aspect, in particular, has made the situation worse by allowing the harassment to continue outside of school hours.
Academic Consequences
The continuous bullying has led A. to avoid school, significantly impacting her attendance. This avoidance has resulted in missed tests and assignments, causing a decline in her grades. The stress and anxiety from being bullied impair A.'s ability to concentrate and perform academically, leading to a noticeable decline in her academic achievements (Eilts & Koglin, 2022). The academic setbacks are severe enough that A. is being considered for repeating the ninth grade, which represents a significant setback in her educational journey. The risk of dropping out is heightened by the persistent fear and anxiety that the bullying instills in A. The school environment, which should be a safe and supportive place for learning, has become a source of stress and trauma, leading to chronic absenteeism as A. tries to avoid her bullies, which leads her to completely withdraw from school. The cyberbullying adds another layer of complexity, contributing to a pervasive sense of insecurity and anxiety, further leading to a lack of desire to return to school.
Conclusion
A.'s case highlights the drastic academic consequences of bullying on students with autism. Despite some support from the school, the persistent nature of the bullying has led to a significant decline in her academic performance and overall well-being, leading her to avoid school and putting her at risk of dropping out altogether. This case highlights the urgent need for comprehensive and effective interventions to support bullied students with SEN, ensuring that they receive the necessary accommodations and protections to thrive academically and personally.

In essence, chronic absenteeism and dropping out limit SEN students' future opportunities (opportunities that are already limited in number in comparison to those available to their neurotypical counterparts), making it difficult for them to achieve their full potential.

THE SOCIAL-EMOTIONAL CONSEQUENCES OF BULLYING ON STUDENTS WITH SEN

The social-emotional toll of bullying on students with SEN cannot be underestimated. This section will delve into the psychological effects (Fink et al., 2015), including increased anxiety, depression, and diminished self-esteem. It will also explore the lived experiences of students with SEN subjected to bullying, highlighting the detrimental effects on their emotional well-being and mental health (Eilts & Koglin, 2022).

Emotional Consequences

The emotional impact of bullying on students with SEN is severe and multifaceted. These students are at a higher risk of developing anxiety, depression, and even suicidal tendencies as a result of persistent bullying (Blake et al., 2012). Victimization often leads to significant emotional distress, including anxiety, depression, and social withdrawal, with SEN students being 45% more likely to exhibit severe anxiety and depression compared to their non-bullied peers (ibid). The chronic stress and emotional trauma associated with bullying can have long-term psychological effects that extend well beyond the school years (deLara, 2019). This sustained emotional distress impacts all aspects of a student's life, including their academic performance, social interactions, and overall quality of life. The following information explores these emotional consequences in greater detail.

Anxiety and Depression

Bullying has a detrimental impact on a child's mental health, leading to heightened levels of anxiety and depression. For example, students with SEN are bullied up to 63% more frequently than their peers and often exhibit symptoms such as sadness, isolation, and changes in sleep and dietary habits (Menesini, 2017). These issues can persist into adulthood, severely affecting their quality of life. Additionally, the correlation between bullying and mental health issues is well-documented, with studies showcasing that victims of bullying display 32% higher levels of depression, emotional symptoms, and hyperactivity/inattention compared to their non-victimized peers in school (Didaskalou et al., 2009; Marengo et al., 2018). Furthermore, children with SEN are more likely to report both bullying victimization and perpetration, which could be attributed to the presence of behavioral and emotional problems (Dasioti & Kolaitis, 2018; Rose & Gage, 2017).

Suicidal Tendencies

The relationship between bullying and suicidal tendencies is complex and alarming. Bullying is linked to increased suicidal ideation and attempts among victims. Research by Reed et al. (2015) indicates that bullied students are up to 50% more likely to experience suicidal ideation compared to their non-bullied peers. Furthermore, a study by the National Center for Injury Prevention and Control (2014) found that victims of severe bullying were 40% more likely to attempt suicide, highlighting the grave implications of bullying on mental health. The severe emotional distress caused by bullying can lead some students to contemplate or attempt suicide. This is particularly concerning for students with SEN, who may already struggle with feelings of inadequacy and isolation – this group already faces significant social and emotional challenges, and the added burden of bullying can exacerbate these issues to a critical level. Studies have shown that bullied SEN students exhibit higher rates of suicidal thoughts and behaviors compared to their non-bullied peers (Dasioti & Kolaitis, 2018). The tragic reality is that in several high-profile school shooting cases, the perpetrators had been bullied, highlighting the potential for bullying to escalate into extreme violence (deLara, 2019).

SOCIAL CONSEQUENCES

The social consequences of bullying for students with SEN are as significant as the emotional consequences. Bullying can lead to social isolation, loneliness, and a sense of exclusion from the peer group (González-Calatayud et al., 2021). These students often struggle to form and maintain healthy social relationships, which can result in a lack of peer support and increased feelings of loneliness. The hostile social environment created by bullying can erode their confidence and self-esteem, making it difficult for them to participate in social activities and integrate into the school community (Andreou et al., 2015). Over time, the social withdrawal and isolation experienced by bullied SEN students can have lasting effects on their social development and emotional well-being. The following information will explore these social consequences in greater detail, examining how bullying impacts the peer relationships of students with SEN.

Isolation and Loneliness

Loneliness and social dissatisfaction are among the most well-documented adverse outcomes of peer rejection and victimization - for instance, Heiman and Olenik-Shemesh (2020) found that students with learning disabilities (LD) reported approximately 15% lower self-efficacy and well-being compared to non-LD students, and about 8% higher loneliness due to being bullied. Victimization leads to exclusion from the group, negative behavior from peers, and the accumulation of negative experiences, making children acutely aware of their social standing (Cullinane, 2020). This exclusion can result in a lack of trust in peers and a decreased sense of safety in school, leading to withdrawal from peer interactions and avoid social and academic activities, reinforcing loneliness and social dissatisfaction (ibid) creating a vicious cycle.

In addition to social withdrawal, the internalization of bullying experiences leads to a heightened sense of vulnerability and mistrust towards others (Heiman & Olenik-Shemesh, 2020). Children who have been victimized frequently report feeling that their peers are generally unfriendly and that they cannot rely on them for support or companionship (Cullinane, 2020). This perception of hostility exacerbates their feelings of isolation and makes it even more challenging to form new relationships (ibid). The social isolation experienced by bullied students also impacts their ability to participate in group activities, which are crucial for social development and building a sense of community. Participation in such activities is often reduced or entirely avoided by bullied students due to fear of further victimization and embarrassment. This avoidance behavior prevents them from developing essential social skills and contributes to their sense of being different or excluded from their peer group (Heiman & Olenik-Shemesh, 2020).

Low Self-Esteem

Low self-esteem is a prevalent and damaging social consequence of bullying for students with SEN. The relentless victimization they endure can erode their confidence and sense of self-worth, affecting their ability to interact socially and form healthy relationships (Rose et al., 2012). Studies indicate that bullied students with special education needs often internalize the negative perceptions and derogatory comments made by their peers, leading to a diminished self-image. This internalization process makes them more likely to believe that they are less capable and less deserving of social acceptance and success than their non-bullied counterparts (Rowley et al., 2012).

The social isolation resulting from bullying further compounds the issue of low self-esteem. Bullied students often experience heightened levels of loneliness and social dissatisfaction, which not only affects their current mental health but also hinders their ability to develop the social skills necessary for building and maintaining healthy relationships (Cullinane, 2020). The lack of peer support and positive social interactions exacerbates feelings of loneliness and rejection, making it difficult for these students to feel confident in social settings. Additionally, the chronic stress associated with bullying can impair cognitive functions essential for social interaction, such as memory and attention. This cognitive impairment can lead to difficulties in social situations, which in turn reinforces the negative self-image and feelings of incompetence among bullied students. The cycle of bullying, social failure, and low self-esteem becomes self-perpetuating, making it increasingly difficult for these students to break free from their negative self-perceptions (Cerda et al., 2018). Table 3 and Table 4 each highlight case studies which delve into the emotional and social consequences of bullying on students with SEN respectively.

Table 3. Case study 3

Case Study 3: Emotional and Social Consequences of Bullying on F., a Student with Autism and Sensory Processing Difficulties

Background

F. is a 9-year-old Year 3 student diagnosed with autism and sensory processing difficulties. He struggles with understanding social cues and is highly sensitive to loud sounds, for which he uses noise-cancelling headphones. F. often says unusual things without understanding their impact and is too naive to recognize when he is being bullied. His lack of assertiveness and tendency to follow others' instructions without understanding the consequences make him vulnerable to manipulation and bullying.

Nature of Bullying

F. has faced multiple instances of bullying from his classmates. In one incident, his classmates told him to remove his pants and jump on a chair, which he did, leading to everyone laughing at him and making fun of him. This resulted in F. being isolated and labelled as a "weirdo" by his peers. The class teacher, unaware that F. was coerced into the behaviour, issued him a warning for what she perceived as bad behaviour.

In another incident, a group of boys confronted F. in the washroom, took his headphones, mocked him, and locked him in a toilet stall. F. was found 30 minutes later by the janitor, crying and confused. These repeated bullying incidents have greatly impacted F.'s emotional well-being.

Emotional Consequences

The bullying has led to significant emotional consequences for F., including feelings of isolation, fear, depression, and anxiety. He feels lonely and disconnected from his peers, who avoid him and label him as different. The fear of further bullying makes F. anxious and wary of interacting with his classmates, leading to increased social withdrawal. The confusion and distress from not understanding why he is being targeted contribute to his depression, further exacerbating his emotional struggles.

Social Consequences

The social consequences of bullying for F. are overwhelming. He has become increasingly isolated, with no friends to support him. His classmates' rejection and mockery have made it difficult for him to form meaningful relationships. The lack of social interactions has deprived F. of the opportunity to develop essential social skills and build self-esteem, leaving him feeling vulnerable and alone.

School Environment and Support

The support provided by the school has been inadequate to address the bullying that F. faces. The lack of awareness among teachers about the coercion and manipulation F. experiences has led to misguided disciplinary actions. The school environment, which should offer safety and support, has become a source of stress and trauma for F. The absence of effective interventions to prevent and address bullying has allowed the harmful behaviour to persist, further impacting F.'s emotional and social well-being.

Conclusion

F.'s case highlights the severe emotional and social consequences of bullying on students with autism. Despite some support from the school, the persistent and pervasive nature of the bullying has led to significant emotional distress and social isolation for F. This case underscores the urgent need for comprehensive and effective interventions to support bullied students with special education needs, ensuring they receive the necessary accommodations and protection to thrive emotionally and socially.

Table 4. Case study 4

Case Study 4: Emotional and Social Consequences of Bullying on J., a Student with Dyslexia **Background** J. is a 12-year-old girl attending a mainstream school who has dyslexia and possibly other specific learning disabilities. J. receives differentiated activities and tasks to accommodate her learning difficulties. She often struggles with reading and writing tasks, which is evident during classroom activities and assignments. **Nature of Bullying** J.'s classmates began to notice her difficulties and the easier, child-friendly worksheets she received in the name of classroom differentiation for her tasks. They started mocking her for being slow at reading and making spelling mistakes. When J. was picked to read in front of the class, she stammered and fumbled, leading to the whole class laughing at her and causing her extreme embarrassment. Her classmates called her "dummy" and "illiterate," isolating her during group activities and recess. This bullying was not addressed adequately by school staff, who viewed it as typical childhood teasing. **Emotional Consequences** The constant bullying led J. to feel ashamed and embarrassed about her condition. She developed significant anxiety about attending school, resulting in frequent absences. J.'s self-esteem plummeted as she internalized the negative labels and mockery from her peers. The shame and embarrassment she felt about her dyslexia made her reluctant to seek help or participate in activities that could highlight her difficulties. **Social Consequences** J. began to withdraw socially, avoiding interaction with her peers and refusing to participate in classroom discussions. She became increasingly isolated, missing out on social interactions that are crucial for her social development. The bullying and subsequent isolation severely impacted her ability to form and maintain friendships, leaving her feeling lonely and unsupported. **School Environment and Support** The school's response to J.'s bullying was inadequate. The staff's perception of the bullying as typical childhood teasing prevented effective intervention. The lack of support and understanding from the school environment exacerbated J.'s emotional and social struggles, making her feel even more isolated and misunderstood. **Conclusion** J.'s case highlights the severe emotional and social consequences of bullying on students with dyslexia. Despite some accommodations for her learning difficulties, the relentless nature of the bullying led to significant emotional distress and social isolation for J. This case underscores the urgent need for comprehensive and effective interventions to support bullied students with specific learning disabilities, ensuring that they receive the necessary accommodations and protection to thrive emotionally and socially.

LONG LASTING IMPACTS

Bullying has enduring impacts on students with SEN, affecting various aspects of their lives beyond the immediate physical and emotional pain. The difficulty in forming healthy relationships is one of the most significant long-term consequences. Trust issues and social anxiety, often developed as a result of prolonged victimization, can make building and maintaining friendships and romantic relationships particularly challenging (Andreou et al., 2015). Additionally, the feelings of isolation and loneliness further complicate their social interactions and ability to connect with others on a deeper level (Begum & Nair, 2023).

The mental health struggles resulting from bullying can be persistent and overwhelming. Many bullied SEN students continue to experience depression, anxiety, and low self-esteem well into adulthood (deLara, 2019; Cerda et al., 2018), leading to difficulties in various life domains. Studies have shown that the psychological scars left by bullying can manifest in chronic mental health conditions that require long-term therapy and support (Eilts & Koglin, 2022). The link between bullying and harsh outcomes such as suicidal ideation is also well-documented, emphasizing the immediate and critical need for early intervention and support for these vulnerable students (Rodríguez-Hidalgo et al., 2019).

Career prospects can be significantly limited for students with SEN who have experienced bullying. Mental health issues can impact their ability to pursue higher education and vocational training, thereby restricting their employment opportunities (Berchiatti et al., 2021). Furthermore, social anxiety and low self-esteem can make it challenging for these individuals to thrive in work environments that require frequent social interactions or assertiveness (Fink et al., 2015). The cumulative effect of these challenges can result in a reduced capacity to secure and maintain employment, which can have long-term financial and social implications (González Contreras et al., 2021).

Hence, bullying impacts not only the current well-being of students with SEN but also their long-term mental health and social development. The consequences of bullying for students with SEN extend far beyond the immediate harm, affecting their social relationships, academic achievements, mental health, and career opportunities. Addressing bullying in schools and providing comprehensive support to victims is crucial to mitigating these long-term effects and helping students with SEN lead fulfilling lives (Heyne, et al., 2011; Marengo et al., 2018).

MITIGATING FACTORS OF CONSEQUENCES OF BULLYING ON CHILDREN WITH SEN

While the majority of the academic and social-emotional consequences of SEN are negative, they can be mitigated by other outcomes which may not necessarily be deemed as 'negative' (Berkowitz et al. 2017, Farrington et al., 2012).

Desire to Overcome Adversity

Students who experience bullying often develop a strong desire to overcome adversity, particularly when they receive support from teachers and peers. This determination can lead to increased academic engagement and resilience (Bunnett, 2021). Research indicates that students from challenging backgrounds, including those who face bullying, can achieve academic success when motivated by the desire to improve their circumstances (Berkowitz et al., 2017). Additionally, Yeager and Dweck (2012) highlight that students who adopt a growth mindset are more likely to view challenges as opportunities for growth, which can enhance their academic performance despite adverse experiences. This resilience in the face of bullying can foster a commitment to overcoming obstacles, thereby promoting academic achievement.

Academic Motivation

The experience of bullying can, paradoxically, enhance a student's academic motivation, especially when they are determined to prove their worth (Lucas-Molina et al., 2022). Farrington et al. (2012) suggest that non-cognitive factors such as grit and perseverance, which are often heightened in response to bullying, play a critical role in academic success. Students who channel their experiences of victimization into academic pursuits may develop a stronger work ethic and a greater focus on their studies (Lucas-Molina et al., 2022). Additionally, support from peers and teachers, as discussed by Wang and Eccles (2012), can bolster a bullied student's motivation to succeed academically, turning negative experiences into a driving force for personal and educational growth.

Emotional Resilience

Emotional resilience is a critical positive outcome that can emerge from overcoming bullying. Sapouna and Wolke (2013) argue that the resilience of bullied students is often strengthened by supportive relationships with family and peers, enabling them to effectively cope with stress. This resilience allows students to maintain emotional stability and continue to engage in their academic and social activities despite the challenges they face (Quintana-Orts et al., 2022). Skinner and Zimmer-Gembeck (2007) further suggest that the development of coping mechanisms contributes to emotional resilience, helping students to manage and overcome the psychological effects of bullying.

School Connectedness and Peer Support

Strong connections to school and peer support can significantly mitigate the negative effects of bullying. Ragusa et al. (2023) found that school connectedness plays a crucial role in adolescents' mental health, providing a buffer against the emotional distress caused by bullying. Peer support, as highlighted by Siddiqui and Schultze-Krumbholz (2023), can empower bystanders to challenge bullying behavior, creating a more supportive school environment. This sense of belonging and connection can encourage bullied students to remain engaged in school, fostering both their emotional well-being and academic success.

Development of Coping Mechanisms

The development of effective coping mechanisms is another positive consequence of facing and overcoming bullying. Stewart and Bernard (2023) and Potard et al. (2022) emphasize that coping strategies are essential for managing stress during childhood and adolescence, particularly for those who experience bullying. Potard et al. (2022) also note that the role of emotions in coping can determine whether a student's response to bullying is adaptive or maladaptive. When students develop healthy coping mechanisms, they are better equipped to handle the emotional and psychological challenges posed by bullying, leading to improved emotional resilience and overall well-being.

THE LINKS BETWEEN ACADEMIC AND SOCIAL-EMOTIONAL CONSEQUENCES OF BULLYING ON STUDENTS WITH SEN

It is important to understand that the academic, emotional, and social consequences of bullying are interconnected and do not necessarily occur separately or individually (Blake et al., 2012). They often have overlapping impacts rather than singular, standalone effects. In essence, the linked nature of academic and social-emotional consequences creates a complex and self-perpetuating cycle of harm for students with special needs. For instance, the fear and anxiety instilled by bullying often lead to school avoidance, which directly impacts academic performance (Kearney & Albano, 2004). This connection highlights how emotional distress translates into academic decline, exacerbating the overall impact of bullying.

The following thematic map (Figure 1) visually depicts the interconnected links between the academic and social-emotional consequences of bullying on students with SEN. Each primary theme highlights the multifaceted negative impacts of bullying, supported by specific sub-themes that further elaborate on these effects.

Figure 1. Thematic map of links between negative academic and social-emotional consequences of bullying on students with SEN

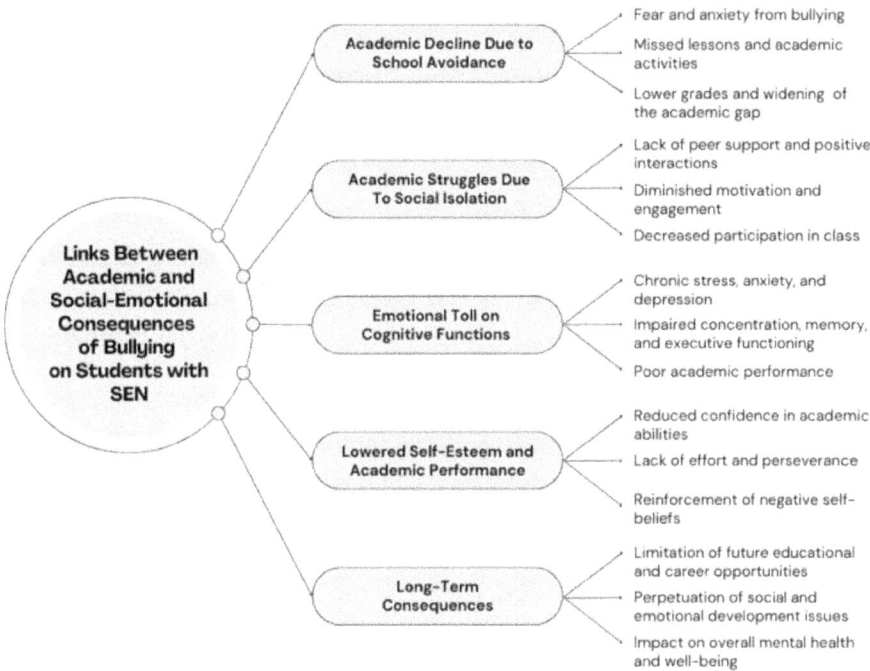

Students with SEN who are bullied frequently experience heightened levels of anxiety and fear, leading to a reluctance to attend school. This avoidance of school stems from a desire to escape the hostile environment and protect oneself from further victimization (Andreou et al., 2015). However, avoiding school results in missed lessons, tests, and important academic activities, which can significantly hinder their educational progress (Blake et al., 2012). The cumulative effect of these absences is often reflected in lower grades and a widening gap between the bullied students and their peers in terms of academic achievement (Abdullah, 2024).

Moreover, the social isolation experienced by bullied SEN students further compounds their academic struggles. The lack of peer support and positive social interactions can diminish their motivation and engagement in school activities (Álvarez-Guerrero et al., 2023). Without a supportive social network, these students may feel disconnected from the school community, which can lead to decreased participation and a lack of interest in their studies (Berchiatti et al., 2021). The absence of a sense of belonging and community within the school environment can create a barrier to academic success, as students may perceive their efforts as futile and unrecognized.

The emotional toll of bullying also directly impacts cognitive functions essential for academic success. Chronic stress, anxiety, and depression associated with bullying can impair concentration, memory, and executive functioning, making it challenging for students with SEN to focus on their studies and perform well academically (Eilts & Koglin, 2022). The persistent worry and emotional turmoil can occupy their mental resources, leaving little room for academic tasks (Fink et al., 2015). This cognitive overload can result in difficulties in understanding and retaining information, completing assignments, and performing well – if at all – in exams (Rodríguez-Hidalgo et al., 2019).

Furthermore, the lowered self-esteem and self-efficacy resulting from bullying can diminish a student's confidence in their academic abilities. Students with SEN who are repeatedly bullied may internalize negative perceptions of themselves, believing they are incapable of achieving academic success (Cerda et al., 2018). This self-doubt and lowered self-esteem can lead to a lack of effort and perseverance in academic tasks, as they may feel that their attempts are 'destined to fail.' The resulting poor academic performance can then reinforce these negative self-beliefs, creating a vicious cycle of low self-esteem and academic underachievement (González Contreras et al., 2021).

In addition to these direct impacts, the academic decline experienced by bullied SEN students can further exacerbate their social-emotional difficulties. Struggling academically can lead to frustration, embarrassment, and a sense of hopelessness, which can intensify feelings of anxiety and depression (Begum & Nair, 2023). This academic stress can spill over into other areas of their lives, affecting their overall mental health and well-being (Rose et al., 2011). Moreover, poor academic performance can limit future educational and career opportunities, perpetuating the long-term effects of bullying on their social and emotional development (Heyne et al., 2011).

In summary, the academic and social-emotional consequences of bullying among students with SEN are deeply interconnected, creating a cycle of harm that affects multiple aspects of their lives. School avoidance due to fear and anxiety directly leads to missed academic opportunities, while the lack of social support and chronic stress directly impairs cognitive functions essential for learning. Additionally, the internalization of negative self-beliefs diminishes academic motivation and effort, further entrenching these students in a cycle of underachievement and emotional distress. Addressing bullying comprehensively and providing holistic support is crucial to breaking this cycle and helping students with SEN thrive both academically and emotionally (Rowley et al., 2012; Zablotsky et al., 2014).

THE INTERSECTIONALITY OF BULLYING AND SPECIAL EDUCATION NEEDS

Understanding the intersectionality of bullying and special education needs is essential for developing targeted interventions. This section will examine how factors such as disability type, severity, and individual coping mechanisms influence the experiences and outcomes of bullying among students with SEN. By recognizing the unique vulnerabilities and strengths within this population, there is a greater opportunity to identify and develop potential interventions and support strategies.

Disability Type and Bullying

The type of disability significantly influences the prevalence and impact of bullying among students with SEN. Research shows that students with autism spectrum disorder (ASD) are particularly vulnerable to bullying due to their social communication difficulties and behavioral characteristics (Rowley et al., 2012; Zablotsky et al., 2014). For instance, Rowley et al. (2012) found that children with ASD who are placed in mainstream schools experience higher levels of bullying compared to those placed in specialized settings. Similarly, Zablotsky et al. (2014) identified that social communication difficulties and behavioral challenges are significant risk factors for bullying among children with ASD.

Students with emotional and behavioral disorders (EBD) also face heightened risks of bullying. Rose and Espelage (2012) highlighted that students with EBD are not only more likely to be victims of bullying but also to perpetrate it. This dual role complicates their social interactions and exacerbates their educational challenges. The study emphasizes the importance of understanding the behavioral and emotional profiles of these students to develop effective anti-bullying strategies.

Severity of Disability

The severity of a student's disability also plays a crucial role in their experiences with bullying. Research by Hartley et al. (2015) demonstrates that students with more severe disabilities are at a greater risk of being bullied. These students often have more visible or pronounced differences, making them easier targets for bullies. The study suggests that interventions should be tailored to address the specific needs of students based on the severity of their disabilities, ensuring that those most at risk receive adequate protection and support.

Individual Coping Mechanisms

Individual coping mechanisms and resilience factors are essential in determining how students with SEN experience and respond to bullying. For example, the presence of strong social support networks, including supportive teachers and peers, can mitigate the negative effects of bullying (Ralph, 2018). Burger et al. (2022) found that students who perceived their teachers as supportive were less likely to report bullying and more likely to feel included in their school communities.

Similarly, Ralph (2018) identified protective factors such as strong peer relationships and effective coping strategies that help SEN students navigate the challenges posed by bullying. These findings highlight the need for schools to foster supportive environments that enhance students' resilience and ability to cope with bullying.

School Environment and Placement

The school environment and placement significantly affect the bullying experiences of SEN students. Rowley et al. (2012) and González Contreras et al. (2021) both emphasize that students with SEN in mainstream schools often face higher levels of bullying compared to those in special education settings. This suggests that mainstream schools need to implement more robust anti-bullying policies and create inclusive environments that protect vulnerable students.

The quality of the student-teacher relationship is another critical factor. Berchiatti et al. (2021) found that positive student-teacher relationships can reduce the incidence of bullying among students with learning difficulties. Teachers play a pivotal role in identifying bullying behaviors and providing the necessary support to affected students (González-Calatayud et al., 2021).

INTERVENTIONS FOR PROTECTING STUDENTS WITH SEN FROM BULLYING

In the context of addressing bullying and supporting students with SEN, it is crucial to implement targeted interventions that can mitigate the negative impacts of bullying. The following table (Table 5) outlines key interventions that have been identified through the literature review as effective in protecting SEN students from bullying incidents.

Table 5. Interventions for protecting students with SEN from bullying

Intervention	Description	Potential Benefits
School-wide Anti-Bullying Programs	Implement comprehensive programs that involve all students and staff (Menesini, 2017).	Creates a supportive and inclusive school culture.
Individual Counseling	Provide one-on-one counseling sessions for bullied students (Rose & Espelage, 2012).	Addresses specific emotional and psychological needs.
Peer Support Groups	Establish peer mentoring and support groups (Álvarez-Guerrero et al., 2023).	Promotes social inclusion and peer support.
Teacher Training	Train teachers to recognize and respond to bullying incidents (Blake et al., 2012).	Enhances early identification and intervention.
Parental Involvement	Encourage active involvement of parents in addressing bullying (Begum & Nair, 2023).	Strengthens home-school collaboration in support of the child.
Social Skills Training	Offer programs to improve social skills and resilience (González-Calatayud et al., 2021).	Helps students develop coping strategies and build self-confidence.
Clear Reporting Mechanisms	Establish and communicate clear procedures for reporting bullying (Eilts & Koglin, 2022).	Ensures incidents are promptly addressed and documented.

School-Wide Anti-Bullying Programs

Comprehensive, school-wide anti-bullying programs create a safe and supportive environment for all students, including those with SEN. These programs involve the entire school community and focus on fostering respect, empathy, and positive behavior. In her research, Menesini (2017) notes that such programs have led to a 20-23% reduction in bullying incidents. A recent example is the "KiVa" program, implemented in various countries including Finland and the Netherlands, which saw a significant reduction in bullying cases and improved overall school climate (Haataja et al., 2016). The program was observed to be effective because it integrated lessons on bullying into the curriculum and actively engaged students and staff in prevention efforts.

Individual Counseling

Individual counseling provides targeted support for students with SEN who have experienced bullying, helping them to address their specific emotional and psychological needs. Rose and Espelage (2012) found that counseling reduced anxiety and depression in bullied students by 15-25%. In the UK, school counselors provided one-on-one sessions that significantly improved the emotional well-being of students with SEN who were victims of bullying, helping them to better manage their stress and develop resilience (Cross et al., 2021).

Table 6. Case study 5

Case Study 5: Academic Consequences of Individual Counseling for YM., a Student with ASD   **Background**   YM. is a 16-year-old student in the twelfth grade diagnosed with Autism Spectrum Disorder (ASD). YM. experiences difficulties with social interactions and communication, which has led to frequent bullying by his peers. As a result, YM suffers from anxiety and depression.   **Nature of Bullying**   YM. has been subjected to verbal bullying, including derogatory comments and exclusion from peer groups. The bullying has led to increased stress and emotional turmoil for YM., which has negatively affected his academics due to impeding his concentration and participation in class.   **School Environment and Support**   The school has implemented individual counseling sessions as an intervention for YM. to address the effects of bullying. The school counselor meets with YM. weekly to provide support and develop coping strategies tailored to his needs. The sessions focus on helping YM. manage his anxiety and build resilience, while also working on social skills and emotional regulation.   **Result**   The introduction of individual counseling has had a notable positive impact on YM's mood and demeanor, subsequently influencing his academics. Prior to counseling, YM. exhibited significant decline in academic achievement due to the stress and distraction caused by bullying. Now, the counseling sessions have helped YM. manage his anxiety and depression more effectively, resulting in improved focus and engagement in classroom activities (Rose & Espelage, 2012). The targeted support has also helped YM. develop coping mechanisms and emotional resilience, thereby reducing the impact of bullying on his academics (Hartley et al., 2015).   **Conclusion**   YM.'s case highlights the significant benefits of individual counseling as an intervention for students with SEN who are victims of bullying. By addressing YM.'s specific emotional and psychological needs, the counseling has alleviated some of the negative academic consequences associated with bullying.

Peer Support Groups

Peer support groups offer a powerful intervention by promoting social inclusion and reducing isolation among students with SEN. Álvarez-Guerrero et al. (2023) reported that peer support groups led to a 30% increase in social connectedness. An example of this is the "Circle of Friends" program, which has been demonstrated to improve social interactions and social acceptance (O'Connor, 2016). O'Connor (2016) used the "Circle of Friends" strategy - via structured group meetings and activities - in a case study of a child with Asperger's Syndrome and other associated needs, and found it to be effective in improving social interactions and acceptance.

Teacher Training

Effective teacher training is essential for recognizing and addressing bullying incidents, especially for students with SEN. Blake et al. (2012) found that trained teachers can identify and intervene in bullying situations 50% faster. A specific application of this intervention is depicted in research highlighting the "Upstander" program in the United States, where teachers received specialized training to recognize signs of bullying and intervene effectively (Bradshaw et al., 2012). This program led to a 15-20% decrease in reported bullying incidents, demonstrating the importance of equipping teachers with the skills necessary to protect vulnerable students (ibid).

Parental Involvement

Active parental involvement is crucial for effectively addressing bullying. Schools that foster strong collaboration with parents report a 12-18% increase in the reporting and resolution of bullying incidents (Begum & Nair, 2023). Additionally, McWood et al. (2023) emphasized in their research the importance of emotional support and advice from parents to their children who might have experienced peer victimization; however, a stress was also put on the requirement of parental involvement to be part of a broader school-based strategic approach to bullying (ibid).

Table 7. Case study 6

Case Study 6: Academic and Emotional Impact of Parental Involvement for M., a Student with Dysgraphia and Low Executive Functioning
Background
M. is an 8-year-old student in the third grade who has been diagnosed with Dysgraphia and low executive functioning. M. experiences difficulties with writing and organizational skills, which have led to frequent bullying at school due to his academic challenges. His parents have actively engaged in addressing these issues through collaboration with the school.
Nature of Bullying
M. has faced both verbal and physical bullying, including derogatory remarks about his handwriting and organizational skills, as well as exclusion from group activities. This bullying has exacerbated M.'s anxiety and low self-esteem, affecting his academic performance and overall school experience.
School Environment and Support
The school has implemented a comprehensive reporting system to facilitate communication between M.'s parents and school staff regarding bullying incidents. This system includes:
1. **Incident Reporting Forms:** Both parents and teachers have access to a digital platform where they can report bullying incidents. The forms allow users to detail the nature of the bullying, including date, time, and parties involved.
2. **Weekly Meetings:** M.'s parents and school staff hold weekly meetings to review reported incidents, discuss M.'s progress, and adjust interventions as needed. Through this measure, issues are addressed promptly and strategies are continuously refined.
3. **Emergency Contact System:** An emergency contact feature on the digital platform allows parents to alert school staff immediately if a bullying incident occurs, ensuring rapid response and intervention.
4. **Feedback Loop:** After each reported incident, a feedback form is provided to parents detailing the actions taken by the school. This transparency helps parents stay informed and involved in resolving issues.
Result
The intervention involving active parental involvement, and the comprehensive reporting system has led to significant improvements in both M.'s academic performance and emotional well-being.
• **Academic Improvement:** M. showed a 20% improvement in his written assignments and organizational skills. The tailored interventions and continuous support from both parents and teachers helped him manage his dysgraphia more effectively and stay on top of his schoolwork.
• **Emotional Well-Being:** The supportive environment created through the collaboration between home and school contributed to a notable reduction in M.'s anxiety and improved his self-esteem. M. reported feeling more confident and less isolated, which positively impacted his participation in school activities and interactions with peers (Begum & Nair, 2023).
The enhanced communication between parents and school staff has facilitated a more responsive and supportive approach to M.'s needs. This case showcases the importance of integrating parental involvement and robust reporting mechanisms into a comprehensive school-based strategy to effectively address bullying and support SEN students (McWood et al., 2023).
Conclusion
M.'s case highlights the critical role of parental involvement and effective communication systems in addressing the academic and emotional impacts of bullying for students with SEN. The active engagement of M.'s parents, combined with the comprehensive reporting system, has been instrumental in supporting his academic progress and emotional resilience.

Social Skills Training

Social skills training programs help students with SEN develop the resilience and confidence needed to navigate social interactions and reduce their vulnerability to bullying. González-Calatayud et al. (2021) found that students who received social skills training were 35% less likely to be victims of bullying. An example of such a training program is the "Social Skills Improvement System" (SSIS) program implemented in various schools in the United States, which significantly improved the social competence and emotional regulation of participants, leading to a 40% reduction in bullying incidents among students with SEN (Diperna et al., 2015).

Clear Reporting Mechanisms

Establishing clear and accessible reporting mechanisms is vital for ensuring that bullying incidents are addressed promptly and effectively. Eilts and Koglin (2022) reported that schools with well-communicated reporting procedures experienced a 25% increase in bullying reports and a 20% improvement in resolution rates. A recent example is the "STOPit" app, widely used in U.S. schools, which allows students to anonymously report bullying incidents. This app has led to an increase in reporting and quicker responses from school authorities, making it easier to address bullying and protect vulnerable students (STOPit Solutions, 2024).

These interventions not only aim to reduce the occurrence of bullying but also to foster a supportive and inclusive school environment. By integrating these strategies into educational practices, schools can better support the emotional, social, and academic well-being of SEN students.

CONCLUSION

As evidenced by the literature and case studies, bullying has tremendous academic and emotional consequences for students with SEN, significantly impacting their overall well-being and development.

The academic consequences are severe and complex. Bullying exacerbates existing learning difficulties, leading to a significant decline in academic performance. The stress and anxiety caused by bullying impair important cognitive functions, making it harder for students with SEN to keep up academically with their peers. Psychological distress caused by bullying detracts from students' ability to concentrate and retain information, resulting in lower grades and reduced academic engagement. Persistent exposure to bullying leads to decreased motivation and general withdrawal from school activities, manifesting in lower participation in class and diminished effort on assignments. This reduced engagement is detrimental as it prevents these students from fully benefiting from educational opportunities, impacting their long-term academic and career prospects.

Emotionally, the impact of bullying is equally profound, encompassing heightened levels of anxiety, depression, and even suicidal tendencies. Students with SEN, who are bullied more frequently than their peers, often exhibit symptoms of sadness, isolation, shifts in sleep and dietary habits, and a lack of interest in previously enjoyed activities. The chronic stress and emotional trauma associated with bullying can lead to long-term psychological effects that extend well beyond the school years, affecting all aspects of a student's life, including their social interactions and overall quality of life. The emotional distress from bullying can also lead to Emotionally Based School Avoidance (EBSA), where students avoid school due to the emotional pain, further impacting their educational outcomes.

Socially, bullied SEN students face significant isolation and loneliness. Bullying can erode their confidence and self-esteem, making it difficult for them to participate in social activities and integrate into the school community. The lack of peer support and positive social interactions diminishes their motivation and engagement in school activities, leading to a sense of exclusion and a barrier to academic success. The intertwined nature of academic and social-emotional consequences creates a complex cycle of harm. School avoidance due to fear and anxiety leads directly to missed academic opportunities, while the lack of social support and chronic stress impairs cognitive functions essential for learning. Additionally, the internalization of negative self-beliefs diminishes academic motivation and effort, further entrenching these students in a cycle of underachievement and emotional distress. Struggling academically can lead to frustration, embarrassment, and a sense of hopelessness, which can intensify feelings of anxiety and depression, affecting their overall mental health and well-being.

While some research indicates that there are certain mitigating factors which are the result of bullying, such as an increase in emotional resilience and the development of coping mechanisms, these alone are not enough to dismiss the harmful impact bullying makes on SEN students.

Addressing bullying comprehensively and providing holistic support is crucial to breaking this cycle and helping students with SEN thrive both academically and emotionally. Effective interventions and supportive school environments can mitigate the adverse effects of bullying, promoting the well-being and success of all students. Ensuring the safety and support of students with SEN in educational settings is essential to helping them lead fulfilling lives and achieve their full potential. By understanding the complex interplay between academic and emotional consequences, educators and policymakers can develop targeted strategies to create safer and more inclusive school environments for students with SEN.

REFERENCES

Abdullah, M. (2024, March). The Impact of Bullying in an Inclusive Classroom Among Students of ASD and Peers in Social Development and Academic Performance in UAE. In *BUiD Doctoral Research Conference 2023: Multidisciplinary Studies* (pp. 49-58). Cham: Springer Nature Switzerland. DOI: 10.1007/978-3-031-56121-4_5

Álvarez-Guerrero, G., García-Carrión, R., Khalfaoui, A., Santiago-Garabieta, M., & Flecha, R. (2023). Preventing bullying of students with special educational needs through dialogic gatherings: A case study in elementary education. *Humanities & Social Sciences Communications*, 10(1), 1–9. DOI: 10.1057/s41599-023-02470-8

Andreou, E., Didaskalou, E., & Vlachou, A. (2015). Bully/victim problems among Greek pupils with special educational needs: Associations with loneliness and self-efficacy for peer interactions. *Journal of Research in Special Educational Needs*, 15(4), 235–246. DOI: 10.1111/1471-3802.12028

Begum, M., & Nair, S. (2023). Understanding bullying experiences among SEN students: A parental perspective. *Asia Pacific Journal of Developmental Differences*, 10(2), 249–288.

Berchiatti, M., Ferrer, A., Galiana, L., Badenes-Ribera, L., & Longobardi, C. (2021). Bullying in students with special education needs and learning difficulties: The role of the student–teacher relationship quality and students' social status in the peer group. In *Child & Youth Care Forum* (pp. 1–23). Springer US.

Berkowitz, R., Moore, H., Astor, R. A., & Benbenishty, R. (2017). A research synthesis of the associations between socioeconomic background, inequality, school climate, and academic achievement. *Review of Educational Research*, 87(2), 425–469. DOI: 10.3102/0034654316669821

Blake, J. J., Lund, E. M., Zhou, Q., Kwok, O. M., & Benz, M. R. (2012). National prevalence rates of bully victimization among students with disabilities in the United States. *School Psychology Quarterly*, 27(4), 210–222. DOI: 10.1037/spq0000008 PMID: 23294235

Bradshaw, C. P., Waasdorp, T. E., & Leaf, P. J. (2012). Effects of school-wide positive behavioral interventions and supports on child behavior problems. *Pediatrics*, 130(5), e1136–e1145. DOI: 10.1542/peds.2012-0243 PMID: 23071207

Bunnett, E. R. (2021). Bullying in pre-adolescents: Prevalence, emotional intelligence, aggression and resilience. *Issues in Educational Research*, 31(4), 1049–1066.

Burger, C., Strohmeier, D., & Kollerová, L. (2022). Teachers can make a difference in bullying: Effects of teacher interventions on students' adoption of bully, victim, bully-victim or defender roles across time. *Journal of Youth and Adolescence*, 51(12), 2312–2327. DOI: 10.1007/s10964-022-01674-6 PMID: 36053439

Cerda, G. A., Salazar, Y. S., Guzmán, C. E., & Narváez, G. (2018). Impact of the school coexistence on academic performance according to perception of typically developing and special educational needs students. *Journal of Educational Psychology-Propositos y Representaciones*, 6(1), 275–300.

Compas, B. E., Connor-Smith, J. K., Saltzman, H., Thomsen, A. H., & Wadsworth, M. E. (2001). Coping with stress during childhood and adolescence: Problems, progress, and potential in theory and research. *Psychological Bulletin*, 127(1), 87–127. DOI: 10.1037/0033-2909.127.1.87 PMID: 11271757

Cross, D., Runions, K. C., & Pearce, N. (2021). Friendly schools' bullying prevention research: Implications for school counsellors. *Journal of Psychologists and Counsellors in Schools*, 31(2), 146–158. DOI: 10.1017/jgc.2021.19

Cullinane, M. (2020). An exploration of the sense of belonging of students with special educational needs. *REACH: Journal of Inclusive Education in Ireland*, 33(1), 2–12.

Dasioti, M., & Kolaitis, G. (2018). Bullying and victimization of children and adolescents with disabilities. In Costello, M. (Ed.), *Handbook of bullying in schools: An international perspective* (pp. 85–97). Routledge.

deLara, E. W. (2019). *Bullying scars: The impact on adult life and relationships*. Oxford University Press.

Didaskalou, E., Andreou, E., & Vlachou, A. (2009). Bullying and victimization in children with special educational needs: Implications for inclusive practices. *Revista Interacções*, 13(1), 249–274.

DiPerna, J. C., Lei, P., Bellinger, J., & Cheng, W. (2015). Efficacy of the social skills improvement system classwide intervention program (SSIS-CIP) primary version. *School Psychology Quarterly*, 30(1), 123–141. DOI: 10.1037/spq0000079 PMID: 25111465

Eilts, J., & Koglin, U. (2022). Bullying and victimization in students with emotional and behavioural disabilities: A systematic review and meta-analysis of prevalence rates, risk and protective factors. *Emotional & Behavioural Difficulties*, 27(2), 133–151. DOI: 10.1080/13632752.2022.2092055

Farrington, C. A., Roderick, M., Allensworth, E., Nagaoka, J., Keyes, T. S., Johnson, D. W., & Beechum, N. O. (2012). *Teaching Adolescents to Become Learners: The Role of Noncognitive Factors in Shaping School Performance—A Critical Literature Review*. University of Chicago Consortium on Chicago School Research.

Fink, E., Deighton, J., Humphrey, N., & Wolpert, M. (2015). Assessing the bullying and victimisation experiences of children with special educational needs in mainstream schools: Development and validation of the Bullying Behaviour and Experience Scale. *Research in Developmental Disabilities*, 36, 611–619. DOI: 10.1016/j.ridd.2014.10.048 PMID: 25462521

González-Calatayud, V., Roman-García, M., & Prendes-Espinosa, P. (2021). Knowledge about bullying by young adults with special educational needs with or without disabilities (SEN/D). *Frontiers in Psychology*, 11, 622517. DOI: 10.3389/fpsyg.2020.622517 PMID: 33488487

González Contreras, A. I., Pérez-Jorge, D., Rodríguez-Jiménez, M. D. C., & Bernadette-Lupson, K. (2021). Peer bullying in students aged 11 to 13 with and without special educational needs in Extremadura (Spain). *Education 3-13*, *49*(8), 945-956.

Haataja, A., Sainio, M., Turtonen, M., & Salmivalli, C. (2016). Implementing the KiVa antibullying program: Recognition of stable victims. *Educational Psychology*, 36(3), 595–611. DOI: 10.1080/01443410.2015.1066758

Hartley, M. T., Bauman, S., Nixon, C. L., & Davis, S. (2015). Comparative study of bullying victimization among students in general and special education. *Exceptional Children*, 81(2), 176–193. DOI: 10.1177/0014402914551741

Heiman, T., & Olenik-Shemesh, D. (2020). Social-emotional profile of children with and without learning disabilities: The relationships with perceived loneliness, self-efficacy and well-being. *International Journal of Environmental Research and Public Health*, 17(20), 7358. DOI: 10.3390/ijerph17207358 PMID: 33050221

Heyne, D., Sauter, F. M., & Maynard, B. R. (2011). School refusal and truancy. In Shackelford, T. K., & Weekes-Shackelford, V. A. (Eds.), *Encyclopedia of Evolutionary Psychological Science*. Springer.

Iqbal, F., Senin, M. S., Nordin, M. N. B., & Hasyim, M. (2021). A qualitative study: Impact of bullying on children with special needs. *Linguistica Antverpiensia*, 2, 1639–1643.

Kearney, C. A., & Albano, A. M. (2004). The functional profiles of school refusal behavior: Diagnostic aspects. *Behavior Modification*, 28(1), 147–161. DOI: 10.1177/0145445503259263 PMID: 14710711

Kochenderfer-Ladd, B. (2004). Peer victimization: The role of emotions in adaptive and maladaptive coping. *Social Development*, 13(3), 329–349. DOI: 10.1111/j.1467-9507.2004.00271.x

Lucas-Molina, B., Pérez-Albéniz, A., Solbes-Canales, I., Ortuño-Sierra, J., & Fonseca-Pedrero, E. (2022). Bullying, cyberbullying and mental health: The role of student connectedness as a school protective factor. *Psychosocial Intervention*, 31(1), 33–41. DOI: 10.5093/pi2022a1 PMID: 37362615

Marengo, D., Jungert, T., Iotti, N. O., Settanni, M., Thornberg, R., & Longobardi, C. (2018). Conflictual student–teacher relationship, emotional and behavioral problems, prosocial behavior, and their associations with bullies, victims, and bullies/victims. *Educational Psychology*, 38(9), 1201–1217. DOI: 10.1080/01443410.2018.1481199

McWood, L. M., Frosch, C. A., Wienke Garrison, C. M., Erath, S. A., & Troop-Gordon, W. (2023). "But There's Only So Much You Can Do…" Parent support-giving within the context of peer victimization. *The Journal of Early Adolescence*, 43(4), 455–489. DOI: 10.1177/02724316221105587

Menesini, E. (2017). Bullying in schools: The state of knowledge and effective interventions. *Psicologia Educativa*, 23(2), 61–71. DOI: 10.1016/j.pse.2017.04.002 PMID: 28114811

National Center for Injury Prevention and Control (U.S). (2014). *The relationship between bullying and suicide: What we know and what it means for schools.* Centers for Disease Control and Prevention. https://stacks.cdc.gov/view/cdc/34163

Norwich, B., & Kelly, N. (2004). Pupils' views on inclusion: Moderate learning difficulties and bullying in mainstream and special schools. *British Educational Research Journal*, 30(1), 43–65. DOI: 10.1080/01411920310001629965

O'Connor, E. (2016). The use of 'Circle of Friends' strategy to improve social interactions and social acceptance: A case study of a child with Asperger's Syndrome and other associated needs. *Support for Learning*, 31(2), 138–147. DOI: 10.1111/1467-9604.12122

Potard, C., Kubiszewski, V., Combes, C., Henry, A., Pochon, R., & Roy, A. (2022). How adolescents cope with bullying at school: Exploring differences between pure victim and bully-victim roles. *International Journal of Bullying Prevention : an Official Publication of the International Bullying Prevention Association*, 4(2), 144–159. DOI: 10.1007/s42380-021-00095-6

Quintana-Orts, C., Mc Guckin, C., Del Rey, R., & Mora-Merchán, J. A. (2022). Overcoming bullying in education. *Overcoming Adversity in Education*, 1, 102–113. DOI: 10.4324/9781003180029-10

Ragusa, A., Caggiano, V., Obregón-Cuesta, A. I., González-Bernal, J. J., Fernández-Solana, J., Mínguez-Mínguez, L. A., León-del-Barco, B., Mendo-Lázaro, S., Di Petrillo, E., & González-Santos, J. (2023). The influence of bullying on positive emotions and their effect as mediators between controllable attributions of success and academic performance. *Children (Basel, Switzerland)*, 10(6), 929. DOI: 10.3390/children10060929 PMID: 37371161

Ralph, N. (2018). *Risk and Protective Factors for Bullying and Peer Victimisation of Children with and Without Special Educational Needs and Disability (SEND)* (Doctoral dissertation, Keele University). https://keele-repository.worktribe.com/OutputFile/463478

Reed, K. P., Nugent, W. R., & Cooper, R. L. (2015). The relationship between bullying and suicide: What we know and what it means for schools. *Adolescent Research Review*, 1(2), 133–146. DOI: 10.1007/s40894-015-0012-8

Rodríguez-Hidalgo, A. J., Alcívar, A., & Herrera-López, M. (2019). Traditional bullying and discriminatory bullying around special educational needs: Psychometric properties of two instruments to measure it. *International Journal of Environmental Research and Public Health*, 16(1), 142–150. DOI: 10.3390/ijerph16010142 PMID: 30621091

Rose, C. A., & Espelage, D. L. (2012). Risk and protective factors associated with the bullying involvement of students with emotional and behavioral disorders. *Behavioral Disorders*, 37(3), 133–148. DOI: 10.1177/019874291203700302

Rose, C. A., & Gage, N. A. (2017). Exploring the involvement of bullying among students with disabilities over time. *Exceptional Children*, 83(3), 298–314. DOI: 10.1177/0014402916667587

Rose, C. A., Monda-Amaya, L. E., & Espelage, D. L. (2011). Bullying perpetration and victimization in special education: A review of the literature. *Remedial and Special Education*, 32(2), 114–130. DOI: 10.1177/0741932510361247

Rose, C. A., Swearer, S. M., & Espelage, D. L. (2012). Bullying and students with disabilities: The untold narrative. *Focus on Exceptional Children*, 45(2), 1–10. DOI: 10.17161/foec.v45i2.6682

Rowley, E., Chandler, S., Baird, G., Simonoff, E., Pickles, A., Loucas, T., & Charman, T. (2012). The experience of friendship, victimization and bullying in children with an autism spectrum disorder: Associations with child characteristics and school placement. *Research in Autism Spectrum Disorders*, 6(3), 1126–1134. DOI: 10.1016/j.rasd.2012.03.004

Sapouna, M., & Wolke, D. (2013). Resilience to bullying victimization: The role of individual, family, and peer characteristics. *Child Abuse & Neglect*, 37(11), 997–1006. DOI: 10.1016/j.chiabu.2013.05.009 PMID: 23809169

Shochet, I. M., Dadds, M. R., Ham, D., & Montague, R. (2006). School connectedness is an underemphasized parameter in adolescent mental health: Results of a community prediction study. *Journal of Clinical Child and Adolescent Psychology*, 35(2), 170–179. DOI: 10.1207/s15374424jccp3502_1 PMID: 16597213

Siddiqui, S., & Schultze-Krumbholz, A. (2023). The Sohanjana Antibullying Intervention: Pilot results of a peer-training module in Pakistan. *Social Sciences (Basel, Switzerland)*, 12(7), 409. DOI: 10.3390/socsci12070409

Skinner, E. A., & Zimmer-Gembeck, M. J. (2007). The development of coping. *Annual Review of Psychology*, 58(1), 119–144. DOI: 10.1146/annurev.psych.58.110405.085705 PMID: 16903804

Stewart, J., & Bernard, M. E. (2023). Empowering the victims of bullying: the 'Bullying: The Power to Cope' program. *Journal of Evidence-Based Psychotherapies*, 23(2), 147–172. DOI: 10.24193/jebp.2023.2.15

STOPit Solutions. (2024). *STOPit: Anonymous Reporting System*. Retrieved from https://www.stopitsolutions.com

Wang, M. T., & Eccles, J. S. (2012). Social support matters: Longitudinal effects of social support on three dimensions of school engagement from middle to high school. *Child Development*, 83(3), 877–895. DOI: 10.1111/j.1467-8624.2012.01745.x PMID: 22506836

Yeager, D. S., & Dweck, C. S. (2012). Mindsets that promote resilience: When students believe that personal characteristics can be developed. *Educational Psychologist*, 47(4), 302–314. DOI: 10.1080/00461520.2012.722805

Zablotsky, B., Bradshaw, C. P., Anderson, C. M., & Law, P. (2014). Risk factors for bullying among children with autism spectrum disorders. *Autism*, 18(4), 419–427. DOI: 10.1177/1362361313477920 PMID: 23901152

Chapter 2
An Analysis of the Cultural and Social Dimensions of Bullying Among Pakistani Children With Special Educational Needs

Kefayat Ullah
Quaid-i-Azam University, Islamabad, Pakistan

Sadia Saeed
https://orcid.org/0000-0002-5977-5658
Quaid-i-Azam University, Islamabad, Pakistan

ABSTRACT

In this study, we examined the social and cultural factors causing bullying of children with special needs, particularly in the socio-cultural context of Pakistan. Despite the global attention on bullying, there remains a significant gap in understanding how cultural norms, social stigmas, and community attitudes affect bullying among children with special needs in Pakistan. This study aims to fill this gap. The study analyzed multiple research studies including research papers, academic articles, books, reports, and policy analyses to examine the different dimensions of bullying of children with special needs in Pakistan. The study findings reveal that embedded cultural norms and social stigmas contribute significantly to the increasing cases of bullying. Community attitudes, lack of awareness, and inadequate anti-bullying policies further aggravate this issue. The insights gained from this study can inform

DOI: 10.4018/979-8-3693-5315-8.ch002

policies that focus on culturally sensitive and inclusive anti-bullying strategies to provide friendlier and more conducive learning environment for all children.

INTRODUCTION

Bullying in educational settings is a global issue that influences millions of students yearly. There are 291 million children with disabilities, representing around 11% of the total children and adolescent population worldwide. Among them, more than 94% live in low-income countries (Columbia Mailman School of Public Health, 2022). According to the United Nations Educational, Scientific and Cultural Organization (UNESCO, 2023a), approximately 32% of students' worldwide report being bullied by their peers at school at least once in the past month. The report further reveals that physical bullying is the most common form of bullying in many regions. Fang et al. (2022) reported in their meta-analysis study that more than 16 million children under the age of 18 with disabilities have experienced violence and bullying around the world. In Pakistan, these figures may be significantly higher due to various socio-cultural dynamics and a lack of comprehensive anti-bullying policies. McFarlane et al. (2017) found that more than 89% of Pakistani children face victimization one or more times, and around 75% reported one or more acts of perpetration within the preceding four weeks. The rise of bullying in schools is undeniable and has been considered as a pressing public issue in Pakistan (Siddiqui & Schultze-Krumbholz, 2023). Naveed et al. (2020) conducted a cross-sectional study at seven public and private schools situated in five districts of Pakistan from children both boys and girls. A total of 26.6% of children reported being bullied at school, and 17% reported being bullied outside of school (Lubna et al., 2022). Special needs schools, which accommodate children with physical, mental, and emotional disabilities, are not safe from this pervasive issue. Children with special needs experience bullying or harassment. They may also be less likely to resist against it (Special Need Alliance, 2015).

The prevalence of bullying among children with special needs in Pakistan is a complex phenomenon deeply intertwined with cultural and social factors. Cultural norms in Pakistan often dictate rigid gender roles and societal hierarchies that can contribute to the marginalization of vulnerable groups, including children with disabilities. Bullying is rooted in the patriarchal and gender-biased structure of Pakistani society (Karmaliani et al., 2017). These children often face social stigma and prejudice, leading to their social exclusion and making them easy targets for bullying. Differences based on gender, class, and disability further complicate their experiences and often leave them without adequate support systems (Saeed et al., 2017).

The need for this study is underscored by the lack of empirical data and comprehensive analyses of bullying among children with special needs in the Pakistani context (Siddiqui & Schultze-Krumbholz, 2023). Existing research has predominantly focused on bullying in mainstream schools (Mbah, 2020; Naveed et al., 2020; Thompson et al., 2007), leaving a significant knowledge gap regarding the unique challenges faced by children with special needs (Berchiatti et al., 2021; Wright, 2020). Despite the global attention on bullying, there remains a significant gap in understanding how cultural norms, social stigmas, and community attitudes specifically influence the occurrence and perception of bullying among children with special needs in Pakistan. This study aims to fill this gap by providing a nuanced understanding of how cultural and social factors contribute to bullying in special needs schools. However, the contribution of this study lies in its potential to influence policy and practice by highlighting the unique cultural and social dynamics that contribute to bullying in special education schools in Pakistan. By providing a detailed analysis of these factors, the study aims to offer evidence-based recommendations for the development of culturally sensitive and context-specific anti-bullying strategies. These recommendations can help educators, policymakers, and community leaders create safer and more inclusive environments for children with special needs.

The research question guiding this study is: How do cultural norms, social stigmas, community attitudes, and institutional inadequacies in Pakistan influence the occurrence and perception of bullying among children with special needs?

The methodological approach involved a comprehensive literature review and secondary data analysis from a range of existing sources, including research papers, academic articles, books, reports, and policy analyses regarding the different social and cultural dimensions of bullying of children with special educational needs. These sources provide a rich and diverse set of data that address the social and cultural dimensions of bullying among children with special needs in Pakistan. The secondary data analysis was designed to synthesize existing findings and provide a broad overview based on established research.

VARIOUS NUANCES OF BULLYING

Bullying is usually rooted in an imbalance of power (Burger et al., 2015). It is an act of intentionally harming someone, verbally, physically, or psychologically. The act of bullying includes pushing, hitting, teasing, and name-calling (Olweus, 2011). There are three major characteristics of bullying: intent, repetition, and power. An individual who bullies intends to cause pain, either through hurtful words or behaviors or through physical harm, and does it repeatedly (Menesini & Salmivalli, 2017). Harassment is a form of bullying that includes rude behavior, threats, annoys, intimidates, or causes fear in another individual (Special Need Alliance, 2015). The frequency of bullying varies between boys and girls. Boys experience more physical forms of bullying while girls experience more psychological bullying (UNICEF, 2023). However, most children at risk of being bullied are from marginalized communities, children with different gender identities, children from poor families, and children with special needs. Bullying is a major issue in Pakistani schools and reports a high prevalence rate among children and adolescents. The most common form of bullying is verbal victimization, followed by social exclusion and physical and emotional bullying.

Most children with special needs may experience some form of bullying (Corcoran et al., 2015; Waseem & Nickerson, 2017). Bullying is classified on various notions of categorization which include intentionality the goal or objective of any individuals through which to cause harm, pressure, and disgrace someone, and secondly, the power disproportion between the socio-culturally or physically unfit among individuals within the societal stratum. Furthermore, bullying is a form of violent behavior that occurs when an individual is subjected to unpleasant activities by one or more people on a regular basis. It is characterized by a power imbalance between the victims and the offenders, as well as intentionality and persistence (Kilic, 2021).

Moreover, social stigma is also one of the cultural factors that contribute to bullying in children with special needs associated with disabilities. Stigma is a social phenomenon that comprises elements of discrimination, stereotyping, labeling, and exclusion (Class, 2021). Disabilities are often viewed as a source of shame and pity, which can lead to the social exclusion of children with special needs. This stigma-based bullying undermines children's well-being and has lifelong consequences (Earnshaw et al., 2018). This stigma is not limited to the children themselves but extends to their families, who may face discrimination and isolation from the broader community. Discrimination is a behavioral expression of stigma or social devaluation (Goffman, 1963). Such societal attitudes can exacerbate the vulnerability of children with disabilities, and make them prime targets for bullying behaviors. The majority of cases of disabilities reported in Pakistani and Afghan schools are associated with a high risk of peer bullying (Karmaliani et al., 2017; Somani et al., 2020). In addition, peer violence and victimization were associated with disability in Pakistan (Somani et al., 2021). These children face a high risk of victimization from their peers and other individuals in society (Corboz et al., 2018).

Additionally, the role of community attitudes and societal norms cannot be ignored. In many Pakistani communities, there is a lack of awareness and understanding about disabilities, which can result in the reinforcement of negative stereotypes and discriminatory behaviors (Bashir & Ahsan, 2023). Community attitudes are often reflected in the school environment, where teachers and peers may unknowingly perpetuate bullying through their actions or inactions. Teachers from rural backgrounds are less likely to intervene in bullying incidents in schools and less likely to punish students who are involved in bullying (Siddiqui et al., 2023a). The lack of adequate training for educators on how to handle bullying, further exacerbates the issue (Siddiqui et al., 2023b).

Similarly, institutional factors also play a significant role in shaping the experiences of children with special needs. Schools often lack the necessary resources and policies to effectively address bullying (Siddiqui et al., 2023b). Data show that children with special needs are being bullied in schools (Berchiatti et al., 2021; Marlina & Sakinah, 2019). Children with disabilities are at risk of high rates of physical violence, particularly those with communication difficulties (Cheshire, 2022). One form of educational inequality related to children with special needs is mistreatment and exclusion from most educational activities (Bashir & Ahsan, 2023).

CONSEQUENCES OF BULLYING

Bullying has many consequences for the children with special needs. These consequences may affect their education and overall well-being. An individual may bully another person while using more than one type. People who experience bullying may have a higher risk of different mental and physical symptoms which can influence their mental health, quality of life, and work or school performance (Geng, 2024). According to the Promoting Relationships & Eliminating Violence Network (2024), physical bullying occurs more during the elementary school years. It has a severe effect on children's development while social and cyber bullying is mostly reported during high school years. However, a very harmful form of bullying is disability bullying which includes mistreating someone or leaving them out because of their disability, making jokes to hurt them, or making someone feel disturbed and uncomfortable because of their disability (Promoting Relationships & Eliminating Violence Network [PREVNET], 2024).

Childhood bullying is a serious public health issue that raises the possibility of negative social, academic, and health consequences in childhood and adolescence. Children who are involved in bullying—bullies, victims, and bully-victims—experience these effects in adulthood (Sigurdson et al., 2015). Wolke et al. (2013) identified that victims and bully-victims faced poor health and social outcomes. Those who were involved in bullying reported poorer psychosocial adjustment and lower educational attainment as adults. Although there is significant regional diversity in the prevalence and nature of bullying, internationally, one in three youngsters had been the victim of bullying in the past thirty days. Three main categories can be used to group the effects of childhood bullying: all effects in adulthood, health effects in childhood, and educational effects in childhood (Armitage, 2021).

Any child can be a victim of harassment or bullying, however, research has identified that children with special needs are more prone and vulnerable to being bullied and more likely to be harmed. (Special Need Alliance, 2015). It can have harmful and long-lasting consequences for children with special needs. Bullying can physically harm a child and may experience emotional and mental effects including depression and anxiety as a result of decreased performance in school (Rigby, 2020; UNICEF, 2023).

Moreover, bullying may vary in special education schools, but that does not mean it does not occur. Children with disabilities including physical, mental, and developmental disabilities, are high at risk of being bullied. It is very important to mention here that sometimes children with special needs also bully others (Cleave & Davis, 2006; Swearer et al., 2012). Bullying has a profound effect on every child but it may be more pervasive for disabled children. Children who face associated academic challenges and unique learning needs being bullied can increase their vulnerability, which affects their ability to learn and their overall development (Taylor, 2022). Bullying is a serious and insidious issue that continues and takes on new forms due to technology and social networking. It is a continuous process full of aggression that exploits a power imbalance between the victim and the perpetrator. The adverse impact may be severe and long-lasting for the child being bullied, the child practicing bullying, and those who witness it. Children who experience bullying may act in ways that seem to instigate or annoy others. However, this behavior does not justify the bullying they experience (Taylor, 2022).

The way bullying is understood varies across nations and is influenced by language and culture. In this context, children's school refusal is becoming an increasingly important issue. The term "school refusal" is an umbrella term that includes different historical terms like truancy, school avoidance, and absenteeism (Kearney et al., 2004). Johnson first coined the phrase "school phobia" in the psychiatric literature for the first time in 1941. The term "school refusal" describes a child's inability to attend school and it has long-term consequences such as academic failure, skipping classes, or coming late and potentially dropping out. Bullying is one of the main reasons why students refuse to attend school (Gusfre, 2022; Ochi et al., 2020). A study has been conducted at the global level which covered the bullying cases. Data were drawn from the Global School-based Student Health Survey of school children aged 12–17 years, in 83 regions during 2003 and 2015. Adolescents worldwide, especially in the Eastern Mediterranean and African regions, are often victims of bullying (Biswas, 2020).

DEMOGRAPHIC FACTORS ASSOCIATED WITH BULLYING

Bullying among children with disabilities is a major issue influenced by several demographic factors. Research studies have highlighted that children with special needs are at higher risk of bullying and victimization as compared to their peers who have no disabilities (Berchiatti et al., 2021). Children with certain types of disabilities, such as autism spectrum disorder, learning disabilities, and attention deficit disorder are reported to be more vulnerable in inclusive environments. Students with emotional, behavioral, and intellectual disabilities, on the other hand, were found to have higher rates of victimization in restrictive educational settings (Rose et al., 2015). The severity of a child's disability can also influence their chances of being bullied. Children with severe disabilities are more likely to be abused due to the visibility of their disability (Rose et al., 2011).

Based on age, younger children with special needs, particularly those in elementary school children are more likely to be bullied. As children grow older and enter into middle and high school, the pattern of bullying may change. So, bullying particularly happens among younger children with special needs due to their developmental stage (Frederickson et al., 2007). Further Saeed et al. (2017) highlight that the intersection of disability with other social categories like gender and class often exacerbates the vulnerability of children with special needs. For instance, girls with disabilities face greater discrimination compared to boys, making them more subjected to bullying. Moreover, the types of bullying can vary based on the child's gender, with boys commonly experience more overt forms of aggression (Marshall & Allison, 2017; Mittleman, 2022). Boys are more likely to face verbal, social and racial bullying, while girls are more likely to experience social exclusion (Khawar & Malik, 2016; Naveed et al., 2020). Research shows that children with special education needs from poor socioeconomic backgrounds are more likely to be victims. Children with special health care needs, especially emotional, behavioral, or developmental problems, are greater likely to face bullying and to engage in bullying behaviors (Berchiatti et al., 2021; Tippett & Wolke, 2014). Moreover, bullying is also associated with social-cultural factors. Children's social vulnerabilities include peer group pressure, social class, being perceived by others as different and weak, and low self-esteem (Colver, 2007). Among the younger generation, the notion of self-esteem is the strongest indicator of victimization among urban youth (Gibson, 2012). Low self-control raises the chances of violent victimization which varies across levels of disadvantaged neighborhoods (Gibson et al., 2014).

Another significant indicator of bullying victimization is the student's socioeconomic status. Research finds that students who belong to low socioeconomic status face more bullying and stigmatization from higher status peers (Babarro & Árias, 2008). Furthermore, the family institution and parental patterns of socialization have been significantly associated with bullying among children with special needs. Further research explored the authoritarian parenting style of parents, lack of emotional support, and interaction can significantly marginalize children with special needs (Alizadeh Maralani et al., 2019; Finardi et al., 2022). Those parents who use an authoritarian style are less involved in their children's academic and social environments, and in contrast, those individuals who recognize their parents' support are less likely to experience bullying victimization in their social surroundings (Gomez-Ortiz et al., 2019; Vlazan & Pintea, 2021; Zhao, 2023).

In addition to this, we have informed this study with different theoretical perspectives such as stigma and labeling theories for understanding this issue in the socio-cultural context of Pakistan. The theory of stigma as it is explained by Erven Goffman (1963), is a key concept and theory that can be engaged for informed analysis of this study. Goffman (1963 p.3) classically defined Stigma as an "attribute that is deeply discrediting." Similarly, Stigma is defined as "a powerful negative label that greatly changes a person's self-concept and social identity" (Clair 2018; Macionis, 2012 p. 200). Thornberg (2015) identified that participants in bullying frequently use dehumanizing labels such as "ugly", "moron", "retarded", "disgusting", "poor man's clothes", etc., as mean names to call victims. Such negative labels and interaction patterns in bullying can be known as a stigma and labeling process (Merten, 1996; Thornberg et al., 2013). These concepts are connected with the secondary data analysis and try to know how children with special educational needs in Pakistan are stigmatized and bullied by their peer groups and others.

Moreover, various studies have found that members of certain social groups are overrepresented as victims of school bullying. For example, students with spluttering and other speech impairments, poor motor skills, hearing impairments, and neuropsychiatric diagnoses like autism spectrum disorders (Blake et al., 2012; Bejerot & Humble, 2013). These students became stigmatized and socially isolated as compared to the mainstream students. The students with hearing issues were mostly considered members of a low-status group, therefore, they were socially marginalized in school and considered second-class citizens which in turn could lead to bullying (Thornberg, 2015).

Moving further, we will now discuss how cultural norms shape responses and stigma toward people with disabilities. We then discuss how the stigma associated with disability results in discriminatory practices. After that, we will analyze community attitudes, internalize the problem of bullying, and then shed light on the policy gap and inadequacy of the support systems. In the final section, we provide answers to our research question and propose possible solutions.

CULTURAL NORMS AND STIGMATIZATION OF DISABILITIES

The review highlighted that cultural norms and stigmatization of disabilities significantly influence the bullying dynamics of children with special needs in Pakistan. Traditional views often frame disabilities negatively, leading to social exclusion and marginalization of children with special needs (United Nations, 2022). Multiple studies (Ahmad & Koncsol, 2022; Hussain et al., 2022) indicate that cultural perceptions in Pakistan often view disabilities as a source of shame and a burden on the family. These views are deeply rooted in historical and societal contexts, where physical and mental impairments are associated with family dishonor and personal failure.

Historically, the traditional practices of bullying and victimization in the particular reference of the South Asian context have been associated with socio-cultural and economic manifestations. In this sense, the imperative notion of children's literary traditions of bullying expressed to illustrate the challenges of socio-cultural and power relations, particularly in the domain of communalism patterns of bullying and marginalization among the disabled (World Health Organization, 1980). Over time traditional bullying has been part of the ongoing debate or discourse which generates various imperative notions and cultural expressions that promote the value of humanism and pluralistic ethos to create a substantive environment of the disabled. However, this academic debate and policy-based narratives promote progressive patterns of the intelligentsia to mobilize the society regarding the fundamental human rights, and their expressions and functionality in the society (Kilic, 2021). Disability as a pattern or source of cultural identity has become evident and has advanced the legitimacy of bullying victimization.

Climaco (2020) identified that some disabled people always carry a certain level of shame. Shame for being as looking disabled while walking, shame for being considered inferior, and shame for not being able to do everything like a normal individual can do. Children with disabilities are at greater risk of school violence due to prejudice and stereotyping (Njelesani et al., 2021). However, the lack of knowledge often leads to negative societal attitudes and irritating behavior towards children with disabilities. Societal norms and culture mostly influence these attitudes. In most cases, disability is seen as a curse that further isolates children with special needs (Peguero & Hong, 2020; Rose et al., 2012a).

Comparisons with studies from other countries, Singh et al. (2016) in India, and Lo et al. (2021) in China show similar patterns of stigmatization, suggesting a broader regional issue but with specific nuances in Pakistan due to its unique cultural and religious fabric. The prevalence incidence of bullying in Bhutan was 25.6%, while in Bangladesh 24.43% (Dema et al., 2019; Irish & Murshid, 2020). Almost one in three students (32%) has been bullied by their peers in school at least once in the last month in all countries except North America and Europe (UNESCO, 2019).

Shaikh et al. (2019) reported that the total incidence of bullying experienced by children in Sri Lanka, Myanmar, and Pakistan was 37.5%. The data further revealed that 15% of the overall sample had experienced bullying in Pakistan (Shaikh et al., 2019). Similarly, in Nepal, 50.86% of respondents had been bullied in the past month (Neupane et al., 2020). In Pakistan, more cases of cyberbullying are reported than in Sweden, which can be attributed to the diverse schooling culture, absence of anti-bullying mechanisms, and lack of supervision (Imran, 2014).

Research shows that children with special educational needs in both Pakistan and Turkey experience higher rates of bullying compared to other developing countries. In Turkey, children with intellectual disabilities and autism spectrum disorder face more verbal and emotional bullying than typically developing children (Eroglu & Kılıç, 2020). Similarly, in Pakistan, children with hearing impairments are at risk of psychological and physical health problems because of bullying (Akram & Munawar, 2016). Cincioğlu and Ergin (2021) conducted a study in Turkey on the perceptions of teachers regarding the bullying behaviors that the students with disabilities are exposed to in inclusive classes. The findings reveal that the teachers do not know how to control bullying in inclusive education, the teachers' attitudes and perceptions in this regard were significantly negative. They even do not want to receive training on bullying.

Moreover, media representations (e.g., television dramas, and news reports) often portray individuals with disabilities in a pitiful or heroic light, rarely showing them as ordinary people. This representation of media reinforces societal stigmas and contributes to their marginalization (Barnes, 1992). The media has a long history record using stereotypes to portray people with disabilities. The media always portrays disability in the form of evil or depravity. There are numerous examples of baddies with individuals with special needs such as Captain Hook, to Shakespeare (Aruma, 2020). However, the way in which disability has been portrayed in the media has changed over the decades. One of the best examples of how disability narratives are changing is the Barbie doll. The representations of animated movies are significant for children because they influence their social, emotional, and cognitive development (Myszograj, 2023).

The above findings reveal that cultural norms and stigmatization of disabilities in Pakistan are deeply intertwined with socio-cultural, and economic factors. The studies show that the developmental perspective of individuals who experience repeated victimization as a result may lose self-esteem and confidence. Particularly when adults do not intervene and provide protection and support. In Pakistani cultural norms, disability is often framed negatively, leading to social exclusion and marginalization of children with special needs. Mostly families hide a disabled member to avoid social embracement. Girls with disabilities face double discrimination of their gender role and their disability. These issues can be addressed through legislation, public awareness, and improving healthcare, education, and economic opportunities to create a truly inclusive society.

Social Stigmas and Discriminatory Practices

The review found that social stigma and discriminatory practices are pervasive and deeply rooted in institutional factors that children with special needs face on a daily basis in Pakistan. These practices exacerbate the vulnerability of these children to bullying.

Children with special needs in Pakistan face social stigma that further complicates their already exacerbated condition of education and integration into society more challenging. Stigma impacts their access to education, the quality of their learning experience, and their overall well-being. Many Pakistanis believe that children with disabilities are a burden. This view is not only prevailing among the general masses but also among the educated public, educators, and administrators in special education schools (Tahirkheli, 2022). In Pakistan, children with disabilities are frequently stigmatized and considered a marginalized segment of society, and their living conditions are very different from those of people who are not disabled (Zahid & Fatima, 2023). Social stigma and discrimination impact children with special educational needs and their caregivers, creating barriers to participation in social activities (Qayyum et al., 2013).

Our review further highlighted that the stigmatization of children with disabilities significantly influences their schooling and overall well-being (Njelesani et al., 2021). Individuals with disabilities struggle with a sense of difference that does not fit into the societal framework. Students with disabilities such as physical, emotional, psychological, and other related issues promote a sense of victimization. Furthermore, according to Wagner (1983) each individual engages in performance under the shared value of the social system where individuals are considered to be normal patterns which shows the actual social characteristics of societal response.

Existing research demonstrates that those students who have certain types of disabilities, like students with a particular spectrum of behavioral and mental health conditions and other health problems and deficiencies, language or speech impairments, have a higher frequency of bullying and victimization over time (Amiola et al., 2023; Rose & Espelage, 2012). Individuals who are engaged in bullying often focus on those students or peers who are poor and physically weak. The prevalence of bullying with disability are vary: Children having neurological, behavioral, and intellectual disorders experienced 35.3% of bullying and victimization, while 20.8% of students experienced bullying at school due to their physical and health impairments (Rose & Espelage, 2012). In contrast, students without disabilities are more concerned about their safety and avoiding bullying from their schoolmates (Iqbal et al., 2021). Furthermore, Doreen et al. (2006) conducted a meta-analysis to explore the bullying practices and victimization of school children and the discriminatory attitude of the community, whereas 35% children aged 12–18 years were involved in bullying process and victimization, and 15% of students experienced cyberbullying.

From the above discussion, the existing empirical data shows that the majority of children with disabilities experience significant discrimination due to social stigma, which affects children and their families. There are significant challenges for children with special needs in Pakistan, but better implementation of anti-stigma policies, increased awareness, and changing societal attitudes are crucial steps for improvement. Providing equal opportunities to these children is essential for decreasing stigma and enhancing an inclusive environment for learning and development.

Community Attitudes and Internalizing Problem of Bullying and Victimization

Children with special needs often internalize the bullying they face, leading to serious psychological and social consequences such as depression, anxiety, and feelings of isolation, as well as poor learning outcomes. Children with special needs are more likely to face bullying as compared to non-disabled children. Mostly these children face psychological impacts leading to increased depression, anxiety, and a decline in academic performance. Similarly, social isolation and reduced participation in community and school activities further aggravate the educational and personal development of these children (Peguero & Hong, 2020). Bullies, victims, and bully-victims all face more problems than students who are not involved in such victimization behaviors. Bully-victims indicate a higher risk of suicidal ideation and are more likely to suffer from mental issues (Kelly et al., 2015). One of the major reasons is the lack of community awareness and understanding regarding special educational needs.

Different factors contribute to an increased risk of bullying for children with disabilities. One of the major factors is the student-teacher relationships. According to Berchiatti et al. (2021), children with special educational needs and learning difficulties frequently experience negative relationships with teachers which can escalate the risk of bullying from the side of peers. Moreover, social status within peer groups also plays a key role. Children with special needs often consider valueless and marginalized, making them more vulnerable to victimization. The prevalence of bullying in Pakistani schools particularly among children with disabilities is a serious issue. Studies have highlighted that harassment and cyberbullying are prevalent among most of the educational institutions in Pakistan, which have adverse effects on the mental health of the victims (Ding et al., 2024; Saeed et al., 2019). Victims of mistreatment behavior often show higher levels of depression, anxiety, and other internalizing problems as compared to their non-bullied peers (Ding et al., 2024).

In Pakistan, many communities lack awareness about the rights and patterns of disabilities, leading to harmful stereotypes and prejudiced behavior (Noor, 2022). These attitudes are reflected in the community's interactions with children with special needs which significantly affect the support, acceptance, and opportunities available to them. Children with severe disabilities in rural Punjab experience lower school enrollment rates and poor learning results in basic reading and math compared to their peers without disabilities (Singal et al., 2018).

The above discussion indicates that community attitudes toward disabilities influence the experiences of children with special needs in Pakistan, these children often internalize the bullying they face leading to severe social and psychological impacts such as depression, anxiety, feelings of isolation, and low education enrollment and learning output. Addressing these issues needs a multifaceted approach such as policy changes, efforts to change societal attitudes towards disabilities, school staff training, and community involvement to eradicate the practice of bullying in educational settings.

Inadequate Institutional Support and Policy Gaps

The review identified major inadequacies in institutional support and clear policy gaps that leave children with special needs vulnerable to bullying in Pakistan. Addressing the issue of bullying among special children in educational settings requires a multifaceted approach, where policy frameworks and institutional support play significant roles. Unfortunately, there are major inadequacies and gaps in this area, which influence the quality of education and the overall development of children with special educational needs (Chisala et al., 2023; Didaskalou et al., 2009). Inadequate institutional support includes a lack of training and awareness. Many schools lack adequate training for teachers and other staff on how to deal with bullying involving children with special needs. Sometimes bullying is not immediately accepted by classroom teachers as annoying behavior (Berchiatti et al., 2021; Rose & Monda-Amaya, 2012). A lack of staff training leads to an inadequate response to bullying cases, as a result leaving affected children at risk. There is sometimes a lack of robust and comprehensive support systems within the school that can facilitate and support children with special needs who are victims and face bullying behavior (Frederickson & Furnham, 2004; UNESCO, 2023b).

Resource allocation is also a major issue in handling bullying. Special needs programs mostly suffer from insufficient resources. These include the unavailability of specialized personnel like counselors and psychologists to provide the necessary support and deal with bullied children with special education needs (Swearer et al.,

2012; UNESCO, 2023b). Sometimes, there is no proper channel or robust mechanism for reporting and addressing bullying incidents. This problem is mostly due to a lack of awareness among teachers and students to report bullying cases (Siddiqui & Schultze-Krumbholz, 2023). Students with observable disabilities and behavioral disorders reported more bullying incidents and they are more victimized than their general education counterparts. This study further compared the bullying among students of special education and general education. Seventh graders in general education show more bullying behavior than sixth graders and ninth graders in general education. Similarly, fifth graders in general education reported more bullying than students of overall graders in general education. The study did not find any gender difference in bullying and victimization (Swearer et al., 2012).

Pakistan's existing policies do not adequately address the problem of bullying faced by children with special needs. Many anti-bullying policies are not inclusive and do not specifically focus on the needs of children with disabilities as a result most children are not protected (UNESCO, 2020; Rigby, 2014). Despite the increased incidents and serious effects of bullying, Pakistan lacks comprehensive policies and interventions to address this dilemma (Ashfaq et al., 2018; Siddiqui & Schultze-Krumbholz, 2023). Most importantly, even if policies are present, there are still significant gaps in their execution and enforcement. This is because there is a lack of resources, training, and accountability mechanisms (Good et al., 2011). Schools frequently lack the administrative capacity to efficiently implement anti-bullying measures, as a result, policies are ineffective in practice (Siddiqui & Schultze-Krumbholz, 2023).

Children with disabilities describe their experience of bullying and victimization that lead them to low self-esteem and poor personality development (O'moore & Kirkham, 2001; Piek et al., 2005). It is helpful to interact with children to listen to their painful stories of marginalization and vulnerabilities. Making positive interactions with children can develop their ability to overcome mental distress and anxieties (World Health Organization, 2001). Further, the existing data reveal that those children who consistently bully and victimize other children are mostly aware of the negative consequences of bullying (Kilic, 2021).

The common strategies and framework to overcome bullying and victimization are to develop capacity-building and robust techniques to train children to avoid embarrassment and shame. In the context of Pakistan, the existing educational policies reveal the lack of specific provisions for anti-bullying measures targeting special needs schools (Nation, 2019). Institutional practices and policies highlight that many special needs schools lack trained staff and adequate resources to effectively address bullying. There is a pressing need for specialized training programs for educators (Ahmad & Yousaf, 2011).

The above discussion shows that there is a glaring policy gap and institutional support issue in Pakistan to address the unique challenges faced by these children with special needs. The substantive consequences of bullying and victimization promote various patterns of distress and mental obsession among children with disabilities. When comparing Pakistan's anti-bullying policies with those countries that have robust anti-bullying policies USA, UK, and Sweden, shows that Pakistan's policy framework is significantly underdeveloped, and lacks both the breadth and depth required to adequately protect vulnerable students (Imran, 2014; Smith et al., 2016). A low-income country like Pakistan has a suitable framework to develop children's capacities. It is recommended to formulate seminal policy to foster learning about the destructive practice of power, subjugation, and prejudice, to form a viable type of literature and children's stories, and curriculum textbooks, thereby often engaging cinema production houses through media and movie promotions to viably promote practical particle solutions to be utilized. These issues can be addressed through a combination of robust policy frameworks and efficient institutional support to protect special needs children in Pakistan from harassment and to ensure their right to safe and inclusive education.

CONCLUSION

This review-based study provides a comprehensive analysis of the cultural and social factors that contribute to bullying in special needs schools in Pakistan. By examining cultural norms, social stigmas, institutional inadequacies, and community attitudes and internalizing problems of bullying and victimization within different socio-cultural contexts, and then contextualizing the study to Pakistan. The study offers critical insights for policymakers, educationists, and children specialists regarding the social and cultural dimension of bullying among children with special needs in Pakistan.

The findings of existing studies on bullying among children with special needs reveal that cultural norms and stigmatization are deeply intertwined with various socio-economic, and demographic factors that significantly influence bullying among special needs schools in Pakistan. Historically disabilities are considered negatively, as a result, most children with special needs face victimization and marginalization. The review identified that social stigmas and discriminatory practices are persistent and deeply rooted in the daily lives of children with special needs. Moreover, community attitudes toward disabilities, significantly influence the experiences of children with special needs in Pakistan, these children often have serious psycho-social impacts such as depression, anxiety, feelings of isolation, poor school enrollment rates, and weak learning outcomes. Pakistan's antibullying policy framework is significantly underdeveloped. There is weak institutional support, lack of proper teacher training, community awareness, and robust mechanisms for reporting and addressing the incidents of bullying at times.

Limitations and Strengths

This study contributes to the broader discourse on disability and education in Pakistan, advocating for culturally sensitive and context-specific anti-bullying strategies to create safer and more inclusive educational environments for all children. This study also has some limitations. Firstly, the study was based on secondary data analysis and limited practical study, the paper suggests for the significance of conducting empirical research within the socio-cultural context of Pakistan to ensure that interventions are both effective and sustainable. The paper further suggests that researchers and practitioners should engage in practical studies that can directly address the Pakistani socio-cultural and educational realities. Secondly, this study was only focused on children with special needs under 18 years of age in Pakistan, while collecting data from a wider range of age groups and regions, and the use of both parametric and non-parametric measures, would enhance the depth and breadth of the research. The study identifies these as important areas for future empirical research.

Recommendation

Addressing bullying among children with special educational needs in Pakistan needs a multifaceted approach that includes social, cultural, and policy-based interventions. The following are some policy-based recommendations to address the incidents of bullying among children with special educational needs in Pakistan:

- There should be implemented and enforced inclusive education policies to integrate children with special needs into mainstream schools.
- Develop comprehensive teacher training and capacity-building programs to address bullying cases of children with special educational needs and promote an inclusive classroom environment.
- Establish and implement strict anti-bullying policies in schools with special provisions for the protection of children with disabilities.
- Initiate national and community-based awareness campaigns to alter community attitudes towards children with disabilities and reduce stigma.
- Organize community programs, seminars, and workshops to educate parents, community elders, and students regarding special education needs and bullying

- Introduce school-based programs and interventions that increase inclusivity and peer support.
- Organize inclusive extracurricular activities that promote interaction and co-operation among all children.
- Organize social skills training programs for children with special educational needs to train them to increase social interactions to reduce the risk of bullying
- Increase cooperation among different stakeholders, including government departments, NGOs, special child protection specialists, educators, and parents to discuss the challenges faced by children with disabilities, share best practices, and coordinate efforts to protect the best interests of children.
- Establish robust mechanisms for monitoring and evaluating the implementation of inclusive education and anti-bullying policies.

REFERENCES

Ahmad, S., & Yousaf, M. (2011). Special education in Pakistan: In the perspectives of educational policies and plans. *Academic Research International*, 1(2), 228.

Ahmad, S. S., & Koncsol, S. W. (2022). Cultural factors influencing mental health stigma: Perceptions of mental illness (POMI) in Pakistani emerging adults. *Religions*, 13(5), 1–21. DOI: 10.3390/rel13050401

Ahmad, S. S., & Koncsol, S. W. (2022, April 28). Perceptions of Mental illness (POMI) in Pakistani emerging adults. *Religions*, 13(5), 401. DOI: 10.3390/rel13050401

Akram, B., & Munawar, A. (2016). Bullying victimization: A risk factor of health problems among adolescents with hearing impairment. *JPMA. The Journal of the Pakistan Medical Association*, 66(1), 13–17. PMID: 26712172

Alizadeh Maralani, F., Mirnasab, M. M., & Hashemi, T. (2019). The Predictive Role of Maternal Parenting and Stress on Pupils' Bullying involvement. *Journal of Interpersonal Violence*, 34(17), 3691–3710. DOI: 10.1177/0886260516672053 PMID: 27701082

Amiola, A. J., Zia, A., Gangadharan, S. K., & Alexander, R. T. (2023). *Intellectual disability services in the Indian subcontinent.* Psychiatry of Intellectual Disability Across Cultures.

Armitage. (2021). Bullying in children: impact on child health. *National Library of Medicine* .

Aruma. (2020, August 24). *Disability stereotypes in the media.* Aruma. Retrieved August 29, 2024, from https://www.aruma.com.au/about-us/blog/run-forest-run-disability-stereotypes-in-the-media/

Ashfaq, U., Waqas, A., & Naveed, S. (2018). Bullying prevention programs in the developing world: Way forward for Pakistan. *Pakistan Journal of Public Health*, 8(4), 174–175. DOI: 10.32413/pjph.v8i4.239

Babarro, J. M., & Árias, R. M. (2008). Socio Program for the Prevention of School Bullying. *Educational Psychology: Journal of Educational Psychologists*, 14(2), 129–146.

Barnes, C. (1992). Disabling imagery and the media. *An Exploration of the Principles for Media Representations of Disabled People. The First in a Series of Reports. Halifax.*

Bartlett, D. J., Macnab, J., Macarthur, C., Mandich, A., Magill-Evans, J., Young, N. L., Beal, D., Conti-Becker, A., & Polatajko, H. J. (2006). Advancing rehabilitation research: An interactionist perspective to guide question and design. *Disability and Rehabilitation*, 28(19), 1169–1176. DOI: 10.1080/09638280600551567 PMID: 17005478

Bashir, S., & Ahsan, H. (2023). *Educational Exclusion of Children with Special Needs* (No. 2023: 109). Pakistan Institute of Development Economics.

Bejerot, S., Plenty, S., Humble, A., & Humble, M. B. (2013). Poor motor skills: A risk marker for bully victimization. *Aggressive Behavior*, 39(6), 453–461. DOI: 10.1002/ab.21489 PMID: 23784933

Berchiatti, M., Ferrer, A., Galiana, L., Badenes-Ribera, L., & Longobardi, C. (2021). Bullying in Students with Special Education Needs and Learning Difficulties: The Role of the Student–Teacher Relationship Quality and Students' Social Status in the Peer Group. *Child and Youth Care Forum*, 51(3), 515–537. DOI: 10.1007/s10566-021-09640-2

Biswas, T., Scott, J. G., Munir, K., Thomas, H. J., Huda, M. M., Hasan, M. M., de Vries, T. D., Baxter, J., & Mamun, A. A. (2020). Global variation in the prevalence of bullying victimisation amongst adolescents: Role of peer and parental supports. *EClinicalMedicine*, 20, 1–8. DOI: 10.1016/j.eclinm.2020.100276 PMID: 32300737

Blake, J. J., Lund, E. M., Zhou, Q., Kwok, O. M., & Benz, M. R. (2012). National prevalence rates of bully victimization among students with disabilities in the United States. *School Psychology Quarterly*, 27(4), 210–222. DOI: 10.1037/spq0000008 PMID: 23294235

Burger, C., Strohmeier, D., Spröber, N., Bauman, S., & Rigby, K. (2015). How teachers respond to school bullying: An examination of self-reported intervention strategy use, moderator effects, and concurrent use of multiple strategies. *Teaching and Teacher Education*, 51, 191–202. DOI: 10.1016/j.tate.2015.07.004

Cheshire, L. (2022). *School Violence and Bullying of Children with Disabilities in the Eastern and Southern African Region: A Needs Assessment*. Retrieved August 2, 2024, from https://www.leonardcheshire.org/sites/default/files/2022-03/Leonard-Cheshire-SVB-report-foreword.pdf

Chisala, M., Ndhlovu, D., & Mandyata, J.M. (2023). Child protection measures on bullying in special education schools. *European Journal of Special Education Research, 9(3),* 57-77. https://doi.org/Cincioğlu, Ş., Ergin, D. Y. (2023). Evaluation of peer bullying towards inclusion students by teachers. *Social Sciences Research Journal, 12*(15), 2017-2027. DOI: 10.46827/ejse.v9i3.4964

Clair, M. (2018). *Stigma: Forthcoming in Core Concepts in Sociology*. Scholars Harvard.

Class, E. (2021, August 30). *Inclusive Perspectives in Primary Education*. Pressbooks.pub; Pressbooks. https://pressbooks.pub/inclusiveperspectives/

Climaco, M. (2020, February 25). *Confronting shame—and accepting my disability—with Judy Heumann - Ford Foundation*. Ford Foundation. Retrieved August 4, 2024, from https://www.fordfoundation.org/news-and-stories/stories/confronting-shame-and-accepting-my-disability-with-judy-heumann/

Columbia Mailman School of Public Health. (2022, March 23). *One in Three Children With Disabilities Has Experienced Violence: Global Study*. Columbia University Mailman School of Public Health. Retrieved July 24, 2024, from https://www.publichealth.columbia.edu/news/one-three-children-disabilities-has-experienced-violence-global-study

Colver, A. (2005). A shared framework and language for childhood disability. *Developmental Medicine and Child Neurology*, 47(11), 780–784. DOI: 10.1111/j.1469-8749.2005.tb01078.x PMID: 16225744

Conti-Becker, A. (2003). Between the ideal and the real: Reconsidering the international classification of functioning, disability and health. *Disability and Rehabilitation*, 25(31), 2125–2129. DOI: 10.3109/09638280902912509 PMID: 19888843

Corboz, J., Hemat, O., Siddiq, W., & Jewkes, R. (2018). Children's peer violence perpetration and victimization: Prevalence and associated factors among school children in Afghanistan. *PLoS One*, 13(2), e0192768. Advance online publication. DOI: 10.1371/journal.pone.0192768 PMID: 29438396

Corcoran, L., Mc Guckin, C., & Prentice, G. (2015). Cyberbullying or cyber aggression?: A review of existing definitions of cyber-based peer-to-peer aggression. *Societies (Basel, Switzerland)*, 5(2), 245–255. DOI: 10.3390/soc5020245

Dema, T., Tripathy, J. P., Thinley, S., Rani, M., Dhendup, T., Laxmeshwar, C., Tenzin, K., Gurung, M. S., Tshering, T., Subba, D. K., Penjore, T., & Lhazeen, K. (2019). Suicidal ideation and attempt among school going adolescents in Bhutan–A secondary analysis of a global school-based student health survey in Bhutan 2016. *BMC Public Health*, 19(1), 1–12. DOI: 10.1186/s12889-019-7791-0 PMID: 31791280

Didaskalou, E., Andreou, E., & Vlachou, A. (2009). Bullying and victimization in children with special educational needs: Implications for inclusive practices. *Revista Interacções, 13,* 249-274. https://doi.org/DOI: 10.25755/INT.406

Ding, J. L., Lv, N., Wu, Y. F., Chen, I. H., & Yan, W. J. (2024). The hidden curves of risk: A nonlinear model of cumulative risk and school bullying victimization among adolescents with autism spectrum disorder. *Child and Adolescent Psychiatry and Mental Health*, 18(1), 1–13. DOI: 10.1186/s13034-023-00694-9 PMID: 38282053

Earnshaw, V. A., Reisner, S. L., Menino, D. D., Poteat, V. P., Bogart, L. M., Barnes, T. N., & Schuster, M. A. (2018). Stigma-based bullying interventions: A systematic review. *Developmental Review*, 48, 178–200. DOI: 10.1016/j.dr.2018.02.001 PMID: 30220766

Eroglu, M., & Kılıç, B. G. (2020). Peer bullying among children with autism spectrum disorder in formal education settings: Data from Turkey. *Research in Autism Spectrum Disorders*, 75, 101572. DOI: 10.1016/j.rasd.2020.101572

Fang, Z., Cerna-Turoff, I., Zhang, C., Lu, M., Lachman, J. M., & Barlow, J. (2022). Global estimates of violence against children with disabilities: An updated systematic review and meta-analysis. *The Lancet. Child & Adolescent Health*, 6(5), 313–323. DOI: 10.1016/S2352-4642(22)00033-5 PMID: 35305703

Finardi, G., Paleari, F. G., & Fincham, F. D. (2022). Parenting a child with learning disabilities: Mothers' self-forgiveness, well-being, and parental behaviors. *Journal of Child and Family Studies*, 31(9), 2454–2471. DOI: 10.1007/s10826-022-02395-x

Frederickson, N., Simmonds, E., Evans, L., & Soulsby, C. (2007). Assessing the social and affective outcomes of inclusion. *British Journal of Special Education*, 34(2), 105–115. DOI: 10.1111/j.1467-8578.2007.00463.x

Frederickson, N. L., & Furnham, A. F. (2004). Peer-assessed behavioral characteristics and sociometric rejection: Differences between pupils who have moderate learning difficulties and their mainstream peers. *The British Journal of Educational Psychology*, 74(3), 391–410. DOI: 10.1348/0007099041552305 PMID: 15296547

Geng, C. (2024, May). *What are the different types of bullying?* Medicalnewstoday.com; Medical News Today. Retrieved August 25, 2024, from https://www.medicalnewstoday.com/articles/types-of-bullying#summary

Gibson, C. L. (2012). An investigation of neighborhood disadvantage, low self-control, and violent victimization among youth. *Youth Violence and Juvenile Justice*, 10(1), 41–63. DOI: 10.1177/1541204011423767

Gibson, C. L., Fagan, A. A., & Antle, K. (2014). Avoiding violent victimization among youths in urban neighborhoods: The importance of street efficacy. *American Journal of Public Health*, 104(2), 154–161. DOI: 10.2105/AJPH.2013.301571 PMID: 24328615

Goffman, E. (1963). *Stigma. Notes on the Management of Spoiled Identity*. Simon & Schuster.

Gómez-Ortiz, O., Apolinario, C., Romera, E. M., & Ortega-Ruiz, R. (2019). The role of family in bullying and cyberbullying involvement: Examining a new typology of parental education management based on adolescents' view of their parents. *Social Sciences (Basel, Switzerland)*, 8(1), 25. Advance online publication. DOI: 10.3390/socsci8010025

Good, J. M., McIntosh, K., & Gietz, C. (2011). Integrating bullying prevention into schoolwide positive behavior support. *Teaching Exceptional Children*, 44(1), 48–56. DOI: 10.1177/004005991104400106

Gusfre, S. A. (2022). Bullying by teachers towards atudents—A scoping review. *International Journal of Bullying Prevention*, 5(4), 331-347.Hussain, S., Alam, A., & Ullah, S. (2022). Challenges to persons with disabilities in Pakistan: A review of literature. *Journal of Social Sciences Review*, 2(3), 35–42.

Imran, S. (2014). Students' perception of cyber bullying : A comparative analysis in Sweden and Pakistan (Dissertation). Retrieved from https://urn.kb.se/resolve?urn=urn:nbn:se:kau:diva-31937

Iqbal, F., Senin, M. S., Nordin, M. N. B., & Hasyim, M. (2021). A qualitative study: Impact of bullying on children with special needs. *Linguistica Antverpiensia*, 2, 1639–1643.

Irish, A., & Murshid, N. S. (2020). Suicide ideation, plan, and attempt among youth in Bangladesh: Incidence and risk factors. *Children and Youth Services Review*, 116, 105215. DOI: 10.1016/j.childyouth.2020.105215

Karmaliani, R., Mcfarlane, J., Somani, R., Khuwaja, H. M., Bhamani, S. S., Ali, T. S., Gulzar, S., Somani, Y., Chirwa, E. D., & Jewkes, R. (2017). Peer violence perpetration and victimization: Prevalence, associated factors and pathways among 1752 sixth grade boys and girls in schools in Pakistan. *PLoS One*, 12(8), e0180833. DOI: 10.1371/journal.pone.0180833 PMID: 28817565

Kearney, C. A., Lemos, A., & Silverman, J. (2004). The functional assessment of school refusal behavior. *The Behavior Analyst Today*, 5(3), 275–283. DOI: 10.1037/h0100040

Kelly, E. V., Newton, N. C., Stapinski, L. A., Slade, T., Barrett, E. L., Conrod, P. J., & Teesson, M. (2015). Suicidality, internalizing problems and externalizing problems among adolescent bullies, victims and bully-victims. *Preventive Medicine*, 73, 100–105. DOI: 10.1016/j.ypmed.2015.01.020 PMID: 25657168

Khawar, R., & Malik, F. (2016). Bullying behavior of Pakistani pre-adolescents: Findings based on Olweus questionnaire. *Pakistan Journal of Psychological Research*, 31(1), 23–43.

Kilic, E. A. (2021). Peer bullying among children with autism spectrum disorder in formal education settings: Data from Turkey. *Research in Autism Spectrum Disorders*, 75, 101572. DOI: 10.1016/j.rasd.2020.101572

Lo, L. L. H., Suen, Y. N., Chan, S. K. W., Sum, M. Y., Charlton, C., Hui, C. L. M., Chang, W. C., & Chen, E. Y. H. (2021). Sociodemographic correlates of public stigma about mental illness: A population study on Hong Kong's Chinese population. *BMC Psychiatry*, 21(1), 1–8. DOI: 10.1186/s12888-021-03301-3 PMID: 34051783

Lubna, Abid, M., & Qamreen (2022). The trends of verbal bullying among university students: A sociolinguistic analysis. *International Journal of Linguistics and Culture*. https://doi.org/DOI: 10.52700/ijlc.v3i2.123

Macionis, J. J. (2012). *Sociology*. Pearson. Fourteen Edition

Marlina, M., & Sakinah, D. N. (2019). Bullying at students with special needs in inclusive schools: Implication for role of special teachers. In: *3rd International Conference on Special Education (ICSE 2019)*, 2019 DOI: 10.31227/osf.io/9q7cw

Marshall, S. A., & Allison, M. K. (2017). Midwestern misfits. *Youth & Society*, 51(3), 318–338. DOI: 10.1177/0044118X17697885

Mbah, R. M. (2020). *The perception of students about school bullying and how it affects academic performance in Cameroon* (Doctoral dissertation, Memorial University of Newfoundland). https://doi.org/DOI: 10.48336/6KA2-2F62

McFarlane, J., Karmaliani, R., Khuwaja, H. M. A., Gulzar, S., Somani, R., Ali, T. S., Somani, Y. H., Bhamani, S. S., Krone, R. D., Paulson, R. M., Muhammad, A., & Jewkes, R. (2017). Preventing peer violence against children: Methods and baseline data of a cluster randomized controlled trial in Pakistan. *Global Health, Science and Practice*, 5(1), 115–137. DOI: 10.9745/GHSP-D-16-00215 PMID: 28351880

Menesini, E., & Salmivalli, C. (2017). Bullying in schools: The state of knowledge and effective interventions. *Psychology Health and Medicine*, 22(sup1), 240–253. DOI: 10.1080/13548506.2017.1279740 PMID: 28114811

Merten, D. E. (1996). Visibility and vulnerability: Responses to rejection by non-aggressive junior high school boys. *The Journal of Early Adolescence*, 16(1), 5–26. DOI: 10.1177/0272431696016001001

Mittleman, J. (2022). Homophobic bullying as gender policing: Population-based evidence. *Gender & Society*, 37(1), 5–31. DOI: 10.1177/08912432221138091

Myszograj, M. (2023). Representation of people with disabilities in children's media. Retrieved August 4, 2024, from https://www.researchgate.net/publication/371044792_Representation_of_people_with_disabilities_in_children's_media

Nation, T. (2019, December 2). *Special Education Policy 2019*. The Nation; The Nation. Retrieved July 22, 2024, from https://www.nation.com.pk/03-Dec-2019/special-education-policy-2019

Naveed, S., Waqas, A., Shah, Z. A., Ahmad, W., Wasim, M., Rasheed, J., & Afzaal, T. (2020). Trends in bullying and emotional and behavioral difficulties among Pakistani schoolchildren: A cross-sectional survey of seven cities. *Frontiers in Psychiatry*, 10, 976. Advance online publication. DOI: 10.3389/fpsyt.2019.00976 PMID: 32009998

Neupane, T., Pandey, A. R., Bista, B., & Chalise, B. (2020). Correlates of bullying victimization among school adolescents in Nepal: Findings from 2015 global school-based student health survey Nepal. *PLoS ONE, 15*(8), 1-13. e0237406. DOI: 10.1371/journal.pone.0237406

Njelesani, J., Lai, J., Gigante, C. M., & Trelles, J. (2021). Will you protect me or make the situation worse?: Teachers' responses to school violence against students with disabilities. *Journal of Interpersonal Violence*, 37(23-24), NP21723–NP21748. DOI: 10.1177/08862605211062996 PMID: 34937449

Noor, W. (2022). Choose not to place 'Dis' in my ability. *Pakistan Journal of Rehabilitation*, 11(1), 5–7. DOI: 10.36283/pjr.zu.11.1/002

O'moore, M., & Kirkham, C. (2001). Self-esteem and its relationship to bullying behaviour. *Aggressive Behavior*, 27(4), 269–283. DOI: 10.1002/ab.1010

Ochi, M., Kawabe, K., Ochi, S., Miyama, T., Horiuchi, F., & Ueno, S. I. (2020). School refusal and bullying in children with autism spectrum disorder. *Child and Adolescent Psychiatry and Mental Health*, 14(1), 1–7. DOI: 10.1186/s13034-020-00325-7 PMID: 32419839

Olweus, D. (2011). Bullying at school and later criminality: Findings from three Swedish community samples of males. *Criminal Behaviour and Mental Health*, 21(2), 151–156. DOI: 10.1002/cbm.806 PMID: 21370301

Peguero, A. A., & Hong, J. S. (2020). Bullying and Youth with Disabilities and Special Health Needs: Victimizing Students with Physical, Emotional/Behavioral, and Learning Disorders. In *School Bullying. Springer Series on Child and Family Studies* (pp. 85–98). Springer., DOI: 10.1007/978-3-030-64367-6_7

Piek, J. P., Barrett, N. C., Allen, L. S., Jones, A., & Louise, M. (2005). The relationship between bullying and self-worth in children with movement coordination problems. *The British Journal of Educational Psychology*, 75(3), 453–463. DOI: 10.1348/000709904X24573 PMID: 16238876

Prevnet. (2024). *Types of Bullying | PREVNet*. Prevnet.ca. Retrieved August 15, 2024, from https://www.prevnet.ca/bullying/types

Qayyum, A., Lasi, S., & Rafique, G. (2013). Perceptions of primary caregivers of children with disabilities in two communities from Sindh and Balochistan, Pakistan. *Disability, CBR and Inclusive Development*, 24(1), 130–142. DOI: 10.5463/dcid.v24i1.193

Rigby, K. (2014). How teachers address cases of bullying in schools: A comparison of five reactive approaches. *Educational Psychology in Practice*, 30(4), 409–419. DOI: 10.1080/02667363.2014.949629

Rigby, K. (2020). How teachers deal with cases of bullying at school: What victims say. *International Journal of Environmental Research and Public Health*, 17(7), 1–11. DOI: 10.3390/ijerph17072338 PMID: 32235651

Rose, C. A., Allison, S., & Simpson, C. G. (2012). Addressing bullying among students with disabilities within a multi-tier educational environment. In D. Hollar (Ed.), *Handbook of children with special health care needs* (pp. 383–397). Springer Science + Business Media. https://doi.org/DOI: 10.1007/978-1-4614-2335-5_20

Rose, C. A., & Monda-Amaya, L. E. (2012). Bullying and victimization among students with disabilities: Effective strategies for classroom teachers. *Intervention in School and Clinic*, 48(2), 99–107. DOI: 10.1177/1053451211430119

Rose, C. A., Monda-Amaya, L. E., & Espelage, D. L. (2011). Bullying perpetration and victimization in special education: A review of the literature. *Remedial and Special Education*, 32(2), 114–130. DOI: 10.1177/0741932510361247

Rose, C. A., Stormont, M. A., Wang, Z., Simpson, C. G., Preast, J. L., & Green, A. L. (2015). Bullying and students with disabilities: Examination of disability status and educational placement. *School Psychology Review*, 44(4), 425–444. DOI: 10.17105/spr-15-0080.1

Rose, C. A., Swearer, S. M., & Espelage, D. L. (2012a). Bullying and students with disabilities: The untold narrative. *Focus on Exceptional Children*, 45(2), 1–10. DOI: 10.17161/foec.v45i2.6682

Saeed, M., Rizvi, M., Saleem, S., & Li, C. (2019). Disasters of cyber world - A question on mental health. *Clinical Research in Psychology*, 2(1), 1–6. DOI: 10.33309/2639-9113.020102

Saeed Ali, T., Karmaliani, R., Mcfarlane, J., Khuwaja, H. M. A., Somani, Y., Chirwa, E. D., & Jewkes, R. (2017). Attitude towards gender roles and violence against women and girls (VAWG): Baseline findings from an RCT of 1752 youths in Pakistan. *Global Health Action*, 10(1), 1342454. DOI: 10.1080/16549716.2017.1342454 PMID: 28758882

Shaikh, M. A., Abio, A., Celedonia, K. L., & Lowery Wilson, M. (2019). Physical fighting among school-attending adolescents in Pakistan: Associated factors and contextual influences. *International Journal of Environmental Research and Public Health*, 16(24), 5039. DOI: 10.3390/ijerph16245039 PMID: 31835671

Siddiqui, S., & Schultze-Krumbholz, A. (2023). Bullying prevalence in Pakistan's educational institutes: Preclusion to the framework for a teacher-led antibullying intervention. *PLoS One*, 18(4), e0284864. Advance online publication. DOI: 10.1371/journal.pone.0284864 PMID: 37104391

Siddiqui, S., Schultze-Krumbholz, A., & Hinduja, P. (2023a). Practices for dealing with bullying by educators in Pakistan: Results from a study using the handling bullying questionnaire. *Cogent Education*, 10(2), 2236442. Advance online publication. DOI: 10.1080/2331186X.2023.2236442

Siddiqui, S., Schultze-Krumbholz, A., & Kamran, M. (2023b). Sohanjana antibullying intervention: Culturally and socially targeted intervention for teachers in Pakistan to take actions against bullying. *European Journal of Educational Research*, 12(3), 1523–1538. DOI: 10.12973/eu-jer.12.3.1523

Sigurdson, J. F., Undheim, A. M., Wallander, J. L., Lydersen, S., & Sund, A. M. (2015). The long-term effects of being bullied or a bully in adolescence on externalizing and internalizing mental health problems in adulthood. *Child and Adolescent Psychiatry and Mental Health*, 9(1), 1–13. DOI: 10.1186/s13034-015-0075-2 PMID: 26300969

Singal, N., Sabates, R., Aslam, M., & Saeed, S. (2018). School enrolment and learning outcomes for children with disabilities: Findings from a household survey in Pakistan. *International Journal of Inclusive Education*, 24(13), 1410–1430. DOI: 10.1080/13603116.2018.1531944

Singh, A., Mattoo, S. K., & Grover, S. (2016). Stigma associated with mental illness: Conceptual issues and focus on stigma perceived by the patients with schizophrenia and their caregivers. *Indian Journal of Social Psychiatry*, 32(2), 134–142. DOI: 10.4103/0971-9962.181095

Smith, P. K., Thompson, F., Craig, W., Hong, I., Slee, P., Sullivan, K., & Green, V. A. (2016). Actions to prevent bullying in western countries. In P. K. Smith, K. Kwak, & Y. Toda (Eds.), *School Bullying in Different Cultures: Eastern and Western Perspectives* (pp. 301–333). chapter, Cambridge: Cambridge University Press. DOI: 10.1017/CBO9781139410878.018

Somani, R., Corboz, J., Karmaliani, R., Chirwa, E. D., Mcfarlane, J., Khuwaja, H. M., Asad, N., Somani, Y., van der Heijden, I., & Jewkes, R. (2020). Peer victimization and experiences of violence at school and at home among school age children with disabilities in Pakistan and Afghanistan. *Global Health Action*, 14(1), 1857084. DOI: 10.1080/16549716.2020.1857084 PMID: 33357165

Special Need Alliance. (2015, March 24). *Bullying of the Special Needs Child and What Parents Can Do*. Special Needs Alliance. https://www.specialneedsalliance.org/the-voice/william-king-self-jr-cela-9/ (Accessed July 20, 2024).

Swearer, S. M., Wang, C., Maag, J. W., Siebecker, A. B., & Frerichs, L. J. (2012). Understanding the bullying dynamic among students in special and general education. *Journal of School Psychology*, 50(4), 503–520. DOI: 10.1016/j.jsp.2012.04.001 PMID: 22710018

Tahirkheli, H. (2022). *Special Education in Pakistan: Hope for Children with Special Needs | socialprotection.org*. Socialprotection.org. Retrieved September 3, 2024, from https://socialprotection.org/discover/blog/special-education-pakistan-hope-children-special-needs-0

Taylor, D. (2022). *Bullying in Special Education: What it is and How to help*. Spero.academy. Retrieved September 2, 2024, from https://www.spero.academy/news/01gg8h7ys8dqvya21rbs5gxkrk/bullying-in-special-education-what-it-is-and-how-to-help

Thompson, D., Whitney, I., & Smith, P. (2007). Bullying of children with special needs in mainstream schools. *Support for Learning*, 9(3), 103–106. DOI: 10.1111/j.1467-9604.1994.tb00168.x

Thornberg, R. (2015). The social dynamics of school bullying: The necessary dialogue between the blind men around the elephant and the possible meeting point at the social-ecological square. *Confero: Essays on Education. Philosophie Politique*, 3(2), 161–203. DOI: 10.3384/confero.2001-4562.1506245

Thornberg, R., Halldin, K., Bolmsjö, N., & Petersson, A. (2013). Victimising of school bullying: A grounded theory. *Research Papers in Education*, 28(3), 309–329. DOI: 10.1080/02671522.2011.641999

Tippett, N., & Wolke, D. (2014). Socioeconomic status and bullying: A meta-analysis. *American Journal of Public Health*, 104(6), 48–59. DOI: 10.2105/AJPH.2014.301960 PMID: 24825231

UNESCO. (2019, November 18). *Behind the numbers: Ending school violence and bullying*. Retrieved November 18, 2024, from https://www.unicef.org/media/66496/file/Behind-the-Numbers.pdf

UNESCO. (2020). *Pakistan is Using Innovative Approaches for Inclusive Education: GEM Report 2020*. Unesco.org. Retrieved July 25, 2024, from https://www.unesco.org/en/articles/pakistan-using-innovative-approaches-inclusive-education-gem-report-2020

UNESCO. (2023a). *Bullying rates higher for children with disabilities*. Unesco.org. Retrieved July 25, 2024, from https://www.unesco.org/en/articles/bullying-rates-higher-children-disabilities

UNESCO. (2023b). *School violence and bullying a major global issue, new UNESCO publication finds*. Retrieved July 29, 2024, from Unesco.org. https://www.unesco.org/en/articles/school-violence-and-bullying-major-global-issue-new-unesco-publication-finds

UNICEF. (2023). *Bullying: What is it and how to stop it*. Unicef.org. Retrieved August 5, 2024, from https://www.unicef.org/parenting/child-care/bullying#understand

United Nations. (2022). *Culture, Beliefs, and Disability*. Retrieved August 1, 2024, from https://www.un.org/esa/socdev/documents/disability/Toolkit/Cultures-Beliefs-Disability.pdf

Van Cleave, J., & Davis, M. M. (2006). Bullying and peer victimization among children with special health care needs. *Pediatrics*, 118(4), e1212–e1219. DOI: 10.1542/peds.2005-3034 PMID: 17015509

Vlazan, A., & Pintea, S. (2021). The relationship between parenting styles, perceived social support and bullying: A cross-sectional retrospective study upon a sample of romanian students. *The Journal of School and University Medicine*. DOI: 10.51546/JSUM.2021.8101

Wagner, H. R. (1983). *Phenomenology of Consciousness and Sociology of the Lifeworld: An Introductory Study*. The University of Alberta Press.

Waseem, M., & Nickerson, A. B. (2017). *Identifying and addressing bullying.* In StatPearls. StatPearls Publishing. https://www.ncbi.nlm.nih.gov/books/NBK441907/ (PMID: 28722959).

Wolke, D., Copeland, W. E., Angold, A. C., & Costello, E. (2013). Impact of bullying in on adult health, wealth, crime, and social outcomes. *Psychological Science*, 24(10), 1958–1970. DOI: 10.1177/0956797613481608 PMID: 23959952

World Health Organization. (1980). *International classification of impairments, disabilities, and handicaps: a manual of classification relating to the consequences of disease, published in accordance with resolution WHA29. 35 of the Twenty-ninth World Health Assembly, May 1976.* World Health Organization.

World Health Organization. (2001). World Health Organization. (2001). International Classification of Functioning, Disability and Health (ICF). Geneva: World Health Organisation. *Int Classif.*

Wright, M. F. (2020). *School Bullying and Students with Intellectual Disabilities.* Accessibility and Diversity in Education., DOI: 10.4018/978-1-7998-1213-5.ch019

Zahid, S., & Fatima, S. (2023, November 27). *Encountering Stigma in Special Education Research - Ideas.* Ideas. Retrieved September 15, 2024, from https://ideasdev.org/the-fieldwork-diaries/encountering-stigma-in-special-education-research/

Zhao, Q. (2023). Relationship between parenting styles and school bullying behaviour among adolescents. *SHS Web of Conferences.* DOI: 10.1051/shsconf/202318002030

Chapter 3
Bullying and Neurodiverse Adolescents:
Mapping Review and Implications

Victoria Maria Ribeiro Lembo
https://orcid.org/0000-0003-3052-9047
Pontifical Catholic University of Campinas, Brazil

Tatiana de Cássia Nakano
Pontifical Catholic University of Campinas, Brazil

Wanderlei Abadio de Oliveira
Pontifical Catholic University of Campinas, Brazil

ABSTRACT

This chapter aims to review the literature on bullying among adolescents with neurodiversity, to determine the prevalence and characteristics of such dynamics among this population. This is a mapping review, and the study search procedures were applied to three databases (SCOPUS, PubMed, and Web of Science). As a result of the entire analysis and selection process, 14 articles were included in the analytical corpus. The articles identified revealed the complexity of the variables and specificities involved in the relationships about bullying and neurodiversity. The findings reveal that students diagnosed with attention deficit hyperactivity disorder and autism spectrum disorder are more frequently involved in bullying situations compared to their neurotypical peers. The chapter, according to the authors, offers some implications for considering care practices in school psychology for neurodivergent adolescents.

DOI: 10.4018/979-8-3693-5315-8.ch003

INTRODUCTION

An individual's neurodivergence can be understood as brain functioning that differs from typical neurology, a collection of heterogeneous characteristics that may manifest early in life and may relate to differences in a person's personal, social, occupational, or academic development (Mahjoob *et al.,* 2024). Usually, these conditions are associated with autism spectrum disorder (ASD) and attention deficit hyperactivity disorder (ADHD) (Lebrón-Cruz & Orvell, 2023). As part of this classification, intellectual disability (ID), motor disorders, and learning disorders are included (Lang *et al.,* 2022).

Particularly in the educational context, these neurodivergent students often receive rejection and exclusion from their peers, they are victimized due to their intense ares of interest, a lack of social skills, and low social status (Accardo *et al.,* 2024; Zablotsky *et al.,* 2014). Therefore, neurodivergent youth are more vulnerable to bullying, often becoming victims of their peers (Morton *et al.,* 2024; Schroeder *et al.,* 2014).

Several studies have examined the incidence of bullying among this population. Bullying is defined as a common form of abuse, defined by an imbalance of power between peers, in which intentional and repetitive behaviors are directed directly or indirectly at victims (Olweus, 2013), attempting to inflict repeated physical or psychological harm on victims (Zablotsky *et al.,* 2014). A person may obtain power through advantages related to their social status, popularity, physical size, strength, age, intellectual capacity, or belonging to a dominant group (Cappadocia *et al.,* 2012).

A bullying experience can lead to a variety of negative outcomes, like psychosomatic symptoms, difficulty adjusting to social and emotional situations, delinquent behavior, and mental health issues (Cappadocia *et al.,* 2012). The consequences of this phenomenon are well documented and include effects on self-esteem, depression, anxiety, self-harm, and even suicidal ideation (Zablotsky *et al.,* 2014).

Generally, most studies have examined bullying in the general educational population, but studies exploring bullying in special education students have not been conducted even though they are at greater risk of victimization (Zablotsky *et al.,* 2014). It is particularly important to pay attention to this phenomenon when it comes to individuals with neurodiversity, given their high prevalence and specific characteristics (Murray *et al.,* 2021).

The current study focuses on attention deficit hyperactivity disorder (ADHD) and autism spectrum disorder (ASD). According to the DSM-V, ADHD is characterized by harmful levels of inattention, disorganization and/or hyperactivity-impulsivity, while ASD is characterized by deficits in communication, social interaction, and repetitive and restricted patterns of behavior, interests, and activities (American Psychiatric Association, 2013).

Young people with ADHD and ASD, who have some type of different functioning, report a 32% greater risk of being victimized by bullying (Accardo *et al.*, 2024). In adolescents with both diagnoses at the same time, the rates are even higher. Approximately 46% of adolescents with autism spectrum disorders and 43 to 65% of those with attention deficit hyperactivity disorder have been bullied in the past year, according to Morton *et al.* (2022).

In terms of bullying types and prevalence rates, a meta-analysis conducted by Park *et al.* (2020) revealed that 67% of people with ASD were victims of bullying, and 29% were perpetrators. Additionally, Fite *et al.* (2014) revealed that adolescents with ADHD were more likely to participate in bullying dynamics as victims or aggressors than their neurotypical peers.

The consequences of this phenomenon for adolescents with these diagnoses include internalizing mental health problems, such as anxiety and depression, and externalizing mental health problems, such as aggressive behavior (Fredrick *et al.*, 2023, Zablotsky *et al.*, 2013). In addition, bullying is associated with difficulties in emotional regulation, low levels of social competence, and externalization of problems (Fredrick *et al.*, 2023, Zablotsky *et al.*, 2013). According to Morton *et al.* (2022), it is essential to identify neurodivergent young people who have been bullied to understand the real risks they face and to adapt interventions specifically to their needs.

Because bullying dynamics have a significant impact on the mental health of neurodivergent adolescents, this study aims to review the literature on bullying among adolescents with neurodiversity, to determine the prevalence and characteristics of such dynamics in this population.

METHOD

Study Type

This study can be considered a mapping review, or a review that does not aim to evaluate the methodological quality of the included studies, but merely to provide the researcher with information on the nature and extent of the production related to the topic under study (Khalil & Tricco, 2022). However, to ensure greater rigor in the data selection and analysis process, this chapter opted to carry out an assessment of the methodological quality of the studies reviewed.

A mapping review was chosen for this study because this type of review allows for a comprehensive and systematic mapping of the available body of literature on a specific topic, rather than an in-depth and interpretive analysis of each individual study. Unlike a systematic review or a narrative review, which aim to deeply evaluate or synthesize the findings of selected studies, a mapping review focuses on providing a broad overview, which is particularly useful when the field of study is still expanding and the research questions are varied or dispersed. This review was structured and developed based on the Preferred Reporting Items for Systematic Reviews and Meta-Analyses (PRISMA) recommendations.

The Search Strategy and the Guiding Question

The guiding question was developed using the PCC (Population, Concept, and Context) strategy (Pollock *et al.*, 2023): Population - what are the experiences of neurodiverse adolescents in bullying dynamics? Concept - how is bullying defined and measured among neurodiverse adolescents? Context - what are the factors and contexts that influence bullying dynamics among neurodiverse adolescents?

Based on the questions outlined above, the terms "bullying" AND "adolescent" AND "neurodiversity" OR "autism" OR "ADHD" were searched in the databases SCOPUS, PubMed, and Web of Science. Outcomes were exported to the Rayyan platform for identification of duplicates and selection of articles for the analytical corpus (Ouzzani *et al.*, 2016).

Inclusion and Exclusion Criteria

This review included quantitative or qualitative studies published in English that addressed the experiences of neurodiverse adolescents in school bullying dynamics. Only scientific articles published in journals between 2019 and 2024 were considered. No review articles or theoretical papers were included. Additionally, studies involving other neurotypical individuals and adults or children were excluded. Editorials, book chapters, letters to the editor, and other types of materials were not included in this study.

Data Extraction and Selection of Studies

Following the search of the databases, the results obtained were entered into the Rayyan platform (Ouzanni et al., 2016) for identification of duplicate articles and to read the titles and abstracts of the articles found. Based on the inclusion and exclusion criteria, 35 scientific articles were selected for further analysis. As a result of reading and recording these texts, a second selection resulted in the inclusion of fourteen studies in this review. In accordance with the PRISMA guidelines, a flowchart was created to explain the selection process and results.

Methodological Quality Assessment

The Joanna Briggs Institute tools were used to assess the methodological quality of the studies included in the analytical corpus (Moola *et al.*, 2024). At this stage, no articles have been deleted.

Data Analysis

Data were analyzed descriptively using the principles of mapping reviews (Khalil & Tricco, 2022). Relevant information, including the study characteristics, sample data, measurement instruments, as well as the main results found, has been extracted and summarized. An understanding of bullying experiences among neurodiverse adolescents has been gained through the identification of themes and patterns across studies.

RESULTS

Searches conducted in the three databases consulted (SCOPUS, WOS and PubMed) resulted in 492 articles submitted for title and abstract analysis. The PRISMA flowchart below explains the selection process in detail.

As a result of the entire analysis and selection process, fourteen articles were included in the analytical corpus. Material was analyzed in three categories: (a) metatheoretical analysis, (b) metamethodological analysis, and (c) metasynthesis. In the first category, the included studies are categorized according to the bibliometric data, theories, or concepts that were used. In the second category, data are provided regarding the methods used to collect data for each article. In addition, there is an assessment of the quality of their methodology. In the third category, the meta-synthesis compiles all the results that are relevant to the objectives of this review.

Category 1: Metatheoretical Analysis

The first table (Table 1) presents the bibliometric data of the articles included in the review corpus, including the year of publication, the title, the authors, the country in which the research was conducted, and the journal in which it was published. The analysis of this content indicates that Taiwan was the country where the most studies were conducted, with a total of nine articles included (n = 9); and the year 2021 had the highest number of publications (n = 6).

In terms of authorship, it is observed that many articles were written by the same researchers, with Hsiao, R. C. and Yen, C. F., each with eight publications (n = 8), and Chou, W. J., with seven publications (n = 7). Most of the authors work in the medical field (medicine or psychology) or in the social sciences field and are either doctors or post-doctoral scholars. A total of eight journals published the included articles, six of which were published in the International Journal of Environmental Research and Public Health.

Table 1. Bibliometric analysis of the articles included in the review

Year	Title	Autorship	Country	Journal
2023	Brief Report Prevalence of Bullying Among Autistic Adolescents in the United States: Impact of Disability Severity Status	Ball, L. E. & Zhu, X.	USA	Journal of Autism and Developmental Disorders
2023	Adolescent–Caregiver Agreement Regarding the School Bullying and Cyberbullying Involvement Experiences of Adolescents with Autism Spectrum Disorder	Liu, T. L., Chen, Y. L., Hsiao, R. C., Ni, H. C., Liang, S. H. Y., Lin, C. F., Chan, H. L., Hsieh, Y. H., Wang, L, J., Lee, M. J., Chou, W. J. & Yen, C. F.	Taiwan	International Journal of Environmental Research and Public Health
2022	Cyberbullying and Empathy Among Elementary School Students: Do Special Educational Needs Make a Difference?	Touloupis, T. & Athanasiades, C.	Greece	Scandinavian Journal of Psychology
2022	School Bullying Behaviors and Victimization in Thai Children and Adolescents With Comorbid Attention Deficit Hyperactivity Disorder, Anxiety Disorders, and Oppositional Defiant Disorder	Prasartpornsirichoke, J., Pityaratstian, N. & Pongparadorn, W.	Thailand	Chulalongkorn Medical Journal
2021a	Perpetration of and Victimization in Cyberbullying and Traditional Bullying in Adolescents With Attention-Deficit/Hyperactivity Disorder: Roles of Impulsivity, Frustration Intolerance, and Hostility	Liu, T. L., Hsiao, R. C., Chou, W. J. & Yen, C. F.	Taiwan	International Journal of Environmental Research and Public Health
2021b	Self-Reported Depressive Symptoms and Suicidality in Adolescents with Attention-Deficit/Hyperactivity Disorder: Roles of Bullying Involvement, Frustration Intolerance, and Hostility	Liu, T. L., Hsiao, R. C., Chou, W. J. & Yen, C. F.	Taiwan	International Journal of Environmental Research and Public Health

continued on following page

Table 1. Continued

Year	Title	Autorship	Country	Journal
2021c	Social Anxiety in Victimization and Perpetration of Cyberbullying and Traditional Bullying in Adolescents With Autism Spectrum Disorder and Attention-Deficit/Hyperactivity Disorder	Liu, T. L, Hsiao, R. C. & Yen, C. F.	Taiwan	International Journal of Environmental Research and Public Health
2021	School Bullying Behavior in Attention-Deficit Hyperactivity Disorder Patients With and Without Comorbid Autism Spectrum Disorder at King Chulalongkorn Memorial Hospital	Pongparadorn, W., Pityaratstian, N., Buathong, N. & Prasartpornsirichoke, J.	Thailand	Chulalongkorn Medical Journal
2021	Relationship between Bullying Victimization and Quality of Life in Adolescents with Attention-Deficit/Hyperactivity Disorder (ADHD) in Taiwan: Mediation of the Effects of Emotional Problems and ADHD and Oppositional Defiant Symptoms	Lin, C. W., Lee, K. H., Hsiao, R. C., Chou, W. J. & Yen, C. F.	Taiwan	International Journal of Environmental Research and Public Health
2021	In-Person Victimization, Cyber Victimization, and Polyvictimization in Relation to Internalizing Symptoms and Self-Esteem in Adolescents With Attention-Deficit/Hyperactivity Disorder	Fogleman, N. D., McQuade, J. D., Mehari, K. R. & Becker, S. P.	USA	Child Care Health Development
2020	Role of School Bullying Involvement in Depression, Anxiety, Suicidality, and Low Self-Esteem Among Adolescents with High-Functioning Autism Spectrum Disorder	Chou, W. J., Wang, P. W., Hsiao, R. C., Hu, H. F. & Yen, C. F.	Taiwan	Frontiers in Psychiatry
2019	Self-Reported and Parent-Reported School Bullying in Adolescents With High Functioning Autism Spectrum Disorder: The Roles of Autistic Social Impairment, Attention-Deficit/Hyperactivity and Oppositional Defiant Disorder Symptoms	Chou, W. J., Hsiao, R. C., Ni, H. C., Liang, S. H. Y., Lin, C. F., Chan, H. L., Hsieh, Y. H., Wang, L. J., Lee, M. J., Hu, H. F. & Yen, C. F.	Taiwan	International Journal of Environmental Research and Public Health

continued on following page

Table 1. Continued

Year	Title	Autorship	Country	Journal
2019	Prevalence of Bullying and Perceived Happiness in Adolescents With Learning Disability, Intellectual Disability, ADHD, and Autism Spectrum Disorder: In the Taiwan Birth Cohort Pilot Study	Lung, F. W., Shu, B. C., Chiang, T. L. & Lin, S. J.	Taiwan	Medicine
2019	Cyberbullying Victimization and Perpetration in Adolescents with High-Functioning Autism Spectrum Disorder: Correlations with Depression, Anxiety, and Suicidality.	Hu, H. F., Liu, T. L., Hsiao, R. C., Ni, H. C., Liang, S. H. Y., Lin, C. F., Chan, H. L., Hsieh, Y. H., Wang, L. J., Lee, M. J., Chou, W. J. & Yen, C. F.	Taiwan	Journal of Autism and Developmental Disorders

In general, researchers used the classic definition of bullying, which refers to an imbalance of power between peers resulting in intentional and continuous aggression directed at victims. According to the thematic scope of this review, bullying/cyberbullying among neurodiverse adolescents, the reviewed articles dealt with the following diagnoses, according to their objective: Attention Deficit Hyperactivity Disorder (ADHD), Autism Spectrum Disorder (ASD), Intellectual Disability (ID), and Learning Disabilities (LD). It should be noted that the researchers defined and discussed the disorders based on the Diagnostic and Statistical Manual of Mental Disorders, 4th or 5th edition (DSM-4 or DSM-5).

Category 2: Metamethod Analysis

Table 2 was developed to analyze the methodological data of each article included in this review. The Table 2 presents the objectives, sample, instruments used, and data analysis employed in each of the studies. The analysis of this material revealed that the research data were collected through scales, structured interviews, and questionnaires completed by elementary and high school students and their caregivers. The samples were a mix of representative and convenience, with the latter being more prevalent (n = 11).

For data analysis, all authors used a quantitative approach, using descriptive and inferential statistics as well as regression and variance analyses. Most researchers (n=12) mentioned utilizing software, with the Statistical Package for the Social Sciences (SPSS), in various versions, being the most mentioned (n=10).

Table 2. Analyses of the methods and objectives of the articles included in the review

Reference	Objectives	Methodological data
Ball and Zhu (2023)	Analyze the prevalence of bullying behaviors among autistic and non-autistic adolescents in the United States; verify the impact of severity of autism on this phenomenon, using the National Survey for Children's Health (NSCH), 2019-2020.	Sample: collected from the National Survey for Children's Health (NSCH), 2019-2020 edition. A representative sample of 29,027 parents of adolescents aged 12 to 17 were selected out of which 28,016 non-autistic peers participated in the study. Instruments: questionnaires on bullying, bullying victims, autism spectrum disorder, and severity of symptoms; demographic information. The instruments were prepared by NSCH and answered by the adolescents' parents. Data Analysis: frequency analysis using the complex sample module and logistic regression analysis using SPSS software version 27.0 (quantitative study).
Liu *et al.* (2023)	Identifying the level of agreement between autistic adolescents and their caregivers regarding bullying and cyberbullying, as well as associated factors.	Sample: participants from outpatient clinics in three Taiwanese hospitals. The convenience sample comprised 219 adolescents diagnosed with autism spectrum disorders, ranging in age from 11 to 18 years, as well as their respective caregivers. Instruments: *School Bullying Experience Questionnaire* (SBEQ) –Chinese version; *Cyberbullying Experiences Questionnaire* (CEQ); *Social Responsiveness Scale* (SRS) – Taiwan version; *Swanson, Nolan, and Pelham Scale version IV* (SNAP-IV) – Chinese version; *Children's Depression Inventory* (CDI) – Taiwan version; M*ultidimensional; Anxiety Scale for Children* (MASC) – Taiwan version Data analysis: descriptive statistics, interclass correlation, and Fisher transformation - no software was mentioned (quantitative study).

continued on following page

Table 2. Continued

Reference	Objectives	Methodological data
Touloupis and Athanasiades (2022)	Examine empathy and involvement in cyberbullying among adolescents with and without special education needs.	Sample: 240 adolescents between the ages of 11 and 12, of whom 120 were neurotypical and 120 needed special education (SEN) due to diagnoses such as ADHD, ASD, and learning difficulties. Instruments: Cyberbullying Questionnaire and Basic Empathy Scale (BES). Data analysis: descriptive statistics; multivariate analysis of variance (MANOVAs); Pearson correlation; and multiple linear regression, but no software was mentioned (quantitative study)
Prasartpornsirichoke *et al.* (2022)	Examine the prevalence of school bullying in Thai children and adolescents with comorbid ADHD, anxiety disorders and ODD at King Chulalongkorn Memorial Hospital, and to investigate the associations and their effects regarding school bullying.	Sample: participants from the outpatient psychiatry clinic at King Chulalongkorn Memorial Hospital in Thailand. Approximately 180 adolescents diagnosed with ADHD and their caregivers, aged 10 to 18 years, were included in the convenience sample. Instruments: Demographic questionnaire; Olweus bully/victim questionnaire (BVQ) - Thai version; Screen for Child Anxiety Related Disorders (SCARED) - Thai version; Swanson, Nolan, and Pelham Rating Scale version IV (SNAP-IV) - Thai version. Data analysis: descriptive statistics, Fisher's exact test, chi square test, and multivariate logistic regression model - software used SPSS 22.0 (quantitative study).

continued on following page

Table 2. Continued

Reference	Objectives	Methodological data
Liu et al. (2021a)	Examine the relationship between impulsivity, frustration intolerance, and hostility among adolescents diagnosed with ADHD who are involved in bullying or cyberbullying.	Sample: participants was selected from outpatient clinics at two hospitals in Taiwan. The convenience sample consisted of 195 adolescents diagnosed with ADHD who were aged 11 to 18 years and their respective caregivers. Instruments: Cyberbullying Experience Questionnaire; School Bullying Experience Questionnaire (C-SBEQ) – Chinese version; Barratt Impulsiveness Scale version 11-Taiwan (BIS-11-TW); Frustration Discomfort Scale (FDS) – Chinese version; Buss–Durkee Hostility Inventory - Chinese Version - Short Form (BDHIC-SF); Child Behavior Checklist for Ages 6-18 (CBCL/6-18) – Chinese version; demographic questionnaire. Data analysis: descriptive statistics, Spearman's rank correlation coefficient, t-test, chi-squared test, logistic regression model - no software was mentioned (quantitative study).
Liu et al. (2021b)	To investigate the relationship between cyberbullying and bullying victimization and perpetration, perception of family function, distress with frustration and hostility and self-reported depressive symptoms and suicidal behaviors in adolescents with attention deficit/ hyperactivity disorder (ADHD).	Participants: selected from outpatient clinics of two Taiwanese hospitals. A convenience sample of 195 adolescents aged 11-18 with ADHD and their respective caregivers was used. Instruments: Center for Epidemiological Studies Depression Scale (CES-D) - Chinese version; Kiddie Schedule for Affective Disorders and Schizophrenia; Cyberbullying Experiences Questionnaire (CEQ); School Bullying Experience Questionnaire (C-SBEQ); *The Frustration Discomfort Scale (FDS) - Chinese version; The Buss–Durkee Hostility Inventory - Chinese Version - Short Form (BDHIC-SF); The Child Behavior Checklist (CBCL) - Chinese version; The Family APGAR - Chinese version; sociodemographic questionnaire.* Data analysis: descriptive statistics, multiple regression model, R-squared, and logistic regression model - software used SPSS 24.0 (quantitative study).

continued on following page

Table 2. Continued

Reference	Objectives	Methodological data
Liu et al. (2021c)	Identify the associations between social anxiety and traditional bullying/cyberbullying in adolescents with ASD or ADHD.	Sample: participants were selected from outpatient clinics at five hospitals in Taiwan. The convenience sample included 219 adolescents with ASD and 287 adolescents with ADHD, all aged between 11 and 18 years, along with their caregivers. Instruments: Cyberbullying Experience Questionnaire (CEQ); School Bullying Experience Questionnaire (C-SBEQ) – Chinese version; Social Anxiety subscale of the Taiwanese version of the Multidimensional Anxiety Scale for Children (MASC-T); Social Responsiveness Scale (SRS) – Chinese version; Swanson, Nolan, and Pelham Version IV (SNAP-IV) – Chinese version; sociodemographic questionnaire Data analysis: descriptive statistics, t-tests, chi-square tests, and logistic regression model; software used was SPSS version 20.0 (quantitative study).
Pongparadorn et al. (2021)	To analyze the prevalence, role, pattern, frequency and behavior of school bullying and victimization in adolescents with ADHD, including personal factors and the degree of severity of ADHD with comorbidities, especially autism spectrum disorders.	Sample: Participants from the psychiatry outpatient clinic at King Chulalongkorn Memorial Hospital in Thailand. In this convenience sample, 210 adolescents with ADHD, aged 10 to 18 years, and their respective caregivers were included. Instruments: a demographic questionnaire; Swanson, Nolan, and Pelham version IV (SNAP-IV); ASSQ - Thai version; and the revised Olweus Bully/Victim Questionnaire (BVQ). Statistics: Pearson's Chi-square test, Fisher's exact test, and logistic regression analysis - SPSS version 22.0 (quantitative study).

continued on following page

Table 2. Continued

Reference	Objectives	Methodological data
Lin *et al.* (2021)	To examine the mediating effects of emotional problems including symptoms of depression, anxiety, attention-deficit/hyperactivity disorder (ADHD), and oppositional defiant disorder (ODD) on the relationship between bullying victimization and quality of life (QoL) among adolescents with ADHD in Taiwan.	Sample: Participants were selected from outpatient clinics of two Taiwanese hospitals. A convenience sample of 171 adolescents diagnosed with ADHD, aged between 12 and 18 years, and their caregivers were included. Instruments: School Bullying Experience Questionnaire (SBEQ) – Chinese version; Taiwanese Quality of Life Questionnaire for Adolescents (TQOLQA); Children's Depression Inventory - Taiwanese Version (CDI-TW); Multidimensional Anxiety Scale for Children (MASC-T) – Taiwanese version; Swanson, Nolan, and Pelham Version IV Scale (SNAP-IV) – Chinese version. Data analysis: structural equation modeling (SEM); goodness-of-fit measures (GFI); comparative fit index (CFI); root mean square error of approximation (RMSEA); and standardized root mean square residual (SRMR) – Amos version 18.0 (quantitative study)
Fogleman *et al.* (2021)	Assess the impact of bullying and cyberbullying on internalizing symptoms (anxiety and depression) and self-esteem.	Sample: 78 adolescents diagnosed with ADHD, aged between 13 and 17, and their respective caregivers - a convenience sample. Instruments: Kiddie Schedule for Affective Disorders and Schizophrenia in School Age Children (K-SADS); Vanderbilt ADHD Diagnostic Parent Rating Scale (VADPRS); Problem Behavior Frequency Scale-Adolescent Report (PBFS-AR); revised Child Anxiety and Depression Scales (RCADS); RCADS-Parent Version (RCADS-P); and Self-Perception Profile for Adolescents (SPPA). Data analysis: Pearson bivariate correlation analysis, multiple regression analysis, and analysis of covariance (ANCOVA) - software used for this study was SPSS version 25.0 (quantitative).

continued on following page

Table 2. Continued

Reference	Objectives	Methodological data
Chou et al. (2020)	Comparing the severity of psychopathologies and the level of self-esteem among 219 adolescents who have high-functioning autism spectrum disorders.	Sample: Participants were selected from outpatient clinics of five Taiwanese hospitals. A convenience sample of 219 adolescents diagnosed with high-functioning autism spectrum disorders, aged between 11 and 18 years, and their caregivers was used. Instruments: School Bullying Experience Questionnaire (C-SBEQ) - Chinese version; Center for Epidemiological Studies Depression Scale (T-CES-D) - Taiwanese version; Multidimensional Anxiety Scale for Children (MASC-T) - Taiwanese version; Kiddie Schedule for Affective Disorders and Schizophrenia - epidemiological version; Rosenberg Self-Esteem Scale (RSES); Chinese Social Responsiveness Scale (SRS); Swanson, Nolan, and Pelham Version IV Scale (SNAP-IV) - Chinese version. Data analysis: Chi-square test, analysis of variance ANCOVA, multivariate analysis of variance and covariance MANCOVA (quantitative study), using SPSS version 20.0.
Chou et al. (2019)	To examine the prevalence of self-reported and parent-reported involvement in school bullying, along with the associations between social impairment and ADHD and oppositional defiant disorder (ODD) symptoms with bullying among adolescents with high-functioning autism spectrum disorders (ASD).	Sample: Participants were selected from outpatient clinics of five Taiwanese hospitals. A convenience sample of 219 adolescents diagnosed with high-functioning autism spectrum disorders, aged between 11 and 18 years, and their caregivers was used. Instruments: School Bullying Experience Questionnaire (C-SBEQ) - Chinese version; Social Responsiveness Scale (SRS) - Chinese version; Swanson Nolan and Pelham Version IV Scale (SNAP-IV) - Chinese version; Demographic Questionnaire. Data analysis: descriptive statistics, a bivariate logistic regression model, and a multivariate logistic regression model using SPSS 20.0 (quantitative study).

continued on following page

Table 2. Continued

Reference	Objectives	Methodological data
Lung et al. (2019)	To investigate the relationship between adolescent psychiatric diagnoses, such as learning disabilities (LD), intellectual disabilities (ID), attention deficit/hyperactivity disorder (ADHD), autism spectrum disorder (ASD), bullying, self-perceived psychological well-being (SPP) and social adaptation status (SAS) in 12-year-old adolescents.	Sample: The fifth round dataset of the Taiwan Birth Cohort Study Pilot (TBCS-P) was used in this study. This study included 1561 12-year-old adolescents diagnosed with ASD, ADHD, ID or learning difficulties (the parents of the adolescents also participated). Representative sample. Instruments: Demographic questionnaire; structured interviews on bullying in schools; Chinese version of the Oxford Happiness Questionnaire. Data analysis: descriptive statistics, regression analysis, chi-square test, and Bayesian analysis - SPSS version 20.0 was used for the quantitative analysis.
Hu et al. (2019)	Examine the association between cyberbullying involvement and sociodemographic characteristics, autistic social impairment, symptoms of attention deficit/hyperactivity disorder (ADHD), and oppositional defiant disorder (ODD).	Sample: participants were selected from outpatient clinics of five Taiwanese hospitals. A convenience sample of 219 adolescents diagnosed with high-functioning autism spectrum disorders, aged between 11 and 18 years, and their caregivers was used. Instruments: Cyberbullying Experiences Questionnaire (CEQ); Chinese Social Responsiveness Scale (SRS); Swanson, Nolan, and Pelham Version IV Short Form (SNAP-IV) - Chinese version; Center for Epidemiological Studies Depression Scale (CESD) - Taiwanese version; Multidimensional Anxiety Scale for Children (MASC-T) - Taiwanese version; Kiddie Schedule for Affective Disorders and Schizophrenia; sociodemographic information. Data analysis: Cohen's kappa coefficient; t-test and Chi-squared tests; multivariate logistic analysis model; logistic and multiple regression analysis model - SPSS version 20.0 (quantitative study).

Critical Analysis of the Included Studies

As part of a literature review, it is crucial to assess the methodological quality of each article included in the analysis. This stage was completed using one tool provided by the Joanna Briggs Institute (Moola *et al.*, 2024).

Specifically, the instrument used enabled the studies to be evaluated in terms of quality, rigor, credibility, and methodological relevance. The instrument consists of eight questions: 1) Were the inclusion criteria for the sample clearly defined?, 2) Are the study subjects and setting described in detail?, 3) Were the measured variables presented in a valid and accurate manner?, 4) Was the measurement of conditions/phenomena based on objective and standardized criteria?, 5) Have confounding factors been identified?, 6) Has a strategy been developed to address confounding factors? 7) Have the results been measured in a valid and reliable manner?, 8) Has the appropriate statistical analysis been conducted? The answers to the questions can be yes, no, unclear, or not applicable (Moola *et al.*, 2024).

The instrument resulted in a score for each article, and it was agreed that studies scoring 7 or 8 had a high level of methodological quality and a low risk of bias. It was determined that articles with a 5 or 6 point score had a moderate risk of bias and, therefore, a moderate methodological quality. Table 3 summarizes the results of this evaluation.

Table 3. Analyses of methodological quality

Reference	Question 1	Question 2	Question 3	Question 4	Question 5	Question 6	Question 7	Question 8	Total
Ball & Zhu, 2023	X	X	X	X	X		X	X	7
Liu et al., 2023	X	X	X	X			X	X	6
Touloupis & Athanasiades, 2022	X	X	X	X			X	X	6
Prasartpornsirichoke et al., 2022	X	X	X	X			X	X	6
Liu et al., 2021a	X	X	X	X	X		X	X	7
Liu et al., 2021b	X	X	X	X	X		X	X	7
Liu et al., 2021c	X	X	X	X	X		X	X	7
Pongparadorn et al., 2021	X	X	X	X			X	X	6
Lin et al., 2021	X	X	X	X	X		X	X	7
Fogleman et al., 2021	X	X	X	X	X	X	X	X	8
Chou et al., 2020	X	X	X	X	X		X	X	7
Chou et al., 2019	X	X	X	X	X		X	X	7

continued on following page

Table 3. Continued

Reference	Question 1	Question 2	Question 3	Question 4	Question 5	Question 6	Question 7	Question 8	Total
Lung et al., 2019	X	X	X	X			X	X	6
Hu et al., 2019	X	X	X	X			X	X	6

As shown in Table 3, the scores ranged from 6 to 8 points. Six articles scored 6 in the methodological assessment, indicating a moderate risk of bias and moderate methodological quality. The other seven articles achieved a score of 7, but only the study by Fogleman et al. (2021) obtained a score of 8, demonstrating a low risk of bias and, therefore, a high level of methodological quality.

Category 3: Meta-Synthesis

The relevant results from each article included in the corpus of this review are presented in Table 4. From the analysis, it is observed that there are contradictions between neurodiverse adolescents diagnosed with ASD or ADHD and their caregivers regarding their involvement in bullying and cyberbullying dynamics (Chou et al., 2019, 2020; Hu et al., 2019; Liu et al., 2023). Additionally, there are controversies regarding the rates of victimization and perpetration in both phenomena, as the studies by Ball and Zhu (2023), Lung et al. (2019), Pongparadorn et al. (2021), and Touloupis and Athanasiades (2022) show that adolescents diagnosed with ASD have a higher likelihood of being victims/perpetrators of bullying or cyberbullying compared to their non-autistic peers. However, the study by Chou et al. (2020) indicated that the involvement of students with ASD in bullying dynamics is like that of the general population.

Regarding adolescents diagnosed with ADHD, the studies by Lin et al. (2021) and Lung et al. (2019) indicated that they have significantly higher rates of bullying victimization compared to their peers. On the other hand, the research by Pongparadorn et al. (2021) found that students with ADHD are more frequently reported to engage in bullying than their peers without the disorder.

Table 4. Main results found in each reviewed article

Reference	Results
Ball & Zhu, 2023	In this sample, 69.9% of adolescents with autism were victims of bullying, and 22.2% were aggressors. There were no significant differences between the severity levels of ASD and bullying victimization/perpetration. Autistic adolescents are considerably more likely to engage in or suffer from bullying than their non-autistic peers.
Liu et al., 2023	Adolescents with ASD and their caregivers showed weak to reasonable levels of agreement regarding their experiences of bullying/cyberbullying victimization and perpetration. Severe inattention, hyperactivity-impulsivity, oppositional defiant disorder (ODD), depressive and anxiety symptoms, and social impairment were associated with multiple types of involvement in bullying. Adolescents with ASD and their caregivers observed and interpreted interactions with peers at school and online differently.
Touloupis & Athanasiades, 2022	Students with special educational needs (SEN) are more involved in cyberbullying (as victims/aggressors) compared to students without SEN. Offensive/threatening messages and online calls on social networks were the most frequently reported forms of involvement in cyberbullying. It was found that students with SEN expressed affective and cognitive empathy to a lesser extent than their peers without SEN. Additionally, the affective dimension of empathy is a greater predictor of cyberbullying behaviors (as victims/aggressors) compared to the cognitive dimension of empathy. The results show that students with ASD and ADHD are more involved in cyberbullying (as victims/aggressors) compared to students with learning difficulties.
Prasartpornsirichoke et al., 2022	The prevalence of bullying among adolescents with ADHD was 69.4%. Verbal bullying was the most reported form in the sample. Additionally, adolescents with ADHD in high school had lower involvement compared to those in elementary and lower secondary school. It was not found that the severity of ADHD symptoms was associated with bullying, either as aggressors or victims, because most patients are undergoing medical treatment. The findings indicated that adolescents with comorbidity of ADHD and anxiety disorder were significantly associated with school victimization, but not with bullying behaviors. The comorbidity of ODD, with moderate to severe symptoms, and male gender are factors that affect bullying behaviors.
Liu et al., 2021a	Hostility increased the risks of adolescents with ADHD being victims and perpetrators of bullying. Impulsivity was not significantly associated with any type of involvement in bullying. Adolescents with ADHD and higher frustration intolerance had greater risks of being victims and perpetrators of cyberbullying. Adolescents with ADHD with high hostility had greater risks of being victims and perpetrators of bullying.
Liu et al., 2021b	Bullying perpetration and frustration intolerance significantly predicted self-reported depressive symptoms; additionally, cyberbullying victimization and hostility significantly predicted suicidal risk in adolescents with ADHD. Suicidal behaviors were significantly predicted by cyberbullying victimization but not by traditional bullying. Adolescents with ADHD who engage in bullying exhibited more severe self-reported depressive symptoms than non-perpetrators. Frustration intolerance and hostility significantly predicted self-reported depressive symptoms and suicidal behaviors, respectively, in adolescents with ADHD. Hostility significantly predicted suicidal behaviors in adolescents with ADHD.

continued on following page

Table 4. Continued

Reference	Results
Liu et al., 2021c	Significant association between social anxiety and bullying victimization in both adolescents with ASD and ADHD. There was also a significant association between social anxiety and cyberbullying victimization in adolescents with ASD. Finally, there was a significant relationship between social anxiety and bullying perpetration in adolescents with ASD but not in adolescents with ADHD.
Pongparadorn et al., 2021	In this study, the prevalence of bullying behaviors among adolescents with ADHD was 70.5%. Most adolescents were victim-aggressors (31.9%). The severity of ADHD in hyperactivity/impulsivity was related only to the aggressor role. Considering the group with mild symptoms by SNAP-IV scores, those mentioned had 2.32 times more chances of being aggressors compared to the "Not Clinically Significant" group, and the group with moderate to severe symptoms had 2.7 times more chances of being aggressors compared to the "Not Clinically Significant" group. The risk of being a victim for the group with comorbidity with ASD was 2.48 times higher compared to children with ADHD without comorbidity with ASD.
Lin et al., 2021	Bullying victimization was indirectly correlated with quality of life (QoL) through the mediation of emotional problems in adolescents with ADHD. Symptoms of ADHD and ODD did not mediate the association between bullying victimization and QoL. Being a bullying victim was positively associated with symptoms of ADHD and ODD among adolescents with ADHD.
Fogleman et al., 2021	Bullying was associated with higher adolescent-reported anxiety, while cyberbullying was associated with higher parent-reported depression. Additionally, adolescents with ADHD who experienced polyvictimization (bullying and cyberbullying) reported the highest levels of anxiety and depression and the lowest self-esteem. Nearly a quarter of adolescents with ADHD reported polyvictimization, and these adolescents also reported the worst emotional functioning in anxiety, depression, and self-esteem domains compared to adolescents with ADHD who did not report victimization or reported experiencing only bullying.
Chou et al., 2020	Self-reported victims-aggressors and victims had more severe depression and anxiety than self-reported neutrals. The results indicated that the rates of various types of bullying involvement in high-functioning adolescents with ASD were similar to those of the general population. High-functioning adolescents with ASD who were victims of bullying had more severe depression and anxiety than those who had never been involved in the phenomenon. A low agreement was found between self-reported bullying involvement and that reported by parents of adolescents with ASD. Parents reported higher rates of bullying victimization and victim-perpetration than those reported by adolescents with ASD. Both pure victims and victim-aggressors had more severe depression and anxiety than neutrals.

continued on following page

Table 4. Continued

Reference	Results
Chou et al., 2019	The agreement between self-reported and parent-reported bullying in adolescents with ASD was low. A difference was found in the roles of autistic social impairment and ADHD and ODD symptoms between adolescents with ASD who were involved in self-reported bullying and those reported by parents. Symptoms of hyperactivity/impulsivity and ODD were associated with parent-reported victimization and victim-perpetration, respectively, but not with self-reported bullying. Self-reported victims and victim-aggressors, as well as parent-reported victim-aggressors, had more severe socio-communication deficits than neutrals, while no difference in socio-communication deficits was found between perpetrators and neutrals. Only socio-communication was significantly associated with bullying involvement in high-functioning adolescents with ASD.
Lung et al., 2019	Nearly a quarter of adolescents reported being victims of bullying. The bullying rate reported by adolescents was 25.4%, while only 2.8% of parents reported knowing that their child had been a victim of bullying. Adolescents diagnosed with ID, ASD, and ADHD all reported significantly higher rates of bullying victimization compared to their peers. ID and ASD were the only diagnoses directly associated with being a bullying victim. Additionally, adolescents who were bullying victims perceived a lower level of happiness. Adolescents diagnosed with ID and ASD reported a bullying rate higher than 60%, followed by ADHD and LD.
Hu et al., 2019	The study found a low level of agreement between self-reported and parent-reported involvement in cyberbullying in adolescents with ASD. The present study found that older individuals were more likely to be victims or perpetrators of cyberbullying. Severe ODD symptoms were significantly associated with both cyberbullying victimization and perpetration in adolescents with ASD. Cyberbullying victims had more severe depression and anxiety and a higher risk of suicide than non-victims.

Regarding comorbidities, adolescents diagnosed with ADHD or ASD who also exhibit symptoms of Oppositional Defiant Disorder (ODD) have an increased risk of being involved, both as victims and aggressors, in bullying and cyberbullying dynamics (Chou et al., 2019; Hu et al., 2019; Lin et al., 2021; Liu et al., 2023; Prasartpornsirichoke et al., 2022). In this sense, it was found that hostility and frustration intolerance observed in students with ADHD also increase the likelihood of engaging in bullying and cyberbullying behaviors (Liu et al., 2021a, 2021b).

Based on this, studies have indicated that adolescents diagnosed with ASD or ADHD who engage in bullying or cyberbullying dynamics, whether as victims or aggressors, exhibit significantly more severe symptoms of anxiety and depression compared to those not involved in such situations (Chou et al., 2020; Fogleman et al., 2021; Liu et al., 2021a, 2021b, 2021c; Prasartpornsirichoke et al., 2022). Considering these results, the complexity of the variables to be analyzed in the relationship between bullying/cyberbullying and neurodiverse adolescents is highlighted.

DISCUSSION

This study aimed to investigate the prevalence and characteristics of bullying dynamics among neurodiverse adolescents. The analysis of the identified articles revealed the complexity of the variables and specificities involved in these relationships. Discrepancies were observed between the perceptions of neurodiverse adolescents diagnosed with autism spectrum disorder (ASD) or attention deficit hyperactivity disorder (ADHD) and those of their caregivers regarding their involvement in bullying and cyberbullying dynamics, which is in line with the specialized scientific literature on the subject (Hwang et al., 2018).

In this direction, it is suggested that adolescents with these diagnoses may have difficulties in identifying emotions, as well as divergences in interpreting interactions with their peers compared to the perceptions of their teachers and parents (Kirst et al., 2022; Roekel et al., 2010). Furthermore, it was found that neurodivergent students who also present Oppositional Defiant Disorder (ODD) are more likely to engage in bullying and cyberbullying behaviors, a result consistent with the specialized literature (Gau et al., 2013). This result may be related to the low emotional and behavioral control, as well as the frustration intolerance of adolescents with this comorbidity (Hussein, 2013; Unnever et al., 2003).

Adolescents with frustration intolerance may face significant difficulties in forming and maintaining interpersonal relationships (Kok et al., 2016). Those diagnosed with ADHD tend to experience social discomfort, which may lead them to spend more time and energy on online activities to achieve a sense of accomplishment, which can increase the risk of involvement in cyberbullying (Lu et al., 2019).

Given this, a disparity is observed in the results regarding the prevalence of neurodiverse adolescents in bullying and cyberbullying dynamics. Despite these differences, it is observed that adolescents diagnosed with ADHD or ASD have higher rates of victimization or perpetration of these phenomena compared to their neurotypical peers, which is corroborated by the scientific literature (Accardo et al., 2024; Heiman & Shemesh, 2019; Morton et al., 2022; Morton et al., 2024; Murray et al., 2021; Perales-Hidalgo et al., 2024; Schroeder et al., 2014).

Another pertinent result of this review refers to the increase in depressive symptoms and suicidal behaviors in adolescents diagnosed with ADHD or ASD who are involved in bullying and cyberbullying dynamics compared to their neurotypical peers, a finding consistent with the specialized literature on the subject (Yen et al., 2014). From this, it is suggested that being a victim of bullying may aggravate the social isolation of neurodiverse adolescents and, consequently, their support, which is a predictor of these symptoms (Factor et al., 2016). Based on this, it is necessary to gain a greater understanding of the individual and social aspects of neurodiverse adolescents to develop anti-bullying coping strategies (Morton et al., 2022).

CONCLUSION: FINAL CONSIDERATIONS

School bullying among neurodiverse adolescents presents particularities that demand specialized attention and specific interventions, which is further supported by the high prevalence rate and the negative impacts on individuals' mental health (Accardo *et al.*, 2024; Zablotsky *et al.*, 2014). Based on this premise, the present study aimed to investigate the prevalence and characteristics of bullying dynamics in neurodiverse adolescents, focusing on identifying specific aspects of this phenomenon and its relationship to these individuals.

The findings reveal that students diagnosed with ADHD and ASD are more frequently involved in bullying situations compared to their neurotypical peers. This involvement is exacerbated by the presence of comorbidities such as Oppositional Defiant Disorder (ODD). Additionally, discrepancies were identified between the perceptions of neurodiverse adolescents diagnosed with ADHD or ASD and their caregivers regarding the involvement of these students in bullying and cyberbullying dynamics. Based on this, it is suggested that these adolescents may have difficulties in recognizing emotions, as well as presenting frustration intolerance and low emotional and behavioral control, factors that may contribute to the results obtained.

It is important to highlight that the results of this review should be interpreted considering its main limitations. Since it is a mapping review, the analyzed studies were scientific articles that, despite undergoing a methodological quality assessment, many (n=6) demonstrated a moderate risk of bias and moderate methodological quality, which constitutes a significant limitation regarding the reviewed evidence. Another relevant issue is the inability to include all the existing scientific literature on the subject, either due to the inclusion/exclusion criteria adopted or the preferential use of certain databases.

Finally, it is recommended that future studies explore the aspects and subjective experiences of these students, with an emphasis on qualitative research, and that they include the investigation of other neurodevelopmental disorders in relation to school bullying.

REFERENCES

Accardo, A. L., Neely, L. C., Pontes, N. M. H., & Pontes, M. C. F. (2024). Bullying victimization is associated with heightened rates of anxiety and depression among Autistic and ADHD youth: National Survey of Children's Health 2016–2020. *Journal of Autism and Developmental Disorders*. Advance online publication. DOI: 10.1007/s10803-024-06479-z PMID: 39034347

American Psychiatric Association. (2013). *Diagnostic and statistical manual of mental disorders* (5th ed.). American Psychiatric Publishing.

Ball, L. E., & Zhu, X. (2023). Brief report prevalence of bullying among autistic adolescents in the United States: Impact of disability severity status. *Journal of Autism and Developmental Disorders*. Advance online publication. DOI: 10.1007/s10803-023-06041-3 PMID: 37380848

Cappadocia, M. C., Weiss, J. A., & Pepler, D. (2012). Bullying experiences among children and youth with Autism Spectrum Disorders. *Journal of Autism and Developmental Disorders*, 42(2), 266–277. DOI: 10.1007/s10803-011-1241-x PMID: 21499672

Chou, W. J., Hsiao, R. C., Ni, H. C., Liang, S. H. Y., Lin, C. F., Chan, H. L., Hsieh, Y. H., Wang, L. J., Lee, M. J., Hu, H. F., & Yen, C. F. (2019). Self-reported and parent-reported school bullying in adolescents with high functioning autism spectrum disorder: The roles of autistic social impairment, attention-deficit/hyperactivity and oppositional defiant disorder symptoms. *International Journal of Environmental Research and Public Health*, 16(7), 1117. Advance online publication. DOI: 10.3390/ijerph16071117 PMID: 30925769

Chou, W. J., Wang, P. W., Hsiao, R. C., Hu, H. F., & Yen, C. F. (2020). Role of school bullying involvement in depression, anxiety, suicidality, and low self-esteem among adolescents with high-functioning autism spectrum disorder. *Frontiers in Psychiatry*, 11(9), 9. Advance online publication. DOI: 10.3389/fpsyt.2020.00009 PMID: 32082201

Factor, P. I., Rosen, P. J., & Reyes, R. A. (2016). The relation of poor emotional awareness and externalizing behavior among children with ADHD. *Journal of Attention Disorders*, 20(2), 168–177. DOI: 10.1177/1087054713494005 PMID: 23839724

Fite, P. J., Evans, S. C., Cooley, J. L., & Rubens, S. L. (2014). Further evaluation of associations between attention-deficit/hyperactivity and oppositional defiant disorder symptoms and bullying-victimization in adolescence. *Child Psychiatry and Human Development*, 45(1), 32–41. DOI: 10.1007/s10578-013-0376-8 PMID: 23516013

Fogleman, N. D., McQuade, J. D., Mehari, K. R., & Becker, S. P. (2021). In-person victimization, cyber victimization, and polyvictimization in relation to internalizing symptoms and self-esteem in adolescents with attention-deficit/hyperactivity disorder. *Child: Care, Health and Development*, 47(6), 805–815. DOI: 10.1111/cch.12888 PMID: 34155671

Fredrick, S. S., Nickerson, A. B., Sun, L., Rodgers, J. D., Thomeer, M. L., Lopata, C., & Todd, F. (2023). ASD symptoms, social skills, and comorbidity: Predictors of bullying perpetration. *Journal of Autism and Developmental Disorders*, 53(8), 3092–3102. DOI: 10.1007/s10803-022-05612-0 PMID: 35678945

Gau, S. S. F., Liu, L. T., Wu, Y. Y., Chiu, Y. N., & Tsai, W. C. (2013). Psychometric properties of the Chinese version of the social responsiveness scale. *Research in Autism Spectrum Disorders*, 7(2), 349–360. DOI: 10.1016/j.rasd.2012.10.004

Heiman, T., & Olenik Shemesh, D. (2018). Predictors of cyber-victimization of higher-education students with and without learning disabilities. *Journal of Youth Studies*, 22(2), 205–222. DOI: 10.1080/13676261.2018.1492103

Hu, H. F., Liu, T. L., Hsiao, R. C., Ni, H. C., Liang, S. H. Y., Lin, C. F., Chan, H. L., Hsieh, Y. H., Wang, L. J., Lee, M. J., Chou, W. J., & Yen, C. F. (2019). Cyberbullying victimization and perpetration in adolescents with high-functioning autism spectrum disorder: Correlations with depression, anxiety, and suicidality. *Journal of Autism and Developmental Disorders*, 49(10), 4170–4180. DOI: 10.1007/s10803-019-04060-7 PMID: 31267285

Hussein, M. H. (2013). The social and emotional skills of bullies, victims, and bully-victims of Egyptian primary school children. *International Journal of Psychology*, 48(5), 910–921. DOI: 10.1080/00207594.2012.702908 PMID: 22853459

Hwang, S., Kim, Y. S., Koh, Y. J., & Leventhal, B. L. (2018). Autism spectrum disorder and school bullying: Who is the victim? Who is the perpetrator? *Journal of Autism and Developmental Disorders*, 48(1), 225–238. DOI: 10.1007/s10803-017-3285-z PMID: 28936640

Khalil, H., & Tricco, A. C. (2022). Differentiating between mapping reviews and scoping reviews in the evidence synthesis ecosystem. *Journal of Clinical Epidemiology*, 149, 175–182. DOI: 10.1016/j.jclinepi.2022.05.012 PMID: 35636593

Kirst, S., Bögl, K., Gross, V. L., Diehm, R., Poustka, L., & Dziobek, I. (2022). Subtypes of aggressive behavior in children with autism in the context of emotion recognition, hostile attribution bias, and dysfunctional emotion regulation. *Journal of Autism and Developmental Disorders*, 52(12), 5367–5382. DOI: 10.1007/s10803-021-05387-w PMID: 34931277

Kok, F. M., Groen, Y., Fuermaier, A. B., & Tucha, O. (2016). Problematic peer functioning in girls with ADHD: A systematic literature review. *PLoS One*, 11(11), e0165119. DOI: 10.1371/journal.pone.0165119 PMID: 27870862

Lang, J., Wylie, G., Haig, C., Gillberg, C., & Minnis, H. (2024). Towards system redesign: An exploratory analysis of neurodivergent traits in a childhood population referred for autism assessment. *PLoS One*, 19(1), e0296077. DOI: 10.1371/journal.pone.0296077 PMID: 38198484

Lebrón-Cruz, A., & Orvell, A. (2023). I am what I am: The role of essentialist beliefs and neurodivergent identification on individuals' self-efficacy. *Journal of Experimental Psychology. General*, 152(11), 2995–3001. DOI: 10.1037/xge0001457 PMID: 37498695

Lin, C. W., Lee, K. H., Hsiao, R. C., Chou, W. J., & Yen, C. F. (2021). Relationship between bullying victimization and quality of life in adolescents with attention-deficit/hyperactivity disorder (ADHD) in Taiwan: Mediation of the effects of emotional problems and ADHD and oppositional defiant symptoms. *International Journal of Environmental Research and Public Health*, 18(18), 9470. Advance online publication. DOI: 10.3390/ijerph18189470 PMID: 34574409

Liu, T. L., Chen, Y. L., Hsiao, R. C., Ni, H. C., Liang, S. H. Y., Lin, C. F., Chan, H. L., Hsieh, Y. H., Wang, L. J., Lee, M. J., Chou, W. J., & Yen, C. F. (2023). Adolescent–caregiver agreement regarding the school bullying and cyberbullying involvement experiences of adolescents with autism spectrum disorder. *International Journal of Environmental Research and Public Health*, 20(4), 3733. Advance online publication. DOI: 10.3390/ijerph20043733 PMID: 36834428

Liu, T. L., Hsiao, R. C., Chou, W. J., & Yen, C. F. (2021a). Perpetration of and victimization in cyberbullying and traditional bullying in adolescents with attention-deficit/hyperactivity disorder: Roles of impulsivity, frustration intolerance, and hostility. *International Journal of Environmental Research and Public Health*, 18(13), 6872. Advance online publication. DOI: 10.3390/ijerph18136872 PMID: 34206834

Liu, T. L., Hsiao, R. C., Chou, W. J., & Yen, C. F. (2021b). Self-reported depressive symptoms and suicidality in adolescents with attention-deficit/hyperactivity disorder: Roles of bullying involvement, frustration intolerance, and hostility. *International Journal of Environmental Research and Public Health*, 18(15), 7829. Advance online publication. DOI: 10.3390/ijerph18157829 PMID: 34360120

Liu, T. L., Hsiao, R. C., Chou, W. J., & Yen, C. F. (2021c). Social anxiety in victimization and perpetration of cyberbullying and traditional bullying in adolescents with autism spectrum disorder and attention-deficit/hyperactivity disorder. *International Journal of Environmental Research and Public Health*, 18(11), 5728. Advance online publication. DOI: 10.3390/ijerph18115728 PMID: 34073617

Lu, W. H., Chou, W. J., Hsiao, R. C., Hu, H. F., & Yen, C. F. (2019). Correlations of internet addiction severity with reinforcement sensitivity and frustration intolerance in adolescents with attention-deficit/hyperactivity disorder: The moderating effect of medications. *Frontiers in Psychiatry*, 10, 268. DOI: 10.3389/fpsyt.2019.00268 PMID: 31105605

Lung, F. W., Shu, B. C., Chiang, T. L., & Lin, S. J. (2019). Prevalence of bullying and perceived happiness in adolescents with learning disability, intellectual disability, ADHD, and autism spectrum disorder. *Medicine*, 98(6), e14483. DOI: 10.1097/MD.0000000000014483 PMID: 30732217

Mahjoob, M., Paul, T., Carbone, J., Bokadia, H., Cardy, R. E., Kassam, S., Anagnastou, E., Andrade, B. F., Penner, M., & Kushi, A. (2024). Predictors of health-related quality of life in neurodivergent children: A systematic review. *Clinical Child and Family Psychology Review*, 27(1), 91–129. DOI: 10.1007/s10567-023-00462-3 PMID: 38070100

Moola, S., Munn, Z., Tufunaru, C., Aromataris, E., Sears, K., Sfetc, R., Currie, M., Lisy, K., Qureshi, R., Mattis, P., & Mu, P. F. (2024). Systematic reviews of Aetiology and risk. In E. Aromataris, C. Lockwood, K. Porritt, B. Pilla, & Z. Jordan (Eds.), *JBI Manual for Evidence Synthesis*. JBI. https://doi.org/DOI: 10.46658/JBIMES-24-06

Morton, H. E., Bottini, S. B., McVey, A. J., Magnus, B. E., Gillis, J. M., & Romanczyk, R. G. (2024). The Assessment of Bullying Experiences Questionnaire (ABE) for neurodivergent youth: Establishing scoring criteria and clinical thresholds. *International Journal of Bullying Prevention : an Official Publication of the International Bullying Prevention Association*, 6(2), 138–148. DOI: 10.1007/s42380-022-00151-9

Morton, H. E., Gillis, J. M., Zale, E. L., Brimhall, K. C., & Romanczyk, R. G. (2022). Development and validation of the Assessment of Bullying Experiences Questionnaire for neurodivergent youth. *Journal of Autism and Developmental Disorders*, 52(11), 4651–4664. DOI: 10.1007/s10803-021-05330-z PMID: 34713376

Murray, A. L., Zych, I., Ribeaud, D., & Eisner, M. (2021). Developmental relations between ADHD symptoms and bullying perpetration and victimization in adolescence. *Aggressive Behavior*, 47(1), 58–68. DOI: 10.1002/ab.21930 PMID: 32895934

Olweus, D. (2013). School bullying: Development and some important challenges. *Annual Review of Clinical Psychology*, 9(1), 751–780. DOI: 10.1146/annurev-clinpsy-050212-185516 PMID: 23297789

Ouzzani, M., Hammady, H., Fedorowicz, Z., & Elmagarmid, A. (2016). Rayyan-a web and mobile app for systematic reviews. *Systematic Reviews*, 5(1), 210. DOI: 10.1186/s13643-016-0384-4 PMID: 27919275

Park, I., Gong, J., Lyons, G. L., Hirota, T., Takahashi, M., Kim, B., Lee, S. Y., Kim, Y. S., Lee, J., & Leventhal, B. L. (2020). Prevalence of and factors associated with school bullying in students with Autism Spectrum Disorder: A cross-cultural meta-analysis. *Yonsei Medical Journal*, 61(11), 909–922. DOI: 10.3349/ymj.2020.61.11.909 PMID: 33107234

Perales-Hidalgo, P., Voltas, N., & Canals, J. (2024). Self-perceived bullying victimization in pre-adolescents on the autism spectrum: EPINED study. *Autism*, 28(11), 2848–2857. Advance online publication. DOI: 10.1177/13623613241244875 PMID: 38623050

Pollock, D., Peters, M. D. J., Khalil, H., McInerney, P., Alexander, L., Tricco, A. C., Evans, C., de Moraes, É. B., Godfrey, C. M., Pieper, D., Saran, A., Stern, C., & Munn, Z. (2023). Recommendations for the extraction, analysis, and presentation of results in scoping reviews. *JBI Evidence Synthesis*, 21(3), 520–532. DOI: 10.11124/JBIES-22-00123 PMID: 36081365

Pongparadorn, W., Pityaratstian, N., Buathong, N., & Prasartpornsirichoke, J. (2021). School bullying behavior in attention-deficit hyperactivity disorder patients with and without comorbid autism spectrum disorder at King Chulalongkorn Memorial Hospital. *Chulalongkorn Medical Journal*, 65(4), 459–465. DOI: 10.58837/CHULA.CMJ.65.4.13

Prasartpornsirichoke, J., Pityaratstian, N., & Pongparadorn, W. (2022). School bullying behaviors and victimization in Thai children and adolescents with comorbid attention deficit hyperactivity disorder, anxiety disorders, and oppositional defiant disorder. *Chulalongkorn Medical Journal*, 66(3), 293–300. DOI: 10.58837/CHULA.CMJ.66.3.6

Roekel, E., Scholte, R. H., & Didden, R. (2010). Bullying among adolescents with autism spectrum disorders: Prevalence and perception. *Journal of Autism and Developmental Disorders*, 40(1), 63–73. DOI: 10.1007/s10803-009-0832-2 PMID: 19669402

Schroeder, J. H., Cappadocia, M. C., Bebko, J. M., Pepler, D. J., & Weiss, J. A. (2014). Shedding light on a pervasive problem: A review of research on bullying experiences among children with Autism Spectrum Disorders. *Journal of Autism and Developmental Disorders*, 44(7), 1520–1534. DOI: 10.1007/s10803-013-2011-8 PMID: 24464616

Touloupis, T., & Athanasiades, C. (2022). Cyberbullying and empathy among elementary school students: Do special educational needs make a difference? *Scandinavian Journal of Psychology*, 63(6), 609–623. DOI: 10.1111/sjop.12838 PMID: 35698831

Unnever, J. D., & Cornell, D. G. (2003). Bullying, self-control, and ADHD. *Journal of Interpersonal Violence*, 18(2), 129–147. DOI: 10.1177/0886260502238731

Yen, C. F., Yang, P., Wang, P. W., Lin, H. C., Liu, T. L., Wu, Y. Y., & Tang, T. C. (2014). Association between school bullying levels/types and mental health problems among Taiwanese adolescents. *Comprehensive Psychiatry*, 55(3), 405–413. DOI: 10.1016/j.comppsych.2013.06.001 PMID: 24529472

Zablotsky, B., Bradshaw, C. P., Anderson, C., & Law, P. A. (2013). The association between bullying and the psychological functioning of children with autism spectrum disorders. *Journal of developmental and behavioral pediatrics. Journal of Developmental and Behavioral Pediatrics*, 34(1), 1–8. DOI: 10.1097/DBP.0b013e31827a7c3a PMID: 23275052

Zablotsky, B., Bradshaw, C. P., Anderson, C. M., & Law, P. (2014). Risk factors for bullying among children with autism spectrum disorders. *Autism*, 18(4), 419–427. DOI: 10.1177/1362361313477920 PMID: 23901152

Chapter 4
Bullying Faced by Children With Special Needs in Pakistan:
Challenges, Interventions, and Societal Implications for Educational Inclusion

Afaf Manzoor
https://orcid.org/0000-0002-1070-4023
University of Education, Lahore, Pakistan

Muhammad Usman Khalid
University of Education, Lahore, Pakistan

Asifa Rashid
University of Education, Lahore, Pakistan

ABSTRACT

The proposed book chapter aims to landscape the case of children with special needs in Pakistan who are victims of persistent bullying and are at high risk of being targeted for facing discrimination due to differences in their physical appearance, communication challenges and social interactions. Based on empirical research and theoretical frameworks, the book chapter consists of five sections; the first section will conceptualize the understanding about the bully and its type, the second section narrates the state of bullying in Pakistan and the challenges of children with special needs within the community and schools. The third section is based on the review of legislation to protect against bullying and support prevention. The fourth

DOI: 10.4018/979-8-3693-5315-8.ch004

section shares the findings of a study conducted as part of this chapter to explore the perspectives of teachers on their knowledge and understanding of bullying and its impact on children with special needs. The final section of the chapter presents the recommendations.

INTRODUCTION AND BACKGROUND

The chapter intends to landscape the case of children with special needs in Pakistan who are the victims of tenacious bullying and are at high risk of being targeted for facing discrimination due to the differences in their physical appearance, communication challenges, and social interactions. The chances of vulnerability for being bullied increase with the expansion of the system and their interaction within the society (Parada,2022). Schools have been reported as one of the most vulnerable places, where children with special needs are bullied in some cases by their peers and school staff (Rogojan &Turda,2022). Bullying is described as aggressive behavior combining repeated undesired actions and systematic misuse of authority (Hassan & Mohammed, 2023). It is a major issue that affects children's mental and physical health. It can be verbal, physical, relational, or cause property damage, among others. Cyberbullying has emerged as a significant concern in the digital age, particularly affecting children with special needs. Kowalski and Toth (2018) defined cyberbullying as the bullying that takes place over digital platforms such as social media, messaging apps, and online forums. Cyberbullying poses unique challenges for vulnerable populations. Children with disabilities are especially susceptible due to their perceived differences and unique challenges, which can exacerbate their experiences of harassment and bullying.

The three main characters in the bullying cycle are: victims, bully-victims, and pure bullies. The long-term effects of bullying have a negative impact on the mental health of children with disabilities, including anxiety, low self-esteem, and even suicidal thoughts in victims (Canales, 2023, Burkhart & Keder, 2020). Despite increased awareness, bullying among students with disabilities is still not well understood. Remarkably, students with disabilities share common characteristics across all roles in the bullying dynamic, especially those with high incidence disorders, including learning disabilities and emotional and behavioral problems (Bussey, 2023). Bullying behaviors in Pakistan are heavily influenced by cultural and socioeconomic elements, such as poverty, long-standing social hierarchies, and attitudes toward disability. These elements often affect how children view and relate to classmates from underrepresented groups, which increases social exclusion and discrimination (Ali & Shah, 2020). Because children from disadvantaged families are more likely to be victims, bullying may be exacerbated by the cultural stigma associated with impairments and economic inequality (Khan & Khan, 2019).

Studies indicate that they are more likely than their peers without disabilities to be both bullies and victims (Boruah, 2022). Pupils who struggle with emotional, behavioral, or developmental issues are more susceptible. In the school setting, social exclusion and isolation exacerbate their susceptibility to bullying (Hakim & Shah, 2017). Although little research has been done on it, it is important to comprehend how prosocial behavior and bullying interact when it comes to students with special needs.

SECTION 1: CONCEPTUALIZING BULLYING AMONG CHILDREN WITH SPECIAL NEEDS

Bulling is a form of aggressive behavior that extends beyond mere aggression (Haru, 2022). Olweus (1994) characterizes bullying as a systematic abuse of power, involving repeated undesirable actions aimed at causing harm to others physically or mentally. This behavior encompasses various forms such as verbal, physical, social, cyber, and sexual bullying, with factors contributing to bullying including individual traits, family dynamics, peer influence, and societal norms (Hassan & Mohammed, 2023). The impacts of bullying are profound, affecting both victims and perpetrators psychologically and physically, leading to long-term adverse health effects (Canales, 2023). Strategies to address bullying include exploring root causes, implementing punishments, providing support and education, and running prevention programs to create a safer environment for students (Hahn, 2023).

Understanding the various roles in the bullying dynamic is crucial for addressing this behavior effectively. Victims who are characterized as passive or provocative, suffer emotional distress, isolation, and academic consequences (Rahma et al., 2022). Bully victims, who both bully others and are victimized, exhibit aggressive behaviors, face social struggles, and experience heightened distress and mental health issues (Rahma et al., 2022). Pure bullies, who engage in bullying without being targeted themselves, display dominance, lack of empathy, and social manipulation, often influenced by factors like family dynamics and exposure to violence (Gomes et al., 2022). Recognizing these roles—victims, bully-victims, and pure bullies—provides insights into the complexities of bullying behavior and its impact on the individuals involved, and effectively guides interventions and support strategies.

Bullying, a pervasive issue globally, affects approximately 1 in 3 students worldwide, with various forms like verbal, social, physical, and cyberbullying (Shahid et al., 2022). Victims often face challenges in forming relationships and may experience academic setbacks due to absenteeism and decreased motivation (Shahid et al., 2022).

Understanding the prevalence and impacts of bullying is crucial for implementing effective interventions and support systems to create a safer environment for all individuals (Academy of Science of South Africa, 2022).

Various Forms of Bullying Among Different Genders

Bullying can be classified into direct and indirect forms. Direct bullying involves physical and verbal harassment, targeting 60% of students (Olweus, 2014; Orpinas et al., 2003; Peskinet al., 2006). Indirect bullying involves relational and cyberbullying, causing social exclusion and spreading rumors (Wolke et al., 2000). There are cultural differences, with older students often bullying younger ones in Western countries (Koo et al., 2008).

While comparing gender, studies highlight that boys are more aggressive and are more directly involved in physical bullying (Kaltsas & Kaltsas, 2023). According to Prinstein et al. (2001), bullying behaviors have become less gender-specific. Indirect kinds of bullying, such spreading rumors and socially isolating people, are more common among girls, according to studies (Khawar & Malik, 2016). In one study, Shujja et al. (2014) investigated the significant predictors of bullying, victimization, and fighting behavior in which the two variables identified were gender and the school type. The study also identified that boys and students from public schools were significant contributors as well as victims of bullying and fighting.

Consequences of Bullying Faced by Children with Special Needs

Children with special needs encounter a multitude of challenges impacting their physical, communicational, and social development, as well as their integration into expanding ecosystems and societal interactions (Wanti et al., 2023). Physical differences, such as mobility issues and health complications, hinder their access to public spaces and participation in activities (Boruah, 2022). Communicational disparities, including speech delays and reliance on assistive technology, contribute to social isolation and stigmatization (Wanti et al., 2023). Social interaction variances, like social skills deficits and sensory sensitivities, lead to peer rejection and avoidance of social situations (Vasylenko et al., 2022). Moreover, increased vulnerability exposes them to bullying, inadequate support, and educational disparities, resulting in social isolation and economic barriers (Khasawneh, 2023).

Theoretical Perspective on Bullying

Theoretical perspectives on bullying offer valuable insights into the complex dynamics underlying this pervasive problem. Theoretical perspective help stakeholders to understand the philosophical aspect of the phenomena that further establish the background and contextual realities. Understanding theoretical perspective also help to know various factors referred to different articles to support the bullying concept. Several theories have been developed to elucidate the causes and mechanisms of bullying behavior, shedding light on various dimensions of social interaction, cognitive processes, and environmental influences. The most widely accepted theories related to bullying are the following:

Dominance Theory emphasizes the pursuit of social status and resources as motivators for bullying, underscoring how individuals may engage in bullying to assert dominance and gain popularity within social groups (Paranti & Hudiyana, 2022).

Humiliation Theory underscores the detrimental effects of humiliation on victims, leading to depression, social disconnection, and a compromised school environment. It emphasizes the violation of fundamental human rights and dignity (Fattore & Mason, 2020).

Social Capital Theory elucidates the role of social resources in either promoting or mitigating bullying behaviors and emphasizes the importance of fostering positive social connections and pro-social bystander interventions (Kim, 2022). In Pakistan, SCT explains the heightened risk of bullying faced by children with special needs, largely driven by societal norms and cultural perceptions of disability. By observing and internalizing adult attitudes toward disability, children may adopt dismissive behaviors as acceptable, and these attitudes become entrenched in school and peer interactions.

Organizational Culture Theory emphasizes the influence of school culture on bullying behavior and suggests that efforts to address bullying must include broader cultural changes within educational institutions (Smith, 2018). In educational institutions, this theory is particularly relevant because each school fosters a unique culture that can either promote inclusivity or perpetuate exclusionary practices. Many schools in Pakistan lack a strong, inclusive organizational culture, leaving children with special needs vulnerable to exclusion and bullying due to limited support or understanding.

The Developmental Theory examines the cognitive processes and social dynamics that contribute to the emergence of bullying behaviors during childhood and adolescence, emphasizing the need for guidance and intervention tailored to developmental stages (Jones & Brown, 2019).

The Theory of Response to Group and Peer Pressure explores how group dynamics and peer influences contribute to bullying behavior, emphasizing the role of social context in shaping attitudes and actions (Rigby, 2024).

Depending on the aspects in which these theoretical perspectives are linked, a realistic picture of how different children and students with special needs are bullied in Pakistan can be reconstructed. The social cognitive theory focuses on the fact that observing negative behaviors towards children with disabilities in a school context is learned, for example, when it is modeled by teachers, peers, and others. In such a context, children are likely to emulate unfriendly gestures towards children with special needs that they believe are appropriate. Dominance theory expands on this point by suggesting that some children, for whatever reason, may bully in order to establish some form of social order, especially when other children are seen as socially inferior due to socially ingrained prejudices. According to Humiliation Theory, such public demonstrations of embarrassment can leave these children with the deepest feelings of shame, further informing them that they are unwanted in a country whose value system is centered on the doctrine of community assimilation. On the one hand, social capital theory points to the lack of bonding and bridging social capital for children with special needs, and on the other hand, the lack of an organizational culture that effective schools should counteract exclusion in schools. It is the Developmental Theory that extends fears for such children, because as they progress through developmental stages in cultures that lack validation of their individuality and support for their differences, they are at increased risk. Finally, the Response to Group and Peer Pressure theory explains that peers exacerbate bullying because many students tend to conform to group norms. In conclusion, all these theories emphasize the appropriateness of multifaceted psychological interventions to change social attitudes, peer behaviors, and policies related to children with special needs in Pakistan.

SECTION 2: STATE OF BULLYING AMONG CHILDREN WITH SPECIAL NEEDS IN PAKISTAN

Children with special needs in Pakistan face increased vulnerability to bullying, which is exacerbated by societal stigma, cultural background, and lack of awareness, impacting their psychological well-being and academic success (Javed et al., 2023; Siddiqui & Schultze-Krumbholz, 2023a). Bullying also disrupts the learning environment, leading to decreased academic performance and higher dropout rates, emphasizing the need for a safe educational setting (Siddiqui & Schultze-Krumbholz, 2023b). Addressing this issue is crucial for promoting social inclusion, preventing long-lasting psychological effects, and driving policy changes and interventions to effectively support children with special needs (Siddiqui & Schultze-Krumbholz, 2023a). By tackling bullying, Pakistan can foster cultural change, challenge negative stereotypes, and promote greater acceptance and inclusion of individuals with disabilities, ultimately contributing to a more inclusive and equal society (Wang, 2023). The societal role of bullying is often overlooked as a minor offense, holds profound societal implications, and warrants serious attention and action in Pakistan. While crimes like robbery and murder receive widespread media coverage and legislative scrutiny, bullying persists as a pervasive issue that is often relegated to the background (Ahmed et al., 2023). Studies indicate that bullying frequently occurs during the school years, with many victims belonging to special needs demographics (Wang, 2023).

The phenomenon cuts across diverse backgrounds, highlighting a societal failure to effectively address its underlying causes. Bullying can be viewed as a precursor to more significant criminal behavior, underscoring the urgency of intervention at an early stage (Mahmoudi, & Keashly, 2021). Superimposing the findings of Naveed et al. (2020) the behavioral issues in children with disabilities are due to peer violence. Malik and Abdullah (2017) reported the opinions of teachers and students that the condition of children with special needs in Pakistan is most vulnerable to bullying because of the programs on the television, social media images, and discussions about cultural disputes, ethnicity, and myths related to disabilities. For provocation to bully, students and teachers were asked to rank different types of bullying and rated verbal bullying highest for students with special needs in schools.

Cyberbullying has emerged as a significant concern in the digital age, particularly affecting children with special needs. Kowalski & Toth (2018) define bullying that takes place over digital platforms such as social media, messaging apps, and online forums, cyberbullying poses unique challenges for vulnerable populations. Children with disabilities are especially susceptible due to their perceived differences and unique challenges, which can exacerbate their experiences of harassment and bullying.

SECTION 3: INTERNATIONAL AND NATIONAL LEGISLATIONS TO SAFEGUARD AND PREVENT BULLYING IN PAKISTAN

Stakeholders in Pakistan need to be aware of the legislation and take proactive measures to prevent and address bullying in all forms for children with special needs. Addressing the existing laws and taking steps to create a safe and respectful environment for children with special needs can promote a culture of dignity and inclusion. The following are the legislations highlighted during the review of various documents:

National Legal Frameworks and Policies

United Nations Convention on the Rights of the Child (UNCRC)

The UNCRC, ratified by Pakistan, is a comprehensive framework that protects the rights of all children, including those with disabilities. Article 23 of the convention specifically addresses the rights of children with disabilities, emphasizing their right to special care, education, and measures to combat discrimination and bullying (Affairs, 1989).

Salamanca Statement and Framework for Action on Special Needs Education

Education for All Handicapped Children Act was adopted in 1994 at the World Conference on Special Needs Education, Salamanca Statement: It mandates policies against bullying to be put in place so that full inclusion can be realized (Education, 2004).

United Nations Convention on the Rights of Persons with Disabilities (UNCRPD)

Pakistan is a signatory to the UNCRPD 2006, which underscores the importance of inclusive education and the protection of persons with disabilities from all forms of abuse, including bullying. Article 24 of the convention highlights the right to inclusive education and the necessity of creating safe learning environments (Nations, 2007).

UNESCO Policy Guidelines on Inclusion in Education

UNESCO provides comprehensive guidelines to promote inclusive education and protect students from bullying. UNESCO's guidelines advocate for a whole-school approach to inclusion, emphasizing the need for changes at all levels of the education system to create inclusive learning environments (United Nations Educational & Organization, 2009).

Sustainable Development Goals (SDGs)

The SDGs, adopted by the United Nations, aim to address global challenges, including those related to poverty, inequality, and education. Goal 4 (Quality Education) emphasizes inclusive and equitable quality education for all. Target 4.5

specifically aims to eliminate disparities in education and ensure equal access for vulnerable populations, including children with disabilities, by addressing issues such as bullying and discrimination (Nations, 2015).

National Legal Frameworks and Policies

Constitution of Pakistan

The Constitution of Pakistan is the supreme law of the country, providing a foundation for all other laws and policies. It enshrines the right to education for all citizens, implicitly including children with special needs (Pakistan, 1982).

The Right to Free and Compulsory Education Act, 2012

This act operationalizes Article 25-A of the Constitution, making education free and compulsory for children aged 5 to 16 years. The act requires schools to provide appropriate facilities and resources to accommodate children with disabilities, and it mandates the establishment of grievance redressal mechanisms to address issues such as bullying and harassment (Bibi, 2018).

National Education Policy 2010 (NEP)

The NEP outlines the government's vision and strategy for the education sector. It emphasizes inclusive education and highlights the need for a safe and supportive learning environment for all children, including those with disabilities. The policy advocates for the integration of children with special needs into mainstream schools and underscores the importance of teacher training programs to equip educators with the skills to handle diversity and prevent bullying (Policy, 2010).

The Disabled Persons (Employment and Rehabilitation) Ordinance, 1981

Although primarily focused on employment, this ordinance also addresses the broader rights of persons with disabilities, including their right to education. The ordinance mandates the creation of an inclusive environment that can help mitigate bullying by fostering acceptance and understanding (Jahanzaib et al., 2021).

SECTION 4: TEACHERS' PERCEPTION REGARDING BULLYING BEHAVIOR OF CHILDREN WITH SPECIAL NEEDS IN PAKISTAN

Bullying awareness and perception vary globally, with teachers often not recognizing bullying incidents due to desensitization or misunderstanding (Bradshaw et al., 2013). This confusion is exacerbated by the lack of a universal definition of bullying, which hinders effective identification and intervention (Yoon & Bauman, 2014). Effective anti-bullying programs rely on staff training, but teachers and school personnel often receive inadequate training in bullying prevention and intervention (Bradshaw et al., 2013; Kennedy et al., 2012; Mishna et al., 2005). This gap in training contributes to inconsistent approaches across schools and districts. Bullying poses a significant threat to the safe learning environments, and increased training can enhance teachers' perceptions of the seriousness of bullying and their confidence in managing situations (Dedousis-Wallace & Shute, 2009; Siddiqui, & Schultze-Krumbholz, 2023a; Yoon, 2004).

As mentioned at the beginning of this chapter, a study has been conducted to understand special education teachers' perceptions regarding bullying of children with special needs.

Method and Procedure

To strengthen the argument and discussion about the bullying in schools to children with special needs, a study was designed to collect data from special education teachers in Punjab, Pakistan. The aim was to understand the knowledge and perceptions of teachers about bullying and its prevention. A sample of 200 special education teachers working in 13 government special schools from 13 cities of Punjab was selected using a purposive sampling technique. The survey was distributed to the teachers, ensuring anonymity to encourage honest and unbiased responses. See table 1 for the demographics of the teachers i.e., experience, age, qualification and location of the sample. A survey questionnaire was adapted from Mobarki et al. (2020) to collect data on the perceptions of special education teachers. The survey included demographic questions and statements designed to gauge teachers' understanding and attitudes toward bullying. Part 1 collected demographic details such as gender, age, academic qualifications, years of experience, and previous training on bullying. Part 2 used a 4-point Likert scale to assess agreement with statements related to the definitions and characteristics of bullying, causes, impacts, and necessary interventions used by the special education teachers. Part 3 was also based on 4-point Likert scale in which teachers were asked to indicate the frequency and context of bullying occurrences in their school environmentwith children with special needs. The study plan was approved by the Ethical Board of the Department of Special Education, University of Education to conduct the study. Initially, a pilot study was conducted on 30 teachers from three cities in Punjab. The reliability analysis of the instrument was run, and Cronbach alpha was found to be 8.89. The data was collected in two ways; through personal visits of the researchers and through Google forms from far-flung areas with a consent form.

Findings and Discussions

The study implies that teachers belonging to different categories recognize the bullying behavior in children with special needs similarly and do not differ in the perceptions of this issue. However, the findings of the study as follows:

Table 1. Demographics of special education teachers in Punjab

Gender	Frequency	Percent
Female	132	66.0
Male	68	34.0
Qualification		
Teaching Diploma	4	2.0
Masters	119	59.5
M.Phil.	64	32.0
Ph.D.	13	6.5
Age		
20-30	13	6.5
31-40	107	53.5
41-50	75	37.5
51 and above	5	2.5
Experience		
0-5	25	12.5
6-10	68	34.0
11-15	62	31.0
16 and above	45	22.5
Have you ever attended a course about bullying		
Yes	25	12.5
No	175	87.5
City/Town		
Lahore	24	12.0

continued on following page

Table 1. Continued

Gender	Frequency	Percent
Kasur	41	20.5
Sahiwal	28	14.0
Sargoda	8	4.0
Bhakhar	9	4.5
Faisalabad	13	6.5
Nankana	11	5.5
Muree	10	5.0
Raiwand	8	4.0
Muridke	21	10.5
Gujranwala	9	4.5
Shekhupura	5	2.5
Okara	13	6.5
Total	200	100.0

The findings in Table 1 provide essential information about the demographic and professional insights of the educators included in the survey. The given gender distribution implies that female teachers dominate in the educational area for children with special needs in Pakistan. In terms of qualifications, a substantial 59% of the teachers hold a Master's degree, suggesting the possibility of them being well positioned, in terms of their learning, to appreciate and deal with issues such as bullying.

By age, distribution it is observed that most of the teachers fall in the age group of 31- 40 years which was 53%. Looking at the teaching experience, the results indicate that the experience of the respondents is fairly spread across the spectrum. Most of the respondents are teachers with 6- 10 years of teaching experience. The distribution of experience points to a good blend of new ideas and experience in the teaching fraternity. However, what is most worrying is that the majority of teachers (87.5%) have never attended any course on bullying. Only 12.5% have received formal training on the topic. The current findings also indicate that despite the professionalism and qualifications of teachers as well as their years of work experience, they may not be trained to handle and prevent bullying behaviors among children with special needs appropriately. This underlines the necessity for continuing professional development focused on enhancing the teachers' knowledge and competencies in the field of anti-bullying initiatives, and, as a result, making learning environments safer for every learner.

Table 2. The factors causing bullying among children with special needs

	N	Minimum	Maximum	Mean	Std. Deviation
Television and Internet	200	1	4	2.91	.751
Lack of a secure school environment to protect victim of bullying.	200	2	4	2.98	.605
Lack of recreational activities	200	2	4	2.93	.634
The variations of social class	200	1	4	3.00	.754
Teacher repeatedly criticize students in the classroom	200	1	4	2.82	.833
Teacher picks on certain students	200	1	4	2.74	.683
Parents nervousness in front of their children.	200	1	4	2.81	.700
Absence of family supervision/ guidance.	200	3	4	3.27	.445

Findings in Table 2 established that several factors are influential in this process. Out of these, the family supervision or guidance is not available in most cases, which has the highest mean score of 3.27 and the least standard deviation of 0.445 which were regarded as critical factors recognized by teachers. Thus, these results raise awareness of the complex nature of bullying behavior and the necessity to implement diverse approaches to eliminate these causes.

Table 3. The impact of bullying on children with special needs

	N	Minimum	Maximum	Mean	Std. Deviation
Low self-esteem	200	1	4	3.39	.648
Achieves success in school.	200	1	4	2.33	.851
Lack of participation in classroom activities.	200	2	4	3.10	.606
Leads to depression in special students.	200	2	4	3.14	.508
Drug abuse.	200	1	4	2.99	.760
Defiance for criminality	200	2	4	3.01	.571
Can contribute to suicide	200	2	4	3.01	.501

Table 3 revealed that teachers have noticed that bullying poses a large impact on these children's self-esteem, as indicated by a mean of 3.39 and SD=.648. Another trend is given by the inclination to fail in school, which receives a mean score of 3.02 and SD=.733 reflecting the adverse academic consequences of bullying. These figures point to the fact that bullying is widespread and causes a negative impact on children with special needs as observed by the teachers. Drug Abuse, is another factor that receives a mean score of 2.99 and SD=.760 reflecting the consequences of bullying.

Table 4. Teacher and school interventions for bullying prevention: Perceptions on the need for increased support

	N	Minimum	Maximum	Mean	Std. Deviation
Bullying is a problem that needs increased attention from teacher.	200	1	4	3.16	.653
The school should have guidance counselor to reduce bullying.	200	2	4	3.43	.571
The school leader should have implemented programs to stop bullying.	200	1	4	3.36	.625
The presence of a school nurse could be useful in promoting a healthy environment and support psychosocial states of students in school.	200	1	4	3.10	.680

Table 4 highlighted findings in the area of study received an average rating of 3.16 and SD=.653 respondents answered in affirmation to the belief that bullying is a major problem that needs more attention. The results imply considerable support for the existence of courses and counselors, with a mean rating of 3.43 and SD=.573 which implies that these professionals are deemed relevant by teachers in the prevention of bullying occurrences. The profile of teachers supports their perception of the complex nature of the problem which requires various strategies to be implemented within the school system.

Table 5. Special education teachers opinion about the school related environment for bulling

In your belief where places do you think bullying occur?	N	Minimum	Maximum	Mean	Std. Deviation
In the school bus	200	1	4	2.95	.678
On the Playground.	200	1	4	2.79	.763
Walking to or from school.	200	1	4	2.66	.724
Inside the classroom.	200	1	4	2.53	.997
In the cafeteria.	200	1	4	2.85	.762
In the school's hallways	200	1	4	2.66	.773

The data in Table 5 presents that bullying is perceived to occur most frequently on the school bus, with a mean score of 2.95 and a standard deviation of 0.678. This is followed by the cafeteria, with a mean of 2.85 and a standard deviation of 0.762. The playground is also seen as a common place for bullying, with a mean score of 2.79 and a standard deviation of 0.763. Bullying while walking to or from school and in the school's hallways both have a mean score of 2.66, with standard deviations of 0.724 and 0.773 respectively. The classroom, although still a notable area for bullying, is perceived to have the lowest occurrence with a mean score of 2.53 and a standard deviation of 0.997. These insights highlight the varied environments within and around the school where bullying is prevalent and emphasize the need for comprehensive anti-bullying strategies that address all these areas to ensure the safety and well-being of children with special needs.

Table 6. The most vulnerable grade level for bulling among special needs children

	N	Minimum	Maximum	Mean	Std. Deviation
1st grade	200	1	3	1.96	.844
2nd grade	200	1	4	2.23	.884
3rd grade	200	1	4	2.47	.763
4th grade	200	1	4	2.77	.843
5th grade	200	1	4	2.84	.895
6th grade	200	1	4	3.12	.734

Table 6 revealed a progressive increase in the mean scores of bullying incidents as students advance in grade level. The standard deviations show some variation in teachers' perceptions within each grade, but the overall trend indicates an increasing prevalence of bullying as children with special needs progress through the primary grades.

Table 7. Most common type/form of bulling at school with special needs children

	N	Minimum	Maximum	Mean	Std. Deviation
Physical bullying	200	1	4	2.33	.838
Verbal bullying.	200	1	4	2.89	.840
Psychological bullying	200	1	4	2.77	.867
Sexual bullying.	200	1	4	1.91	.968
Cyberbullying	200	1	3	1.96	.804

The findings in Table 7 outlined that physical bullying, with a mean score of 2.33, and a standard deviation of 0.838 which shows, that the rate of physical aggression reported was moderate. It is established that the mean of verbal bullying is higher at 2.89 and SD. 840, pointing out that threatening by words, labeling, calling names is more frequent than other types of bullying for children with special needs.

Table 8. Teachers' perception toward their role in bullying behavior

	N	Minimum	Maximum	Mean	Std. Deviation
I responded to students when they are bullied.	200	1	4	3.22	.869
I refer the victim and bully to academic counselor	200	2	4	3.28	.651
I do nothing/ ignore, when the bullying occurs.	200	1	4	2.07	1.132
I would try to make these students talk together and resolve the problem.	200	1	4	3.32	.762
I observe students when they are being on bullied.	200	1	4	2.97	.992
I would control the bullies by applying penalties	200	1	4	3.06	.724
I talk to the parents of perpetrators of bullying about this issue	200	1	4	3.28	.708
I conduct a lecture to raise students' awareness of bullying.	200	1	4	3.03	.871

Table 8 showed a high mean score in using reactive approach to bullying as reported by teachers, where the mean value is 3.22 with SD= 0.869 for responding to students when they are being bullied, and a slightly higher mean of 3.28 with SD=. 651 for referring both victims and perpetrators to academic counselors. This low score means that while most teachers may not condone bullying, they do nothing about it or turn a blind eye to the situation, and this is a gap that could be very bad for students. Overall, the findings presented the teachers as receptive and willing to address the bullying issue in school, however, certain more specific aspects of their monitoring and intervention activities could be considered to be less consistent.

Table 9. Teacher's perception regarding bullying among children with special needs based on gender

		Levene's Test for Equality of Variances || t-test for Equality of Means							
		F	Sig.	t	df	Sig. (2-tailed)	Mean Difference	Std. Error Difference	95% Confidence Interval of the Difference	
									Lower	Upper
Gender	Equal variances assumed	.093	.761	-1.428	198	.155	-.06350	.04446	-.15117	.02417
	Equal variances are not assumed.			-1.420	133.2	.158	-.06350	.04472	-.15195	.02495

The analysis in Table 9 yielded no statistically significant difference in teachers' perceptions based on gender, as the p-value exceeds the 0.05 threshold. These findings suggest that gender does not significantly influence teachers' perceptions of bullying among children with special needs.

Research consistently supports the finding that there is no significant difference in the perceptions of bullying between male and female teachers, with both groups demonstrating similar levels of awareness and concern regarding bullying among children with special needs. For instance, a study by Yoon et al. (2016) found that gender did not play a significant role in teachers' recognition of bullying incidents or their intervention strategies. Similarly, research by Bauman and Del Rio (2006) indicated that both male and female teachers exhibited comparable levels of empathy and commitment to addressing bullying in their classrooms. These studies, along with others like those conducted by Troop-Gordon & Ladd (2015), reinforce the notion that gender does not significantly influence teachers' perceptions or responses to bullying among special needs students, highlighting a shared professional dedication to creating safe and inclusive learning environments.

Table 10. Teacher's perception regarding bullying among children with special needs based on experience

	Sum of Squares	Df	Mean Square	F	Sig.
Between Groups	.683	3	.228	2.614	.052
Within Groups	17.062	196	.087		
Total	17.745	199			

The ANOVA results in Table 10 indicated a marginal trend toward significance (p = 0.052), but the findings remain statistically insignificant as the p-value exceeds the 0.05 threshold. This suggests that perceptions of bullying may vary slightly among teachers with differing levels of experience. The trend implies that more experienced teachers might hold more nuanced perspectives on bullying, potentially stemming from their extended exposure and the strategies they have developed over time to address such issues. However, these interpretations should be approached with caution, given the lack of statistical significance.

The findings of this study are consistent with few other studies. Yoon & Kerber (2003) found that both novice and veteran teachers exhibit similar levels of awareness and concern about bullying, indicating that experience does not substantially alter their perceptions. Additionally, Bradshaw et al. (2013) concluded that teachers' attitudes toward bullying interventions remain consistent regardless of their years of teaching experience. These findings might be different because of the different school culture in Pakistan.

Table 11. Teachers' perception regarding bullying among children with special needs based on qualification

	Sum of Squares	Df	Mean Square	F	Sig.
Between Groups	.071	3	.024	.264	.851
Within Groups	17.673	196	.090		
Total	17.745	199			

The ANOVA results in Table 11 indicate no significant variation (p = 0.851) in teachers' perceptions of bullying based on their academic qualifications.

A review of various studies indicates the same findings, that there is no significant difference in teachers' perceptions of bullying among children with special needs based on their academic qualifications. Studies by Jones (2019) and Combs-Jones (2021) have demonstrated that teachers' awareness and concern about bullying are not markedly influenced by their level of formal education. These findings suggest that regardless of whether teachers hold advanced degrees or basic teaching credentials, their perceptions of bullying remain relatively uniform. This consistency is further supported by research by Lepley's (2023) study, which emphasizes the role of practical experience and ongoing professional development over formal academic qualifications in shaping teachers' understanding and responses to bullying.

Table 12. Teacher's perception regarding bullying among children with special needs based on locality

	Sum of Squares	Df	Mean Square	F	Sig.
Between Groups	.583	12	.049	.529	.894
Within Groups	17.162	187	.092		
Total	17.745	199			

The results in Table 12 show no statistically significant difference in teachers' perceptions of bullying among children with special needs based on their locality. The consistency in perception across different cities/towns highlights the universality of concerns related to bullying in special needs children context, regardless of geographic location across Punjab.

Studies support, the findings of this study as there is no significant difference in teachers' perceptions regarding bullying among children with special needs across urban, suburban, or rural settings. Studies such as those conducted by Farmer et al. (2012) and Waasdorp et al. (2012) demonstrate that teachers in diverse geographic locations share similar concerns and awareness levels of bullying issues in special education contexts. These findings suggest that the challenges and complexities associated with bullying are universally recognized by educators, regardless of their teaching environment.

These findings collectively underscore the uniformity in teachers' awareness and concerns regarding bullying across diverse backgrounds, suggesting a consistent need for inclusive anti-bullying strategies in special education contexts.

SECTION 5: INTERVENTIONS AND RECOMMENDATIONS FOR INCLUSIVE AND SUPPORTIVE ENVIRONMENTS IN PAKISTAN TO COMBAT BULLYING IN SCHOOLS FOR CHILDREN WITH SPECIAL NEEDS

The interventions that have been implemented or taken to manage the bullying issues in educational institutions of Pakistan are very few and most of the interventions are used to target only a specific component of the training such as engaging in movement activities (McFarlane et al., 2017), proper physical arrangement (Hakim & Shah, 2017), or developing social skills and managing anger of the victims (Maryam & Ijaz, 2018). Another limitation of these training programs is that they focus more on children in regular classrooms and don't talk much about the preventive measures for children with special needs. According to the intervention plan proposed by Maryam and Ijaz (2018), the victims were empowered with the appropriate social skills and the self-defense skills to combat bullying; in this regard, general data shows a shift in the upward improvement of skills and decrease in the level of bullying. While outlining the framework of the Right to Play's intervention which strengthens school attendance and prevents violence among children, in addition to fostering life skills among children. McFarlane et al. (2017) stated that Pakistan seems to be a demanding context for evaluating school-based interventions because children cannot attend school regularly in Pakistan hence affecting all school-focused interventions. For enhancing the anti-bullying strategies, school-based mental health services and the procedures related to the psychosocial counseling should be initiated and developed (Saleem et al., 2021). Naveed et al. (2020) further emphasize the importance of understanding the underlying patterns of behavioral difficulties. It is also challenging for educational institutions to engage in whole-school intervention design where everybody at school, including teachers, parents, and the learners are involved in anti-bullying stances (Arslan & Zaman, 2014; Rehman et al., 2015).

Hakim and Shah (2017) conducted a study to analyze the techniques employed in the management of bullying in primary schools in Haripur – Pakistan. According to their study, they discovered that the majority of the teachers practice the strategy of creating a safe physical environment by providing information about rules before the possibility of the child misbehaving or engaging in any form of bullying or other related vices by using instructional methods to promote activities, games, and management to address bullying and other concerning behaviors among students and ward off fights (Hakim & Shah, 2017).

The review of literature highlighted that there is a need for bullying and cyber bullying interventions, in Pakistan especially for children with special needs. Additionally, most of the interventions that were adopted/adapted and applied have focused on a single domain of training such as performing exercises (Karmaliani et al., 2020), creation of safe environment (Hakim & Shah, 2017). Naveed et al. (2020) stressed the need to understand the 'form' or the patterns of the behavioral difficulties to formulate meaningful, realistic and pragmatic anti-bully interventions, that include school-based mental health services and psychosocial counseling in the case of children with special needs. The findings of the study shared in the previous section based on a survey, it is identified that teachers are aware about bullying occurrences and they try to prevent, deter, and fight bullying while working with students with special needs. Teachers have a wider role to play rather than teaching, they can also participate to plan and execute various policies and plans of schools (Shah et al., 2015). The main source of intervention can be the teacher who can bring changes in the whole school climate and prevent the bullying perpetration and victimization especially for learners with diverse needs (Strohmeier et al., 2012).

In order to effectively and comprehensively eliminate or prevent bullying in special school, prevention, and intervention together with the promotion of positive and inclusive cultures are required to be adopted and implemented (Pearce et al., 2024). Research based interventions for children with special needs to include them in school with a sense of belonging, dignity and respect are:

Whole-School Approaches: Interventions such as PBIS (Positive Behavioral Interventions and Supports) for students with special needs (Department of Education, 2014) and Olweus Bullying Prevention Program (OBPP) (Olweus, 2014).

Social-Emotional Learning (SEL): This intervention enhances core aspects of social and emotional learning, namely self-awareness, self-management, social awareness, interpersonal skills, and responsible decision-making in diverse learners (CASEL, 2021).

Respecting and Positive School Environment: Teaching of respect can be done through school rules and policies, specific lesson plans and using different teaching strategies (Rogojan & Turda, 2022). Respectful attitudes play a very important part in setting up a safe and welcoming school climate (Quintana-Orts et al., 2022). Creating a positive school climate that teaches students to be empathetic, kind, and tolerant should always be adopted to prevent bullying (Kaltsas & Kaltsas, 2023).

Raising Awareness: Harper (2015) emphasizes that school programs should focus on raising awareness among students and staff about bullying behaviors and their negative impact.

Individualized Support: Individualized Education Programs (IEPs.) help the students to enhance their basic skills and adjust in school in better way which protects the special students from bullying behavior (Kartika et al., 2017).

Peer Support Programs: Introducing Buddy systems to increase social contact and decrease loneliness because students with special needs who are lonely have a difficult time managing their daily activities (Carter et al., 2009).

Staff Training: Training is essential for the staff to prevent the dismantling of such behaviors' and to cultivate the positive behaviors among the students with special needs (Najdowski et al., 2021).

Anti-Bullying Policies and Legislation: Anti-bullying policies and the laws provide the proper guidelines for bullying prevention and enhance parent and community involvement for the betterment and increase the confidence among students with special needs (ACER's National Bullying Prevention Center, 2021).

Use of Technology: Whistleblowing and open reporting and/or data collection mechanisms are very useful to control bullying among special students (Gaffney et al., 2021). Through resources such as anonymous reporting platforms, empathy-building simulations, and assistive communication apps, incorporating technology into anti-bullying campaigns for children with special needs can increase safety and promote inclusivity (Anderson & Jiang, 2018). By empowering students and fostering understanding, this method makes the classroom climate more encouraging (Kowalski et al., 2014).

Restorative Practices: These practices basically promote active listening, inclusivity, open and honest communication reduce conflict which related to accountability and community involvement and provide a safe and healthy environment (Vissing, 2023).

Recommendations in the Context of Pakistan

In light of the discussion in this chapter, the authors find the following recommendations useful in addressing bullying among children with special needs in the context of Pakistan:

Policy Interventions and Advocacy

Preventing bullying is based on a human rights framework in compliance with rules and regulations within a school setting and an overall understanding of dignity, equality, autonomy, and solidarity. Establishing clear anti-bullying policies with specific provisions for children with special needs is crucial. Pakistan's educational policies should include guidelines for schools on handling bullying cases involving students with disabilities, along with state or provincial-level monitoring systems to ensure compliance.

School-Wide Positive Behavioral Interventions and Supports (SWPBIS)

Schools also use systemic prevention that involves multiple tiers: universal, targeted, and individualized to combat bullying and related concerns. SWPBIS is a framework aimed at promoting positive behaviors and reducing problem behaviors through proactive interventions (Bradshaw et al., 2013). It involves setting clear behavioral expectations, communicating those expectations, and reinforcing positive behaviors. For schools in Pakistan, implementing SWPBIS can foster a culture of respect and inclusion, which is especially essential for children with special needs who are at higher risk of being bullied. In order to reduce cases of bullying in institutions while also addressing the trauma experienced by victims, it is suggested that female counselors should be on duty for female students and male counselors be assigned to male students.

Professional Development and Training for the Teachers and Education Leaders

As highlighted in the review of the literature and the findings of the study discussed above, teachers lack awareness and training in combating bully. Teachers need skills to recognize subtle bullying signs and to intervene constructively. Therefore, trainings may be designed with the focus on empathy-building exercises, classroom management strategies, and tailored approaches for supporting children with special needs. Management and organizational leadership in preventing and handling of bullying and positive school climate is pivotal too. It may be mandatory for these leaders to have adequate knowledge about special needs of the children to create conducive environment for children with learning disabilities to learn and grow.

Active Parental Involvement and Engagement Programs

Families of children with special needs should be actively involved in anti-bullying programs in schools. In Pakistan, parents often lack the awareness and resources to address bullying. Schools can organize seminars and workshops for parents, focusing on recognizing signs of bullying, effective communication with teachers, and supporting their children in navigating social situations, including cyber bullying.

Peer-Mediated Interventions

Encouraging peer support through structured peer buddy programs can reduce bullying and foster friendships. In Pakistan, implementing peer-buddy systems with students who have received awareness training can support children with special needs and help prevent them from being socially isolated and more vulnerable to bullying. Incorporating advanced interventions like these can help create a holistic approach to preventing and responding to bullying, ensuring a safer and more inclusive environment for children with special needs in Pakistan.

REFERENCES

Academy of Science of South Africa (ASSAf). (2022). *Webinar on Mental Health and Bullying.* http://dx.doi.org/.DOI: 10.17159/assaf.2022/0085

ACER's National Bullying Prevention Center. (2021). *Bullying and students with disabilities.* Retrieved from https://www.pacer.org/bullying/info/students-with-disabilities/

Affairs, U. N. O. O. (1989). The Law of the Sea: Navigation on the High Seas: Legislative History of Part VII, Section I (Articles 87, 89, 90-94, 96-98) of the United Nations Convention on the Law of the Sea (Vol. 18). New York: United Nations.

Ahmed, B., Yousaf, F. N., Ahmad, A., Zohra, T., & Ullah, W. (2023). Bullying in educational institutions: College students' experiences. *Psychology Health and Medicine*, 28(9), 2713–2719. DOI: 10.1080/13548506.2022.2067338 PMID: 35440249

Ali, F., & Shah, A. (2020). Cultural influences on peer victimization in Pakistani schools. *Journal of Social Sciences*, 15(3), 78–90.

Anderson, M., & Jiang, J. (2018). *Teens, Social Media & Technology 2018.* Pew Research Center.

Arslan, M., & Zaman, R. (2014). Unemployment and its determinants: A study of Pakistan economy (1999-2010). *Journal of Economics and Sustainable Development*, 5(13), 20–24.

Bauman, S., & Del Rio, A. (2006). Preservice teachers' responses to bullying scenarios: Comparing physical, verbal, and relational bullying. *Journal of Educational Psychology*, 98(1), 219–231. DOI: 10.1037/0022-0663.98.1.219

Bibi, T. (2018). Article 25th A: Implications of free and compulsory secondary education. *VFAST Transactions on Education and Social Sciences*, 6(1), 57–63.

Boruah, A. S. (2022). Problems faced by the teachers in educating the physically challenged children in special schools. *Towards Excellence*, 14(4), 78–93. DOI: 10.37867/TE140409

Bradshaw, C. P., Waasdorp, T. E., O'Brennan, L. M., & Gulemetova, M. (2013). Teachers' and education support professionals' perspectives on bullying and prevention: Findings from a National Education Association study. *School Psychology Review*, 42(3), 280–297. DOI: 10.1080/02796015.2013.12087474 PMID: 25414539

Burkhart, K., & Keder, R. D. (2020). Bullying: The role of the clinician in prevention and intervention. In *Clinician's Toolkit for Children's Behavioral Health* (pp. 143-173). Academic Press.

Bussey, K. (2023). The contribution of social cognitive theory to school bullying research and practice. *Theory into Practice*, 62(3), 293–305. DOI: 10.1080/00405841.2023.2226549

Canales, M. U.Miguel Urra Canales. (2023). Bullying. Description of the roles of victim, bully, peer group, school, family and society. *Influence: International Journal of Science Review*, 5(2), 184–194. DOI: 10.54783/influencejournal.v5i2.148

Carter, E. W., Cushing, L. S., & Kennedy, C. H. (2009). Peer support strategies for improving the social interactions and job skills of adolescents with disabilities. *Education and Training in Autism and Developmental Disabilities*, 44(4), 440–450.

Collaborative for Academic, Social, and Emotional Learning (CASEL). (2021). *What is SEL?* Retrieved from https://casel.org/what-is-sel/

Combs-Jones, W. L. (2021). An Investigation of Teachers' Descriptions, Understandings, and Perceptions of Intervention and Prevention Tactics Addressing Students with Disabilities: A Collective Case Study [Doctoral Dissertation, University of Liberty]

Dedousis-Wallace, A., & Shute, R. H. (2009). Indirect bullying: Predictors of teacher intervention, and outcome of a pilot educational presentation about impact on adolescent mental health. *Australian Journal of Educational & Developmental Psychology*, 9, 2–17.

Department of Education (ED). (2014). *Guiding principles: A resource guide for improving school climate and discipline*. ERIC Clearinghouse.

Education (2004). The Salamanca statement and framework for action on special needs education. Special Educational Needs and Inclusive Education: Systems and contexts, 1, 382.

Farmer, T. W., Petrin, R., Brooks, D. S., Hamm, J. V., Lambert, K., & Gravelle, M. (2012). Bullying involvement and the school adjustment of rural students with and without disabilities. *Journal of Emotional and Behavioral Disorders*, 20(1), 19–37. DOI: 10.1177/1063426610392039

Fattore, T., & Mason, J. (2020). Humiliation, resistance and state violence: Using the sociology of emotions to understand institutional violence against women and girls and their acts of resistance. *International Journal for Crime. Justice and Social Democracy*, 9(4), 104–117. DOI: 10.5204/ijcjsd.1693

Ferrer-Cascales, R., Albaladejo-Blázquez, N., Sánchez-SanSegundo, M., Portilla-Tamarit, I., Lordan, O., & Ruiz-Robledillo, N. (2019). Effectiveness of the TEI program for bullying and cyberbullying reduction and school climate improvement. *International Journal of Environmental Research and Public Health*, 16(4), 580. DOI: 10.3390/ijerph16040580 PMID: 30781543

Gaffney, H., Ttofi, M. M., & Farrington, D. P. (2021). What works in anti-bullying programs? Analysis of effective intervention components. *Journal of School Psychology*, 85, 37–56. DOI: 10.1016/j.jsp.2020.12.002 PMID: 33715780

Gomes, A., Martins, M. C., Silva, B., Ferreira, E., Nunes, O., & Caldas, A. C. (2022). How different are girls and boys as bullies and victims? Comparative perspectives on gender and age in the bullying dynamics. *International Journal of Educational Psychology*, 11(3), 237–260. DOI: 10.17583/ijep.9310

Hahn, G. (2023). Bullying: Violência na linguagem e sua dimensão perlocucionária/ Language violence and its perlocutionary dimension. *Revista Linguagem em Foco/ Language in Focus Journal, 15*(1), 152-176.

Hakim, F., & Shah, S. A. (2017). Investigation of bullying controlling strategies by primary school teachers at district Haripur. [PJPBS]. *Peshawar Journal of Psychology and Behavioral Sciences*, 3(2), 165–174.

Harper, K. M. (2015). *Teacher perceptions of the use of school-wide positive behavior interventions and supports at reducing the presence of bullying in middle schools*. The University of Southern Mississippi.

Haru, E. (2022). Perilaku bullying di kalangan pelajar/ Bullying behavior among students. *Jurnal Alternatif WacanaI lmiah Interkultural/ Journal of Alternative Intercultural Academic Discourse, 11*(2), 59-71.

Hassan, B. A. R., & Mohammed, A. H. (2023). Overview of bullying. *Studies in Social Science & Humanities*, 2(4), 69–71. DOI: 10.56397/SSSH.2023.04.07

Jahanzaib, M., Fatima, G., & Shoaib, M. (2021). Review of policy documents in perspective of rehabilitation of persons with special needs in Pakistan. *Journal of ISOSS*, 7(4), 419–432.

Javed, K., Malik, S., Younus, W., & Shahid, A. (2023). Confronting the destructive impact of Bullying: The harmful consequences and laws for anti-bullying initiatives. *Journal of Social Sciences Review*, 3(2), 666–675. DOI: 10.54183/jssr.v3i2.309

Jones, A., & Brown, B. (2019). Developmental Theory: Understanding the emergence of bullying behavior. *Child Development Perspectives*, 13(4), 321–335.

Jones, S. (2019). *Bullying in schools: A shared understanding* (Doctoral dissertation, Cardiff University).

Kaltsas, E. P., & Kaltsas, J. (2023). Combatting bullying in school and its consequences. In *Research Highlights in Language, Literature and Education* (Vol. 6, pp. 28-35). B P International. ISBN 978-81-19217-91-5. DOI: 10.9734/bpi/rhlle/v6/9918F

Karmaliani, R., McFarlane, J., Khuwaja, H. M. A., Somani, Y., Bhamani, S. S., Saeed Ali, T., Asad, N., Chirwa, E. D., & Jewkes, R. (2020). Right To Play's intervention to reduce peer violence among children in public schools in Pakistan: A cluster-randomized controlled trial. *Global Health Action*, 13(1), 1836604. DOI: 10.1080/16549716.2020.1836604 PMID: 33138740

Kartika, A., Suminar, D. R., Tairas, M. M., & Hendriani, W. (2017). *Individualized education program (IEP) paperwork: A narrative review*. In: Asia International Multidisciplinary Conference 2017, 1-2 May, 2017, Universiti Teknologi Malaysia, Johor Bahru, Malaysia.

Kennedy, T. D., Russom, A. G., & Kevorkian, M. M. (2012). Teacher and administrator perceptions of bullying in schools. *International Journal of Education Policy and Leadership*, 7(5), 1–12. DOI: 10.22230/ijepl.2012v7n5a395

Khan, M., & Khan, S. (2019). Socioeconomic factors in school bullying: A Pakistani perspective. *International Journal of Educational Research*, 28(1), 45–57.

Khasawneh, M. A. S. (2023). Social attitude of children with special needs in the learning process. *Acta Scientiae. Journal of Science*, 24(6), 32–43.

Khawar, R., & Malik, F. (2016). Bullying behavior of Pakistani pre-adolescents: Findings based on Olweus questionnaire. *Pakistan Journal of Psychological Research*, 31(1), 23–43.

Kim, S. (2022). The role of social capital in the onset of victimization against children. *Child Indicators Research*, 15(1), 67–86. DOI: 10.1007/s12187-021-09859-4

Koo, H., Kwak, K., & Smith, P. K. (2008). Victimization in Korean schools: The nature, incidence, and distinctive features of Korean bullying or wang-ta. *Journal of School Violence*, 7(4), 119–139. DOI: 10.1080/15388220801974084

Kowalski, R. M., Giumetti, G. W., Schroeder, A. N., & Lattanner, M. R. (2014). Bullying in the digital age: A critical review and meta-analysis of cyberbullying research among youth. *Psychological Bulletin*, 140(4), 1073–1137. DOI: 10.1037/a0035618 PMID: 24512111

Kowalski, R. M., & Toth, A. (2018). Cyberbullying among youth with and without disabilities. *Journal of Child & Adolescent Trauma*, 11(1), 7–15. DOI: 10.1007/s40653-017-0139-y PMID: 32318133

Lepley, C. (2023). *Bullying in Schools: Teacher Perceptions on Effectiveness of the Current Bullying Program*. Immaculata University.

Mahmoudi, M., & Keashly, L. (2021). Filling the space: A framework for coordinated global actions to diminish academic bullying. *Angewandte Chemie/Applied Chemistry, 133*(7), 3378-3384.

Malik, A., & Abdullah, N. A. (2017). Level of aggression among college teachers and students in Pakistan: An analysis. *Pakistan Journal of Social Sciences*, 37(2), 343–353.

Maryam, U., & Ijaz, T. (2018). Efficacy of a school based intervention plan for victims of bullying. *e-Academia Journal, 8*, 206-216.

McFarlane, J., Karmaliani, R., Khuwaja, H. M. A., Gulzar, S., Somani, R., Ali, T. S., Somani, Y. H., Bhamani, S. S., Krone, R. D., Paulson, R. M., Muhammad, A., & Jewkes, R. (2017). Preventing peer violence against children: Methods and baseline data of a cluster randomized controlled trial in Pakistan. *Global Health, Science and Practice*, 5(1), 115–137. DOI: 10.9745/GHSP-D-16-00215 PMID: 28351880

Mishna, F., Scarcello, I., Pepler, D., & Wiener, J. (2005). Teachers' understanding of bullying. *Revue canadienne de l'éducation. Canadian Journal of Education*, 28(4), 718–738. DOI: 10.2307/4126452

Mobarki, A. A., Morsi, N. M. A., & Hamouda, G. M. (2020). *Teachers' Perception Regarding Bullying Behavior in Elementary Schools at Jizan City* (Doctoral dissertation, King Abdul Aziz University, Jeddah).

Najdowski, A. C., Gharapetian, L., & Jewett, V. (2021). Toward the development of antiracist and multicultural graduate training programs in behavior analysis. *Behavior Analysis in Practice*, 14(2), 462–477. DOI: 10.1007/s40617-020-00504-0 PMID: 34150459

Nations, U. (2007). Convention on the Rights of Persons with Disabilities. *European Journal of Health Law*, 14(3), 281–298. PMID: 18348362

Nations, U. (2015). Transforming our world: The 2030 agenda for sustainable development. New York: United Nations, Department of Economic and Social Affairs, 1, 41.

Naveed, S., Waqas, A., Shah, Z., Ahmad, W., Wasim, M., Rasheed, J., & Afzaal, T. (2020). Trends in bullying and emotional and behavioral difficulties among Pakistani schoolchildren: A cross-sectional survey of seven cities. *Frontiers in Psychiatry*, 10, 976. DOI: 10.3389/fpsyt.2019.00976 PMID: 32009998

Olweus, D. (1994). Bullying at school: Long-term outcomes for the victims and an effective school-based intervention program. In *Aggressive behavior: Current perspectives* (pp. 97–130). Springer US. DOI: 10.1007/978-1-4757-9116-7_5

Olweus, D. (2014). Victimization by peers: Antecedents and long-term outcomes. In *Social withdrawal, inhibition, and shyness in childhood* (pp. 315–341). Psychology Press.

Orpinas, P., Horne, A. M., & Staniszewski, D. (2003). School bullying: Changing the problem by changing the school. *School Psychology Review*, 32(3), 431–444. DOI: 10.1080/02796015.2003.12086210

Pakistan. (1982). The Constitution of Islamic Republic of Pakistan, with the Provisional Constitution Order, 1981: As amended up-to-date. Lahore: All Pakistan Legal Decision.

Parada, R. H. (2022). Bullying prevention and prosocial skill development in school settings. In *School-Wide Positive Behaviour Support* (pp. 170–188). Routledge. DOI: 10.4324/9781003186236-9

Paranti, S. M., & Hudiyana, J. (2022). Current Social Domination Theory: Is it still relevant. *Psikostudia: Jurnal Psikologi Psychostudia. The Journal of Psychology*, 11(2), 324–340.

Pearce, N., Monks, H., Alderman, N., Hearn, L., Burns, S., Runions, K., Francis, J., & Cross, D. (2024). 'It's all about context': Building school capacity to implement a whole-school approach to bullying. *International Journal of Bullying Prevention : an Official Publication of the International Bullying Prevention Association*, 6(1), 53–68. DOI: 10.1007/s42380-022-00138-6

Peskin, M. F., Tortolero, S. R., & Markham, C. M. (2006). Bullying and victimization among Black and Hispanic adolescents. *Adolescence*, 41(163), 467–484. PMID: 17225662

Policy, N. (2010). *National Education Policy*. Ministry of Education.

Prinstein, M. J., Boergers, J., & Vernberg, E. M. (2001). Overt and relational aggression in adolescents: Social-psychological adjustment of aggressors and victims. *Journal of Clinical Child Psychology*, 30(4), 479–491. DOI: 10.1207/S15374424JCCP3004_05 PMID: 11708236

Quintana-Orts, C., Mc Guckin, C., Del Rey, R., & Mora-Merchán, J. A. (2022). Overcoming bullying in education. In *Overcoming adversity in education* (pp. 102–113). Routledge. DOI: 10.4324/9781003180029-10

Rahma, A., Istima, F., Addinullah, M. A., & Nihayah, U. (2022). Konseling interpersonal dalam menumbuhkan kesehatan mental korban bullying/ Interpersonal counseling in promoting the mental health of bullying victims. *Nosipakabelo: Jurnal Bimbingan Dan Konseling Islam/ Journal of Islamic Guidance and Counseling, 3*(2), 68-84.

Rehman, A., Jingdong, L., & Hussain, I. (2015). The province-wise literacy rate in Pakistan and its impact on the economy. *Pacific Science Review B. Humanities and Social Sciences*, 1(3), 140–144.

Rigby, K. (2024). Theoretical perspectives and two explanatory models of school bullying. *International Journal of Bullying Prevention : an Official Publication of the International Bullying Prevention Association*, 6(2), 101–109. DOI: 10.1007/s42380-022-00141-x

Rogojan, L., & Turda, E. (2023). Educational Intervention Program for the Prevention of Bullying Behaviour in Primary School. In I. Albulescu, & C. Stan (Eds.), Education, Reflection, Development - ERD 2022, vol 6. European Proceedings of Educational Sciences (pp. 464-475). European Publisher. https://doi.org/DOI: 10.15405/epes.23056.42

Saleem, S., Khan, N. F., & Zafar, S. (2021). Prevalence of cyberbullying victimization among Pakistani youth. *Technology in Society*, 65, 101577. DOI: 10.1016/j.techsoc.2021.101577

Shah, S. S., Ali, N., Anwer, M., & Jaffar, A. (2015). Nurturing sustainable teachers' leadership culture: Possibilities, challenges, stakeholders' behavior analysis in the context of Pakistan. [IJR]. *International Journal of Research*, 2(3), 593–600.

Shahid, M., Rauf, U., Sarwar, U., & Asif, S. (2022). Impact of bullying behavior on mental health and quality of life among pre-adolescents and adolescents in Sialkot-Pakistan. Pakistan. *Journal of the Humanities and Social Sciences*, 10(1), 324–331. DOI: 10.52131/pjhss.2022.1001.0200

Shujja, S., Atta, M., & Shujjat, J. M. (2014). Prevalence of bullying and victimization among sixth graders with reference to gender, socio-economic status and type of schools. *Journal of Social Sciences*, 38(2), 159–165. DOI: 10.1080/09718923.2014.11893246

Siddiqui, S., & Schultze-Krumbholz, A. (2023a). Bullying prevalence in Pakistan's educational institutes: Preclusion to the framework for a teacher-led antibullying intervention. *PLoS One*, 18(4), e0284864. DOI: 10.1371/journal.pone.0284864 PMID: 37104391

Siddiqui, S., & Schultze-Krumbholz, A. (2023b). The Sohanjana Antibullying Intervention: Pilot results of a peer-training module in Pakistan. *Social Sciences (Basel, Switzerland)*, 12(7), 409. DOI: 10.3390/socsci12070409

Smith, J. (2018). Organizational Cultural Theory and bullying behavior: Implications for educational institutions. *Journal of School Psychology*, 40(3), 211–225.

Strohmeier, D., Hoffmann, C., Schiller, E. M., Stefanek, E., & Spiel, C. (2012). ViSC social competence program. *New Directions for Youth Development*, 2012(133), 71–84. DOI: 10.1002/yd.20008 PMID: 22504792

Troop-Gordon, W., & Ladd, G. W. (2015). Teachers' victimization-related beliefs and strategies: Associations with students' aggressive behavior and peer victimization. *Journal of Abnormal Child Psychology*, 43(1), 45–60. DOI: 10.1007/s10802-013-9840-y PMID: 24362767

United Nations Educational& Organization. (2009). Policy guidelines on inclusion in education. In: UNESCO Paris.

Vasylenko, O., Chaikovskyi, M., Dobrovitska, O., Ostrovska, N., Kondratyuk, S., & Luchko, Y. (2022). Peculiarities of adaptive and rehabilitation processes of children with special educational needs. *Broad Research in Artificial Intelligence and Neuroscience*, 13(4), 398–420. DOI: 10.18662/brain/13.4/395

Vissing, Y. (2023). Children's Lives Are Different Today: More Reasons for Building a Children's Human Rights Framework. In *Children's Human Rights in the USA: Challenges and Opportunities* (pp. 147–178). Springer International Publishing. DOI: 10.1007/978-3-031-30848-2_7

Waasdorp, T. E., Bradshaw, C. P., & Leaf, P. J. (2012). The impact of schoolwide positive behavioral interventions and supports on bullying and peer rejection: A randomized controlled effectiveness trial. *Archives of Pediatrics & Adolescent Medicine*, 166(2), 149–156. DOI: 10.1001/archpediatrics.2011.755 PMID: 22312173

Wang, J. (2023). The Impacts and Interventions of School Bullying. In *SHS Web of Conferences* (Vol. 157, p. 04023). EDP Sciences. DOI: 10.1051/shsconf/202315704023

Wanti, L. P., Romadloni, A., Somantri, O., Sari, L., Prasetya, N. W. A., & Johanna, A. (2023). English learning assistance using interactive media for children with special needs to improve growth and development. *Pengabdian: JurnalAbdimas/ Devotion. Journal of Community Service*, 1(2), 46–58.

Wolke, D., Woods, S., Bloomfield, L., & Karstadt, L. (2000). The association between direct and relational bullying and behaviour problems among primary school children. *Journal of Child Psychology and Psychiatry, and Allied Disciplines*, 41(8), 989–1002. DOI: 10.1111/1469-7610.00687 PMID: 11099116

Yoon, J., & Bauman, S. (2014). Teachers: A critical but overlooked component of bullying prevention and intervention. *Theory into Practice*, 53(4), 308–314. DOI: 10.1080/00405841.2014.947226

Yoon, J., Sulkowski, M. L., & Bauman, S. A. (2016). Teachers' responses to bullying incidents: Effects of teacher characteristics and contexts. *Journal of School Violence*, 15(1), 91–113. DOI: 10.1080/15388220.2014.963592

Yoon, J. S. (2004). Predicting teacher interventions in bullying situations. *Education & Treatment of Children*, 27(1), 37–45.

Yoon, J. S., & Kerber, K. (2003). Bullying: Elementary teachers' attitudes and intervention strategies. *Research in Education*, 69(1), 27–35. DOI: 10.7227/RIE.69.3

Chapter 5
Collaboration Between Parents, Children With Disabilities, and School Personnel:
A Key Component of School-Based Bullying Prevention

Hannah Rapp
https://orcid.org/0000-0001-8036-3044
University at Buffalo, SUNY, USA

Julianna Casella
https://orcid.org/0000-0001-5188-4414
University at Buffalo, SUNY, USA

Amanda Nickerson
University at Buffalo, SUNY, USA

ABSTRACT

School-aged children with disabilities face heightened rates of bullying victimization compared to their typically developing peers. This chapter emphasizes the important role that parents of children with disabilities play in bullying prevention and intervention. First, school-based interventions for reducing bullying victimization among children with disabilities, such as inclusion, social-emotional learning, and multi-component programming, are reviewed. Furthermore, this chapter reviews recommendations for how parents can engage in communication with their child regarding bullying and strategies to help children with disabilities develop skills for

DOI: 10.4018/979-8-3693-5315-8.ch005

handling such situations. Guidelines are provided for parents who seek to report bullying incidents to school personnel. This chapter also outlines helpful responses to bullying by school personnel as perceived by parents of children with disabilities. Lastly, this chapter explores considerations for schools and parents when supporting children with disabilities who are both bullied and bully others.

INTRODUCTION

Bullying is any unwanted aggressive behavior(s) by another youth or group of youths that involves an observed or perceived power imbalance and is repeated multiple times or is highly likely to be repeated (Gladden et al., 2014). Children with disabilities often experience increased rates of bullying victimization, including physical, psychological, social, or educational harm. Data collected by the World Health Organization (WHO) from 11 nations suggest that adolescents with a long-term illness, disability, or medical condition were about 1.3 to 2 times more likely to have been bullied than typically developing adolescents from the same country (Sentenac et al., 2013). Approximately 20% of U.S. children in grades 6 to 12 report being bullied (National Center for Education Statistics, 2019), whereas the rate of bully victimization for school-aged children with disabilities is estimated to be 39.5% (Iyanda, 2021).

Parents of children with disabilities play a significant role in recognizing, preventing, and responding to bullying. Parents of children with disabilities are often involved in their child's social life (Buttimer & Tierney, 2005; Walton & Tiede, 2020) and educational programs (Freeman & Kirksey, 2023; Kirksey et al., 2022; Zhang & Chen, 2023). They may also notice a change in their child's behavior (e.g. school phobia; Lydecker et al., 2023) that could signal bullying. In addition, children are more likely to tell their parents rather than school personnel about experiencing bullying (Demaray et al., 2013).

This chapter explores the vital role that parents of children with disabilities play in supporting their child during bullying incidents and in collaborating with school personnel to address bullying. It starts by reviewing the literature about bullying interventions for reducing bullying victimization among children with disabilities, followed by a brief overview of the unique relationship between parents and children with disabilities. The chapter is divided into two parts: parent-child communication and parent-school communication. The first part outlines how parents engage in communication and problem-solving strategies with their child with disabilities regarding bullying. The second part offers guidelines to parents seeking to communicate with school personnel regarding bullying. Additionally, the chapter outlines school responses to bullying that parents of children with disabilities perceived as helpful and unhelpful. Furthermore, this chapter discusses parent-school collaboration in addressing bullying perpetrated by students with disabilities. Finally, the chapter considers ways in which parents' involvement in a school-based bullying prevention can vary based on the type of disability of the child (i.e., developmental disability, physical disability, emotional disturbance).

SCHOOL-BASED INTERVENTIONS FOR DECREASING BULLYING VICTIMIZATION AMONG CHILDREN WITH DISABILITIES

Several interventions in school settings have been aimed at mitigating bullying victimization among children with disabilities, such as inclusion, social and emotional learning, and multi-component programming. Regarding inclusive programming, interactive peer groups have been implemented for children with and without disabilities (Bradley, 2016; Graybill et al., 2016). In Bradley's (2016) study, 12 children with autism spectrum disorder (ASD), 10 of whom had experienced at least one incident of bullying, met in groups of four (one child with ASD to three neurotypical peers) every two weeks for seven months to discuss topics like friendship, bullying, interests, work skills, and behaviors. Graybill et al. (2016) selected 13 children with disabilities (those with Individualized Education Programs or 504 plans[1]) from elementary and middle schools, who had relatively high bullying victimization scores, to meet in groups with typically developing peers for seven sessions to discuss topics related to bullying, such as empathy, problem-solving, assessing safe spaces, and self-esteem. In both studies, children with disabilities reported significantly less bullying victimization following the inclusive programs. Similarly, Saylor and Leach (2009) implemented Peer EXPRESS in which middle and high school children with and without disabilities took part in recreation-focused activities such as arts, sports, and service projects, held once a week for 24 weeks. This study also reported success in reducing bullying victimization among children with disabilities. Collectively, these studies suggest that facilitating inclusive activities among children with and without disabilities can reduce peer victimization. However, they are limited in their generalizability due to their small sample sizes and the absence of control groups.

School-based social and emotional learning (SEL) programs have also been evaluated for reducing bullying victimization among children with disabilities. SEL programs, such as *Second Step*, are designed to build children's self-awareness, social awareness, self-management, problem solving, and relationship management skills (Durlak et al., 2011). Following a 15-week *Second Step* program involving 457 sixth graders (ages 10 to 14), teachers reported a significant decrease in relational victimization (i.e., exclusion) for children with disabilities (Sullivan et al., 2015). However, the children with disabilities themselves did not report significant decreases in relational victimization compared to children with disabilities in control classrooms. Furthermore, in a study involving 123 middle school children (ages 11 to 12) with disabilities, those in the *Second Step* group ($n = 47$) showed significant reductions in bullying perpetration over the course of three years but did not report significant reductions in bullying victimization (Espelage et al., 2015). Given these mixed findings, more research is necessary to determine the effectiveness of SEL programming in reducing bullying victimization among children with disabilities.

Schools also address the complex issue of bullying by employing multiple interventions strategies simultaneously. Humphrey et al. (2013) measured the effects of an 18-month intervention program called "Achievement for All" (AFA), which targeted bullying victimization and other outcomes for 4,758 children with disabilities (ages 5 to 15) across 323 schools in England. The AFA program comprised three main components: (a) monitoring academic progress and providing teacher support, (b) conducting three structured conversations per school year with parents about their child's learning plan, and (c) implementing school-wide interventions such as restorative justice approaches to conflict, use of social and emotional learning materials, buddy benches, circle time, peer-based mentoring, and staff trainings in behavioral reward systems. The findings revealed a significant reduction in bullying victimization among children with disabilities in schools implementing the AFA program compared to control schools. However, it is difficult to tell which of the many AFA initiatives were most effective in targeting bullying behaviors. Additionally, the study did not specify whether the AFA program incorporated explicit anti-bullying lessons.

Furthermore, educator training programs focused on bullying victimization among children with disabilities have been used as an anti-bullying strategy. Through an online professional development training, educators participated in psychoeducational modules covering topics such as special education services, definitions of disabilities, definitions of bullying, and associated risk factors among students with disabilities (Espelage et al., 2023; Robinson et al., 2023). The training also entailed how to recognize and implement a multi-tiered system of supports (MTSS), including interventions at school-wide (Tier 1), classroom-level (Tier 2) and individualized (Tier 3) levels. Following the training, interviews with 33 educators revealed several key insights (Robinson et al., 2023). Educators identified the importance of conducting a school climate survey to identify how and when school bullying occurs, the necessity of addressing social and communication challenges among all students in their classrooms, and the need to use students' individual behavior plans to improve students' self-determination, foster student-teacher relationships and reduce students' verbal aggression. Despite these positive learning outcomes among educators, no formal evaluations have been conducted to assess the impact of the training on reducing bullying among children with disabilities.

In sum, several school-based interventions have aimed to reduce bullying victimization among children with disabilities. However, it is important to consider interventions beyond the school environment, as parents play a critical role in the support system for children with disabilities. In the next section, the role parents can play in bullying intervention and prevention is examined.

Parental Involvement in the Lives of Children with Disabilities

The parent-child relationship for children with disabilities is a unique relationship which requires specific consideration when working to prevent bullying for children with disabilities. Parents of children with disabilities, in general, may experience increased caregiving (Hayes et al., 2013; Pinquart, 2018; Plant & Sanders, 2007; Smith et al., 2001) and financial stress (Goudie, 2014). These parents may also be more involved in their children's leisure activities (Buttimer & Tierney, 2005) and educational programs (Freeman & Kirksey, 2023; Kirksey et al., 2022) than parents of typically developing children. Caregiving responsibilities for children with developmental disabilities tend to fall more heavily on mothers than on fathers in the United States (Crowe, 2000), Spain (Vilaseca et al., 2023), and Australia (Rowbotham et al., 2011). In a systematic literature review of 24 studies from China, Taiwan, and Turkey about disability and parenting, mothers predominantly managed care activities like obtaining diagnoses, accessing services, and communicating with professionals (Acar et al., 2021).

Research has shown that the parent-child relationship for children with disabilities, specifically autism spectrum disorder (ASD) and intellectual disability (ID), can be characterized by highly involved caregiving (i.e., "enmeshment") and dependency on caregivers (Walton & Tiede, 2020). Examples of enmeshment can include behaviors that hinder children from developing their own identity and independence, such as feeling pressured to spend most their free time with their family. However, research has also evidenced that parents of children with disabilities seek to promote their children's autonomy by fostering self-determination, which includes making independent choices, solving problems, and expressing their needs (Carter et al., 2013; Chu, 2018; Ward, 2005). Thus, parents must consider how socially distancing children with disabilities from their peers, either before or after negative relational experiences, might reduce their ability to cope with and problem-solve during future negative experiences (Limber et al., 2016, p. 137). Given that parents are involved in the education, social life, and mental and physical well-being of their children with disabilities, they play an important role in communicating with their children and school personnel about bullying.

Communicating with Children about Bullying Victimization

Open communication between parents and children about bullying is important. Telling an adult about bullying has been reported to be an effective strategy (Black et al., 2010; Craig et al., 2007; Nixon et al., 2020). Emotionally supportive relationships between adolescents and parents following bullying victimization were found to be associated with lower levels of emotional and behavioral problems over time (Yeung & Leadbeater, 2010). Similarly, adolescents experienced fewer depressive symptoms after bullying experiences when they perceived that their parents listened to them, understood them, gave them advice, and helped them to solve problems (Conners-Burrow et al., 2009). Table 1 offers specific examples of helpful parent and child communication regarding bullying experiences based on recommendations from the Youth Voice Project (Davis & Nixon, 2010) and Lovegrove et al. (2013).

Table 1. Helpful and unhelpful parent communication for conversations regarding bullying

Helpful Communication	Examples
• Listening without interrupting.	"Tell me more." "Tell me what happened."
• Avoiding extreme emotional reactions and maintain a neutral expression while listening.	
• Empathizing with your child's feelings.	"That must have been scary for you." "That must have been very frustrating."
• Allowing the child to take the lead to problem solve.	"What do you think you want to do about this?" "How can I help?"
• Keep checking in with the child afterwards to see if the behavior has stopped.	
Unhelpful Communication	**Examples**
• Victim blaming	"If you acted different, this wouldn't happen to you." "Stop tattling."
• Recommending strategies that are often not effective due to the power imbalance of bullying and convey that the parent does not take the report of bullying seriously.	"Ignore it." "Things will work out on their own." "Fight back."
• Ignoring what is going on.	"Solve it yourself."

continued on following page

Table 1. Continued

Helpful Communication	Examples
• Acting as if there is a single quick fix for bullying.	"If you just ___, this won't happen again."
• Minimizing your child's feelings.	"I think you're overreacting."

A parent who already has an open communication with their child about friends, feelings and school is more likely to learn of their child's experiences with bullying (Lovegrove et al., 2013). In comparison, Unnever and Cornell (2004) found that middle school-aged children were less likely to report being bullied when parents used power-assertive parenting methods. For conversation starters and other discussion protocols, parents can visit *Stopbullying.gov* (stopbullying.gov/prevention/how-to-prevent-bullying#Keep0) or the *Bully Free World* website (bullyfreeworld-bully.nationbuilder.com/conversation_starters).

Not every child is able to communicate about bullying experiences, such as a child who has severe communication challenges. In this case, parents can also pay attention to common signs of bullying. Some indicators of bullying at school include refusal or reluctance to go to school, a request to come home for lunch, loss of interest in schoolwork, persistent stomachaches or headaches, unexplained injuries, avoidance of social situations, sudden loss of friends, and missing or damaged clothing, books, electronics or jewelry (ASPA, 2021). Additionally, among children with hearing loss, signs of bullying included sleep issues and anxiety (Bouldin et al., 2021).

Counselling: Evidence-Based Responses to Bullying

Parents play a crucial role in helping their child to effectively deal with bullying by providing guidance and support (Lovegrove et al., 2013). Therefore, it is important for parents understand which bullying response strategies are effective. Research indicates that strategies like telling a friend or adult and using humor can be effective for coping with relational bullying (such as emotional hurt or exclusion), but not as effective for physical bullying (Nixon et al., 2020). Specifically, younger children often find telling an adult at school helpful, while older children tend to use humor to handle relational bullying situations. Children with disabilities, as compared to peers, are more likely to report that telling an adult worsens the situation (Hartley et al., 2017). Physical retaliation, such as fighting back, can be perceived as an effective response to bullying by children in general (Black et al., 2010). However, other research supports that for children with and without disabilities, physical retaliation is not effective (Hartley et al., 2017), and can increase victimization over time (Mahady-Wilton et al., 2000). Avoidance, such as pretending not to be bothered by the bullying, is a common response to bullying among all children, but it tends to be less effective and leads to poorer outcomes for children with disabilities (Hartley et al., 2017). Moreover, children with disabilities are more likely to express their feelings to the person who bullies, although this strategy is also perceived as less effective for them compared to their peers (Hartley et al., 2017).

These disparities underscore how strategies that are effective for the general student population may not be as effective for children with disabilities who can face additional challenges such as fewer friends, lower self-esteem, and weaker social skills (Rose et al., 2011). Therefore, combining individual response strategies with environmental supports like buddy systems, SEL programs, and clear reporting guidelines, is critical to supporting children with disabilities. Overall, understanding which strategies are effective for different types of bullying situations and for different age groups can help parents provide appropriate guidance and support to their children facing bullying incidents.

Parents can proactively demonstrate appropriate behavioral skills for bullying situations to help children with disabilities avoid responses like retaliation or physical confrontation.

Practicing Behavioral Skills to Respond to Bullying

Practicing behavioral skills to respond to bullying can be particularly important for children with disabilities. Video-modeling and self-modeling interventions that involve demonstrating appropriate response behaviors, engaging children in rehearsing these behaviors through role-playing or verbal scenarios, and providing constructive feedback, have been effective in teaching social skills to children with autism spectrum disorders (ASD; Bellini et al., 2007; Nikopoulous & Keenan, 2004; Sancho et al., 2010). Rex (2014) and Segura (2012) implemented video-modeling interventions to help children with ASD to practice responding to bullying. In Rex's (2014) study, six children with ASD were presented with three different bullying scenarios (e.g., "What would you do if someone shared their cookies with everyone but you?", "What would you do if someone would not stop tapping you?", etc.) and were coached to assertively respond (e.g., "Please don't do that.") and to inform an adult when necessary (e.g., "Mom, someone was not nice to me today."). In Segura's study (2012), three children with ASD learned how to differentiate between bullying and nonbullying behavior (e.g. friendly teasing), report bullying, and to ask an adult for help when needed. The program also coached children on steps to take when experiencing bullying: (1) stay calm and be cool, (2) ask yourself, "Do I need help?", (3) act confident (i.e., face the person, use eye contact, stand tall, hold your head high, and use a strong firm voice.), and (4) choose what to do: ignore, tell the bully to stop, walk away and look for friends, and/or talk to an adult.

Behavioral skills training is not limited to children with ASD. Behavioral skills trainings for responding to bullying have also been beneficial for adults with intellectual disabilities, both for those preparing to transition from high school into the workforce (Peterson, 2020) and those residing in group homes (Stannis et al., 2019). For example, Peterson (2020) helped to prepare high school students with intellectual disabilities (ages 19-20) to respond to workplace bullying, such as theft (e.g., "I lost my credit card. Can I use yours to buy my lunch?") and infantilization (e.g., "you'll get it next time, let me do [the task] for you."). In both studies, researchers provided instruction on appropriate responses (e.g., avoiding retaliation like scoffing or crying, declining requests, acknowledging victimization, and walking away or turning away), role-played scenarios, helped participants to rehearse responses, and provided feedback.

Additionally, the U.S. Department for Health and Human Services released a series of children's videos that explain how to respond to bullying behaviors (ASPA, 2022). These videos were presented to children with a variety of disabilities and physical conditions, such as depression, ADHD, cerebral palsy, severe food allergies, and epilepsy (Vessey & O'Neill, 2011). The series includes 12 videos featuring cartoon animals addressing topics like verbal, physical, and cyberbullying. When children with disabilities watched the video series and participated in discussion groups, they became more resilient in managing bullying situations, were significantly less bothered by teasing, and developed a more positive self-concept (Vessey & O'Neill, 2011).

In sum, there is evidence that the use of behavior modeling can be helpful for children with disabilities. This method could be a resource for parents to help their child to respond to bullying behaviors.

Communicating with the School Regarding Bullying Victimization

The guidelines so far have focused on how parents can work directly with their child, but it is also very important that parents communicate with school personnel if their child is being bullied. Parents of children with disabilities (Pimm, 2012) and without disabilities (Greeff & Van den Berg 2013; Lindstrom Johnson et al., 2019) report incidents of school bullying to school personnel as a first response.

Additionally, parents often advise their children to report bullying incidents to school personnel (Cooper et al., 2013; Stives et al., 2021).

School personnel also seek to inform parents about bullying incidents. In fact, as of 2011, 31 U.S. state laws required that district policies outline procedures for investigating bullying, and several of these laws also specify how schools should communicate the results of a bullying investigation to parents and guardians (Stuart-Cassel et al., 2011, p. 38). For example, in accordance with the state of New Jersey's Anti-Bullying Bill of Rights Act, bullying must be reported to the principal the same day it occurs, the principal must inform the parents of all suspected student victims and offenders as soon as possible and start an investigation of the act one day after receiving the report (Cerf et al., 2012, p. 17). These formal bullying policies can be beneficial for all parties involved. Research has suggested that schools with high-quality bullying policies (e.g., clear definition of bullying; procedures and consequences for bullying) have lower rates of bullying victimization than schools with lower-quality policies (Ordonez, 2006; Woods & Wolke, 2003).

To effectively support children with disabilities in navigating bullying incidents, it is essential for parents and school personnel to be aware of federal laws concerning disability-based harassment, which are considered violations of civil rights (e.g., Section 504 and Title II of the Rehabilitation Act of 1973). These laws underscore the school's responsibility to address bullying that is based on factors such as race, gender, ethnicity, nationality, sexual orientation, or disability, as it creates a hostile environment. Schools are mandated to investigate such incidents promptly, eliminate any discriminatory environment, and take preventive actions against future bullying (See *II. School's Obligations to Address Disability-Based Harassment* in Lhamon, 2014). For example, if a child is being made fun of in school for a behavior related to their disability, and a teacher witnesses the bullying and fails to report it or follow supports outline in a 504 plan, it constitutes a disability-based harassment violation and/or a violation to a free appropriate public education (FAPE). Upon investigation, the Office of Civil Rights and the school district must enter a resolution agreement (Lhamon, 2014). This agreement may include various components such as providing counseling to the student, monitoring bullying incidents, implementing school-wide bullying prevention strategies based on positive behavior supports, devising a voluntary monitoring system for parent volunteers during lunch and recess, or offering ongoing education to students regarding the district's anti-bullying policies (Lhamon, 2014). Understanding these legal frameworks and school policies empowers parents to advocate effectively for their children. It also emphasizes the importance of collaborative efforts between parents and school personnel to ensure a safe and supportive school environment for all students.

Many schools provide channels for parents seeking to report acts of bullying, harassment, and intimidation. These may include options such as using the school's website or filling out a bullying report form. A straightforward way to begin is by visiting the school's website and searching for terms like "bully report" in the search box. *PACER's National Bullying Prevention Center* (2019) provides specific recommendations for parents seeking to report an incident to a school. PACER's guidelines include:

1) Keeping documentation, or written history of the child's experience with bullying (i.e., when it happened, where, who was involved, how it made the child feel or impacted the child's ability to learn).
2) Learning about the school's policy on bullying from the website or school handbook.
3) Reporting the bullying to the teacher or an adult at school that the child interacts with and sharing ideas for action plan to stop the bullying.
4) Documenting all conversations with school personnel. For example, who the parent talked to, a summary of the conversation, the school's response, actions taken, and whether a follow-up is needed.
5) Assessing whether the action plan is working. If the child continues to be bullied, a parent may need to contact school administration or district personnel to request an in-person meeting. At the meeting they should be prepared to report what has been done so far, and what they would like to see happen. The parent should bring all documentation to the meeting.

Furthermore, *The Bully Project* (n.d.) provides a sample letter template for parents to write to school personnel which includes sections to describe the circumstances, steps that have been taken, and a request for a meeting to discuss a resolution. PACER points out that parents can begin communication with their children's teachers prior to any incidents of bullying to communicate concerns or collaborate on preventative measures.

During communications between school personnel and parents, knowledge of previous bullying prevention strategies used to support individuals with disabilities can be beneficial. In *Perspectives on Bullying and Difference*, McNamara (2013) provides several examples of specific bullying prevention strategies for individual education programs (IEP). However, IEP meetings typically occur only once a year and follow a mandated agenda of topics to be discussed, so they may not be the best venue for discussing specific bullying concerns. A response to bullying must be timely for there to be follow-up communication; therefore, the following bullying prevention strategies could be considered at general meetings with school personnel (Jordan & Austin, 2012; McNamara, 2013):

1) Monitoring the child during unstructured times (i.e., hallways, bathrooms, playground), and/or allowing the child to leave class early to avoid hallway incidents.
2) Increasing the child's understanding of how their disability may impact social situations.
3) Keeping the child away from the person bullying or children who tend to bully.
4) Keeping the child away from charged competitive situations.
5) Fostering the child's positive social interactions or relationships with peers, teachers, and school staff persons.
6) Setting up regular times, people, or spaces where a child can check in.
7) Helping a child to know the difference between tattling and reporting an incident as well as the difference between playful teasing and hurtful teasing.
8) Developing the child's social skills by setting focused behavioral goals like taking turns and sharing.
9) Helping a child to practice direct (i.e., "Stop that!") or indirect ways (i.e., walking away) ways to respond to, handle, or avoid bullying.
10) Teaching child about computer technology, online safety, and online etiquette.

Schools may also consider involving parents in bullying prevention initiatives, such as parent trainings, workshops, and education. A meta-analytic review of 16 studies found that these parent programs significantly reduced rates of bullying and victimization (Chen et al., 2021). However, future research is needed to explore the effectiveness of parent trainings, workshops, and education on reducing victimization outcomes among children with disabilities, and how they can be better tailored to support parents of children with disabilities.

In summary, effective communication between parents and school personnel is essential for addressing and preventing bullying. Parents should report incidents, document their child's experiences, and engage with school policies and procedures. Schools are required by law in many states to inform parents of bullying incidents and have formal policies in place, which are linked to lower rates of bullying. Proactive strategies and timely responses, along with parental involvement in prevention programs, further support reducing bullying victimization.

Parents' Perceptions of Helpful and Unhelpful School Bullying Responses

Two studies highlight parents' perceptions of helpful and unhelpful school bullying responses (Pimm, 2012; Rapp, 2023). A survey conducted by Pimm (2012) involving 80 parents of children with disabilities found that 68% of parents believed the school's response was unhelpful, noting that schools had downplayed the problem, blamed their child, penalized their child through the "solutions" offered, and did not keep them informed about the bullying. Parents felt supported when school personnel responded to bullying situations by taking direct action to address the person doing the bullying behavior, implementing school-wide programs to prevent bullying behaviors, and educating children about disabilities. Examples of schools taking direct action included teachers or other school staff speaking to the person who bullied about his/her behavior right after it happened, or physically moving the person who had bullied away from the victim. Examples of programming that parents perceived as helpful were peer protection systems such as "Circle of Friends" in which six to eight volunteers create a support network for a child with a disability, and disability education such as inviting an expert on a child's disability into the school to speak to support staff regarding his/her reactions. Pimm (2012) noted that programs perceived as effective by parents were generally aimed at increasing children's empathy towards peers, awareness of school procedures regarding bullying, and understanding about disabilities.

Similarly, in a survey of 65 parents of children with developmental disabilities who had been bullied, 89% of the parents felt that schools could have handled the bullying situations better (Rapp, 2023). A major theme that emerged from parents' suggestions for schools included improved communication about the bullying between parents and school personnel. The communication guidelines in Table 1 can be adapted by school personnel for discussing bullying incident(s) with parents and their children. Communication about bullying can be mutually beneficial to both parents and school personnel. In the study, several parents shared that they were able to reduce their own anger and resentment about the bullying incident(s) by processing it with school personnel (Rapp, 2023). On the other hand, school personnel could benefit from listening to bullying prevention suggestions from parents of children with disabilities, as these parents have a unique understanding of their child's needs. For instance, when asked how the school could have better handled a bullying situation, a parent recommended starting a "lunch bunch" social group to help their child develop social skills and to provide closer supervision during lunch. Taken together, these studies emphasize that parents perceived several school bullying responses as helpful, including prompt action and consequences for persons who bully, school-wide programs, and parent-school communication.

Perpetration of Bullying by Children with Disabilities

A common misconception about children with disabilities is that they are only victims - and not perpetrators - of bullying behaviors; however, studies have also shown that children with certain types of disabilities disproportionately perpetuate bullying. In a national study using data from over 90,000 United State public schools, students with disabilities were about 40% more likely to be disciplined for bullying perpetration when compared to their peers without disabilities (Gage et al., 2021). Specific disabilities which are related to social, emotional, and behavioral difficulties have been found to be at increased risk for involvement in bullying (Lebrun-Harris et al., 2018; Rose & Espelage, 2012; Rose et al., 2015). Students with behavioral disabilities, in particular, have been found to be more likely to receive disciplinary actions for bullying perpetration (Swearer et al., 2012).

One disability which has been studied for its bullying perpetration is Attention-Deficit/Hyperactivity Disorder (ADHD) (Bustinza et al., 2022). In a national survey of 5,932 children and adolescents with ADHD, 16% of the sample endorsed that they bullied others, compared to 6% of the general population (Bustinza et al., 2022). This study also found that risk factors for bullying perpetration included being male, receiving government assistance, being less engaged with school, and having social difficulties, such as friendship problems, difficulties staying calm, and arguing frequently (Bustinza et al., 2022).

Another specific disability which has been found to be associated with increased rates of perpetration of bullying is ASD (Fredrick et al., 2022; Sterzing et al., 2012). It is important to note there have been controversial results when comparing rates of bullying perpetration between students with ASD and their peers. Some studies find similar levels of bullying perpetration between students with ASD and their typically developing peers (Maïano et al., 2016), whereas other studies find less self-reported bullying perpetration behaviors compared to other disability groups (Rose et al., 2015), and some studies report significantly higher rates of perpetration when compared to those with other development disabilities (Sterzing et al., 2012). In a study of 390 students with ASD and without intellectual disability (ID), children with more significant social deficits, externalizing symptoms (particularly hyperactivity, aggression and conduct problems), and depressive symptoms were rated as engaging in greater levels of bullying perpetration (Fredrick et al., 2023). Interestingly, there was not a significant relationship between the severity of ASD symptoms and anxiety with bullying perpetration when controlling for other risk factors (Fredrick et al., 2023).

While the majority of the literature focuses on these specific disorders, there has also been some exploration into considerations for other disability types, as well. For example, one systematic review examined perpetration and victimization among school-aged youth with intellectual disabilities across 11 studies (Maiano et al., 2012). This study indicated that while about 15% of students with ID engaged in bullying perpetration, there were no clear differences when compared to their typically developing peers (Maiano et al., 2012). Swearer and colleagues (2012) examined differences in students with behavioral disabilities (i.e., behavioral disorder and other health impaired), observable disabilities (i.e., speech language impairment, hearing impaired, mild intellectual disability), non-observable disabilities (i.e., specific learning disabilities), and students without disabilities. They found that students with behavioral disabilities engaged in the highest level of bullying perpetration. They also found that students with observable disabilities engaged in higher levels of bullying than their peers without disabilities, whereas peers with non-observable disabilities did not differ from their peers without disabilities.

It is also important to note that bullying perpetration and bullying victimization of students with disabilities should not be viewed in isolation. Oftentimes, individuals who have been bullied will go onto bully others, in a unique bullying role known as bully-victims (Haynie et al., 2001). As students with disabilities are at increased rate of bullying victimization, as discussed previously in this chapter, it is important to consider whether this may play a part in why a student with a disability is engaging in bullying perpetration, and whether the student has become frustrated with their experience of victimization and engage in bullying perpetration to cope with these experiences (Rose, 2010; Swearer et al., 2012). One study found that about 30 to 50 percent of students with disabilities were bully victims, with more than half of students with a behavioral disability acting in this role (Swearer et al., 2012). Within this context, it may be most effective to address both concerns with bullying victimization and bullying perpetration concurrently.

When addressing bullying perpetration by students with disabilities, schools and parents can use specific strategies that have been proven to be effective at addressing this concern in students without disabilities. Some of these strategies may include:

1. Behavioral Intervention Plans (BIPs) or informal behavioral intervention strategies which discourage bullying behaviors and encourage prosocial interactions with their peers, such as daily report cards, check-in/check-out, and progress monitoring of the effectiveness of these interventions (Swearner & Givens, 2006).
2. Explicit skill instruction to promote empathy, perspective taking, and coping strategies, specifically for managing anger, such as Coping Power Program (Gansle, 2005; Lochman & Wells, 2002).
3. Psychoeducation regarding the impact of bullying (Nickerson et al., 2017).
4. Restorative justice approaches as appropriate to repair relationships and harm caused as a result of bullying incidents (Lodi et al., 2022).

Considerations: Type of Disability

The type of disability a child has can influence the nature of bullying they may experience, as well as the involvement of parents in a school's prevention or intervention strategy. In this section, disability types were categorized as developmental disabilities (i.e., ASD, Down syndrome, etc.), physical disabilities (i.e., visual impairment, hearing impairment, orthopedic impairment, etc.), and emotional disturbance (i.e., obsessive-compulsive disorder, conduct disorder, schizoaffective disorder, etc.) in order to address the nuances in bullying prevention strategies.

Developmental Disabilities

Among children with developmental disabilities, social skills development is critical to bullying prevention. For example, parents who perceived their children with disabilities as more gullible, or easily tricked or manipulated, reported higher rates of peer victimization (Werth, 2017). Additionally, when specifically looking at children with ASD, social skill deficits have been found to predict bullying perpetration, as they may not understand the social nuances of what is considered to be typical peer interactions and what would be considered bullying (Fredrick et al., 2023). School personnel can support a child's social skills development through IEP objectives, SEL programming, behavioral modeling, and by encouraging parents to help their child practice social skills outside of school.

Several studies have evidenced the positive effects of the *Program for the Education and Enrichment of Relational Skill* (PEERS) parent-assisted social skills program, on the social skills of children and adolescents with ASD (Laugeson et al., 2009; Mendelberg et al., 2014; Tripathi et al., 2022). The PEERS program includes psychologist-led concurrent sessions for parents and their children that instruct them on key elements about making and keeping friends, including conversational skills, peer entry and exit skills, developing friendship networks, handling teasing, bullying, and arguments with peers, practicing good sportsmanship and good host behavior during get-togethers with friends, and changing bad reputations (Laugeson et al., 2009). During a PEERS program among preschool children with ASD and their parents, parents received psychoeducation on prosocial and challenging behaviors, socialization practices, and friendship development, in order to become effective social coaches (Tripathi et al., 2022).

Physical Disabilities

In a national longitudinal study, high school children with orthopedic impairments were at a significantly greater risk of repeated victimization than were children with other types of disabilities (Blake et al., 2012). A possible explanation for this finding may be that children look physically different or use equipment like wheelchairs (Lightfoot et al., 1999). Additionally, children with orthopedic impairments may be in contact with more children during their typical school day. According to the U.S. National Center for Education Statistics (2023), children ages 6 to 21 with orthopedic impairments, speech impairments and visual impairments spend 70 to 88% of their school day in general education classes, while children with intellectual disabilities and deaf blindness spend only 20 to 30% of their school day in general education classes.

Thus, school personnel should consider implementing educational trainings for children to learn more about disabilities, particularly those that affect their classmates. For example, the *Kids on the Block* educational puppetry troupe features life-size puppets with disabilities who perform skits and answer questions about any requested disability. *Kids on the Block* has been shown to promote elementary school children's positive attitudes towards individuals with disabilities and increase children's accurate knowledge about individuals with disabilities (Dunst, 2014). Furthermore, a meta-analytic review involving 20 interventions studies to promote disability awareness and positive attitudes towards disability (Chae et al., 2019) found that interventions that involved direct interactions with individuals with disabilities, followed by programs that used materials such as media, activities and books and role-playing activities, had the strongest effects on improving children's attitudes across all school levels. These effects were impacted by the length of the intervention, specifically, the number of sessions in the program increased the likeliness of its effectiveness. Furthermore, parents can play a role in informally educating other parents and children about a disability, creating opportunities for their child to socialize with peers without disabilities, and encouraging their child to participate socially and academically (Baker & Donelly, 2010).

Children with disabilities who are unable to fully participate in school activities are significantly more likely to report bullying victimization than children with disabilities who can fully participate (Sentenac et al., 2011). In a systematic review that examined studies on bullying in physical education classes (Ball et al., 2022), 86% of children with visual impairments or blindness from the combined 14 studies reported experiencing relational bullying, or repeated exclusion and social isolation, by peers and P.E. teachers. Ball et al. (2022) contend that there needs to be balance between keeping children with visual impairments safe and allowing them to participate in physical education activities that have a reasonable risk because excluding them leads to decreased independence, competence, poorer fundamental motor skills, and can indirectly lead to obesity. Additionally, organized sports can foster interactions, friendships, social acceptance, and identity formation for people with disabilities (Klenk et al., 2019). Guidelines for universal design in physical education or adapting specific sports or activities to make them accessible for all children, can be found in *Strategies for Inclusion: Physical Education for Everyone* by Lieberman and Houston-Wilson (2018). Adaptions might include equipment (e.g., using longer rackets and/or softer balls), rules (e.g., slowing the pace of the game, allowing more chances, not using a defender, including everyone before a team can score), environment (e.g., decreasing distractions, limiting noise, changing lighting), and instruction (e.g., task-analyzing skill instruction). Similarly, parents can encourage their children, especially older children, to self-advocate for the assistance or accommodations that they may need to participate (e.g., asking to be moved to a better position to be able to see the activity being demonstrated).

Emotional Disturbance

Children with emotional disturbance (ED) report the highest rates of bullying victimization when compared to children with all other types of disabilities (Blake et al., 2012). Emotional disturbance is characterized by an inability to learn that cannot be explained by intellectual or health factors, inappropriate behaviors, and an inability to form or maintain interpersonal relationships (IDEA, 2017). In interviews among teachers who worked with parents of children with ED, one teacher noted that parents of children with ED mostly receive calls from schools regarding children's negative behaviors (Buchanan & Clark, 2017). Suggestions for improving communication with parents of children with ED include establishing regular parent-school check-ins that are not contingent on a child's behaviors, proactively talking about how parents want to be communicated with about behavior problems, utilizing parent-teacher conferences more effectively to build trust between teachers and parents, and helping parents feel more comfortable at IEP meetings (Buchanan & Clark, 2017).

The *Students with Involved Families and Teachers* (SWIFT) program demonstrates effective collaboration between parents of children with ED and school personnel. SWIFT, an intensive four-component intervention, was implemented for three to five months to support nine children with ED as they transitioned from day-treatment school to public school (Buchanan et al., 2015). During the SWIFT intervention, parents were set up to receive weekly trainings from "parent-coaches" to help them develop strategies at home for setting up consistent rules, expectations, and systems of reinforcement. Second, children received weekly sessions from "skills coaches" to develop prosocial skills and reinforce the use of positive adaptive skills and peer relations. Changes in children's home and school behaviors (i.e., arguing, destructiveness, flexible, on-task etc.) were monitored by teachers and parents through daily assessments. Lastly, a case manager and the two coaches analyzed daily assessment data and developed individualized interventions for the child. Thus, coordination of communication between the school and the parent was a team effort. This study highlights the benefits of intensive supports for children with ED when going through difficult circumstances, such as a school transition. A similar team response might be adopted for children with ED who are perpetrating or experiencing bullying behaviors.

CONCLUSION

This chapter contributes to the growing body of knowledge on bullying prevention and intervention efforts, with a focus on the critical role of parent-child and parent-school communication in supporting children with disabilities. It begins with a review of school-based interventions aimed at preventing bullying victimization among students with disabilities. Next, the chapter outlines communication guidelines regarding how school personnel, parents, and children can talk about bullying to promote an atmosphere of emotional validation and effective problem-solving. Lastly, it challenges readers to consider how parent-school collaboration in bullying prevention can vary based on child's specific disability type and the type of bullying occurring. For example, children with developmental disabilities or emotional disturbances might benefit more from social skills trainings, while children with physical impairments report higher rates of exclusionary bullying in physical education classes.

The chapter also identifies gaps in the literature. Although parents of children with disabilities perceive several school-based bullying prevention strategies as beneficial —such as disability education, inclusive programming, and clear anti-bullying procedures—more research is needed to confirm these perceptions. Additionally, existing communication guidelines for discussing bullying behaviors are not tailored to children with disabilities. Further research is needed to develop communication guidelines specific to children with disabilities, their teachers, and their families.

REFERENCES

Acar, S., Chen, C. I., & Xie, H. (2021). Parental involvement in developmental disabilities across three cultures: A systematic review. *Research in Developmental Disabilities*, 110, 103861. DOI: 10.1016/j.ridd.2021.103861 PMID: 33482560

Assistant Secretary for Public Affairs (ASPA). (2021, Novemeber 10). *Warning Signs for Bullying*. StopBullying.gov. https://www.stopbullying.gov/bullying/warning-signs

Assistant Secretary for Public Affairs (ASPA). (2022, May 27). *Kid Videos*. StopBullying.gov. https://www.stopbullying.gov/kids/kid-videos

Baker, K., & Donelly, M. (2010). The social experiences of children with disability and the influence of environment: A framework for intervention. *Disability & Society*, 16(1), 71–85. DOI: 10.1080/713662029

Ball, L., Lieberman, L., Haibach-Beach, P., Perreault, M., & Tirone, K. (2022). Bullying in physical education of children and youth with visual impairments: A systematic review. *British Journal of Visual Impairment*, 40(3), 513–529. DOI: 10.1177/02646196211009927

Bellini, S., & Akullian, J. (2007). A meta-analysis of video modeling and video self-modeling interventions for children and adolescents with autism spectrum disorders. *Exceptional Children*, 73(3), 264–287. DOI: 10.1177/001440290707300301

Black, S., Weinles, D., & Washington, E. (2010). Victim strategies to stop bullying. *Youth Violence and Juvenile Justice*, 8(2), 138–147. DOI: 10.1177/1541204009349401

Blake, J. J., Lund, E. M., Zhou, Q., Kwok, O. M., & Benz, M. R. (2012). National prevalence rates of bully victimization among students with disabilities in the United States. *School Psychology Quarterly*, 27(4), 210–222. DOI: 10.1037/spq0000008 PMID: 23294235

Bouldin, E., Patel, S. R., Tey, C. S., White, M., Alfonso, K. P., & Govil, N. (2021). Bullying and children who are deaf or hard-of-hearing: A Scoping Review. *The Laryngoscope*, 131(8), 1884–1892. DOI: 10.1002/lary.29388 PMID: 33438758

Bradley, R. (2016). 'Why single me out?' Peer mentoring, autism and inclusion in mainstream secondary schools. *British Journal of Special Education*, 43(3), 272–288. DOI: 10.1111/1467-8578.12136

Buchanan, R., & Clark, M. (2017). Understanding parent–school communication for students with emotional and behavioral disorders. *The Open Family Studies Journal, 9* (Suppl 1 M5), 122. https://doi.org/DOI: 0.2174/1874922401709010122

Buchanan, R., Nese, R. N., Palinkas, L. A., & Ruppert, T. (2015). Refining an intervention for students with emotional disturbance using qualitative parent and teacher data. *Children and Youth Services Review*, 58, 41–49. DOI: 10.1016/j.childyouth.2015.08.014 PMID: 28966422

Buttimer, J., & Tierney, E. (2005). Patterns of leisure participation among adolescents with a mild intellectual disability. *Journal of Intellectual Disabilities*, 9(1), 25–42. DOI: 10.1177/1744629505049728 PMID: 15757870

Carter, E. W., Lane, K. L., Cooney, M., Weir, K., Moss, C. K., & Machalicek, W. (2013). Self-determination among transition-age youth with autism or intellectual disability: Parent perspectives. *Research and Practice for Persons with Severe Disabilities: the Journal of TASH*, 38(3), 129–138. DOI: 10.1177/154079691303800301

Cerf, C., Gantwerk, B., Martz, S., Hespe, D., & Vermeire, G. (2012, September). *Guidance for parents on the anti-bullying bill of rights act*. https://www.nj.gov/education/safety/sandp/hib/docs/ParentGuide.pdf

Chae, S., Park, E. Y., & Shin, M. (2019). School-based interventions for improving disability awareness and attitudes towards disability of students without disabilities: A meta-analysis. *International Journal of Disability Development and Education*, 66(4), 343–361. DOI: 10.1080/1034912X.2018.1439572

Chen, Q., Zhu, Y., & Chui, W. H. (2021). A meta-analysis on effects of parenting programs on bullying prevention. *Trauma, Violence & Abuse*, 22(5), 1209–1220. DOI: 10.1177/1524838020915619 PMID: 32242506

Chu, S. Y. (2018). Family voices: Promoting foundation skills of self-determination for young children with disabilities in Taiwan. *Asia Pacific Education Review*, 19(1), 91–101. DOI: 10.1007/s12564-018-9519-8

Conners-Burrow, N. A., Johnson, D. L., Whiteside-Mansell, L., McKelvey, L., & Gargus, R. A. (2009). Adults matter: Protecting children from the negative impacts of bullying. *Psychology in the Schools*, 46(7), 593–604. DOI: 10.1002/pits.20400

Cooper, L., & Nickerson, A. (2013). Parent retrospective recollections of bullying and current views, concerns, and strategies to cope with children's bullying. *Journal of Child and Family Studies*, 22(4), 526–540. DOI: 10.1007/s10826-012-9606-0

Crowe, T. K., VanLeit, B., & Berghmans, K. K. (2000). Mothers' perceptions of child care assistance: The impact of a child's disability. *The American Journal of Occupational Therapy*, 54(1), 52–58. DOI: 10.5014/ajot.54.1.52 PMID: 10686627

Davis, S., & Nixon, C. (2010). *The youth voice project: Preliminary results from the youth voice project: victimization and strategies*. Research Press Publishers.

Demaray, M. K., Malecki, C. K., Secord, S. M., & Lyell, K. M. (2013). Agreement among students', teachers', and parents' perceptions of victimization by bullying. *Children and Youth Services Review*, 35(12), 2091–2100. DOI: 10.1016/j.childyouth.2013.10.018

Dunst, C. J. (2014). Meta-analysis of the effects of puppet shows on attitudes toward and knowledge of individuals with disabilities. *Exceptional Children*, 80(2), 136–148. DOI: 10.1177/001440291408000201

Durlak, J. A., Weissberg, R. P., Dymnicki, A. B., Taylor, R. D., & Schellinger, K. B. (2011). The impact of enhancing students' social and emotional learning: A meta-analysis of school-based universal interventions. *Child Development*, 82(1), 405–432. DOI: 10.1111/j.1467-8624.2010.01564.x PMID: 21291449

Espelage, D. L., Forber-Pratt, A., Rose, C. A., Graves, K. A., Hanebutt, R. A., Sheikh, A. E., Woolswaever, A., Milarsky, T. K., Ingram, M. K., Robinson, L., Gomez, A. M., Chalfant, P. K., Salama, C., & Poekert, P. (2024). Development of online professional development for teachers: Understanding, recognizing and responding to bullying for students with disabilities. *Education and Urban Society*, 56(5), 601–623. DOI: 10.1177/00131245231187370

Espelage, D. L., Rose, C. A., & Polanin, J. R. (2015). Social-emotional learning program to reduce bullying, fighting, and victimization among middle school students with disabilities. *Remedial and Special Education*, 36(5), 299–311. DOI: 10.1177/0741932514564564

Fredrick, S. S., Nickerson, A. B., Sun, L., Rodgers, J. D., Thomeer, M. L., Lopata, C., & Todd, F. (2023). ASD symptoms, social skills, and comorbidity: Predictors of bullying perpetration. *Journal of Autism and Developmental Disorders*, 53(8), 3092–3102. DOI: 10.1007/s10803-022-05612-0 PMID: 35678945

Freeman, J. A., & Kirksey, J. (2023). Linking IEP status to parental involvement for high school students of first-generation and native-born families. *Exceptional Children*, 89(2), 197–215. DOI: 10.1177/00144029221108402

Gage, N. A., Katsiyannis, A., Rose, C., & Adams, S. E. (2021). Disproportionate bullying victimization and perpetration by disability status, race, and gender: A national analysis. *Advances in Neurodevelopmental Disorders*, 5(3), 256–268. DOI: 10.1007/s41252-021-00200-2

Gansle, K. A. (2005). The effectiveness of school-based anger interventions and programs: A meta-analysis. *Journal of School Psychology*, 43(4), 321–341. DOI: 10.1016/j.jsp.2005.07.002

Gladden, M. R., Vivolo-Kantor, A. M., Hamburger, M. E., & Lumpkin, C. D. (2014). *Bullying surveillance among youths: uniform definitions for public health and recommended data elements, Version 1.0*. National Center for Injury Prevention and Control, (U.S.). Division of Violence Prevention. https://stacks.cdc.gov/view/cdc/21596

Goudie, A., Narcisse, M. R., Hall, D. E., & Kuo, D. Z. (2014). Financial and psychological stressors associated with caring for children with disability. *Families, Systems & Health*, 32(3), 280–290. DOI: 10.1037/fsh0000027 PMID: 24707826

Graybill, E. C., Vinoski, E., Black, M., Varjas, K., Henrich, C., & Meyers, J. (2016, March). Examining the Outcomes of Including Students With Disabilities in a Bullying/Victimization Intervention. *School Psychology Forum*, 10(1), •••.

Greeff, A. P., & Van den Berg, E. (2013). Resilience in families in which a child is bullied. *British Journal of Guidance & Counselling*, 41(5), 504–517. DOI: 10.1080/03069885.2012.757692

Hartley, M. T., Bauman, S., Nixon, C. L., & Davis, S. (2017). Responding to bullying victimization: Comparative analysis of victimized students in general and special education. *Journal of Disability Policy Studies*, 28(2), 77–89. DOI: 10.1177/1044207317710700

Hayes, S. A., & Watson, S. L. (2013). The impact of parenting stress: A meta-analysis of studies comparing the experience of parenting stress in parents of children with and without autism spectrum disorder. *Journal of Autism and Developmental Disorders*, 43(3), 629–642. DOI: 10.1007/s10803-012-1604-y PMID: 22790429

Haynie, D. L., Nansel, T., Eitel, P., Crump, A. D., Saylor, K., Yu, K., & Simons-Morton, B. (2001). Bullies, victims, and bully/victims: Distinct groups of at-risk youth. *The Journal of Early Adolescence*, 21(1), 29–49. DOI: 10.1177/0272431601021001002

Humphrey, N., Lendrum, A., Barlow, A., Wigelsworth, M., & Squires, G. (2013). Achievement for All: Improving psychosocial outcomes for students with special educational needs and disabilities. *Research in Developmental Disabilities*, 34(4), 1210–1225. DOI: 10.1016/j.ridd.2012.12.008 PMID: 23380579

Individuals with disabilities education act (IDEA; 2017). Sec. 300.8 (c) (4). https://sites.ed.gov/idea/regs/b/a/300.8/c/4

Iyanda, A. E. (2021). Bullying Victimization of Children with Mental, Emotional, and Developmental or Behavioral (MEDB) Disorders in the United States. *Journal of Child & Adolescent Trauma*, 15(2), 221–233. DOI: 10.1007/s40653-021-00368-8 PMID: 35600527

Jordan, K., & Austin, J. (2012). A review of the literature on bullying in US schools and how a parent–educator partnership can be an effective way to handle bullying. *Journal of Aggression, Maltreatment & Trauma*, 21(4), 440–458. DOI: 10.1080/10926771.2012.675420

Kirksey, J. J., Gottfried, M. A., & Freeman, J. A. (2022). Does parental involvement change after schools assign students an IEP? *Peabody Journal of Education*, 97(1), 18–31. DOI: 10.1080/0161956X.2022.2026717

Klenk, C., Albrecht, J., & Nagel, S. (2019). Social participation of people with disabilities in organized community sport: A systematic review. *German Journal of Exercise and Sport Research*, 49(4), 365–380. DOI: 10.1007/s12662-019-00584-3

Laugeson, E. A., Frankel, F., Mogil, C., & Dillon, A. R. (2009). Parent-assisted social skills training to improve friendships in teens with autism spectrum disorders. *Journal of Autism and Developmental Disorders*, 39(4), 596–606. DOI: 10.1007/s10803-008-0664-5 PMID: 19015968

Lebrun-Harris, L. A., Sherman, L. J., Limber, S. P., Miller, B. D., & Edgerton, E. A. (2018). Bullying victimization and perpetration among U.S. children and adolescents: 2016 national survey of children's health. *Journal of Child and Family Studies*, 28(9), 2543–2557. DOI: 10.1007/s10826-018-1170-9

Lhamon, C. E. (2014, October 21). Dear colleague letter: Responding to bullying of students with disabilities from the assistant secretary for civil rights. https://www2.ed.gov/about/offices/list/ocr/letters/colleague-bullying-201410.pdf

Lieberman, L. J., & Houston-Wilson, C. (2018). *Strategies for inclusion: physical education for everyone* (3rd ed.). Human Kinetics.

Lightfoot, J., Wright, S., & Sloper, P. (1999). Supporting pupils in mainstream school with an illness or disability: Young people's views. *Child: Care, Health and Development*, 25(4), 267–284. DOI: 10.1046/j.1365-2214.1999.00112.x PMID: 10399032

Limber, S. P., Kowalkski, R. M., Agatston, P. W., & Huynh, H. V. (2016). Bullying and children with disabilities. In Saracho, O. (Ed.), *Contemporary Perspectives on Research on Bullying and Victimization in Early Childhood Education* (pp. 129–155). Information Age Publishing.

Lindstrom Johnson, S., Waasdorp, T. E., Gaias, L. M., & Bradshaw, C. P. (2019). Parental responses to bullying: Understanding the role of school policies and practices. *Journal of Educational Psychology*, 111(3), 475–487. DOI: 10.1037/edu0000295

Lochman, J. E., & Wells, K. C. (2002). The Coping Power program at the middle-school transition: Universal and indicated prevention effects. *Psychology of Addictive Behaviors*, 16(4, Suppl, 4S), S40–S54. DOI: 10.1037/0893-164X.16.4S.S40 PMID: 12502276

Lovegrove, P. J., Bellmore, A. D., Green, J. G., Jens, K., & Ostrov, J. M. (2013). "My voice is not going to be silent": What can parents do about children's bullying? *Journal of School Violence*, 12(3), 253–267. DOI: 10.1080/15388220.2013.792270

Lydecker, J. A., Winschel, J., Gilbert, K., & Cotter, E. W. (2023). School absenteeism and impairment associated with weight bullying. *Journal of Adolescence*, 95(7), 1478–1487. DOI: 10.1002/jad.12220 PMID: 37487590

Mahady Wilton, M. M., Craig, W. M., & Pepler, D. J. (2000). Emotional regulation and display in classroom victims of bullying: Characteristic expressions of affect, coping styles and relevant contextual factors. *Social Development*, 9(2), 226–245. DOI: 10.1111/1467-9507.00121

Maiano, C., Normand, C. L., Salvas, M. C., Moullec, G., & Aime, A. (2016). Prevalence of school bullying among youth with autism spectrum disorders: A systematic review and meta-analysis. *Autism Research*, 9(6), 601–615. DOI: 10.1002/aur.1568 PMID: 26451871

Mandelberg, J., Laugeson, E. A., Cunningham, T. D., Ellingsen, R., Bates, S., & Frankel, F. (2014). Long-term treatment outcomes for parent-assisted social skills training for adolescents with autism spectrum disorders: The UCLA PEERS program. *Journal of Mental Health Research in Intellectual Disabilities*, 7(1), 45–73. DOI: 10.1080/19315864.2012.730600

McNamara, B. E. (2013). *Bullying and students with disabilities: strategies and techniques to create a safe learning environment for all*. Corwin.

National Center for Education Statistics. (2019, July). *Student reports of bullying results from the 2017 school crime supplement to the national crime victimization survey*. https://nces.ed.gov/pubs2019/2019054.pdf

National Center for Education Statistics. (2023). *Students with Disabilities*. Condition of Education. U.S. Department of Education, Institute of Education Sciences. https://nces.ed.gov/programs/coe/indicator/cgg

Nickerson, A. B., Guttman, D., & Cook, E. (2017). Prevention and early intervention efforts for targets of bullying and youth who bully. In Bradshaw, C. P. (Ed.), *Handbook on bullying prevention: A life course perspective*. NASW Press.

Nikopoulous, C. K., & Keenan, M. (2004). Effects of video modeling on social initiations by children with autism. *Journal of Applied Behavior Analysis*, 37(1), 93–96. DOI: 10.1901/jaba.2004.37-93 PMID: 15154221

Nixon, C. L., Jairam, D., Davis, S., Linkie, C. A., Chatters, S., & Hodge, J. J. (2020). Effects of students' grade level, gender, and form of bullying victimization on coping strategy effectiveness. *International Journal of Bullying Prevention : an Official Publication of the International Bullying Prevention Association*, 2(3), 190–204. DOI: 10.1007/s42380-019-00027-5

Ordonez, M. A. (2006). *Prevalence of bullying among elementary school children as a function of the comprehensiveness of anti-bullying policies and programs in the school* [Doctoral dissertation, Ball State University].

PACER's National Bullying Prevention Center. (2019). *Working with the school- What parents should know about bullying*. https://www.pacer.org/bullying/parents/working-with-school.asp

Peterson, A. M. (2020). *Teaching young adults with intellectual and developmental disabilities how to recognize and respond to coworker victimization scenarios.* [Master's Thesis, Michigan State University].

Pimm, C. (2012). The perspectives of parents, carers. and families. In C., McLaughlin, Colleen., R. Byers, & C. Oliver (Ed.), *Perspectives on bullying and difference supporting young people with special educational needs and/or disabilities in school* (1st ed., pp. 54-65). National Children's Bureau.

Pinquart, M. (2018). Parenting stress in caregivers of children with chronic physical condition—A meta-analysis. *Stress and Health*, 34(2), 197–207. DOI: 10.1002/smi.2780 PMID: 28834111

Plant, K. M., & Sanders, M. R. (2007). Predictors of care-giver stress in families of preschool-aged children with developmental disabilities. *Journal of Intellectual Disability Research*, 51(2), 109–124. DOI: 10.1111/j.1365-2788.2006.00829.x PMID: 17217475

Rapp, H. (2023). *An Exploratory Mixed Methods Study Considering Parents of Adolescents with Developmental Disabilities as Secondary Victims of Bullying Abuse.* [Doctoral Dissertation, The University of Wisconsin-Madison].

Rex, C. (2014). An Anti-Bullying Intervention for Children with Autism Spectrum Disorder. https://scholarship.claremont.edu/cmc_theses/803

Robinson, L. E., Clements, G., Drescher, A., El Sheikh, A., Milarsky, T. K., Hanebutt, R., Graves, K., Delgado, A. V., Espelage, D. L., & Rose, C. A. (2023). Developing a multi-tiered system of support-based plan for bullying prevention among students with disabilities: Perspectives from general and special education teachers during professional development. *School Mental Health*, 15(3), 826–838. DOI: 10.1007/s12310-023-09589-8 PMID: 37359153

Rose, C. A. (2010). Bullying among students with disabilities: Impact and implications. In *Bullying in North American schools* (pp. 54–64). Routledge.

Rose, C. A., & Espelage, D. L. (2012). Risk and protective factors associated with the bullying involvement of students with emotional and behavioral disorders. *Behavioral Disorders*, 37(3), 133–148. DOI: 10.1177/019874291203700302

Rose, C. A., Monda-Amaya, L. E., & Espelage, D. L. (2011). Bullying perpetration and victimization in special education: A review of the literature. *Remedial and Special Education*, 32(2), 114–130. DOI: 10.1177/0741932510361247

Rose, C. A., Simpson, C. G., & Moss, A. (2015). The bullying dynamic: Prevalence of involvement among a large-scale sample of middle and high school youth with and without disabilities. *Psychology in the Schools*, 52(5), 515–531. DOI: 10.1002/pits.21840

Rowbotham, M., Carroll, A., & Cuskelly, M. (2011). Mothers' and fathers' roles in caring for an adult child with an intellectual disability. *International Journal of Disability Development and Education*, 58(3), 223–240. DOI: 10.1080/1034912X.2011.598396

Sancho, K., Sidener, T. M., Reeve, S. A., & Sidener, D. W. (2010). Two variations of video modeling interventions for teaching play skills to children with autism. *Education & Treatment of Children*, 33(3), 421–442. DOI: 10.1353/etc.0.0097

Saylor, C. F., & Leach, J. B. (2009). Perceived bullying and social support in students accessing special inclusion programming. *Journal of Developmental and Physical Disabilities*, 21(1), 69–80. DOI: 10.1007/s10882-008-9126-4

Segura, B. P. (2012). *The superheroes social skills program: a study examining an evidence-based program for elementary-aged students with autism spectrum disorders who are frequently bullied.* [Doctoral dissertation. University of Utah].

Sentenac, M., Gavin, A., Arnaud, C., Molcho, M., Godeau, E., & Gabhainn, S. N. (2011). Victims of bullying among students with a disability or chronic illness and their peers: A cross-national study between Ireland and France. *The Journal of Adolescent Health*, 48(5), 461–466. DOI: 10.1016/j.jadohealth.2010.07.031 PMID: 21501804

Sentenac, M., Gavin, A., Gabhainn, S. N., Molcho, M., Due, P., Ravens-Sieberer, U., Gaspar de Matos, M., Malkowska-Szkutnik, A., Gobina, I., Vollebergh, W., Arnaud, C., Emmanuelle, G., & Godeau, E. (2013). Peer victimization and subjective health among students reporting disability or chronic illness in 11 Western countries. *European Journal of Public Health*, 23(3), 421–426. DOI: 10.1093/eurpub/cks073 PMID: 22930742

Smith, T. B., Oliver, M. N., & Innocenti, M. S. (2001). Parenting stress in families of children with disabilities. *The American Journal of Orthopsychiatry*, 71(2), 257–261. DOI: 10.1037/0002-9432.71.2.257 PMID: 11347367

Stannis, R. L., Crosland, K. A., Miltenberger, R., & Valbuena, D. (2019). Response to bullying (RTB): Behavioral skills and in situ training for individuals diagnosed with intellectual disabilities. *Journal of Applied Behavior Analysis*, 52(1), 73–83. DOI: 10.1002/jaba.501 PMID: 30168600

Sterzing, P. R., Shattuck, P. T., Narendorf, S. C., Wagner, M., & Cooper, B. P. (2012). Bullying involvement and autism spectrum disorders: Prevalence and correlates of bullying involvement among adolescents with an autism spectrum disorder. *Archives of Pediatrics & Adolescent Medicine*, 166(11), 1058–1064. DOI: 10.1001/archpediatrics.2012.790 PMID: 22945284

Stives, K. L., May, D. C., Mack, M., & Bethel, C. L. (2021, May). Understanding responses to bullying from the parent perspective. In Frontiers in Education (Vol. 6). Frontiers Media SA. https://doi.org/DOI: 10.3389/feduc.2021.642367

Stuart-Cassel, V., Bell, A., & Springer, J. F. (2011). *Analysis of state bullying laws and policies*. U.S. Department of Education, Office of Planning, Evaluation and Policy Development, Policy and Program Studies Service., https://www2.ed.gov/rschstat/eval/bullying/state-bullying-laws/state-bullying-laws.pdf

Sullivan, T. N., Sutherland, K. S., Farrell, A. D., & Taylor, K. A. (2015). An evaluation of Second Step: What are the benefits for youth with and without disabilities? *Remedial and Special Education*, 36(5), 286–298. DOI: 10.1177/0741932515575616

Swearer, S. M., & Givens, J. E. (2006). Designing an alternative to suspension for middle school bullies. Paper presented at the annual convention of the National Association of School Psychologists, Anaheim, CA.

Swearer, S. M., Wang, C., Maag, J. W., Siebecker, A. B., & Frerichs, L. J. (2012). Understanding the bullying dynamic among students in special and general education. *Journal of School Psychology*, 50(4), 503–520. DOI: 10.1016/j.jsp.2012.04.001 PMID: 22710018

The Bully Project. (n.d.). *Tools for Parents*. https://www.thebullyproject.com/parents

Tripathi, I., Estabillo, J. A., Moody, C. T., & Laugeson, E. A. (2022). Long-term treatment outcomes of PEERS® for preschoolers: A parent-mediated social skills training program for children with autism spectrum disorder. *Journal of Autism and Developmental Disorders*, 52(6), 1–17. DOI: 10.1007/s10803-021-05147-w PMID: 34302574

Unnever, J. D., & Cornell, D. G. (2004). Middle school victims of bullying: Who reports being bullied? *Aggressive Behavior*, 30(5), 373–388. DOI: 10.1002/ab.20030

Vessey, J. A., & O'Neill, K. M. (2011). Helping students with disabilities better address teasing and bullying situations: A MASNRN study. *The Journal of School Nursing: the Official Publication of the National Association of School Nurses*, 27(2), 139–148. DOI: 10.1177/1059840510386490 PMID: 20956579

Vilaseca, R., Rivero, M., Leiva, D., & Ferrer, F. (2023). Mothers' and fathers' parenting and other family context variables linked to developmental outcomes in young children with intellectual disability: A two-wave longitudinal study. *Journal of Developmental and Physical Disabilities*, 35(3), 387–416. DOI: 10.1007/s10882-022-09856-7

Walton, K. M., & Tiede, G. (2020). Brief report: Does "healthy" family functioning look different for families who have a child with autism? *Research in Autism Spectrum Disorders*, 72, 101527. Advance online publication. DOI: 10.1016/j.rasd.2020.101527 PMID: 32123539

Ward, M. J. (2005). An historical perspective of self-determination in special education: Accomplishments and challenges. *Research and Practice for Persons with Severe Disabilities : the Journal of TASH*, 30(3), 108–112. DOI: 10.2511/rpsd.30.3.108

Werth, J. M. (2017). *Parent Perceptions of Social Vulnerability of Students with Disabilities: Experience of and Coping with Victimization*. [Doctoral Dissertation, State University of New York at Buffalo].

Woods, S., & Wolke, D. (2003). Does the content of anti-bullying policies inform us about the prevalence of direct and relational bullying behaviour in primary schools? *Educational Psychology*, 23(4), 381–401. DOI: 10.1080/01443410303215

Yeung, R., & Leadbeater, B. (2010). Adults make a difference: The protective effects of parent and teacher emotional support on emotional and behavioral problems of peer-victimized adolescents. *Journal of Community Psychology*, 38(1), 80–98. DOI: 10.1002/jcop.20353

Zhang, H., & Chen, C. (2023). "They just want us to exist as a trash can": Parents of children with autism spectrum disorder and their perspectives to school-based bullying victimization. *Contemporary School Psychology*, 27(1), 8–18.

ENDNOTE

[1] An Individualized Education Program (IEP) is a detailed document developed for each public school child in special education. IEPs are mandated by the Individuals with Disabilities Education Act (IDEA). A 504 Plan, mandated by Section 504 of the Rehabilitation Act of 1973, provides accommodations and modifications to help students with disabilities access the general education curriculum and participate fully in school activities.

Chapter 6
Fostering Inclusion and Safety:
A Case Study of Anti-Bullying Practices at the Praxis Inclusive School

Mahwish Kamran
https://orcid.org/0000-0002-0572-1603
Iqra University, Pakistan

Sohni Siddiqui
https://orcid.org/0000-0002-4001-5181
Technische Universität Berlin, Germany

ABSTRACT

While inclusive education is a cornerstone of contemporary civil rights movements, concerns persist among educators regarding the widespread placement of students with learning disabilities (LD) in mainstream classrooms. One of the most compelling reasons for this apprehension is the potential for increased bullying incidents in inclusive settings. This chapter delves into the experiences of bullying faced by children with LD in inclusive environments and explores strategies for fostering safe and secure classrooms. It further examines pedagogical practices that can equip teachers to effectively manage the learning needs of both students with LD and their typically developing peers. The chapter's primary objective is to present the findings from a case study conducted within an inclusive school in Pakistan. It analyzes how the pedagogical practices adopted by this specific school can be leveraged to promote the inclusion of children with LD by mitigating bullying and fostering greater educational equity.

DOI: 10.4018/979-8-3693-5315-8.ch006

INTRODUCTION

A child-centered approach within inclusive education fosters the identification of children's potential for positive societal contributions. This is achieved by exposing them to inclusive settings that offer differentiated learning experiences tailored to develop their potential, self-confidence, and a sense of belonging within the school community and broader society (Cerna, 2021; Murray, 1999; Reicher, 2010).

Moreover, inclusion operates as a proactive strategy to prevent the exclusion of students with disabilities from general education settings. By anticipating and addressing barriers, inclusion aims to facilitate their full participation (Shaukat, 2023). The significance of inclusion is categorically emphasized at the international level, particularly with regard to children with special educational needs (SEN). The literature also underscores the benefits of inclusion for all children, irrespective of gender, race, personality traits, or socioeconomic background (GoP, 2009; Kazimi & Kazmi, 2018; National Education Policy, 2017).

Moreover, inclusion is not solely advantageous for children with SEN, hence their mainstreaming is advocated for in policy documents (GoP, 2009; National Education Policy, 2017). However, despite a decade of promotion in both developed and developing nations, inclusive schools continue to face challenges such as inaccessible infrastructure, limited resources, a lack of qualified teachers, inadequate individualized instruction, and, most notably, bullying of children with disabilities (Kamran & Bano, 2023; Leijen et al., 2021).

In this context, the onus falls upon schools to provide the necessary support, as without such measures, inclusive education remains a mere rhetorical ideal. Therefore, this study investigates the pedagogical practices employed by a successful inclusive school, herein referred to as "The Praxis School," (pseudonym), to cultivate a bullying-free environment for students with and without disabilities. The research delves into the various elements implemented at The Praxis School that accommodate the specific needs of students with disabilities, particularly those with learning disabilities.

The current research study focuses on how these elements facilitate a positive learning experience within an inclusive environment where students with disabilities learn alongside their typically developing peers. The study emphasizes the proactive measures taken by the school staff to ensure a learning environment free from disability-based bullying.

Furthermore, by exploring these practices, the chapter aims to provide educators with a comprehensive understanding of how to prevent bullying in inclusive classrooms, ultimately fostering a more accessible learning environment for all students, particularly those with learning disabilities.

Research Gap and Objectives

There are many studies conducted in the context of accommodating children with learning disabilities in an inclusive setting. However, very few research studies have been conducted in the context of mitigating bullying of children with LD in an inclusive setting (Shaukat, 2023). Moreover, this type of research study is rare in the context of Pakistan (Kamran & Bano, 2023). The key research questions are as follows

RQ 1. What are the experiences of bullying faced by children with LD in inclusive settings and how are the challenges overcome?

RQ 2. How can the pedagogical practices adopted by the practice school be used to promote the inclusion of children with LD by mitigating bullying and promoting greater educational equity?

LITERATURE REVIEW

Pedagogical Practices to Prevent Bullying in an Inclusive School

The dilemma is that the literature indicates that teachers are reluctant to include children with learning disabilities. One of the reasons they discuss is that they are bullied and it becomes difficult for teachers to accommodate them. Teachers not only need pedagogy for them but also to prevent them from being bullied (Azad, 2016; Kamran et al., 2023). The emotional toll of navigating the educational journey for children with learning disabilities (LD) is well-documented, impacting both the children and their parents (Ehsan, 2018). A critical concern voiced by parents is the issue of bullying faced by children with LD in mainstream classrooms (Ehsan, 2018). This concern is highly pertinent and warrants further discussion. While some parents presented recommendations from psychologists specializing in LD, advocating for successful inclusion through appropriate pedagogical strategies (Lodhi et al., 2016), the reality often falls short. Despite integrating children with LD into regular classrooms, schools may lack the necessary pedagogical expertise and resources to effectively support their needs.

Inclusive education, while a laudable goal, presents a complex challenge, often hampered by various obstacles that necessitate focused attention (Shaukat, 2023). A primary concern lies in the social maturity of young children in primary schools. They may lack the necessary understanding and empathy to interact compassionately with new classmates who have learning disabilities (Georgiadi et al., 2012;

Odom et al., 2006). To bridge this gap, school administrators and teachers must prioritize pre-inclusion training for typically developing peers (Ebersold & Meijer, 2016). This training equips students with the skills to interact effectively with children with special education needs (SEN), thereby fostering a supportive learning environment. The absence of such sensitization efforts within the described context emerges as a significant hurdle in the successful implementation of inclusive practices. The current situation suggests a potential lack of awareness regarding inclusive education practices within schools, leading to the uncritical inclusion of children with disabilities (Azad, 2016). Literature emphasizes the importance of fostering a specific "culture of inclusion" within schools (Hameed & Manzoor, 2019). This culture requires the creation of appropriate conditions that facilitate genuine inclusion, potentially including the establishment of bullying-free zones for children with disabilities. For example, the school in this study has a resource room with resources such as playdough, indoor plants, and arts and crafts. Teachers reported that doing activities with playdough, caring for indoor plants, and using art supplies kept students engaged. As a result, bullying behavior has been prevented. They work together, sometimes in groups or pairs, which is a perfect example of group work and teamwork.

This chapter presents the findings from a case study of an inclusive school that exemplifies a successful implementation of these principles. The school actively embraces inclusion by fulfilling the specific needs and prerequisites for children with learning disabilities, fostering an environment where they are accepted without judgment or ridicule. The realization of an inclusive school community hinges upon the establishment of a corresponding culture and environment, fostered through the active participation and cooperation of all stakeholders (Engelbrecht et al., 2016). This process necessitates an "enculturation" of learning and teaching practices. Educators and the broader school community must transition from a set of rigid norms, beliefs, customs, and practices that prioritize the status quo. Instead, they must embrace a transformative approach, characterized by a commitment to ongoing change and the provision of continuous support that facilitates and sustains this evolution (Engelbrecht et al., 2016).

Building upon this notion, a critical understanding of the multifaceted role of schools in fostering inclusion becomes paramount (Ainscow et al., 2004). This role encompasses a wide range of aspects within the school environment, including pedagogical practices, leadership approaches, student-teacher interactions, and peer-to-peer dynamics. Additionally, it necessitates the provision of the necessary material resources. The case study presented offers valuable insights into how these interconnected elements can collectively facilitate a school's progress towards establishing a truly inclusive environment. This holistic model serves as a potential framework for adaptation and implementation within other educational settings. Furthermore, a key objective of this research is to identify and analyze the pedagogical practices employed by The Praxis School, a successful inclusive school environment. Exploring and potentially replicating these practices in other educational settings holds significant promise for advancing inclusion efforts. The study delves into how The Praxis School caters to the specific needs of students with learning disabilities, fostering a positive learning experience. The underlying motivation is to unveil the key factors that contribute to this school's established reputation for inclusion. By investigating these practices, the research aims to provide valuable insights that can be adapted and implemented in schools striving to create inclusive environments free from bullying, particularly for students with learning disabilities.

Materials and Methods

This research investigates the pedagogical practices employed by teachers to facilitate inclusion and address the needs of students with learning disabilities (LD) within the classroom environment. The study specifically explores: (1) the prevalence of bullying faced by students with LD, and (2) effective measures to create a safe learning environment. Furthermore, it examines pedagogical practices that can equip teachers to manage the diverse needs of both students with LD and their typically developing peers. This includes a focus on differentiated instructional strategies implemented to cater to individual learning styles. The research also explores the challenges face by teachers in the areas of instruction, learning, and assessment. To achieve these objectives, a case study approach was employed, focusing on a unique inclusive school, The Praxis School, established in 1996. This school has a long-standing commitment to inclusive educational practices and caters specifically to the needs of learners with disabilities. The Praxis School was selected due to its local reputation for implementing policies and practices aimed at successfully integrating children with special educational needs (SEN) into mainstream classrooms. Operating as a private, primary-level inclusive school, The Praxis School strives to deliver high quality education to students with SEN in an inclusive environment.

This research investigates the current state of inclusive education practices within a private, primary school located in Karachi that serves a diverse student population. This school has been serving children with various disabilities for over 30 years. The school is unique because it has existed for such a long time. It also has professionally trained teachers, and most importantly, it is documented in the UNICEF document for its inclusive pedagogy (UNICEF, 2003).

The study employs a qualitative research design to gain in-depth understanding of teachers' pedagogical practices from multiple perspectives (Merriam, 2009; Patton, 1999; St. Pierre, 2000). A single case embedded design was chosen because it lends itself to studying one specific case (The Praxis School) over time through extensive data collection from multiple sources (Creswell, 2007, p. 73). This approach aligns well with the research goal of understanding "how" and "why" inclusion is implemented in the school. Case studies provide a rich contextual understanding and facilitate data collection from multiple participants, allowing the researcher to examine the current situation regarding the inclusion of children with special educational needs (CWSN).

The qualitative case study design utilized a purposive sample (N=16) consisting of teachers (N=11), coordinators (N=3), the taekwondo/physical education teacher (N=1), and the school administrator (N=1). For further details on demographics, refer to Table 1. These participants were interviewed to explore their perspectives on pedagogical practices for CWSN. They were selected because of their professional development and experience. They had more than 10 years of teaching experience and worked with students with a variety of disabilities in their classrooms. In addition, classrooms from grades I to V were included as units of analysis through classroom observations.

Table 1. Details of the participants

S. No.	Designation and gender (m/f)	Experience with Inclusive School	Job Responsibilities
1	Director/Administrator (m)	25 years	Founder/Administrative affairs
2	Coordinator (f)	10 years	Communication, collaboration, and delegation of tasks, monitoring and supervision
3	Coordinator (f)	12 years	Communication, collaboration, and delegation of tasks, monitoring and supervision
4	Coordinator (f)	10 years	Communication, collaboration, and delegation of tasks, monitoring and supervision
5	Teacher (f)	6 years	English, Mathematics and Science
6	Teacher (f)	9 years	Social Studies and General knowledge
7	Teacher (f)	10 years	English
8	Teacher (f)	6 years	Urdu and Islamic Studies
9	Teacher (f)	6 years	Social Studies and General knowledge
10	Teacher (f)	8 years	English, Mathematics and Science
11	Teacher (f)	6 years	English, Mathematics and Science
12	Teacher (f)	10 years	Science
13	Teacher (f)	10 years	Mathematics

continued on following page

Table 1. Continued

S. No.	Designation and gender (m/f)	Experience with Inclusive School	Job Responsibilities
14	Teacher (f)	6 years	Urdu and Islamic Studies
15	P.E. Teacher (m)	10 years	Taekwondo teacher/sports teacher
16	Teacher (f)	6 years	English, Mathematics and Science

The research design followed a three-phase structure. The initial phase involved establishing rapport with the school administration and teachers, culminating in securing permission for data collection. Data collection commenced with a pilot study, followed by interviews with the administrator, coordinators, and teachers (including the taekwondo/sports teacher). Next, classroom observations were conducted (The schedule for the classroom observations can be found in Table 2.).

Table 2. Schedule of classroom observations

Classrooms Observations	# of Observations
Grade - I	5 Week-Days
Grade - II	5 Week-Days
Grade - III	5 Week-Days
Grade - IV	5 Week-Days
Grade - V	5 Week-Days
Activity Room/library/labs/	5 Week-Days
All COs	**30 Week-Days**

Data analysis commenced with transcribing interviews, followed by coding and thematic development, ultimately leading to the reporting of research findings. This process was followed in a linear, step-by-step manner (refer to Figure 1). It is important to clarify here that the interviews with all stakeholders and the classroom observations facilitated data triangulation. The informal field notes also helped the researchers to triangulate the findings. Data analysis also followed a rigorous process of axial coding, followed by focused and selective coding. Themes were generated and thematic analysis was conducted (Braun & Clarke, 2006).

Figure 1. Process of data collection

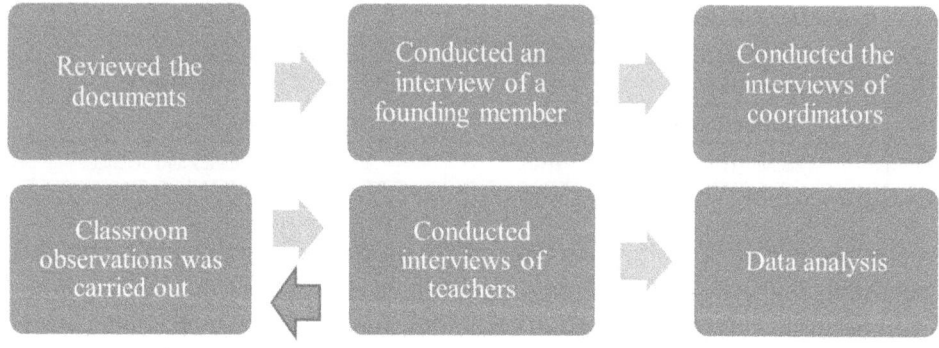

Reviewed the documents → Conducted an interview of a founding member → Conducted the interviews of coordinators

Classroom observations was carried out ← Conducted interviews of teachers → Data analysis

(Source: Created by Author)

Study Strengths and Limitations

This embedded single case study research design has both strengths and limitations. A limitation of all qualitative research is that it is not generalizable to the larger population (Miles & Huberman, 1994). It cannot be replicated exactly because a researcher in another context will see and hear things that are different from what was studied in the researcher's context. Even if the researcher is able to duplicate the context and participants exactly, the researcher will relate to the data through the prism of his or her reality (Lincoln & Guba, 1985). In addition, this study is limited to teachers and leaders belonging to the primary level, its results are not generalizable to other levels of education. The sample population of the study represents the teachers and leaders of the inclusive school in the research site. Thus, it follows that the results of this study cannot be generalized to the entire population of teachers and leaders in schools across Karachi.

However, this is a unique study of its kind in Pakistan and the findings of the exploratory research study have provided the recommendations that can be done to fill the gaps in the educational provision for children with special educational needs. In addition, the practical side of the research study was presented in terms of disseminating research findings of positive practices that can provide some direction for policy makers, schools and other professionals to follow. The previous research studies conducted in the field of inclusive education in Pakistan have not explored the relationship between the whole school approach and pedagogical practices (Hameed & Manzoor, 2019; Qureshi & Razzaq, 2019; Singal, 2019). Also, the case study in the context of an inclusive institution serving the middle to lower middle class is yet to be explored (Azad, 2016). Moreover, the school has been documented as a pioneer in providing inclusive education in the context of

Pakistan (UNICEF, 2003). This research study presented the inclusive practices of a unique and unexplored institution.

The study used self-reported data collected through semi-structured interviews and classroom observation, and the data could not be independently corroborated as the study had to be completed within a specified time period. However, the classroom observations and teacher data are informative of each other and help to increase the consistency and reliability of the findings.

Ethical Considerations

This passage outlines the ethical considerations guiding a qualitative research study on inclusive education. The researcher emphasizes the importance of respecting participants and ensuring research benefits the school community.

Key Ethical Principles

> **Relationships and Informed Consent:** The study adheres to a "relationships paradigm" (Sheehy, 2005), prioritizing informed consent and building trust with participants (Brooks et al., 2014). This involved treating participants as partners and obtaining consent through an information sheet and consent form. Parental consent was acquired for observations involving children with special needs.
> **Confidentiality and Privacy:** The study prioritizes anonymity and confidentiality. Data is kept confidential, with only the researcher and supervisor having access to raw data. Pseudonyms are used throughout the research to protect participants' identities (Amjad & Malik, 2024).
> **Minimizing Risk:** The researcher minimized risk by building rapport with participants and seeking gatekeeper assistance. Participation was voluntary, and informed consent ensured participants were aware of potential risks (Amjad & Malik, 2024).
> **Transparency and Benefit:** The research aimed for mutual benefit (Brooks et al., 2014). Participants were involved in the research process, receiving a clear explanation of the study's purpose, methodology, and data usage. Findings were fed back to the school community through coded transcripts.

Overall, the research demonstrates a commitment to ethical principles in qualitative research, particularly regarding informed consent, confidentiality, risk minimization, and participant benefit.

Research Findings

Pedagogical Practices for Preventing Bullying Among Children with Learning Disabilities

The teachers at The Praxis School believed that to make inclusion a reality without any fear of mocking and bullying of children with disabilities: three features are a need of the day: (i) professionally developed teachers, (ii) availability of teachers, and (iii) accessibility to the resources to accommodate children with disability in an inclusive school.

Bullying thrives on power imbalances, with perpetrators often targeting those perceived as weaker (Burger et al., 2015). Children with disabilities are especially vulnerable due to characteristics that differ from typical development (Davis & Nixon, 2010; National Autistic Society, 2017; Van Geel et al., 2014). This can make them seem less physically or intellectually capable, leading to social exclusion and academic challenges (Faith et al., 2015). To address this, The Praxis School prioritizes providing human and material resources to empower these students. By building their skills and fostering independence, the school aims to bridge the gap between children with and without disabilities. This not only enhances their academic performance but also reduces the risk of mocking and humiliation.

Many studies support adapting the curriculum to accommodate students with disabilities (Mehmood & Parveen, 2021; Nwankwo & Nnatu, 2018). This approach not only fosters inclusion but also empowers these students to achieve academic success, build self-confidence, and avoid potential feelings of humiliation due to learning differences. The study found that teachers embraced various strategies to support students with learning disabilities in both mainstream classrooms and beyond. They viewed easy access to the curriculum as a key resource and ensured this by implementing all activities in an inclusive setting. The school is implementing the Montessori curriculum by modifying it to accommodate children with learning disabilities. A teacher explained:

"Modification is need-based. There are different approaches to teaching them, which are derived and modified from the Montessori curriculum. I have discussed many examples of modification. For children with learning disabilities, we make use of audio-recorded lectures. We permit extra time on assignments and essays. Also, allow for preferential seating to facilitate better listening".

A major concern for The Praxis School's teachers is the lack of a government-designed curriculum for children with special needs (CWSN). They view this as a significant missing resource. All teachers strongly agree on the urgent need for a curriculum tailored to meet the unique needs of CWSN effectively. Moving on to book-related challenges, a math teacher shared:

"We choose accessible electronic versions of course readings. We convert the reading into the format required, whether we let them use a screen reader, an enlarger, or another technology".

The absence of a curriculum designed for children with disabilities was compounded by a lack of suitable learning materials. In response, the school, as the Coordinator explains, implemented strategies to address these needs.

"The problem is that children with learning disabilities are required to repeat many times. The workbook offers only 4 to 5 pages for practice. They need many practice pages. We cannot do that here. The books of GABA and Spectrum (Publishing Houses) were available at a low cost. We used it here, but the issue with these books is that they are not colorful. Now we download worksheets from the internet and get them photocopied to ensure the availability of practice pages. There are no specially designed specific books for them. We use books from Oxford, Paramount, Learning Star, and Nexus. These are colorful and activity-based. We use erasable books and they are available. After practicing a child rubs it and attempts again".

While textbooks play a role, activity-based learning is crucial for children with special needs (CWSN) (Richards et al., 2015). Since textbooks often lack sufficient practice opportunities, downloading worksheets can be a valuable alternative. This approach is both cost-effective and can be supplemented with appropriate textbooks. However, teachers emphasize the need for readily available resources to implement activity-based learning fully.

A teacher commented on the use of activity-based learning:

There should be as many activities and resources as possible for children with learning disabilities. These are very important and we made resources with our hands. In math we use objects like blocks, abacus, etc. When we teach action words in English, we do actions like clapping, laughing and jumping. For this we need audio-visual aids. In science, we make them grow plants. We study leaves, stems, roots, and soil, and we show them and teach them. They can never learn by verbal teaching alone, and they do not like writing. They have to perform. They participate and learning is enhanced and this is not possible without resources/teaching aids.

In a creative activity, the art teacher used colorful Styrofoam steps to engage a hearing-impaired child with learning disabilities. The teacher asked the child to take a specific number of steps, then another, and finally inquired about the total number. Interestingly, not only did the child correctly answer '6,' but the entire class unknowingly mirrored the answer. This simple exercise demonstrates how activity-based learning can promote addition and subtraction skills in a fun and inclusive way. Notably, the activity was brief, reusable, and addressed a common concern – that activity-based learning can be time-consuming. It serves as a perfect example of a practical and effective teaching method, as the coordinator explained:

"Through art, we teach them science concepts. For example, when we ask them to do project work/research, they are happy to do a Google search. They bring ideas. For example, planets can be made from thermopile or Scotch tape paper balls. Planets can be made out of paint. When we ask them to see how a caterpillar becomes a butterfly. When we ask them to do something practical, they enjoy it. If we ask them to learn about life cycles/plants, they enjoy it. They do the activity of germination by putting in seeds and finding out how they grow. These activities involve them well/ engage them/ this develops interest and learning becomes easier for them. This helps with retention. Hands-on activities and project-based learning work well with these children. They do two to three science/social studies activities in a month. For written work, we ask them to make booklets. [Project work works well for all subjects.] In English, we ask them to bring information about some author and we ask them to make booklets with colorful pictures. In math, we teach them fractions by dividing a model of a pizza into four pieces. This makes a pizza/burger interesting to a child and he understands fractions. The same is done in other subjects. In Urdu they make booklets. It is a written activity by taking colored paper and tying it with a ribbon and pasting pictures. It is made for a poet or a country. The children feel happy with their research work. However, the information is in English, then a teacher gets involved and translates it into Urdu. For example, it is about a writer, his life story is written with pictures, his publications are written with pictures. The same thing happens in English".

Similarly, during classroom observation, it was noted that a teacher photocopied the textbook in a larger font which aided CWSNs in reading and they showed amazing academic performance. The observed activities demonstrated that expensive resources aren't always necessary. For instance, teachers creatively used cardstock models of pizza and burgers to teach fractions. Furthermore, all classrooms from grades 1 to 5 have designated learning corners and libraries. A teacher explained how these engaging spaces play a vital role in including all children, regardless of abilities. Here, students can find displays showcasing the various activities they've participated in.

For students with challenges related to sitting tolerance, the school implemented a station-based learning approach. As one educator aptly described, these stations are *'Children's play areas that foster self-directed learning through deep engagement'*. This activity-based method benefits both children with and without disabilities, promoting inclusive participation and mutual learning (Kamran & Siddiqui, 2024). It's not about creating separate provisions, but rather an environment where all students can thrive together. This reduces feelings of superiority, inferiority, and power imbalances, ultimately contributing to a classroom culture that minimizes bullying.

Bhargava (2015) emphasizes the importance of balanced timetables, acknowledging that students come with diverse abilities, experiences, and needs (OECD, 2008). A rigid schedule can't cater to everyone effectively. This is particularly true for students with disabilities, who may require modifications to the regular timetable to stay engaged, and motivated, and learn at their own pace. The study's researcher noted a focus on understanding student mood during classroom visits. Rather than imposing a rigid schedule, teachers gauge student interest. If math isn't engaging them initially, they might switch to a subject like English, catering to their current preference. This flexibility extends beyond the schedule. After breaks, if students seem tired, playful activities like painting might be offered. Teachers even solicit student input on preferred activities. This focus on engagement, through play and choice, appears to be a powerful motivator for learning.

A key challenge in inclusive settings is ensuring all students, including those with disabilities, feel comfortable and supported. The Praxis School addresses this by identifying individual needs and then adapting the classroom environment accordingly. This allows everyone to participate fully and fosters a sense of belonging for all. One teacher shared an incident of a child with autism and learning disability, who usually has good concentration and interest, but sometimes takes much longer to complete his work. As she says:

"In the case of Ahmed (pseudonym), the light should be dim for an autistic child because light irritates him and he gets hyper. But other children need bright light, so we make him sit where the light is not directly on him. Our environment needs to be comfortable and then only a child will enjoy learning".

Assistive technologies are instrumental in integrating students with disabilities into inclusive classrooms (Kamran & Siddiqui, 2023). These tools empower students to participate and learn alongside their peers, minimizing differences and promoting a more equitable learning environment.

A coordinator of inclusive setup stated:

"The benefits of using technology are many, and its incorporation can be multifunctional. Children with special educational needs can significantly benefit from technology. With the help of technology, children with disabilities can overcome difficulties in all four basic skills: speaking, reading, listening, and writing, as well as mathematical reasoning and problem-solving".

The teacher stated:

"To implement assistive technology in the school for catering to special needs children, teachers should be professionally developed. Teachers who cater to children with special needs are given augmented tasks in inclusive education classrooms. The struggle is planned to connect children with disabilities to class-

room activities that their peers are relishing, resulting in a sense of achievement, collective actions with distinct outcomes, and unbiased didactic knowledge. Additionally, the use of assistive technology can also lessen frustration, increase zeal, foster a feeling of peer acceptance, and develop efficiency in school and at home. It is therefore required to emphasize the fact that the application of assistive technology boosts a sense of accomplishment and collective effort in the classroom set up for children with special educational needs. Assistive technology improves and contributes to greater motivation and assistive technology can act as a provision for the education of children with special educational needs, in that way decreasing the pressure of work and stress levels of teachers".

During classroom observations, a noteworthy modified resource was a special chair for a child with learning disabilities and autism. This child struggles with balance and risks falling off a regular chair. This chair exemplifies Assistive Technology (AT), which refers to any device, tool, equipment, or software program that enhances the capabilities of people with disabilities (PWD), children with special educational needs (CWSN), or children with disabilities (CWD). AT can also encompass tools that promote self-reliance in daily tasks (Kamran & Siddiqui, 2023). A wide range of assistive technologies (AT) can empower students with special educational needs. Carefully planned and managed AT devices, like hearing aids for children with hearing loss (Genc et al., 2021), can significantly support students. Research suggests these tools benefit individuals with various disabilities, including hearing and visual impairments, Autism Spectrum Disorder, and physical limitations (Kamran & Siddiqui, 2023). AT fosters not only, academic independence but also social independence, ultimately allowing children with special needs to lead fulfilling lives. Active users of AT can even contribute to a nation's economic development (Hameed & Manzoor, 2019). Through AT, education for these students can be revolutionized, enabling them to become valued members of society and active contributors.

The Praxis School effectively enhanced learning for children with special needs (CWSN) through various strategies. Teachers created learning corners, worksheets, and additional resources to cater to diverse learning styles. This, along with assistive devices like those brought in by parents (e.g., hearing aids), provided CWSN with multiple learning opportunities through different media, experiences, and play-based activities. However, compared to Western contexts, The Praxis School had limited access to electronic assistive technology. This might be due to the school prioritizing resource allocation to meet the broader needs of all CWSN. While the lack of advanced assistive technology presents a challenge, the school demonstrates a commendable commitment to maximizing student learning with the resources available

Research underlines that simply having resources isn't enough; effective implementation requires qualified educators (Shaukat, 2023). This study is heartening in that The Praxis School boasts a team of expert teachers who are keenly aware of the specific needs of children with special needs (CWSN). The school demonstrates a strong commitment to teacher development through in-service training, and they also recruit teachers who have been professionally trained in their pre-service pieces of trainings.

Empowering Teachers, Peers and Victims in Mitigating Bullying of Children with Learning Disabilities

The detrimental impact of bullying on students' psychological, social, and physical well-being is a well-established concern (Siddiqui et al., 2023). While a significant body of research has explored bullying within general education settings, a dearth of experimental studies exists regarding prevention or intervention strategies specifically tailored to students with disabilities (Houchins et al., 2016). Siddiqui et al. (2023) posit that professional development programs for educators are a crucial tool for curbing bullying in educational institutions. These programs equip teachers with the skills to identify and confront bullying behavior (Siddiqui et al., 2023). The rationale behind such programs lies in the belief that teachers, by virtue of their constant presence and influence within the school environment, are ideally positioned to enact positive change (Siddiqui et al., 2023; Strohmeier et al., 2012). Their enhanced competencies can be instrumental in introducing initiatives that prevent bullying perpetration and victimization (Siddiqui et al., 2023). Furthermore, teachers' ongoing presence throughout the academic year creates a safe space for students to seek immediate assistance in instances of witnessed or experienced bullying (Siddiqui et al., 2023).

The Praxis School prioritizes professional development for its educators, offering both pre-service and in-service training programs (Kamran & Siddiqui, 2024). This commitment to continuous professional growth is evident in their practices and their understanding of Children with Special Needs (CWSN). The school fosters a collaborative environment where teachers engage in peer-to-peer learning, fostering a shared teaching and learning experience. This is further illustrated by a teacher's statement:

"The best way is to train each other through shared learning experiences. The school has professional development within a community system. We are training each other alongside getting pieces of training from outside. The school pays for our diploma courses. We attend training workshops and seminars. It is like continuous professional development. The diploma in behavioral management is done by almost all teachers, and a famous psychologist was the facilitator.

We conduct workshops for parents, too. If we have a teacher trained from some other institution, then we involve them to train others. We conduct workshops on weekends, usually on Saturdays. If workshops are conducted by other renowned institutions, our school pays and we attend the workshops. The training helps us to help mitigate bullying-related issues".

Even in schools with established zero-tolerance policies against bullying, children with disabilities may still be targeted due to their perceived differences from their peers (Henson et al., 2012). However, research suggests that professionally trained teachers can play a significant role in mitigating such incidents (Siddiqui et al., 2023). This notion is further supported by a teacher at The Praxis School, who stated:

"Children and young people with a learning disability often experience bullying at school, singled out for being seen as different. This could be because of reasons such as speaking or moving differently, showing emotions differently, having specialist equipment, making loud noises in class, etc.".

Research emphasizes the importance of empowering victims to advocate for themselves as a means to prevent further victimization (Bourke & Burgman, 2010). This aligns with the approach taken by The Praxis School, where the coordinator explained that children with disabilities receive clear instructions on how to respond to situations of humiliation, mocking, or bullying. Recognizing that some victims may be hesitant to speak up due to shyness or shame, The Praxis School has also implemented a bully box system. This anonymous reporting mechanism allows students to confidentially report bullying incidents (Smith et al., 2016).

The coordinator stated:

We told our children that If you feel that you can talk to the person bullying you and ask them to stop, that is the first place to start. If you feel uncomfortable or unable to do this, speak to your teacher, parent, or someone else you trust. Our school has a bully box, report the incident there.

Fostering peer acceptance and empathy towards Children with Special Needs (CWSN) through teacher training is recognized as a crucial element for successful inclusive education (Georgiadi et al., 2012; Odom et al., 2006; Siddiqui et al., 2023). The importance of preparing both peers and students to welcome classmates with disabilities is underscored by Tzani-Pepelasi et al. (2019), who advocate for training and awareness sessions as a key strategy. This aligns with the perspective shared by an educator at The Praxis School, who stated.

As far as bullying is concerned, it happens, but it is rare in our setup. Our school categorically explained to learners without disabilities that bullying is strictly prohibited. We have both in-house awareness seminars regarding bullying. We trained them to report if anyone witnessed bullying.

At The Praxis School, a majority of educators emphasized the importance of direct communication with teachers. Participants highlighted the school's approach, which encourages students to report bullying incidents calmly and provide specific details. The school recognizes that some students might feel nervous about verbal reporting, and offers alternative methods such as written reports or email communication. A summary of the findings is shown in Figure 2.

Figure 2. Practices of the Praxis School to mitigate bullying in inclusive setup

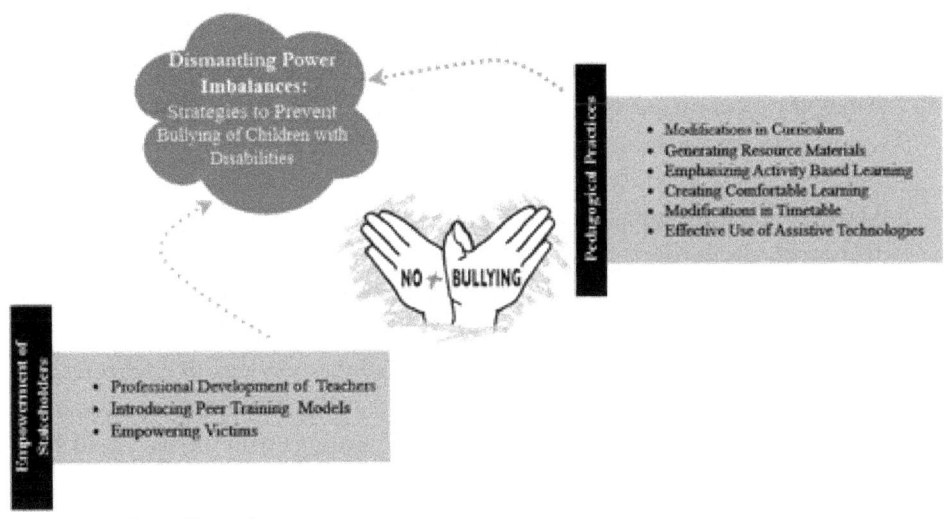

(Source: Created by Author)

CONCLUSION

This chapter explores effective teaching practices for inclusive classrooms, with a focus on reducing bullying. Thematic analysis revealed that schools with well-trained teachers are better equipped to address the developmental needs of children with learning disabilities (Shaukat, 2023). The Praxis School staff highlighted several key strategies.

- **Activity-Based Learning:** Research suggests this approach is particularly beneficial for students with special needs (Richards et al., 2015). The teachers use multiple activities to teach a single concept, as repetition is crucial for students with learning difficulties (short-term memory limitations).

- **Modification:** The curriculum and timetable were modified to fit the needs of each student (Mehmood & Parveen, 2021; Nwankwo & Nnatu, 2018). The data confirms there's no single solution for managing aggressive behavior in students with disabilities within inclusive classrooms. Effective strategies require an individualized approach. A strong foundation can be built by establishing clear classroom rules, expectations, and responsibilities. Additionally, creating a differentiated, individualized, and integrated curriculum ensures a meaningful learning experience for all students. Unnecessary details are skipped, and content is simplified for children with disabilities. Teachers break down instructions into smaller steps, ensuring comprehension.
- **Universal Design for Learning (UDL):** The Praxis School follows UDL principles, acknowledging that students learn differently. Lessons are designed with varied materials, activities, and engagement strategies to cater to diverse learning styles (OECD, 2008).
- **Assistive Technology (AT):** The school effectively uses AT to support students with disabilities, promoting academic achievement and social inclusion. Research confirms that AT can foster independence for students with disabilities, both academically and socially (Anna & Angharad, 2021). AT encompasses a wide range of tools, from mobility devices like wheelchairs to software programs that address specific learning difficulties or visual/auditory impairments (Anuruddhika, 2018). This aligns with the No Child Left Behind Act's emphasis on technology to improve learning outcomes (U.S. Department of Education). When AT helps students overcome challenges, they experience academic success (Asghar et al., 2017) and get fewer target for bullying victimization.
- **Professional Development of Teachers:** Research highlights that professional development for teachers is crucial, not only for improving inclusive teaching practices but also for equipping them to prevent bullying and protect students with disabilities from humiliation and insults (Kamran & Siddiqui, 2024; Siddiqui et al., 2023). Recognizing this importance, The Praxis School dedicates resources to ongoing teacher training. This investment fosters a supportive learning environment that minimizes differences and promotes a culture free from bullying.
- **Training of Peers:** Research worldwide, including studies in Pakistan (Bjereld, 2018; Siddiqui & Schultze-Krumbholz, 2023), suggests that peer support programs can be effective in controlling bullying incidents. The Praxis School implements several steps to foster this approach. These include peer awareness sessions where students learn about the challenges faced by children with disabilities, developing empathy towards their peers with disabilities with the help of activities and discussions, peer supporter training

where students are equipped with the skills and knowledge to support their classmates and prevent bullying, etc. By implementing these strategies, The Praxis School empowers students to create a more inclusive and supportive learning environment for all.
- **Empowering Victims to Stand-Up for Themselves:** Children with disabilities can face social challenges and may find it difficult to express themselves compared to their peers (Cowden, 2010). This can make them more susceptible to bullying. The Praxis School recognizes this vulnerability and implements a multi-pronged approach to address it, the school establishes clear rules against bullying for all students, the school provides guidelines and strategies to help children with disabilities stand up for themselves, students are encouraged to report bullying to teachers or trusted adults and for those who may feel uncomfortable speaking up directly, an anonymous reporting system, like a "bully box," is available.

The complex issue of bullying disproportionately affects children with disabilities (CWD). The Praxis School addresses this concern by creating a comprehensive support system. This system not only ensures inclusion, accommodation, and preparation for the future through modern pedagogical practices but also empowers CWD to self-advocate and resist bullying and victimization. Notably, participating coordinators and teachers expressed strong confidence in the school's support for CWD, aligning with the school's mission statement. This perspective is further supported by research, suggesting that the teachers' practices often reflect these beliefs.

All of the strategies discussed above have reduced the problems of bullying, and it is worth noting that this facility is a bullying-free zone, as stated by the school administrator.

Significance of the Study

The intensive literature review revealed that most elite mainstream institutions are studied, leaving a gap by not studying the inclusive schools that cater to the middle class (Azad, 2016). The current research study explored how disabilities are addressed in the Praxis School, which is designed to cater to students from middle-income backgrounds. In addition, the current study identifies the gap in terms of pedagogical practices. This study is particularly significant given the existing difficulties that schools in Pakistan seem to be suffering from in terms of moving towards the adoption of inclusive educational policies and practices. It needs to be clarified that the practice inclusive school that is the focus of this research study is an example of an inclusive school that is documented as a good inclusive school in the UNICEF report (2003). The attributes mentioned as documented in the UNICEF report are that the Praxis Inclusive School has created opportunities for the inclusion of children with disabilities in mainstream schools by creating a welcoming and accommodating environment for all children. Although there are contextual differences, it may be useful for schools in Pakistan to read about the current practices and values of this school. It could provide understanding, awareness and motivation for schools that seem to be struggling with their approach to diversity. It is a general observation that there is by no means a "one size fits all" approach to both education and inclusion due to contextual differences. However, an explicit focus on one school's approaches to diversity can be both motivating and relevant for other schools and society at large (Ian & Stuart, 2015).

Another inspiring factor for conducting this research study is that it is also significant to expose such a school to the wider educational community, as it is often easy to be overwhelmed with pessimism about the situation in some schools in Pakistan. This study is an optimistic way of presenting that there may be schools that, despite difficulties, are rising above them and creating cultures that truly embrace diversity with a mission to create appropriate learning practices for all students.

Previous research has shown that teachers have negative attitudes toward disabilities when they are not trained (Kamran et al., 2022; Sharma et al., 2015). Teachers who are trained are prepared to include children with disabilities. Therefore, in an inclusive setting, teachers are trained to effectively serve children with disabilities. The research study can help in terms of studying their practices which can be a source of promoting inclusive educational practices. This research will help to investigate and study inclusive educational practices.

Recommendations for the Future Researchers

What needs to be done in the context of Pakistan is more research aimed at exploring how inclusion can be implemented and where the problems lie. Pakistan is ready to implement successful inclusive education practices and the current research study is a practical example of it. However, acceptance of differences is a need of the hour and it can be facilitated through inclusion of diverse children and more vigorous research (Anna & Angharad, 2021). Schools must try to start this by including children with disabilities. Rather than searching for the conditions needed to create more inclusive school communities for children with disabilities, it is necessary to further explore the everyday life of schools to clearly understand how and why schools face many problems in responding to the demands of developing collective or individual potentials (Shaukat, 2023).

- It is recommended to conduct surveys with larger samples from all four provinces of Pakistan to get a more accurate picture. It is a need of the hour to

collect data on the total number of children with special needs enrolled in mainstream schools and how they are served in terms of pedagogy and other resources.
- It is necessary to carry out research studies involving parents, as they are very important stakeholders.
- In-depth studies are needed in relation to the academic performance and management of children with special educational needs.

The results of the study present a model of an inclusive school that can be replicated in other schools with a similar context. The potential long-term impact is the fulfillment of the Sustainable Development Goals, which require an equitable and inclusive setup.

REFERENCES

Ainscow, M., Booth, T., & Dyson, A. (2004). Understanding and developing inclusive practices in schools: A collaborative action research network. *International Journal of Inclusive Education*, 8(2), 125–139. DOI: 10.1080/1360311032000158015

Amjad, A. I., & Malik, M. A. (2024). Interviewing students with special needs: Developing ethical considerations and interviewing protocols. *Journal of Research in Special Educational Needs*, 24(4), 1161–1174. Advance online publication. DOI: 10.1111/1471-3802.12702

Anna, L., & Angharad, E. B. (2021). The social and human rights models of disability: Towards a complementarity thesis. *The International Journal of Human Rights*, 25(2), 348-379. https://doi.org/DOI: 10.1080/13642987.2020.1783533

Anuruddhika, B. (2018). Teachers' instructional behaviors towards inclusion of children with visual impairment in the teaching learning process. *European Journal of Special Education Research*, 3(3), 164–182. DOI: 10.5281/zenodo.1246950

Asghar, I., Cang, S., & Yu, H. (2017). Assistive technology for people with dementia: An overview and bibliometric study. *Health Information and Libraries Journal*, 34(1), 5–19. DOI: 10.1111/hir.12173 PMID: 28191727

Azad, T. (2016). *Exploring inclusive practice: The beliefs and practices of classroom teachers in two mainstream primary schools in Karachi* [Unpublished doctoral dissertation, King's College London, University of London] London.

Bhargava, D. (2015). Balanced Timetable Key to Student Engagement. Retrieved from https://www.carsonst.wa.edu.au/wp-content/uploads/2012/11/Balanced-Timetable-Manual-1.pdf

Bjereld, Y. (2018). The challenging process of disclosing bullying victimization: A grounded theory study from the victim's point of view. *Journal of Health Psychology*, 23(8), 1110–1118. DOI: 10.1177/1359105316644973 PMID: 27153857

Bourke, S., & Burgman, I. (2010). Coping with bullying in Australian schools: How children with disabilities experience support from friends, parents and teachers. *Disability & Society*, 25(3), 359–371. DOI: 10.1080/09687591003701264

Braun, V., & Clarke, V. (2006). Using thematic analysis in psychology. *Qualitative Research in Psychology*, 3(2), 77–101. DOI: 10.1191/1478088706qp063oa

Brooks, R., TeRiele, K., & Maguire, M. (2014). *Ethics and Education Research*. Sage. DOI: 10.4135/9781473909762

Burger, C., Strohmeier, D., Spröber, N., Bauman, S., & Rigby, K. (2015). How teachers respond to school bullying: An examination of self-reported intervention strategy use, moderator effects, and concurrent use of multiple strategies. *Teaching and Teacher Education*, 51, 191–202. DOI: 10.1016/j.tate.2015.07.004

Cerna, L., Mezzanotte, C., Rutigliano, A., Brussino, O., Santiago, P., Borgonovi, F., & Guthrie, C. (2021). Promoting inclusive education for diverse societies: A conceptual framework. *OECD Education Working Papers*, No. 260, OECD Publishing, Paris. https://doi.org/DOI: 10.1787/19939019

Convention on the Rights of Persons with Disabilities. (2007). Resolution/Adopted by the General Assembly, 24 January 2007, A/RES/61/106. Available online: https://www.refworld.org/docid/45f973632.html

Cowden, P. A. (2010). Social anxiety in children with disabilities. *Journal of Instructional Psychology*, 37(4), 301–305.

Creswell, J. W. (2007). *Qualitative Inquiry and Research Design: Choosing Among Five Traditions* (2nd ed.). Sage Publications.

Davis, S., & Nixon, C. (2010). Preliminary results from the Youth Voice Research Project: Victimization & Strategies. Retrieved from http://www.youthvoiceproject.com/YVPMarch2010.pdf

Ebersold, S., & Meijer, C. (2016). Financing inclusive education: Policy challenges, issues and trends, implementing inclusive education: Issues in bridging the policy-practice gap. *International Perspectives on Inclusive Education*, 8, 37–62. DOI: 10.1108/S1479-363620160000008004

Ehsan, M. (2018). Inclusive education in primary and secondary Schools of Pakistan: Role of teachers. *American Academic Scientific Research Journal for Engineering, Technology, and Sciences, 40*(1), 40–61. Retrieved from https://asrjetsjournal.org/index.php/American_Scientific_Journal/article/view/3684

Engelbrecht, P., Swart, E., & Eloff, I. (2016). Stress and coping skills of teachers with a learner with Down's syndrome in inclusive classrooms. *South African Journal of Education*, 21(4), 256–259.

Faith, M. A., Reed, G., Heppner, C. E., Hamill, L. C., Tarkenton, T. R., & Donewar, C. W. (2015). Bullying in medically fragile youth: A review of risks, protective factors, and recommendations for medical providers. *Journal of Developmental and Behavioral Pediatrics*, 36(4), 285–301. DOI: 10.1097/DBP.0000000000000155 PMID: 25923529

Genc, Z., Babieva, N. S., Zarembo, G. V., Lobanova, E. V., & Malakhova, V. Y. (2021). The views of special education department students on the use of assistive technologies in special education. [iJET]. *International Journal of Emerging Technologies in Learning*, 16(19), 69–80. DOI: 10.3991/ijet.v16i19.26025

Georgiadi, M., Kalyva, E., Kourkoutas, E., & Tsakiris, V. (2012). Young children's attitudes toward peers with intellectual disabilities: Effect of the type of school. *Journal of Applied Research in Intellectual Disabilities*, 25(6), 531–541. DOI: 10.1111/j.1468-3148.2012.00699.x PMID: 23055287

Gladden, R. M., Vivolo-Kantor, A. M., Hamburger, M. E., & Lumpkin, C. D. (2014). Bullying surveillance among youths: Uniform definitions for public health and recommended data elements, version 1.0.

GoP. (2009). National Education Policy Islamabad: Government of Pakistan. http://itacec.org/document/2015/7/National_Education_Policy_2009.pdf

Hameed, A., & Manzoor, A. (2019). Similar agenda, diverse strategies: A review of inclusive education reforms in the Subcontinent. *Bulletin of Education and Research*, 41(2), 53–66.

Henson, M. (2012). *Issues of crime and school safety: Zero tolerance policies and children with disabilities* [Master's Thesis, University of Central Florida]

Houchins, D. E., Oakes, W. P., & Johnson, Z. G. (2016). Bullying and students with disabilities: A systematic literature review of intervention studies. *Remedial and Special Education*, 37(5), 259–273. DOI: 10.1177/0741932516648678

Ian, H., & Stuart, W. (2015). Inclusive education policies: Discourses of difference, diversity and deficit. *International Journal of Inclusive Education*, 19(2), 141–164. DOI: 10.1080/13603116.2014.908965

Kamran, M., & Bano, N. (2023). A systematic review of literature on inclusive education with special emphasis on children with disability in Pakistan. *International Journal of Inclusive Education*, •••, 1–19. DOI: 10.1080/13603116.2023.2256321

Kamran, M., & Siddiqui, S. (2023). Assistive technology integration: Promoting inclusion and achieving sustainable development goals. In Escudeiro, P., Escudeiro, N., & Bernardes, O. (Eds.), *Handbook of research on advancing equity and inclusion through educational technology* (pp. 1–25). IGI Global., DOI: 10.4018/978-1-6684-6868-5.ch001

Kamran, M., Siddiqui, S., & Adil, M. S. (2023). Breaking barriers: The influence of teachers' attitudes on inclusive education for students with mild learning disabilities (MLD). *Education Sciences*, 13(6), 606. Advance online publication. DOI: 10.3390/educsci13060606

Kamran, M., Thomas, M., & Siddiqui, S. (2022). Teachers' opinions about promoting inclusive classroom settings: An investigation regarding the presence of special needs assistants. *The Government: Research Journal of Political Science*, 11, 57–71.

Kamran, & Siddiqui, S. (2024). Roots of resilience: Uncovering the secrets behind 25+ years of inclusive education sustainability. *Sustainability 16*(11), 4364. https://doi.org/DOI: 10.3390/su16114364

Kazimi, A. B., & Kazmi, S. W. (2018). Developing Inclusive education approaches among stakeholders in Pakistan. *Journal of Education & Social Sciences*, 6(1), 86–95. DOI: 10.20547/jess0611806106

Leijen, A., Arcidiacono, F., & Baucal, A. (2021). The dilemma of inclusive education: Inclusion for some or inclusion for all. *Frontiers in Psychology*, 12, 633066. DOI: 10.3389/fpsyg.2021.633066 PMID: 34566742

Lincoln, Y. S., & Guba, E. G. (1985). *Naturalistic inquiry*. Sage. DOI: 10.1016/0147-1767(85)90062-8

Lodhi, S. K., Thaver, D., Akhtar, I. N., Javaid, H., Masoor, M., Bano, S., Malik, F. N., Iqbal, M. R., Hashmi, H. R., Siddiqullah, S., & Saleem, S. (2016). Assessing the knowledge, attitudes and practices of school teachers regarding dyslexia, attention-deficit/ hyperactivity and autistic spectrum disorders in Karachi, Pakistan. *Journal of Ayub Medical College, Abbottabad: JAMC*, 28(1), 99–104. PMID: 27323572

McKenna, J. W., Muething, C., Flower, A., Bryant, D. P., & Bryant, B. (2015). Use and relationships among effective practices in co-taught inclusive high school classrooms. *International Journal of Inclusive Education*, 19(1), 53–70. DOI: 10.1080/13603116.2014.906665

Mehmood, M. U., & Parveen, Z. (2021). Explore areas of needed support, competencies, attitudes, and concerns of elementary school teachers for inclusion of CWDS in elementary schools of Punjab. *Global Educational Studies Review, VI*, 6(III), 109–120. DOI: 10.31703/gesr.2021(VI-III).12

Merriam, S. B. (2009). *Qualitative Research: A Guide to Design and Implementation*. Jossey-Bass.

Miles, M. B., & Huberman, A. M. (1994). Qualitative data analysis: An expanded sourcebook. *Sage (Atlanta, Ga.)*.

Murray, J. (1999). An Inclusive School Library for the 21st Century: Fostering Independence.

National Autistic Society. (2017). Bullying: A guide for parents. Retrieved from http:// researchautism.net

National Education Policy. (2017). Ministry of Federal Education and Professional Training Government of Pakistan. Available online: https://dgse.gov.pk/SiteImage/Downloads/National%20Policy%20for%20Persons%20with%20Disability.pdf (accessed on 5 February 2023)

Nwankwo, I. U., & Nnatu, S. O. (2018). Exploring inclusive education strategy for optimization of learning capacity and access to health information among children with disabilities (CWD) in Nigeria. *International Journal of Academic Research in Business & Social Sciences*, 8(9), 1147–1163. DOI: 10.6007/IJARBSS/v8-i9/4687

Odom, S. L., Zercher, C., Li, S., Marquart, J. M., Sandall, S., & Brown, W. H. (2006). Social acceptance and rejection of preschool children with disabilities: A mixed-method analysis. *Journal of Educational Psychology*, 98(4), 807–823. DOI: 10.1037/0022-0663.98.4.807

Organisation for Economic Cooperation and Development (OECD). (2008). 21st century learning: Research, innovation and policy directions from recent OECD analyses. Retrieved on the 19th of January 2015, from www.oecd.org/dataoecd/39/8/40554299.pdf

Patton, M. Q. (1999). Enhancing the quality and credibility of qualitative analysis. *Health Services Research*, 34(5), 1189–1208. PMID: 10591279

Qureshi, R., & Razzaq, F. (2019). I am not against Inclusive education but': Teachers' Voices from Pakistan. *Journal of Inclusive Education*, 3(1).

Reicher, H. (2010). Building inclusive education on social and emotional learning: Challenges and perspectives–A review. *International Journal of Inclusive Education*, 14(3), 213–246. DOI: 10.1080/13603110802504218

Richards, K. A. R., Eberline, A. D., Padaruth, S., & Templin, T. J. (2015). Experiential learning through a physical activity program for children with disabilities. *Journal of Teaching in Physical Education*, 34(2), 165–188. DOI: 10.1123/jtpe.2014-0015

Sharma, U., Simi, J., & Forlin, C. (2015). Preparedness of pre service teachers for inclusive education in the Solomon Islands. *The Australian Journal of Teacher Education*, 40(5). Advance online publication. https://ro.ecu.edu.au/ajte/vol40/iss5/6. DOI: 10.14221/ajte.2015v40n5.6

Shaukat, S. (2023). Challenges for education of children with disabilities in Pakistan. *Intervention in School and Clinic*, 59(1), 75–80. DOI: 10.1177/10534512221130082

Sheehy, K. (Ed.). (2005). *Ethics and research in inclusive education: Values into practice*. Psychology Press.

Shinde, S., Weiss, H. A., Varghese, B., Khandeparkar, P., Pereira, B., Sharma, A., Gupta, R., Ross, D. A., Patton, G., & Patel, V. (2018). Promoting school climate and health outcomes with the SEHER multi-component secondary school intervention in Bihar, India: A cluster-randomised controlled trial. *Lancet*, 392(10163), 2465–2477. DOI: 10.1016/S0140-6736(18)31615-5 PMID: 30473365

Siddiqui, S., & Schultze-Krumbholz, A. (2023). The Sohanjana Antibullying Intervention: Pilot results of peer-training module in Pakistan. *Social Sciences (Basel, Switzerland)*, 12(7), 409. Advance online publication. DOI: 10.3390/socsci12070409

Siddiqui, S., Schultze-Krumbholz, A., & Kamran, M. (2023). Sohanjana Antibullying Intervention: Culturally and socially targeted intervention for teachers in Pakistan to take actions against bullying. *European Journal of Educational Research*, 12(3), 1523–1538. DOI: 10.12973/eu-jer.12.3.1523

Singal, N. (2019). Challenges and opportunities in efforts towards inclusive education: Reflections from India. *International Journal of Inclusive Education*, 23(7-8), 827–840. DOI: 10.1080/13603116.2019.1624845

Smith, P. K., Thompson, F., Craig, W., Hong, I., Slee, P., Sullivan, K., & Green, V. A. (2016). *15 Actions to prevent bullying in western countries. School Bullying in Different Cultures: Eastern and Western Perspectives*. Cambridge University Press. DOI: 10.1017/CBO9781139410878

St. Pierre, E. (2000). Post structural feminism in education: An overview. *International Journal of Qualitative Studies in Education : QSE*, 13(5), 477–515. DOI: 10.1080/09518390050156422

Strohmeier, D., Hoffmann, C., Schiller, E.-M., Stefanek, E., & Spiel, C. (2012). ViSC Social Competence Program. *New Directions for Youth Development*, 2012(133), 71–84. DOI: 10.1002/yd.20008 PMID: 22504792

Tzani-Pepelasi, C., Ioannou, M., Synnott, J., & McDonnell, D. (2019). Peer support at schools: The buddy approach as a prevention and intervention strategy for school bullying. *International Journal of Bullying Prevention : an Official Publication of the International Bullying Prevention Association*, 1(2), 111–123. DOI: 10.1007/s42380-019-00011-z

UNICEF. (2003). *Examples of Inclusive Education in Pakistan*. The United Nations Children's Fund.

Van Geel, M., Vedder, P., & Tanilon, J. (2014). Relationship between peer victimization, cyberbullying, and suicide in children and adolescents: A meta-analysis. *JAMA Pediatrics*, 168(5), 435–442. DOI: 10.1001/jamapediatrics.2013.4143 PMID: 24615300

KEY TERMS AND DEFINITIONS

Bullying: Bullying is characterized by repeated aggressive behavior intended to inflict physical, emotional, or mental harm, often arising from a power imbalance (Burger et al., 2015). To distinguish different forms, bullying that occurs without the use of electronic or digital means is categorized as "traditional bullying." Conversely, bullying that employs technology to intentionally inflict harm is classified as "cyberbullying" (Gladden et al., 2014). School and neighborhood bullying are prime examples of traditional bullying, while cyberbullying emerges from the use of technology like the internet.

Disability: Results from the interaction between people with impairments and attitudinal and environmental barriers that hinder their full and effective participation in society on an equal basis with others (Convention on the Rights of Persons with Disabilities, 2007).

Inclusive Education: Inclusive education is conceptualized as a dynamic process that addresses the diverse needs of all learners (Kamran et al., 2023). This approach emphasizes increased participation in learning activities, cultural experiences, and school communities, while striving to minimize exclusion within and from the educational system. It necessitates adjustments and modifications to content, instructional approaches, school structures, and learning strategies. Guiding this process is a shared vision that encompasses all children within a designated age range and a firm belief that educating all students is the responsibility of the mainstream education system (Kamran & Siddiqui, 2024). The benefits of inclusion extend beyond children with special needs; it fosters a positive learning environment for all students, regardless of gender, ethnicity, individual characteristics, or socioeconomic background (National Education Policy 2017).

Learning Disability: The term "learning disability" does not reflect intellectual capacity. Rather, it signifies that students may encounter challenges across physical, educational, emotional, and environmental domains (Kamran et al., 2023). Within academic settings, students grapple with a spectrum of learning disabilities, each posing hurdles to their educational progress and development. These disabilities, encompassing various conditions, can impact the acquisition and application of skills in listening, speaking, reading, writing, critical thinking, and mathematics (Kamran & Siddiqui, 2024). Common examples include dyslexia, dysgraphia, dyscalculia, and auditory processing disorder. Despite possessing average or above-average intellectual abilities, students with learning challenges often experience difficulty with academic tasks and require specific guidance and support to flourish in their educational endeavors.

Peer Support Programs to Control Bullying: Peer training programs can be implemented within homogeneous or heterogeneous age groups. These structured learning environments leverage reciprocal knowledge and experience exchange among students. In the context of bullying prevention, peer training empowers students to actively contribute to a safe and respectful learning environment, fostering a culture of kindness and inclusion (Siddiqui & Schultze-Krumbholz, 2023).

Teachers' Professional Development to Control Aggressive Behaviors: Teacher professional development (PD) programs are grounded in the principle that educators play a pivotal role in shaping the school environment (Strohmeier et al., 2012). By equipping teachers with the necessary skills, PD programs aim to empower them to reduce student social misconduct. Research suggests that comprehensive teacher PD initiatives can effectively address behaviors that interfere with student learning. Specifically, these programs can equip educators with the skills needed to manage challenging behaviors and address issues of antisocial conduct (McKenna et al., 2015; Shinde et al., 2018).

Chapter 7
Lifting the Veil:
Exploring Bullying Towards Students With Special Needs in Inclusive Settings

Marie Gomez Goff
https://orcid.org/0009-0006-7613-615X
Southeastern Louisiana University, USA

ABSTRACT

This chapter is about bullying towards students with special needs in inclusive educational settings. By examining the various forms of bullying that these students may encounter, including physical aggression, verbal abuse, social exclusion, cyber harassment, mistreatment by teachers and staff, and the intersectionality of discrimination, this segment aims to illuminate the complexities and challenges faced by this vulnerable population. The chapter also explores the prevalence, impact, and contributing factors of bullying, emphasizing the urgent need for targeted interventions and prevention strategies. By fostering a deeper understanding of the dynamics of bullying towards students with special needs, educators, policymakers, and stakeholders can work collaboratively to create safe, inclusive environments where every student is valued, respected, and supported in their academic and social development. This chapter underscores the importance of addressing bullying in inclusive educational settings as a critical step towards promoting empathy, inclusivity, and equity for all students with special needs.

DOI: 10.4018/979-8-3693-5315-8.ch007

INTRODUCTION

In the landscape of inclusive education, where students with special needs are integrated into mainstream classrooms, the promise of diversity, acceptance, and equal opportunities shines brightly. However, this vision is shadowed by a troubling reality: the pervasive issue of bullying that plagues students with special needs within these inclusive educational settings. Bullying, in its various insidious forms, poses a significant threat to the well-being, emotional health, and academic success of these vulnerable students (Kuriakose et al., 2023). These forms of bullying not only undermine the fundamental principles of inclusivity and respect, but also perpetuate cycles of marginalization and discrimination (Anderson, 2006; Killen & Rutland, 2022).

Statistics reveal a distressing prevalence of bullying among students with special needs, highlighting the urgent need for a deeper understanding of this complex issue (Blake et al., 2012; Iqbal et al., 2021; Swearer et al., 2012). The impact of bullying on these students is profound, extending beyond the immediate emotional distress to hinder their academic engagement, social connections, and overall well-being. The scars left by bullying can endure long after the incidents themselves, shaping the self-perception and life trajectories of students with special needs (Iqbal et al., 2021; Swearer et al., 2009, Swearer et al., 2012).

To provide readers with a global understanding of bullying of students with special needs, a thorough review of the current literature was conducted. Key search terms for the literature review included: (a) bullying, (b) students with disabilities, (c) special needs, (d) bullying prevention, (e) school bullying, (f) inclusive education, (g) bullying intervention, (h) victimization, (i) peer victimization, (j) bullying experiences, (k) bullying effects, (l) bullying behaviors, (m) bullying prevalence, (n) bullying risk factors, and (o) bullying impact on academic performance. A variety of sources were utilized to gather a diverse set of literature and other important information including: (a) ERIC database, (b) PsycINFO database, (c) Proquest database, (d) national, state, and local websites, (e) journals, and (f) books.

In this chapter, we lift the veil shrouding the different forms of bullying that students with special needs face in inclusive educational settings. By shedding light on the root causes, dynamics, and consequences of bullying, we aim to empower educators, policymakers, and advocates with the knowledge and tools to combat this pervasive problem.

UNDERSTANDING BULLYING IN INCLUSIVE EDUCATIONAL SETTINGS

Establishing inclusive educational environments that foster a sense of safety and support for all students is paramount for enhancing student learning outcomes and overall well-being. The repercussions of bullying can wield a profound and detrimental influence on the educational journeys of students with special needs. Therefore, it becomes crucial to define the concept of bullying, shed light on its prevalence, clarify the various forms it can take, and thoroughly scrutinize the profound effects that bullying can have on students with special needs.

Definitions of Bullying

Bullying remains a persistent and widespread challenge that educational institutions confront on a daily basis. Traditionally, it is seen as a societal norm (Carter & Spencer, 2006; Dawkins, 1996; Wiener et al., 2013). By acknowledging and grasping these fundamental aspects, stakeholders can collaborate on crafting comprehensive approaches to effectively address bullying and foster safer, more inclusive learning environments for everyone.

Bullying manifests in both direct and indirect forms, each capable of inflicting harm on the victim. Direct bullying entails the aggressor directly confronting the victim through verbal or physical means, as described by Olweus (2023). This form of bullying encompasses actions like teasing, physical assault, threats, property damage, or coercion to compel the victim to act against their will, as delineated by the NEA (2020). Conversely, bullying can also take on an indirect guise, where aggression is executed through subtle and covert methods (Olweus, 2023). Indirect bullying involves social aggression, characterized by behaviors such as spreading rumors, ostracizing individuals, or manipulating social dynamics to undermine or harm others. Additionally, cyberbullying emerges as another form of indirect bullying, where technology is utilized to harass, intimidate, or harm individuals. This modern manifestation of bullying involves the use of digital platforms to spread harmful content, engage in online harassment, or target individuals anonymously, amplifying the reach and impact of the aggression on the victim. The diverse nature of bullying emphasizes the importance of recognizing and addressing these various forms to create safe and inclusive environments for all individuals.

Bullying directed at individuals with special needs may transcend mere peer aggression and can escalate into a more dangerous form of bullying known as disability harassment. As articulated by the U.S. Department of Education (2020), disability harassment entails "intimidation or abusive behavior towards a student based on disability that fosters a hostile environment by impeding or withholding a student's access to benefits, services, or opportunities within the institution's program" (para. 7). Disability harassment is expressly prohibited under Section 504 of the Rehabilitation Act of 1973 and Title II of the Americans with Disabilities Act (1990), underscoring the legal imperative to safeguard individuals with disabilities from discriminatory and abusive treatment.

Prevalence of Bullying Among Students with Special Needs

Within educational settings, bullying emerges as one of the most frequently reported disciplinary challenges among all students, with data from the Centers for Disease Control and Prevention (CDC, 2023) indicating that close to 14% of public schools acknowledge the occurrence of bullying on a weekly basis. Notably, reports of bullying are most prevalent in middle schools, with a striking 28% incidence rate, followed by high schools at 16% and elementary schools at 9%. These statistics underscore the pervasive nature of bullying within school environments and accentuate the urgent need for proactive measures to address and mitigate the detrimental impact of bullying on students with special needs.

Students who become targets of bullying often stand out from their peers due to perceived differences in characteristics such as weight, gender, sexual orientation, religious beliefs, and disability (Nabuzoka, 2003; NEA, 2020). Extensive research underscores that students with special needs are particularly vulnerable to bullying, facing a heightened risk compared to their peers without special needs (Christensen et al., 2012; Eilts & Koglin, 2022; Estell et al., 2009; Knox & Conti-Ramsden, 2007; Norwich & Kelly, 2004; Rose et al., 2011; Swearer et al., 2012; Van Cleave & Davis, 2006; Wiener & Mak, 2009). Various factors contribute to this increased susceptibility, including physical vulnerability, social-skill deficits, special health requirements, and challenging social environments (Card & Hodges, 2008; Carter, 2009; Fox & Boulton, 2006; Hawker & Boulton, 2000; Little, 2002). These factors collectively heighten the risk of students with special needs becoming targets of bullying.

Statistics on bullying reveal the alarming frequency and widespread nature of this behavior in educational settings. This data offers a crucial understanding of the prevalence of various forms of bullying, the demographics of individuals involved, and the repercussions for victims. According to the U.S. Department of Education (2019), bullying incidents occur approximately once every seven minutes, with one in five students reporting that they are experiencing acts of bullying on a weekly basis. A slightly higher percentage of female students (24%) compared to male students report being bullied at school. Among students who reported being bullied, 13% indicated that they were subjected to being made fun of, called names, or insulted. Additionally, 13% of bullied students reported being the target of hurtful rumors, with a higher proportion of female students (18%) experiencing this compared to male students (9%). Physical bullying was reported by 5% of students, with a greater percentage of male students (6%) than female students (4%) experiencing incidents such as being pushed, shoved, tripped, or spit on. Moreover, 5% of bullied students stated that they were purposefully excluded from activities, with a higher percentage of female students (7%) than male students (4%) reporting such incidents. Despite these alarming statistics, only 46% of students who were bullied reported the incident to an adult at school, and a concerning 41% of bullied students believe that the bullying would likely happen again. These figures underscore the need for continued efforts to address and prevent bullying in educational environments to ensure the safety and well-being of all students.

The type of disability a student has can significantly increase their vulnerability to bullying. Research has shown that individuals with conditions such as attention deficit hyperactivity disorder (ADHD), learning disabilities, and autism spectrum disorder (ASD) are at a heightened risk of being targeted by their peers for bullying. Studies have highlighted the increased likelihood of bullying for students with ADHD (Twyman et al., 2010; Unnever & Cornell, 2003; Wiener & Mak, 2009). Similarly, research by Mishna (2003) and Twyman et al. (2010) has underscored the elevated risk faced by individuals with learning disabilities. Moreover, individuals on the autism spectrum are also more prone to bullying compared to their peers without disabilities. These findings emphasize the importance of addressing bullying specifically targeting students with disabilities and implementing strategies to create inclusive and supportive environments that protect all students from harm and discrimination.

Research suggests that bullying incidents may be underreported by both students with special needs and school staff (Bradshaw et al., 2007; Frith & Hill, 2003), leading to potential underestimation of the true extent of the issue. Conversely, there are instances where bullying of students with special needs may be overestimated (Frith & Hill, 2003; Van Roekel et al., 2010). To improve the precision of data concerning bullying of students with special needs, it is crucial to establish a uniform definition and description of bullying within the educational environment. By ensuring that all students, staff members, and stakeholders share a common understanding of what constitutes bullying, a more accurate picture of the prevalence and nature of bullying targeting students with special needs can be obtained.

Forms of Bullying Towards Students With Special Needs

Bullying behaviors manifest in various ways, spanning physical, verbal, and social dimensions (Craig & Pepler, 2003; Yudin, 2019). Physical bullying may involve acts such as hitting, pushing, or damaging personal belongings, while verbal bullying encompasses insults, taunts, and derogatory remarks aimed at undermining a student's self-esteem. Social bullying can manifest through exclusion, spreading rumors, or manipulating social relationships to ostracize the targeted student. Furthermore, students with special needs are also susceptible to cyberbullying, which involves the use of digital platforms to harass, intimidate, or humiliate individuals. Disturbingly, instances of bullying by school staff members can exacerbate the challenges faced by students with special needs, perpetuating a hostile and unsupportive environment. Recognizing and addressing these diverse forms of bullying is essential to safeguarding the well-being and fostering the inclusion of students with special needs in educational settings.

Bullying by Teachers and Staff

Acts of aggression towards students with special needs are not limited to their peers; teachers and school staff can also partake in bullying directed at these students. As outlined by McEvoy (2013), bullying of students with special needs by educators and school personnel is characterized as "a repetitive pattern of behavior, driven by a power imbalance, that poses a threat, causes harm, induces humiliation, instills fear, or leads to significant emotional distress for students" (para. 3). Teachers and staff members may employ punitive measures, manipulation, or derogatory language that exceeds appropriate disciplinary actions (Twemlow & Fonagy, 2005). Further, McEvoy (2013) suggests that aggressive behaviors exhibited by educators and staff often involve humiliating students in the confines of the classroom, shielded from the oversight of other adults. Unfortunately, this type of bullying is frequently downplayed or disregarded by colleagues, normalized and rationalized by both students and staff, and may go unnoticed by external observers. Such covert and overt behaviors can profoundly impact the well-being and academic advancement of students with special needs in lasting ways.

Impact of Bullying on Students With Special Needs

Bullying that targets students with special needs often precipitates a myriad of adverse academic and emotional outcomes. It is imperative to recognize that the repercussions of bullying extend beyond the immediate targets, as bystanders can also be impacted by the negative effects of bullying, with lasting consequences that may persist into adulthood (APA, 2024; Boden et al., 2007; Cornell et al., 2013; Ellery et al., 2010; Nconsta & Shumba, 2013). Students that experience bullying are more likely to be depressed or anxious, suffer from low self-esteem, be absent a lot from school, and become suicidal (ASPA, 2021). These students are also more likely to experience headaches, stomach aches, fatigue, and poor appetite.

Students with special needs frequently encounter challenges in academic settings, experiencing diminished academic performance and an elevated risk of school dropout due to the detrimental effects of bullying. Moreover, victims of bullying among students with special needs are particularly vulnerable to a range of emotional difficulties, including depression, anxiety, sleep disturbances, changes in eating habits, disengagement from once-enjoyed activities, reduced school attendance, and compromised academic achievement (Cook et al, 2010; Espelage et al., 2012; Ferrara et al., 2019; Hong & Espelage, 2012; Rose & Espelage, 2012; Rose et al., 2011; Swearer et al., 2012; Ttofi et al., 2011; Yudin, 2019). These emotional consequences can have profound and enduring effects on the overall well-being and educational trajectories of students with special needs, underscoring the critical importance of addressing and preventing bullying in educational environments to safeguard the mental health and academic success of all students.

The statistics concerning the impact of bullying paint a troubling picture of its wide-ranging consequences. As reported by the National Center for Education Statistics (NCES, 2019), a substantial 27% of students reveal that being subjected to bullying has detrimentally altered their self-perception and self-esteem. Additionally, 14% of students report that their physical health has suffered as a result of bullying, highlighting the detrimental effects on their overall well-being. Moreover, 19% of students express that bullying has had a negative impact on their relationships with both friends and family, underscoring the social repercussions of such mistreatment. Furthermore, a concerning 19% of students attribute a decline in their academic performance to the experience of bullying, indicating the disruptive influence it has on their schoolwork and educational outcomes.

The prevalence of cyberbullying presents a significant challenge, with reports highest among middle school students, followed by high school students, and then elementary school students, as indicated by the CDC (2023). The statistics on cyberbullying paint a disturbing picture of its impact and escalation over the years.

Between 2007 and 2019, the percentages of individuals who have encountered cyberbullying more than doubled, increasing from 18% to 37%, underscoring the pervasive nature of this digital form of harassment (CDC, 2023). A staggering 69% of students who fell victim to cyberbullying reported that it had a detrimental effect on their self-esteem, highlighting the profound psychological toll of such online abuse. Additionally, 13% of students revealed that their physical health suffered as a result of cyberbullying, emphasizing the tangible health consequences associated with this form of harassment. Furthermore, 32% of students disclosed that their friendships were negatively impacted by cyberbullying, pointing to the strain it places on social relationships and support networks. In a worrying trend, 7% of students expressed that their academic performance and schoolwork were adversely affected by cyberbullying, highlighting the disruptive influence of online harassment on their educational experience. These concerning cyberbullying statistics underscore the urgent need for proactive measures to address this growing issue, safeguard the well-being of students, and foster a safe and inclusive online environment for all.

Factors Contributing to Bullying of Students with Special Needs

Bullying of students with special needs is a complex issue influenced by various factors that create a challenging environment for these vulnerable individuals. One contributor is the pervasive lack of awareness and understanding of disabilities among students and even teachers. Moreover, power dynamics within inclusive classrooms play a crucial role, as some students may exploit perceived differences to exert control and dominance over their peers. Additionally, the school climate and culture can either perpetuate or prevent bullying, depending on the values and norms upheld within the institution. Finally, inadequate support and resources for students with special needs leave them more vulnerable to bullying, as they may struggle to advocate for themselves or access the necessary assistance to address such instances effectively (Raskauskas & Modell, 2011).

Lack of Awareness and Understanding of Disabilities

A significant factor contributing to the bullying of students with special needs is the pervasive lack of awareness and understanding of disabilities within school communities. This lack of knowledge often stems from misconceptions, stereotypes, and a general ignorance about the diverse range of disabilities that exist (Ison et al., 2010; NASEM, 2016; Shigri, 2018). When students, teachers, and staff members do not have a comprehensive understanding of the challenges faced by students with special needs, it can lead to unintentional discrimination, exclusion, and even hostility towards these individuals.

In the context of bullying, this lack of awareness can manifest in various ways. Peers may mock or belittle students with special needs due to their differences without realizing the impact of their actions. Teachers may fail to intervene effectively in bullying situations involving students with disabilities because they do not fully comprehend the specific vulnerabilities or communication needs of these students (Burger et al., 2022). Furthermore, the absence of disability awareness programs and education in schools contributes to a culture where students with special needs are seen as "others" rather than valued members of the community (Ison et al., 2010; Shigri, 2018).

Power Dynamics in Inclusive Classrooms

Power dynamics within inclusive classrooms play a significant role in contributing to bullying of students with special needs. In any social setting, including schools, power imbalances can arise based on factors such as social status, perceived abilities, and popularity (Nelson et al., 2019). Students with special needs often find themselves in a position of vulnerability due to their differences, which can make them easy targets for those seeking to assert control or dominance.

In inclusive classrooms, where students with and without special needs are integrated, power dynamics can become even more pronounced. Students who perceive themselves as more "typical" or socially dominant may use their status to marginalize or mistreat their peers with special needs (Ison et al., 2010; Shigri, 2018). This can take the form of verbal or physical aggression, exclusion from social activities, or manipulation of social relationships to isolate and control students with disabilities.

Moreover, teachers and school staff may also inadvertently reinforce power imbalances by failing to address or intervene in bullying situations effectively (Burger et al., 2022). If educators do not actively promote a culture of respect and equality within the classroom, students may feel empowered to assert their dominance over their peers with special needs without fear of consequences.

Peer Influence and Social Dynamics

Peer influence and social dynamics are crucial factors that contribute significantly to the bullying of students with special needs in school settings. The social environment within a school plays a pivotal role in shaping the behaviors and attitudes of students, and peer interactions can either support or undermine the well-being of students with disabilities (Pan et al., 2020). In many cases, peer influence can perpetuate bullying behaviors towards students with special needs. Peers may model negative behaviors they observe from others, seek social approval by participating in bullying, or target individuals perceived as different to align themselves with the social group. Additionally, social dynamics within peer groups can create hierarchies that marginalize students with disabilities, leading to exclusion, ridicule, or even physical harm. Furthermore, the fear of being ostracized or bullied themselves can pressure students to conform to negative behaviors directed at their peers with special needs (Søndergaard, 2014). This creates a cycle of bullying where students may engage in harmful actions to avoid becoming targets themselves or to gain acceptance within their social circles.

School Climate and Culture

The notions of school climate and culture are pivotal in molding the general atmosphere and, ultimately, the academic achievement of students.

School climate encompasses the overall atmosphere, environment, and quality of life in a school, including safety, relationships, and academic expectations, involving the physical, emotional, and social dimensions of the school experience, as well as the perceptions and attitudes of students, staff, and parents (Mehta, 2011; Strobel Education, 2023). In contrast, school culture comprises the values, beliefs, norms, and traditions that influence the functioning of a school and guide the behavior of its members, encompassing the shared expectations and attitudes of teachers, administrators, students, and parents, along with the rituals and practices that define the school's identity (Strobel Education, 2023). While school climate and culture are interconnected, they are separate concepts that significantly impact the overall school environment and educational journey.

The school environment of a school plays a critical role in shaping the dynamics of bullying, especially concerning students with special needs. Acts of bullying can instill fear and disrespect, adversely impacting the overall school experience, norms, and relationships within the school community (OSERS, 2013, Yudin, 2019). School structures, social norms, and institutional values all contribute to either preventing or perpetuating bullying behaviors directed at students with disabilities (Pan et al., 2020; Reyes-Rodriguez et al., 2021). The notion of "school cliques" and social hierarchies can create settings where students with special needs face marginalization or exclusion due to their differences. In certain instances, specific groups may leverage their social standing to target and mistreat students with disabilities as a means of asserting dominance or preserving their position within the social hierarchy.

Additionally, the prevailing culture within a school can influence how bullying of students with special needs is perceived and addressed. Schools that prioritize inclusivity, empathy, and respect are more likely to create an environment where bullying is less tolerated and where students feel safe and supported (Reyes-Rodriguez et al., 2021; Yudin, 2019). Conversely, schools that overlook or downplay incidents of bullying, particularly towards students with disabilities, may inadvertently condone such behaviors and contribute to a culture of intolerance and exclusion.

Inadequate Support and Resources for Students with Special Needs

When students with disabilities do not receive the necessary support and accommodations to address their unique needs, they may struggle to navigate social interactions, advocate for themselves, or access help when faced with bullying situations (Berchiatti et al., 2021). This lack of support can leave students feeling isolated, powerless, and more susceptible to mistreatment by their peers.

Moreover, a scarcity of resources for students with special needs can also impact their overall well-being and social integration within the school environment. Without appropriate support services, such as counseling, individualized education plans, or assistive technology, students with disabilities may face additional challenges that make them more visible targets for bullying (Berchiatti et al., 2021). The absence of trained staff members or programs dedicated to promoting inclusivity and understanding of disabilities further exacerbates the risk of bullying for these students.

Inadequate support and resources not only affect the individual student with special needs but also contribute to a broader culture within the school that may inadvertently condone or overlook instances of bullying targeting these individuals (Pan et al., 2020; Reyes-Rodriguez et al., 2021). When schools fail to prioritize the needs of students with disabilities and provide the necessary resources to foster their academic and social development, they send a message that these students are less valued or deserving of equal protection and support.

Addressing and Preventing Bullying in Inclusive Educational Settings

After reviewing the prevalence, forms, and factors of bullying, it should be noted that bullying and the effects of bullying are preventable (NEA, 2020). Addressing and preventing bullying in inclusive educational settings necessitates a comprehensive strategy that cultivates a climate of inclusiveness, respect, and assistance for every student. All parties involved, including administrators, educators, school personnel, and students, must collectively commit to diminishing and thwarting bullying within the school environment (Rose & Monda-Amaya, 2012).

By creating a welcoming environment where diversity is celebrated, schools can lay the foundation for positive social interactions and mutual understanding among students (Rillotta & Nettlebeck, 2007; Shigri, 2018). This should entail integrating anti-bullying initiatives into school-wide programs that includes all school staff members (Bradshaw et al., 2011; Olweus, 1993; Olweus et al., 2007; Ttofi & Farrington, 2011). Robust anti-bullying policies and protocols that explicitly delineate expectations and repercussions for bullying behaviors to create a secure and respectful school climate should be enforced (Biggs et al., 2009; Stickl Haugen et al., 2019). Providing comprehensive training and support for teachers and staff equips them with the tools and knowledge needed to recognize, address, and prevent bullying effectively (Raskauskas & Modell, 2011). Developing intervention and support plans tailored to the individual needs of students can help mitigate the risk of bullying and provide targeted assistance to those who may be more vulnerable.

Encouraging peer support and advocacy empowers students to stand up against bullying, support their peers, and promote a culture of kindness and inclusion (Fox & Boulton, 2006; Robertson et al., 2003; StopBullying.gov, 2023). Promoting social and emotional learning initiatives that cultivate empathy, resilience, and positive relationship skills can further strengthen the social fabric of the school community (StopBullying.gov, 2023). Engaging parents and caregivers in bullying prevention efforts ensures a collaborative approach to creating a safe and supportive environment both at school and at home. By implementing these strategies collectively, schools can work towards creating a nurturing and inclusive environment where every student feels valued, respected, and empowered to reach their full potential. Strategies for addressing and preventing bullying in inclusive educational settings are discussed in more detail below and summarized in Table 2.

Creating a Culture of Inclusivity and Respect

Creating a culture of inclusivity and respect is foundational to fostering a supportive and safe educational environment for students with special needs. Inclusivity refers to the practice of ensuring that all individuals, regardless of their abilities, backgrounds, or differences, are welcomed, valued, and included in the school community (Kozleski & Choi, 2018). Respect, on the other hand, entails treating others with dignity, understanding, and consideration, acknowledging their unique qualities and perspectives. For students with special needs, inclusivity means providing them with equitable opportunities for learning, participation, and social interaction, while respect involves recognizing their strengths, challenges, and individuality with empathy and compassion (Schuelka et al., 2019).

A positive school culture that embraces inclusivity and respect plays a crucial role in preventing bullying among students with special needs. When students feel accepted, supported, and valued for who they are, they are less likely to engage in harmful behaviors such as bullying. A culture that celebrates diversity, promotes empathy, and upholds kindness creates a sense of belonging and community where all students can thrive academically, socially, and emotionally (Schuelka et al., 2019). In such an environment, bullying is seen as unacceptable, and students are encouraged to uphold values of tolerance, understanding, and mutual respect.

To create an inclusive and respectful environment for students with special needs, schools can implement various strategies. These may include promoting awareness and understanding of disabilities among students and staff, fostering positive peer relationships through inclusive activities and initiatives, providing opportunities for collaboration and teamwork among students of diverse abilities, and celebrating individual differences through cultural events and educational programs (Schuelka et al., 2019). Additionally, schools can establish clear expectations for behavior, actively address instances of discrimination or disrespect, and involve students in discussions and decision-making processes related to inclusivity and respect. By embedding these strategies into the fabric of the school culture, educators can cultivate a supportive and nurturing environment that empowers students with special needs to thrive and reach their full potential. These strategies are summarized in Table 1 below.

Table 1. Strategies for creating an inclusive environment for students with special needs

Strategies
● Promoting awareness and understanding of disabilities among students and staff ● Fostering positive peer relationships through inclusive activities and initiatives ● Providing opportunities for collaboration and teamwork among students of diverse abilities ● Celebrating individual differences through cultural events and educational programs ● Establish clear expectations for behavior ● Actively address instances of discrimination or disrespect ● Involve students in discussions and decision-making processes related to inclusivity and respect

Implementing Anti-Bullying Policies and Procedures

In the prevention and management of bullying incidents within school communities, school administrators hold a pivotal role. As detailed by Ward (1995), administrators bear the responsibility of formulating comprehensive policies, executing proactive measures, and endorsing anti-bullying campaigns to combat bullying effectively. Numerous states have passed laws mandating school and district policies to address bullying (Swearer et al., 2009). The Office of Special Education and Rehabilitation Services (OSERS, 2013) underscores the significance of school administrators reviewing and harmonizing their existing bullying policies and procedures with federal and state legal mandates.

School anti-bullying policies must clearly define bullying so all community members have a shared understanding (NEA, 2020). In addition to ensuring that bullying is defined, it is also suggested that the school policy should include detailed procedures for reporting and addressing incidents, and specific steps for intervention. With the prevalence of state laws addressing bullying in schools, school-level policies must also align with state legislation (Maag & Katsiyannis, 2012; PACER, 2024). To reinforce the established anti-bullying policy, administrators can actively support these policies through regular classroom visits and conducting private meetings with students on an individual basis, as needed (Biggs et al., 2009).

Implementing anti-bullying policies and procedures is a critical step in creating a safe and inclusive learning environment for students with special needs. Anti-bullying policies outline the rules, expectations, and consequences related to bullying behavior, emphasizing the school's commitment to promoting respect, empathy, and kindness among students (Raskauskas & Modell, 2011). These policies serve as a framework for preventing and addressing bullying incidents, setting clear boundaries and standards for behavior that protect all students from harm.

When tailoring anti-bullying policies for students with special needs, schools must consider the unique challenges and needs of these students to ensure their effective protection and support. This may involve providing additional resources, accommodations, or specialized interventions to address the specific vulnerabilities or communication barriers that students with special needs may face in bullying situations (Raskauskas & Modell, 2011). Moreover, anti-bullying policies for students with special needs should emphasize the importance of individualized support, collaboration with families and caregivers, and a proactive approach to preventing bullying incidents through targeted interventions and education.

Procedures for reporting and addressing bullying incidents involving students with special needs should be clear, accessible, and responsive to the unique circumstances of these students (Raskauskas & Modell, 2011). Schools should establish multiple avenues for reporting bullying, including channels for students, teachers, staff, and parents to raise concerns and seek assistance. Collaborative efforts involving educators, support staff, parents, and external resources may be necessary to address the complex needs of students with disabilities who experience bullying. By implementing tailored policies and procedures that consider the specific needs of students with special needs, schools can create a supportive and inclusive environment where all students feel valued, respected, and protected from bullying.

Providing Training and Support for Teachers, Staff, and Students

Training plays a crucial role in equipping educators, school staff, and students with the necessary knowledge, skills, and resources to recognize, prevent, and respond to bullying incidents (Raskauskas & Modell, 2011). These may include identifying the different forms of bullying, understanding the root causes and consequences of bullying behavior, learning effective communication and conflict resolution skills, promoting empathy and inclusivity, and recognizing the signs of bullying victimization or perpetration. Additionally, training should emphasize the importance of creating a supportive and nurturing environment where students feel safe, respected, and valued.

Best practices for supporting individuals involved in bullying situations include fostering a culture of open communication and trust, providing timely and appropriate interventions, and offering ongoing support to both the victim and the perpetrator (Raskauskas & Modell, 2011). Educators and staff should be trained to respond promptly to reports of bullying, conduct thorough investigations, and implement tailored intervention strategies that address the needs of all parties involved. Encouraging empathy, understanding, and accountability among students is crucial in promoting positive relationships and preventing future incidents of bullying. By providing comprehensive training and support, schools can empower their community members to work together towards building a culture of respect, empathy, and kindness that rejects bullying in all its forms.

Classroom Activities and Interventions

Incorporating classroom activities and interventions is a crucial method for preventing bullying and nurturing a positive learning environment. It is essential for students to have sufficient opportunities to acquire, practice, and reinforce age-appropriate social skills within a secure setting (Baker & Donelly, 2010). By weaving engaging and educational activities into the curriculum, teachers can proactively tackle the underlying causes of bullying behavior and instill values of empathy, kindness, and respect in students. These activities might involve role-playing various scenarios, facilitating group discussions on conflict resolution, and organizing collaborative projects that emphasize teamwork and collaboration (Rose & Monda-Amaya, 2012). Furthermore, interventions like peer mediation programs and initiatives focused on social-emotional learning can empower students to cultivate vital social skills and forge meaningful relationships grounded in mutual understanding and acceptance (Meadan & Monda-Amaya, 2008). Through the consistent implementation of these methods in classrooms, educators can establish a supportive and inclusive atmosphere that actively addresses bullying and cultivates a culture of empathy and tolerance among students.

Develop Intervention and Support Plans for Students

Developing intervention and support plans for students, especially those with special needs, is essential to address bullying and promote their well-being in the school environment. Individualized intervention plans tailored to the unique needs and circumstances of each student are crucial in providing targeted support and protection from bullying incidents (Raskauskas & Modell, 2011). These plans may include specific strategies to enhance social skills, build self-esteem, improve coping mechanisms, and foster resilience in students with special needs who are more vulnerable to bullying.

Collaborative approaches involving teachers, parents, and support staff are key components of effective intervention plans. By working together as a team, these stakeholders can share insights, coordinate efforts, and provide consistent support to the student (Raskauskas & Modell, 2011). Teachers can implement strategies in the classroom to promote a positive and inclusive atmosphere, while parents and support staff can offer additional guidance and reinforcement outside of school hours. This collaborative approach ensures a holistic and comprehensive support system for the student, addressing their needs across different settings and contexts.

Monitoring and evaluating the effectiveness of intervention plans is essential to ensure that the support provided is helping the student and preventing further instances of bullying. By collecting data, observing changes in behavior, and seeking feedback from all parties involved, educators can assess the impact of the intervention strategies and make necessary adjustments to better support the student (Raskauskas & Modell, 2011). Continuous evaluation allows for ongoing refinement of the intervention plans, ensuring that they remain relevant, effective, and responsive to the evolving needs of the student. Through individualized plans, collaboration among stakeholders, and regular monitoring and evaluation, schools can create a supportive and empowering environment that promotes the well-being and success of students with special needs.

Encouraging Peer Support and Advocacy

Encouraging peer support and advocacy among students, especially those with special needs, is crucial for creating inclusive and supportive school environments. Peer support can significantly benefit students with special needs by fostering a sense of belonging, enhancing social skills, and improving self-esteem (StopBullying.gov, 2023). When students receive support from their peers, they feel accepted and valued, which can positively impact their academic performance and overall well-being.

Peer advocacy programs play a vital role in promoting inclusivity and combating bullying in schools. By empowering students to advocate for their peers with special needs, these programs help create a culture of understanding and empathy (StopBullying.gov, 2023). Peer advocates can intervene in bullying situations, educate their peers about disabilities, and promote acceptance and respect among students. This proactive approach not only prevents bullying but also fosters a sense of community and solidarity among students.

To foster positive peer relationships, schools can implement various strategies. Encouraging collaboration through group projects and team-based activities helps students develop empathy, communication skills, and mutual respect (StopBullying.gov, 2023). Peer mentoring programs pair students with special needs with supportive peers who provide guidance and encouragement. Additionally, promoting diversity awareness and organizing disability awareness events can help educate students about different abilities and reduce stigma.

Promoting peer support and advocacy, especially for students with special needs, is essential for creating a more inclusive and compassionate school environment. By harnessing the power of peer relationships, schools can enhance the well-being of all students and foster a culture of respect, empathy, and acceptance.

Promoting Social-Emotional Learning and Empathy

Promoting social-emotional learning (SEL) and empathy is essential for supporting the holistic development of all students, including those with special needs. Social-emotional learning equips students with the necessary skills to understand and manage their emotions, build positive relationships, and make responsible decisions (Smith & Low, 2013). For students with special needs, developing these skills is particularly crucial as it can enhance their social interactions, self-awareness, and overall well-being.

Teaching empathy and emotional regulation skills is a key component of social-emotional learning for students of all abilities. By fostering empathy, students learn to understand and respect the feelings of others, leading to more compassionate and inclusive interactions (Smith & Low, 2013). Additionally, teaching emotional regulation skills helps students effectively manage their emotions, cope with stress, and navigate challenging situations. These skills are especially beneficial for students with special needs as they provide them with tools to communicate their emotions and navigate social interactions more effectively.

Incorporating social-emotional learning into the curriculum is vital for promoting the overall development of students. Schools can integrate SEL into various subjects and activities, such as through storytelling, role-playing exercises, and cooperative learning tasks (Smith & Low, 2013). Providing explicit instruction on empathy, emotional regulation, and interpersonal skills helps students practice and internalize these important skills in different contexts. By embedding social-emotional learning into the curriculum, schools can create a supportive and nurturing environment that fosters emotional intelligence, empathy, and positive social behaviors among all students, including those with special needs.

Engaging Parents and Caregivers in Bullying Prevention Efforts

Engaging parents and caregivers in bullying prevention efforts is crucial for creating a comprehensive and effective approach to combating bullying in schools. Parents and caregivers play a significant role in preventing bullying by fostering a safe and supportive home environment, teaching empathy and respect, and modeling positive behaviors for their children. By actively involving parents in bullying prevention efforts, schools can reinforce these values and promote a consistent message of kindness and inclusivity across home and school settings (PACER, 2024; Raskauskas & Modell, 2011; StopBullying.gov, 2023).

Communication strategies are key for involving parents in bullying prevention efforts. Schools can engage parents through regular communication channels such as newsletters, emails, and parent-teacher meetings to provide information about bullying prevention initiatives, resources, and strategies. Open and transparent communication allows parents to stay informed and actively participate in discussions about bullying prevention, intervention, and support for students (PACER, 2024; Raskauskas & Modell, 2011; StopBullying.gov, 2023). If an incident of bullying arises, it is imperative that schools promptly notify not only the parents of the victims but also the parents of the perpetrators. Astor et al. (2001) found that parents are often unaware of their children's involvement in bullying incidents, emphasizing the critical need for transparent communication channels between schools and families.

Collaborative approaches between schools and families are essential for creating a unified front against bullying. Schools can establish partnerships with parents and caregivers by inviting them to participate in anti-bullying workshops, training sessions, and awareness campaigns (PACER, 2024; Raskauskas & Modell, 2011; StopBullying.gov, 2023). By working together, schools and families can share resources, exchange ideas, and develop coordinated strategies to address bullying behaviors effectively. Collaborative efforts foster a sense of shared responsibility and commitment to creating a safe and inclusive school environment for all students.

Engaging parents and caregivers in bullying prevention efforts strengthens the partnership between home and school, amplifies the impact of prevention initiatives, and reinforces a culture of respect and empathy among students. By fostering collaboration and communication between schools and families, we can create a united front against bullying and promote a positive and supportive environment where all students can thrive.

Table 2. Strategies for addressing and preventing bullying in inclusive educational settings

Strategies
● Develop a comprehensive and strategic plan that supports inclusiveness, respect, and assistance for all students ● Create a welcoming environment where diversity is celebrated ● Establish anti-bullying initiatives ● Implement robust anti-bullying policies and protocols ● Provide comprehensive training and support for all teachers and staff ● Develop intervention and support plans tailored for individual students ● Encourage peer support and advocacy ● Promote social and emotional learning initiatives ● Engage parents and caregivers in bullying prevention efforts ● Create a positive school culture of inclusivity and respect

CONCLUSION

This chapter sheds light on the complexities and challenges faced by students with special needs, who are disproportionately vulnerable to various forms of bullying that can have lasting impacts on their well-being, academic performance, and overall quality of life. As we reflect on the prevalence, impact, and contributing factors of bullying towards students with special needs, it is crucial to recognize that creating a safe, supportive, and inclusive environment is not merely a goal but a moral imperative. Every student, regardless of their abilities or differences, deserves to learn and thrive in an environment that nurtures their potential, values their unique contributions, and safeguards their dignity and rights.

Moving forward, it is essential for educators to implement targeted interventions and prevention strategies that address the root causes of bullying, promote empathy, and foster a culture of respect and inclusivity. By equipping teachers, staff, students, and parents with the knowledge, skills, and resources to identify, intervene, and prevent bullying, we can cultivate a school climate where diversity is celebrated, differences are embraced, and every student feels valued and supported.

Furthermore, collaboration between schools, families, and community organizations is paramount in creating a unified front against bullying towards students with special needs. By engaging all stakeholders in dialogue, advocacy, and action, we can amplify our impact, share best practices, and work towards a collective vision of equity, justice, and empowerment for all students.

The journey towards combating bullying towards students with special needs in inclusive educational settings is ongoing and multifaceted. It requires a commitment to continuous learning, reflection, and action to dismantle barriers, challenge prejudices, and create a more inclusive and equitable educational landscape for all.

By working together with determination and compassion, we can transform the narrative of inclusivity from rhetoric to reality, ensuring that every student has the opportunity to learn, grow, and thrive in a safe and supportive environment.

REFERENCES

American Psychological Association [APA]. (2024). *Bullying*. APA. Retrieved April 22, 2024, from https://www.apa.org/topics/bullying

Americans with Disabilities Act of 1990, 42 U.S.C. § 12101 et seq. (1990).

Anderson, D. W. (2006). Inclusion and interdependence: Students with special needs in the regular classroom. *Journal of Education & Christian Belief*, 10(1), 43–59. DOI: 10.1177/205699710601000105

Assistant Secretary for Public Affairs [ASPA]. (2020). *Bullying and youth with disabilities and special health needs*. StopBullying.gov. Retrieved April 22, 2024, from https://www.stopbullying.gov/bullying/special-needs

Astor, R. A., Meyer, H. A., & Pitner, R. O. (2001). Elementary and middle school students' perceptions of safety: An examination of violence-prone school sub-context. *The Elementary School Journal*, 101, 511–528. DOI: 10.1086/499685

Baker, K., & Donelly, M. (2010). The social experiences of children with Disability and the influence of environment: A framework for intervention. *Disability & Society*, 16(1), 71–85. DOI: 10.1080/713662029

Berchiatti, M., Ferrer, A., Galiana, L., Badenes-Ribera, L., & Longobardi, C. (2021). Bullying in students with special education needs and learning difficulties: The role of the student–teacher relationship quality and students' social status in the peer group. *Child and Youth Care Forum*, 51(3), 515–537. DOI: 10.1007/s10566-021-09640-2

Biggs, M. J., Simpson, C. G., & Gaus, M. D. (2009). A case of bullying: Bringing together the disciplines. *Children & Schools*, 31(1), 39–42. DOI: 10.1093/cs/31.1.39

Blake, J. J., Lund, E. M., Zhou, Q., Kwok, O., & Benz, M. R. (2012). National prevalence rates of bully victimization among students with disabilities in the United States. *School Psychology Quarterly*, 27(4), 210–222. DOI: 10.1037/spq0000008 PMID: 23294235

Boden, J. M., Horwood, L. J., & Fergusson, D. M. (2007). Exposure to childhood sexual and physical abuse and subsequent educational achievement outcomes. *Child Abuse & Neglect*, 31(10), 1101–1114. DOI: 10.1016/j.chiabu.2007.03.022 PMID: 17996302

Bradshaw, C., Sawyer, A., & O'Brennan, L. (2007). Bullying and peer victimization at school: Perceptual differences between students and school staff. *School Psychology Review*, 36(3), 361–382. DOI: 10.1080/02796015.2007.12087929

Bradshaw, C. P., Waasdorp, T. E., O'Brennan, L. M., & Gulemetova, M. (2013). Teachers' and education support professionals' perspectives on bullying and prevention: Findings from a National Education Association Study. *School Psychology Review*, 42(3), 280–297. DOI: 10.1080/02796015.2013.12087474 PMID: 25414539

Burger, C., Strohmeier, D., & Kollerová, L. (2022). Teachers can make a difference in bullying: Effects of teacher interventions on students' adoption of bully, victim, bully-victim or defender roles across time. *Journal of Youth and Adolescence*, 51(12), 2312–2327. DOI: 10.1007/s10964-022-01674-6 PMID: 36053439

Card, N. A., & Hodges, E. V. (2008). Peer victimization among schoolchildren: Correlations, causes, consequences, and considerations in assessment and intervention. *School Psychology Quarterly*, 23(4), 451–461. DOI: 10.1037/a0012769

Carter, B., & Spencer, V. G. (2006). The fear factor: Bullying and students with disabilities. *International Journal of Special Education*, 21, 11–23.

Carter, S. (2009). Bullying of students with asperger syndrome. *Issues in Comprehensive Pediatric Nursing*, 32(3), 145–154. DOI: 10.1080/01460860903062782 PMID: 21992104

Center for Disease Control and Prevention [CDC]. (2023). *Fast facts: Preventing bullying*. CDC. Retrieved April 22, 2024 from, https://www.cdc.gov/violenceprevention/youthviolence/ bullyingresearch/fastfact.html

Christensen, L., Fraynt, R. J., Neece, C. L., & Baker, B. L. (2012). Bullying adolescents with intellectual disability. *Journal of Mental Health Research in Intellectual Disabilities*, 5(1), 49–65. DOI: 10.1080/19315864.2011.637660

Cook, C. R., Williams, K. R., Guerra, N. G., Kim, T. E., & Sadek, S. (2010). Predictors of bullying and victimization and childhood and adolescents: A meta-analytic investigation. *School Psychology Quarterly*, 25(2), 65–83. DOI: 10.1037/a0020149

Cornell, D., Gregory, A., Huang, F., & Fan, X. (2013). Perceived prevalence of teasing and bullying predicts high school dropout rates. *Journal of Educational Psychology*, 105(1), 138–149. DOI: 10.1037/a0030416

Craig, W. M., & Pepler, D. J. (2003). Identifying and targeting risk for involvement in bullying and victimization. *Canadian Journal of Psychiatry*, 48(9), 577–582. DOI: 10.1177/070674370304800903 PMID: 14631877

Dawkins, J. L. (1996). Bullying, physical disability, and the pediatric patient. *Developmental Medicine and Child Neurology*, 38(7), 603–612. DOI: 10.1111/j.1469-8749.1996.tb12125.x PMID: 8674911

Eilts, J., & Koglin, U. (2022). Bullying and victimization in students with emotional and behavioural disabilities: A systematic review and meta-analysis of prevalence rates, risk and protective factors. *Emotional & Behavioural Difficulties*, 27(2), 133–151. DOI: 10.1080/13632752.2022.2092055

Ellery, F., Kassam, N., & Bazan, C. (2010). *Prevention pays: The economic benefits of ending violence in schools*. Plan International.

Espelage, D. L., Green, H. D., & Polanin, J. (2012). Willingness to intervene in bullying episodes among middle school students: Individual and peer group influences. *The Journal of Early Adolescence*, 32(6), 776–801. Advance online publication. DOI: 10.1177/0272431611423017

Estell, D. B., Farmer, T. W., Irvin, M. J., Crowther, A., Akos, P., & Boudah, D. J. (2009). Students with exceptionalities and the peer group context of bullying and victimization in late elementary school. *Journal of Child and Family Studies*, 18(2), 136–150. DOI: 10.1007/s10826-008-9214-1

Ferrara, P., Franceschini, G., Villani, A., & Corsello, G. (2019). Physical psychological and social impact of school violence on children. *Italian Journal of Pediatrics*, 45(1), 76. DOI: 10.1186/s13052-019-0669-z PMID: 31248434

Fox, C., & Boulton, M. (2006). Friendship as a moderator of the relationship between social skills problems and peer victimization. *Aggressive Behavior*, 32(2), 110–121. DOI: 10.1002/ab.20114

Frith, U., & Hill, E. (2003). *Autism: Mind and brain*. Oxford University Press.

Hawker, D. S., & Boulton, M. J. (2000). Twenty years' research on peer victimization and psychosocial maladjustment: A meta-analytic review of cross-sectional studies. *Journal of Child Psychology and Psychiatry, and Allied Disciplines*, 41(4), 441–455. DOI: 10.1111/1469-7610.00629 PMID: 10836674

Hong, J. S., & Espelage, D. L. (2012). A review of research on bullying and peer victimization in school: An ecological system analysis. *Aggression and Violent Behavior*, 17(4), 311–322. DOI: 10.1016/j.avb.2012.03.003

Iqbal, F., Senin, M. S., Nordin, M. N. B., & Hasyim, M. (2021). A qualitative study: Impact of bullying on children with special needs. *Linguistica Antverpiensia*, 2, 1639–1643. DOI: 10.14264/294169

Ison, N., McIntyre, S., Rothery, S., Smithers-Sheedy, H., Goldsmith, S., Parsonage, S., & Foy, L. (2010). 'just like you': A disability awareness programme for children that enhanced knowledge, attitudes and acceptance: Pilot study findings. *Developmental Neurorehabilitation*, 13(5), 360–368. DOI: 10.3109/17518423.2010.496764 PMID: 20828333

Killen, M., & Rutland, A. (2022). Promoting fair and just school environments: Developing inclusive youth. *Policy Insights from the Behavioral and Brain Sciences*, 9(1), 81–89. DOI: 10.1177/23727322211073795 PMID: 35402700

Knox, E., & Conti-Ramsden, G. (2007). Bullying in young people with a history of specific language impairment (SLI). *Educational and Child Psychology*, 24(4), 130–141. DOI: 10.53841/bpsecp.2007.24.4.130

Kozleski, E. B., & Choi, J. H. (2018). Leadership for equity and inclusivity in schools: The cultural work of inclusive schools. *Inclusion (Washington, D.C.)*, 6(1), 33–34. DOI: 10.1352/2326-6988-6.1.33

Kuriakose, V., Bishwas, S. K., & Mohandas, N. P. (2023). Does bullying among students hamper their well-being? Roles of helplessness and psychological capital. *International Journal of Educational Management*, 37(5), 1104–1123. DOI: 10.1108/IJEM-10-2022-0437

Little, L. (2002). Middle-class mothers' perceptions of peer and sibling victimization among children with asperger's syndrome and nonverbal learning disorders. *Issues in Comprehensive Pediatric Nursing*, 25(1), 43–57. DOI: 10.1080/014608602753504847 PMID: 11934121

Maag, J. W., & Katsiyannis, A. (2012). Bullying and students with disabilities: Legal and practice considerations. *Behavioral Disorders*, 37(2), 78–86. DOI: 10.1177/019874291203700202

McEvoy, A. (2013). *Abuse of Power.* Learning for Justice. Retrieved April 22, 2024 from, https://www.learningforjustice.org/magazine/fall-2014/abuse-of-power

Meadan, H., & Monda-Amaya, L. (2008). Collaboration to promote social competence for students with mild disabilities in the general classroom: A structure for providing social support. *Intervention in School and Clinic*, 43(3), 158–167. DOI: 10.1177/1053451207311617

Mehta, S. B. (2011). *School climate and the assessment of bullying* (Order No. 3501727). Available from ProQuest Dissertations & Theses Global. (929145544). Retrieved April 22, 2024 from, https://www.proquest.com/dissertations-theses/school-climate-assessment-bullying/docview/929145544/se-2

Mishna, F. (2003). Learning disabilities and bullying: Double jeopardy. *Journal of Learning Disabilities*, 36(4), 1–15. DOI: 10.1177/00222194030360040501 PMID: 15490906

Nabuzoka, D. (2003). Teacher ratings and peer nominations of bullying and other behavior of children with and without learning disabilities. *Educational Psychology*, 23(3), 307–321. DOI: 10.1080/0144341032000060147

National Academies of Science, Engineering, and Medicine. (2016). *Preventing bullying through science, policy, and practice*. National Academies Press. Retrieved April 22, 2024 from, https://www.sciencedirect.com.proxy.library.nyu.edu/science/article/pii/S0273229717300138?via%3Dihub#b0440

National Center for Educational Statistics [NCES] (2019). The Condition of Education 2019. NCES 2019-144. *National Center for Education Statistics*.

National Education Association. (2020). *How to identify bullying*. NEA. Retrieved April 22,2024 from https://www.nea.org/professional-excellence/student-engagement/tools-tips/how-identify-bullying

Ncontsa, V. N., & Shumba, A. (2013). The nature, causes and effects of school violence in South African high schools. *South African Journal of Education*, 33(3), 15. DOI: 10.15700/201503070802

Nelson, H. J., Burns, S. K., Kendall, G. E., & Schonert-Reichl, K. A. (2019). Preadolescent children's perception of power imbalance in bullying: A thematic analysis. *PLoS One*, 14(3), e0211124. Advance online publication. DOI: 10.1371/journal.pone.0211124 PMID: 30849078

Norwich, B., & Kelly, N. (2004). Pupils' views on inclusion: Moderate learning difficulties and bullying in mainstream and special schools. *British Educational Research Journal*, 30(1), 43–65. DOI: 10.1080/01411920310001629965

Office of Special Education and Rehabilitation Services [OSERS]. (2013). *OSERS August 20, 2013 dear colleague letter to educators*. United State Department of Education [USDOE]. Retrieved April 22, 2024 from, https://sites.ed.gov/idea/files/bullyingdcl-8-20-13.pdf

Olweus, D. (1993). *Bullying at school: What we know and what we can do*. Blackwell Publishing.

Olweus, D. (2023). *Olweus bullying prevention program*. Olweus bullying prevention program, Clemson University. Retrieved April 22, 2024 from, https://olweus.sites.clemson.edu/olweusinfo.php

Olweus, D., Limber, S. P., Flerx, V. C., Mullin, N., Riese, J., & Snyder, M. (2007). *Olweus bullying prevention program: Schoolwide guide.* Hanzelden., DOI: 10.15700/201503070802

PACER National Bullying Prevention Center. (2024). *What is bullying?* PACER. Retrieved April 22, 2024 from, https://www.pacerkidsagainstbullying.org/what-is-bullying/

Pan, B., Zhang, L., Ji, L., Garandeau, C. F., Salmivalli, C., & Zhang, W. (2020). Classroom status hierarchy moderates the association between social dominance goals and bullying behavior in middle childhood and early adolescence. *Journal of Youth and Adolescence,* 49(11), 2285–2297. DOI: 10.1007/s10964-020-01285-z PMID: 32661845

Raskauskas, J., & Modell, S. (2011). Modifying anti-bullying programs to include students with disabilities. *Teaching Exceptional Children,* 44(1), 60–67. DOI: 10.1177/004005991104400107

Reyes-Rodríguez, A. C., Valdés-Cuervo, A. A., Vera-Noriega, J. A., & Parra-Pérez, L. G. (2021). Principal's practices and school's collective efficacy to preventing bullying: The mediating role of school climate. *SAGE Open,* 11(4), 215824402110525. DOI: 10.1177/21582440211052551

Rillotta, F., & Nettlebeck, T. (2007). Effects of an awareness program on attitudes of students without an intellectual disability towards persons with an intellectual disability. *Journal of Intellectual & Developmental Disability,* 32(1), 19–27. DOI: 10.1080/13668250701194042 PMID: 17365364

Robertson, K., Chamberlain, B., & Kasari, C. (2003). General education teachers' relationships with included students with special educational autism. *Journal of Autism and Developmental Disorders,* 33(2), 123–130. DOI: 10.1023/A:1022979108096 PMID: 12757351

Rose, C. A., & Espelage, D. L. (2012). Risk and protective factors associated with the bullying involvement of students with emotional and behavioral disorders. *Behavioral Disorders,* 37(3), 133–148. DOI: 10.1177/019874291203700302

Rose, C. A., Espelage, D. L., Aragon, S. R., & Elliot, J. (2011). Bullying and victimization among students and special education in general education curriculum. *Exceptionality Education International,* 21(3), 2–14. DOI: 10.5206/eei.v21i3.7679

Rose, C. A., Espelage, D. L., & Monda-Amaya, L. E. (2009). Bullying and victimization rates among students in general and special education: A comparative analysis. *Educational Psychology,* 29(7), 761–776. DOI: 10.1080/01443410903254864

Rose, C. A., & Monda-Amaya, L. E. (2012). Bullying and victimization among students with disabilities: Effective strategies for classroom teachers. *Intervention in School and Clinic*, 48(2), 99–107. DOI: 10.1177/1053451211430119

Schuelka, M. J., Johnstone, C. J., Thomas, G., & Artiles, A. J. (2019). *The sage handbook of inclusion and diversity in education*. Sage Publications. DOI: 10.4135/9781526470430

Section 504 of the Rehabilitation Act of 1973, 29 U.S.C § 794 et seq. (1973).

Shigri, N. (2018). *The importance of disability awareness: Home and school*. Medium. Retrieved April 22, 2024 from, https://medium.com/arise-impact/the-importance-of-disability-awareness-home-and-school-eead2276f349

Smith, B. H., & Low, S. (2013). The role of social-emotional learning in bullying prevention efforts. *Theory into Practice*, 52(4), 280–287. DOI: 10.1080/00405841.2013.829731

Søndergaard, D. M. (2014). Social exclusion anxiety: Bullying and the forces that contribute to bullying amongst children at school. *School Bullying*, 47–80. DOI: 10.1017/CBO9781139226707.005

Stickl Haugen, J., Sutter, C. C., Tinstman Jones, J. L., & Campbell, L. O. (2019). School district anti-bullying policies: A state-wide content analysis. *International Journal of Bullying Prevention : an Official Publication of the International Bullying Prevention Association*, 2(4), 309–323. DOI: 10.1007/s42380-019-00055-1

StopBullying.gov. (2023). *Bullying and youth with disabilities and special health needs*. StopBullying.gov. Retrieved April 22, 2024 from, https://www.stopbullying.gov/bullying/special-needs

Strobel Education. (2024). *Climate culture in schools: Understanding the difference*. Retrieved April 22, 2024 from, https://strobeleducation.com/blog/climate-culture-in-schools-understanding-the- difference/

Swearer, S. M., Espelage, D. L., & Napolitano, S. A. (2009). *Bullying prevention and intervention: Realistic strategies for schools*. Guilford.

Swearer, S. M., Wang, C., Maag, J. W., Siebecker, A. B., & Frerichs, L. J. (2012). Understanding the bullying dynamic among students in special and general education. *Journal of School Psychology*, 50(4), 503–520. DOI: 10.1016/j.jsp.2012.04.001 PMID: 22710018

Ttofi, M. M., Farrington, D. P., Losel, F., & Loeber, R. (2011). Do the victims of school bullies tend to become depressed later in life? A systematic review and meta-analysis of longitudinal studies. *Journal of Aggression, Conflict and Peace Research*, 3(2), 63–73. DOI: 10.1108/17596591111132873

Twemlow, S. W., & Fonagy, P. (2005). The prevalence of teachers who bully students in schools with differing levels of behavior problems. *The American Journal of Psychiatry*, 16(12), 2387–2389. DOI: 10.1176/appi.ajp.162.12.2387 PMID: 16330608

Twyman, K. A., Saylor, C. F., Saia, D., Macias, M. M., Taylor, L. A., & Spratt, E. (2010). Bullying and ostracism experiences in children with special health care needs. *Journal of Developmental and Behavioral Pediatrics*, 31(1), 1–8. DOI: 10.1097/DBP.0b013e3181c828c8 PMID: 20081430

Unnever, J. D., & Cornell, D. G. (2003). Bullying, self-control, and ADHD. *Journal of Interpersonal Violence*, 18(2), 129–147. DOI: 10.1177/0886260502238731

U.S. Department of Education [USDOE]. (2019). Student reports of bullying results from the 2017 school crime supplement to the national crime victimization survey. National Center for Educational Statistics [NCES]. Retrieved April 22, 2024, from https://nces.ed.gov/pubs2019/2019054.pdf

U.S. Department of Education [USDOE]. (2020). *Dear colleague letter regarding disability harassment*. Office of Civil Rights [OCR]. Retrieved April 22, 2024, from https://www2.ed.gov/about/offices/list/ocr/docs/disabharassltr.html

Van Cleave, J., & Davis, M. (2006). Bullying and peer victimization among children with special health care needs. *Pediatrics*, 118(4), 1212–1219. DOI: 10.1542/peds.2005-3034 PMID: 17015509

Van Roekel, E., Scholte, R., & Didden, R. (2010). Bullying among adolescents with autism spectrum disorders: Prevalence and perception. *Journal of Autism and Developmental Disorders*, 40(1), 63–73. DOI: 10.1007/s10803-009-0832-2 PMID: 19669402

Ward, B. R. (1995). The school's role in the prevention of youth suicide. *Social Work in Education*, 17(2), 92–100. DOI: 10.1093/cs/17.2.92

Wiener, J., & Mak, M. (2009). Peer victimization in children with attention-deficit/hyperactivity disorder. *Psychology in the Schools*, 46(2), 116–131. DOI: 10.1002/pits.20358

Wiener, M. T., Day, S. J., & Galvan, D. (2013). Deaf and hard of hearing students' perspective on bullying and school climate. *American Annals of the Deaf*, 158(3), 324–343. DOI: 10.1353/aad.2013.0029

Yudin, B. M. (2019). *Keeping students with disabilities safe from bullying.* Stop-Bullying.gov. Retrieved April 22, 2024, from https://www.stopbullying.gov/blog/2013/08/23/keeping-students-disabilities-safe- bullying

KEY TERMS AND DEFINITIONS

Disability Harassment: A form of repeated aggressive behavior towards an individual on the sole basis of their disability which can include creating a hostile environment and/or withholding services or opportunities.

Chapter 8
Peer Bullying of Inclusion Students:
Understanding Prevention and Intervention Strategies

Sahin Cincioglu
https://orcid.org/0009-0005-7566-3348
Trakya University, Turkey

ABSTRACT

Students in inclusive education settings are at greater risk of being bullied because of their special needs. Bullying can manifest itself in harmful behaviors that negatively impact these students socially, emotionally, or physically. At the heart of peer bullying is a power imbalance, and research shows that students with special needs are more likely to be bullied than their peers without disabilities. To address this, a comprehensive strategy involving all stakeholders is essential to understand, prevent, and respond to bullying of students in inclusive settings. Recognizing the signs and effects of peer bullying on these students is critical. To effectively prevent bullying, schools must implement programs that promote tolerance and empathy and ensure a safe, inclusive environment for all students.

INTRODUCTION

Peer bullying is defined as a set of actions involving psychological, physical, or verbal aggression and underlying repetitive behaviors that result from an imbalance of power (Rose et al., 2009). Peer bullying refers to a behavioral dimension that is prevalent to a degree that exceeds the expectations of teachers and parents, especially in school environments. Peer bullying refers to an aggression that arises

DOI: 10.4018/979-8-3693-5315-8.ch008

from a certain power imbalance and is repeatedly applied to the victims. It takes place regardless of gender, language, religion, race and culture, and is based on maintaining a hegemony over the victim who is socially, emotionally and physically harmed (Ramirez, 2017).

Peer bullying refers to a negative situation that people may encounter in interpersonal relationships not only today, but also since the earliest periods of human existence. Although peer bullying has a very ancient history, it is thought-provoking that there is no fully accepted definition of peer bullying, despite the fact that it can occur in any environment, country, and culture where people are present. This situation shows that peer bullying has a complex structure that includes abstract situations (Houchins et al., 2016; Olweus, 1995).

When we examine the definitions of peer bullying, there is a consensus that bullying behaviors should include three elements; 1- Bullying behavior is not a behavior that occurs in one situation, it must be repeated in different situations and therefore covers a period of time, 2- There is an imbalance of power between the bully and the victim in different areas, 3- The bullying behavior is psychological, verbal or physical and as a result of this behavior the bully has nothing to gain other than satisfaction (Olweus, 1995).

Many countries around the world, such as America, England, Spain, Turkey, China, and Australia, suffer from peer bullying in the school environment and the situation is reflected in various studies (Bourke & Burgman, 2010; Cincioğlu & Ergin, 2023a; Li et al., 2017; Ramirez, 2017). It has been found that approximately 30% of adolescents in the United States are victims of bullying (Sabramani et al., 2021). However, the fact that this rate exceeds 50% due to peer bullying against students with special needs calls for urgent action in this regard (Rose et al., 2010). Bakker and Bossman (2003) found that students with learning disabilities are exposed to peer bullying more often and more frequently than their typically developing peers. Svetaz et al. (2000) collected data from the National Longitudinal Studies of Adolescent Health using a sample of more than 20,000 students in the United States and found that students with learning disabilities in inclusive education were exposed to more violent behavior than typically developing students. Luciano & Savage (2007) found in their study that 40% of students with learning disabilities are regularly exposed to peer bullying compared to 25% of general education students. They also found that 60% of students with learning disabilities were exposed to verbal bullying, 35% were exposed to physical bullying, and 25% were exposed to social bullying.

Inclusive education refers to the least restrictive environment that contributes to the development of students with special needs in areas such as academic success, socialization, and self-confidence, where students with special needs are educated together with students without special needs. Typically developing students in general education classrooms and students with special needs benefit from supportive educational services provided in special education settings (Dölek, 2002; Olweus, 1995). However, students with special needs are at higher risk for peer bullying due to their special needs (Chan et al., 2018; Savage, 2005; Saylor & Leach, 2009; Özdemir, 2020; Van Cleave & Davis, 2006; Woods & Wolke, 2004; Yong et al., 2011).

Students from inclusive educational settings become targets of peer bullying because they have limited defense mechanisms due to their special needs and difficulties in social and adaptive skills (Cincioğlu, 2023). Students who are bullied may experience physical symptoms such as unexplained wounds, bruises, persistent headaches, or abdominal pain (Mynard et al., 2000). Students with special needs may also experience emotional symptoms such as anxiety, depression, low self-esteem, constant worrying, and not wanting to go to school. In addition, behaviors of students with special needs such as truancy, declining course grades, social withdrawal, sleep disturbances, and extreme irritability may also be signs that they are being bullied by peers (Çetinkaya et al., 2009; Fleming & Jacobsen, 2009; Konishi et al., 2010; Mynard et al., 2000; Sabuncuoğlu et al., 2006).

Peer bullying is a serious issue that creates problems in educational settings. When a student is bullied, it can have traumatic consequences and negatively impact the learning experience (Humphrey et al., 2013). Because inclusive education is a model that brings together students with different abilities, there are studies that show that peer bullying occurs more because of the differences between these students and that inclusive students are more likely to be victims (Ball et al., 2021; Bourke & Burgman, 2010; Chan et al., 2018; Rose et al., 2010).

In this chapter, we will focus on understanding, prevention, and intervention strategies for peer bullying for students with special needs in an inclusive setting.

Purpose of the Research

The aim of our research is to provide a comprehensive and detailed analysis of the most commonly used peer bullying prevention and intervention programs, with a particular focus on their integration into inclusive education and an examination of their basic components. The study undertook a review of peer bullying prevention and intervention programmes for inclusion students. It aimed to reflect the most widely used prevention and intervention programmes worldwide and to provide insight into the nature of peer bullying towards students with special needs receiving inclusive education, taking into account demographic variables within certain bases.

Research Gap

Recent research highlights the growing attention to the issue of bullying among children with special needs, which only began to receive scholarly attention in 2003. While studies on this topic have increased in recent years, they remain inadequate in both scope and depth. In particular, there is a significant disparity in the quantity and quality of research on peer bullying among students with special needs compared to typically developing students. A major limitation of existing studies is the paucity of evidence-based research and the fact that most implemented programs lack rigorous experimental evaluation. Despite these shortcomings, evidence suggests that students with special needs can be effectively protected from peer bullying in inclusive educational settings. This chapter reviews peer-based anti-bullying interventions to prevent bullying of children with special needs and provides a guide for further research.

Research Questions

This chapter addresses the following questions

- What are the basic components of peer bullying prevention and intervention programs for students in inclusive schools?
- What are the demographic characteristics of peer bullying among students with special needs?
- What peer bullying prevention and intervention programs are commonly used around the world?
- What studies have been conducted on peer bullying prevention and intervention for students with special needs?

THE EFFECTS OF PEER BULLYING ON STUDENTS WITH SPECIAL NEEDS

Studies conducted in different countries have shown that children exposed to peer bullying experience severe effects of bullying such as suicidal tendencies, school massacres, depression, introversion, and decreased academic success (Diamanduros et al., 2008; Gökler, 2009; Karataş, 2011; Ramirez, 2017; Rigby, 2002). Students who are bullied by their peers may experience negative outcomes such as low self-esteem, depression, emotional withdrawal, and anxiety (Lebrun-Harris et al., 2019).

Children exposed to bullying during the school years are not only negatively affected temporarily, but the effects continue for many years (Halliday, 2021; Ramirez, 2017).

Peer bullying can have traumatic and devastating effects on all students. However, inclusive students with special needs are more vulnerable to bullying incidents (Luciano & Savage, 2007). These students may feel the effects of bullying more deeply because they demonstrate a lack of coping skills to deal with bullying incidents. These challenges and limitations faced by students with special needs can lead to a power imbalance between them and typically developing students due to the unique requirements of these children (Cincioğlu & Ergin, 2023b; Rose et al., 2009).

Students in inclusive settings often have difficulty communicating and interacting socially in the school environment. Conditions such as learning disabilities, autism spectrum disorder, attention deficit hyperactivity disorder, and other neurodevelopmental disorders can make it difficult for these students to adapt to the social environment and behave appropriately (Horisna, 2022). In their study, Rose & Espelage (2012) identified the disability group and bullying rate of students with special needs and found that 35.3% of students who were bullied were students with behavioral and emotional disorders, 33% were students with autism spectrum disorders, 24.3% were students with intellectual disabilities, and 20.8% were students with health disorders. In addition, it was found that 19% of students with learning disabilities faced high levels of bullying victimization. Iyanda (2022) found similar results in her study and further elaborated that due to their lack of social skills, these students may be prevented from forming healthy relationships with their peers and participating in group activities. These students, who are socially different from their peers, may feel excluded and isolated when they are ostracized by other students and have problems with peer acceptance and therefore avoid social interactions (Hajdukova et al., 2015). Students with special needs may feel inadequate and worthless if they feel they are constantly being ridiculed or criticized. The low self-esteem experienced by inclusive students can negatively affect these students socially and academically (Halliday, 2021; Rose et al., 2015). Students with intellectual disabilities may be vulnerable to bullying because of their cognitive difficulties. Students with intellectual disabilities are at risk for exposure to verbal and social bullying behaviors because they lag behind their peers in understanding social cues and academic skills. Frederickson et al. (2007) found that students with intellectual disabilities are at risk of being bullied by their peers due to difficulties with social skills. In addition, the decrease in inclusive students' overall quality of life due to anxiety and depression can reduce their participation in school activities (Cook & Friend, 2010; Lebrun-Harris et al., 2019; Rose et al., 2015). Such emotional problems can limit the social and academic abilities of inclusive students now and in the years to come.

Inclusive education students may experience bullying that negatively affects their academic performance. Inclusive students who are bullied may have difficulty concentrating in class (Konishi et al., 2010). They may be absent because they are afraid to go to school and may even consider dropping out. This can lead to lower grades in their courses and cause them to fail academically (Gottfried & Kirksey, 2017). When inclusive students who are bullied by their peers avoid or run away from school, they miss out on the socialization opportunities that inclusive education provides. This deprivation hinders their acquisition of social skills and access to supportive educational services (Kamran & Siddiqui, 2024). Studies have shown that students with attention deficit hyperactivity disorder, intellectual disabilities, or other developmental delays are 1.5 times more likely to be absent from school than typical students (Black & Zablotsky, 2018; Cincioğlu, 2023; Theobald et al., 2017; U.S. Department of Education, 2016). Luciano and Savage (2007) conducted a study in Montreal, Canada and found that 55% of students with learning disabilities who were exposed to bullying experienced a significant decrease in their academic performance, 40% of these students had problems with absenteeism, and 20% were at risk of dropping out of school. The physical bullying they may face can cause injuries to students and lead to chronic health problems if the physical violence continues (Malecki et al., 2020). These negative symptoms can limit students' ability to participate in daily school activities and reduce their overall quality of life. (Karatas & Ozturk, 2011). Several studies have found that students with learning disabilities experience significantly more academic anxiety than students without disabilities (Grills-Taquechel et al., 2012; Nelson & Harwood, 2012; Swanson & Howell, 1996). Students with learning disabilities are at a greater disadvantage because anxiety negatively affects working memory and academic performance (Owens et al., 2012). Students with learning disabilities often have memory problems, and higher rates of anxiety may exacerbate memory problems (Owens et al., 2012).

Peer bullying can have serious and long-term negative effects on students in inclusive settings. Students with special needs, who face a variety of physical, emotional, social, and academic challenges, are more vulnerable to peer bullying and therefore at risk. It is important to address the needs of inclusion students in order to prevent and intervene in peer bullying. This requires addressing the situation with comprehensive and holistic approaches. When educators, families, and students work together, it is possible to reduce bullying behaviors and provide a safe and supportive learning environment for inclusion students. For peer bullying programs, all stakeholders must take the necessary steps to create an educational environment where inclusion students can reach their full potential.

KEY COMPONENTS OF PEER BULLYING PREVENTION PROGRAMS

To prevent peer bullying for students with special needs in the school environment, awareness and training programs for students, teachers, and parents should provide information about the definition and symptoms of peer bullying and how to deal with peer bullying (Kamran & Siddiqui, 2024; Windsor et al., 2022). In addition to raising awareness among families and school staff through these programs, awareness and education programs play a critical role in protecting students, reporting peer bullying, and coping with bullying, as students with special needs may find it difficult to defend themselves when bullied. It is very important for teachers to be aware of peer bullying and its underlying factors. The fact that teachers recognize the individual characteristics of students with special needs and have information about the students' special needs can prevent possible bullying incidents (Dölek, 2002; Evans et al., 2014; Karataş, 2011; Saylor & Leach, 2009).

Teachers should create a positive climate in their classrooms. When the difficulties that students with special needs may experience with socialization and play skills are addressed with the methods and strategies that teachers use, significant gains can be made in both classroom management and the prevention of bullying incidents (Lindsay & McPherson, 2012).

It is critical that students receive comprehensive training on special needs within a structured program. In addition, they should be informed about who to contact if they are bullied in order to prevent peer bullying (Bourke & Burgman, 2010; Wood & Orpinas, 2020). Providing all of this training, especially to students with special needs, within a program can ensure that the student with special needs is not bullied or that the period of victimization is shortened. In addition to providing comprehensive training to students to protect them from being victimized by bullying, it is also important for teachers to explain the characteristics of these students to typically developing students in the classroom during the time when the students are not in the classroom, to explain the behaviors they may or may not exhibit depending on the need group and level, and to explain the reasons for this in order to understand and recognize the special needs of the students in the classroom. An aware and conscious classroom environment can act as a shield for the prevention of peer bullying incidents for students with special needs (Cincioğlu & Ergin, 2023b; Saylor & Leach, 2009).

Empathy training provided to typically developing students in the classroom environment can lead students with special needs to understand the negative effects of bullying and avoid bullying behaviors. Students in an empathetic environment may be more willing and cooperative in supporting their bullied friends. Empathy training provided to students contributes to the prevention of bullying by developing their emotional intelligence (Boske & Osanloo, 2015).

Families can play an important role in addressing bullying and reducing its impact. If families can provide an environment where they can empathize with their children at home, peer bullying of students with special needs can be prevented (Lösel & Farrington, 2012; Shaheen et al., 2019). The home environment, where students spend a significant amount of time outside of school, can play an important role in preventing peer bullying. Parents should work closely with teachers and school administrators to prevent their children from engaging in bullying behavior. Parents should know the signs of bullying, recognize when their child is being bullied, and report the situation to the teacher and school administration. In order to prevent peer bullying, training programs that raise awareness about peer bullying, students with special needs, and empathy, as well as training programs that raise family awareness about peer bullying, can play an important role in this regard.

As a result, awareness and empathy training programs aimed at preventing peer bullying for students with special needs are very important to ensure that these students in inclusive education receive an education in a supportive and safe learning environment. These programs can address bullying behaviors and increase students' social and academic success. Collaboration among students, teachers, school administrators, and families can play a critical role in preventing bullying. Teachers and school staff need to be trained to intervene quickly and effectively in cases of bullying against students with special needs. In addition, teachers and school administrators should be supported and counseling services should be provided to enhance the ability of inclusive students to cope with bullying.

BULLYING PATTERNS IN INCLUSION STUDENTS: A DEMOGRAPHIC PERSPECTIVE

Students' exposure to peer bullying may vary depending on their demographic characteristics. Demographic variables may include characteristics such as gender, age, socioeconomic status, ethnicity, and family structure.

The Influence of Age on Peer Bullying Incidents Involving Inclusion Students

Students with special needs may be at risk for peer bullying at certain ages. Students with special needs who are educated at the elementary level may become targets for peer bullying because they are in the process of developing their social skills. The reports received indicate that bullying of younger children is more prevalent, and that the incidence of bullying decreases but the severity increases as the victims age from 8 to 16 years (Fox & Boulton, 2005; McNicholas et al., 2017; Winters et al., 2018).

The Influence of Gender on Peer Bullying Incidents Involving Inclusion Students

Gender is an important variable in relation to peer bullying victimization. In terms of peer bullying, female students are generally more exposed to verbal and emotional bullying, while male students are more exposed to physical bullying (Iyanda, 2022; Malecki et al., 2020). Female students with special needs may be at a double disadvantage when it comes to peer bullying. While they may be targets of bullying because of their social skills, they may also be exposed to forms of social and emotional bullying because of their gender. In general, male students with special needs are more likely to be physically bullied. Regardless of the type of bullying students experience, their quality of life is significantly impacted (Rose et al., 2009).

The Influence of Ethnic Origin on Peer Bullying Incidents Involving Inclusion Students

Students' ethnicity may also play an important role in peer bullying. Students who are minorities in terms of ethnic groups may be exposed to peer bullying more than the majority groups (Blake et al., 2016). According to the researches, it has been found that ethnic discrimination, exclusion and bullying events are associated with prejudice. Students with special needs of immigrant origin may be at risk of peer bullying due to their special requirements, in addition to the bidirectional disadvantage of being bullied due to their ethnic origin (Bromand, 2012). The impact of ethnicity on peer bullying may be further complicated by language barriers and cultural differences (Basilici et al., 2022). Inclusive students may be exposed to exclusion and discrimination because of their ethnicity, which may lead them to experience more bullying incidents in the school and social settings they enter. In addition, the fact that integrated students' social support networks may be weak due to their ethnic origin is likely to create barriers to the development of their coping skills with bullying (Chan et al., 2018).

The Influence of Social Economic Status on Peer Bullying Incidents Involving Inclusion Students

Students' socioeconomic status is an important determinant of bullying experiences. Students with low socioeconomic status may experience more peer bullying than students with higher socioeconomic status (Çetinkaya et al., 2009; Malecki et al., 2020). This may be due to factors such as lack of social support, financial deprivation, and low family educational status. Among inclusive students, those with low socioeconomic status are at significant risk of being bullied. The financial deprivation of special needs students with low socioeconomic status may prevent students from benefiting from special education services. In addition, families may face various disadvantages in meeting their children's needs and accessing support and resources to address bullying. This may limit inclusion students' ability to cope with peer bullying and make them more vulnerable (Fleming & Jacobsen, 2009; Laftman et al., 2017).

The Influence of Family Structure on Peer Bullying Incidents Involving Inclusion Students

Family structure is an important variable that affects students' exposure to bullying incidents. Students growing up in single-parent families may be bullied more than their peers in two-parent families. This may be due to stress and lack of social support in the family. Among students with special needs, those who grow up in single-parent families are also at higher risk (Laftman et al., 2017). Students with special needs who grow up in single-parent families may not receive adequate attention and care from their parents, and may also have difficulty meeting their needs. As a result, inclusion students may not be able to adjust emotionally to the school environment, may have difficulty concentrating, and may have limited ability to cope with bullying (Erdoğan et al., 2023; Wu et al., 2023).

The Influence of School Climate and Environment on Peer Bullying Incidents Involving Inclusion Students

The school environment plays an important role in the bullying experiences of inclusion students with special needs. A supportive and inclusive school environment, one of the most important characteristics of the least restrictive environment for the inclusion student, can reduce the incidents of peer bullying of students with special needs and help them improve their coping skills in the process.

In a school climate that is positive for the inclusion student, teachers and school staff must be sensitive to the needs of the inclusion student and provide appropriate support services for these students. It is also critical that positive school climate policies are designed to prevent and address peer bullying and focus on ensuring the safety of all students in the school. Friendships and positive relationships are very important in ensuring a positive school climate (Gage & Larson, 2014). Ensuring tolerance and empathy among students makes it easier for students with special needs to adjust to school and can reduce peer bullying behavior toward inclusive students (Bourke & Burgman, 2010; Savage, 2005).

The Influence of Type of Disability on Peer Bullying Incidents Involving Inclusion Students

A learning disability is a group of impairments in reading, writing, speaking, reasoning, listening, or mathematical processing that are believed to be caused by impaired functioning of an individual's central nervous system (American Psychiatric Association 2000). Although these disabilities are not caused by mental retardation, sensory impairment, cultural differences, or inadequate education, they may occur with these conditions. Students with learning disabilities may often need help from peers or teachers with tasks that their peers can usually perform in a school setting (Kuhne & Wiener 2000). In addition, students with learning disabilities may be separated from their classmates during the day, or they may be learning in a completely different environment. These situations can place the student with learning disabilities in a different and vulnerable situation. This, in turn, can lead to them being bullied by their peers.

Previous research studies have shown that students with special needs who are bullied differ depending on the type of disability. Students with physical needs may receive more attention because of their obvious physical differences and mobility limitations. This may make inclusion students with physical disabilities a target for bullies. In their study, Rose et al. (2009) found that students with physical needs were exposed to higher levels of verbal and physical bullying than typically developing students. These students may be ostracized, ridiculed, and physically attacked.

Students with emotional and behavioral disorders may be bullied by peers because they have problems controlling their behavior and showing their emotional reactions. Bullies can take advantage of these difficulties to provoke these students and manipulate their responses (Iyanda, 2021). Estell et al. (2009) stated that students with conduct disorders have problems with peer acceptance and are more likely to be excluded and exposed to social bullying.

Students with autism spectrum disorder are at risk of being bullied by their peers due to their difficulties with communication skills and social interaction. These difficulties may not be adequately understood by other students in the inclusive environment. This can lead to misunderstandings and negative reactions toward students on the autism spectrum. The sudden and harsh reactions of students with autism spectrum disorder may result in these students not being accepted within their peer groups (Campbell et al., 2017; Forrest et al., 2019; Zablotsky et al., 2014). Typically developing students' negative perceptions of students with autism spectrum disorder and inadequate information about the needs of these students can be identified as the primary reasons for peer bullying. Humphrey and Symes (2011) found that students with autism spectrum disorder were ostracized and emotionally bullied by their peers. Zablotsky et al (2014) studied students with autism spectrum disorder who were educated in inclusive settings. According to their findings, students with autism spectrum disorder were most likely to be victims, bullies, and bully-victims. It was found that these children who are educated in a full-time inclusive environment are more likely to be bullied by their peers than children who are educated in a special education environment. This situation has shown that teachers and school staff should be more cautious and knowledgeable in this regard.

Students with hearing and visual impairments may be bullied because of their sensory impairments. Students who are deaf may face social exclusion and bullying due to difficulties in their communication skills. Students with visual needs may face social isolation and physical bullying. Sacks and Wolffe (2006) found that students with hearing and visual impairments experienced more social exclusion.

Depending on the types of needs that inclusive students have in the school environment, their exposure to peer bullying differs depending on the type of need. The literature states that students with special needs are more exposed to peer bullying than typically developing students, depending on their needs (Chan et al., 2018). Therefore, it is very important for all stakeholders in the school environment to implement prevention and intervention programs to provide an inclusive and empathetic environment in inclusive education. These programs should be prepared by taking into account the types of needs of inclusion students, the needs of the students, and the risk situations they face. In order to prevent and intervene in peer bullying for inclusive students, it is possible to identify the needs of students with special needs and demographic variable characteristics, to develop individualized educational programs and policies, and to better focus on peer bullying incidents and develop better solution strategies.

APPROACHES TO PREVENT PEER BULLYING FOR INCLUSIVE STUDENTS

Several approaches can be put into practice to prevent peer bullying of students with special needs who are educated in mainstream, inclusive, or integrated settings. These approaches include creating a positive school culture, implementing peer mentoring and support systems, implementing social-emotional learning programs, and ensuring the development of all school stakeholders. Creating an inclusive school culture aims to create an environment where all students are equal, respect differences, are empathetic, and feel respected and valued (Good et al., 2011). Peer mentoring and support systems aim to prevent peer bullying by utilizing friendship relationships in an environment where inclusive students are accepted (Bourke & Burgman, 2010). Training all school stakeholders on this issue helps to ensure that inclusion students receive a safe and inclusive education (Lodi et al., 2021).

Restorative Justice Approach

It is an approach that brings together students who have been harmed by bullying incidents and those who have harmed them to discuss the causes and consequences of the bullying incidents and to work together to find solutions to the problem. The restorative justice approach can be an effective intervention strategy for peer bullying of inclusion students. This approach can be used to ensure that the problems caused by peer bullying are repaired and that the bullying student takes responsibility for the bullying behavior (Katic et al., 2020). Through restorative justice processes, students are helped to develop empathy and understanding for students who are being bullied by their peers. A student who bullies a peer tries to understand the physical or emotional harm experienced by students with special needs who are being victimized. In this way, this process helps the bullying student not to engage in bullying behavior in the future and to develop empathy. The bullying student is given the opportunity to correct negative behaviors and establish social interactions. This process allows school stakeholders to work together and encourages them to address incidents of peer bullying against inclusive students and victimized students receive support to help them process and heal from the trauma of peer bullying. As a result of this support, students feel safer at school.

Mediation

It refers to a process in which the parties who have been harmed and bullied by peer bullies come together and discuss the bullying incident and its consequences through a mediator. Thanks to mediation, an empathetic understanding is developed between the parties and together they can find a solution to the peer bullying incident (Du et al., 2018).

Restorative Circles

A restorative circle is a method that brings together members of the school community to discuss incidents of bullying and offer solutions to the problem. These circles provide a safe and supportive environment where everyone has an equal voice and can express their opinions. When a bullying incident occurs in a classroom, students gather in a circle, accompanied by the classroom teacher or guidance counselor. Students in the circle try to understand the impact of the bullying behavior on the classroom, and the whole class develops solutions to the problem (Hopkins, 2002).

Conferences

Conferencing refers to a formal process that brings together bullies, victims, school staff, and families to discuss the incident and seek a solution. In this way, all parties involved in peer bullying incidents understand what happened and have the opportunity to take corrective action together (Gökler, 2009).

Restorative Justice Approaches in Schools

In research study by Hopkins (2002), it was found that an increasing number of schools internationally have launched initiatives and projects that promote restorative approaches and practices:

a-) As an approach that promotes social and emotional skills (e.g., self-esteem, peaceful conflict resolution, empathy, and non-violent communication).
b-) To support all school personnel through training in disciplinary and cultural policies.
c-) Responding to and managing incidents of conflict, bullying, aggressive and/or inappropriate violent behavior.

Lodi et al. (2021) reviewed 34 studies on restorative justice and restorative practices published between 2010 and 2021. They found that the most commonly used restorative practices included restorative circles (76%), restorative conferences (50%), peer mediation (29%), restorative conversations (24%), and community building circles (15%). Restorative justice and restorative practices have been found to improve school climate, reduce discipline problems, and provide positive conflict management. In addition, positive peer interactions and student-teacher relationships have been shown to be promoted through the development of social and emotional skills.

School-Based Programs

Peer bullying can have a negative impact on students' social, emotional, physical, and psychological health. It can reduce students' academic performance and disrupt the overall school climate. Therefore, school-based prevention programs can be effective against peer bullying of students with special needs in an inclusive setting.

Zero-Tolerance Policies

In order for all school stakeholders to be effective in combating peer bullying, schools should develop and implement clear and unambiguous policies. These policies should emphasize that peer bullying is unacceptable, set clear rules, and require every student to behave in accordance with these rules. Sanctions for students who do not follow these policies and rules should also be clearly communicated. The school administration establishes a written policy on bullying and communicates this policy to students, teachers, and parents. School rules include a zero-tolerance policy for bullying and clearly state how to respond to bullying. This creates a positive school climate against peer bullying (Fleming & Jacobsen, 2009; Good et al., 2011).

Information Sessions

In addition, information sessions, workshops and seminars organized in schools are activities to raise awareness about bullying. Training programs for school staff and teachers provide knowledge and skills to recognize and intervene in bullying (Gökler, 2009).

Developing Social Skills

Social skills training is designed to improve students' ability to manage social interactions and to cope with bullying. Topics such as emotional regulation, empathy, and problem-solving skills are taught to students. School-based social skills training programs help students develop their ability to empathize, express their emotions, and resolve conflicts. These programs are implemented through classroom activities, group work, and role-playing. Ttofi and Farrington (2011) found that school-based programs reduced bullying by 20-23 percent and victimization by 17-20 percent.

Student Councils and Antibullying Clubs

It is extremely important for the success of anti-bullying programs that students in the school take an active role in addressing peer bullying (Siddiqui & Schultze-Krumbholz, 2023). They can also create a barrier to peer bullying by receiving training on how to report incidents of bullying. Wood & Orpinas (2020) study aimed to increase the advocacy of students with special needs against peer bullying, trainings were given to increase the knowledge of students with special needs and develop a positive attitude towards students with special needs. As a result of this study, it was ensured that students with special needs together with their peers defended their needs in the school environment and caused students with special needs to cope with victimization and avoid victimization. Student councils and anti-bullying clubs allow students to take an active role in the fight against bullying. These groups organize campaigns about bullying and guide students in reporting incidents of bullying. Bourke & Burgman (2010) highlighted the support of friends in their study. The study found that friend support plays a critical role in coping with bullying. Friends provided emotional support to students with special needs and increased resilience in the face of bullying.

Parental and Community Involvement in School Based Antibullying Programs

Parental involvement is extremely important to increase the effectiveness of school-based anti-bullying programs. Families should be made aware of the issue and provide positive support to their children regarding peer bullying in the home environment. The school administration provides information to parents by organizing information sessions and workshops on bullying. Families are given guidance on how to understand and support their children's experiences with bullying. In addition, social awareness of the fight against bullying is raised through cooperation with local community organizations (Karataş, 2011; Li, 2017).

School Based Counselling Sessions

Responding quickly and effectively to bullying incidents is essential to ensure the safety of victims and to correct the behavior of bullies. Support and intervention strategies include elements such as providing emotional support to victims and taking disciplinary action against bullying students. School counselors who intervene in bullying incidents provide psychological support to victimized students and guide them to correct their behavior by conducting individual interviews with bullying students. In addition, reporting systems for bullying incidents are established to ensure that incidents are monitored and necessary actions are taken (Chalamandaris & Piette, 2015).

International Antibullying Intervention Programs

Many bullying prevention and intervention programs have been developed and implemented around the world. However, only a few of the programs that have been extensively researched and have the potential to be modified to prevent bullying of children with special needs are highlighted here. These programs have been developed by gathering data from large sample groups. Summary information about these prevention and intervention programs is presented in Table 1.

Table 1. Summary information about these prevention and intervention programs

İntervention Program	Title of the Publication	Aims of the Program
Olweus Bullying İntervention Program	A useful evaluation design, and effects of the Olweus Bullying Prevention Program (Olweus, 2005)	Reduction of aggressive behavior and incidents of bullying, creation of a more supportive and safe school environment.
"Steps to Respect" İntervention Program	The Steps to Respect Program uses a multilevel approach to reduce playground bullying and destructive bystander behaviors. (Frey et al.,2005)	To develop students' social skills, resolve conflicts, promote good communication and friendship.
Kiva Anti-Bullying Program	Counteracting bullying in Finland: The KiVa program and its effects on different forms of being bullied (Salmivalli et al., 2011)	Develop friendship support systems and teach teachers strategies for identifying, monitoring, and intervening in bullying incidents.
Bullying Prevention and İntervention Program (BPIP)	Elementary school psychologists' experiences with school-based bullying prevention and intervention efforts (Faas, 2015)	Train teachers, students, school staff, and parents to intervene in bullying; establish school rules and policies against bullying.
Bernese Antibullying Program	The Bernese Program against victimization in kindergarten and elementary school (Alsaker & Valkanover, 2012)	Train teachers to recognize and prevent bullying behaviors, change classroom attitudes about bullying through meetings and discussions with children, and intervene when bullying occurs.
Schoolwide Positive Behaviour Support System	Evaluation of social and academic effects of school-wide positive behaviour support in a Canadian school district (McIntosh & Bennett, 2011).	To ensure a good inclusive environment, adopt common rules and disciplinary policies and establish a common language in the school.

Olweus Bullying Intervention Program

It is an intervention program designed to improve student behavior in schools and to prevent bullying and aggressive behavior. This program was developed by Dan Olweus and the first step in the intervention is to assess the current level of bullying and aggression in the school. This is done with the participation of teachers, school administrators, students, and families. The strengths and weaknesses of the school in relation to bullying are identified. Later, an anti-bullying committee is established in the school. This committee consists of students, teachers, families, and school administration. The committee oversees the process of designing, implementing, and evaluating the program. The program provides students with information about peer bullying, exercises to help students recognize and prevent bullying, and activities to help students develop positive communication, problem-solving, and empathy skills. This program trains teachers to recognize and intervene in peer bullying and aggressive behavior. As a result, teachers build stronger relationships with students in the school environment and learn strategies to prevent bullying incidents and the behaviors that lead to them. Families are provided with training and guidance on how to communicate with their children at home, how to talk with their children about bullying and aggressive behaviors, and how to help families encourage positive behaviors in their children at home. Families are actively involved in the school so that they are an important part of the program. Regular monitoring and evaluation processes are in place to measure the success of the program. This includes assessing whether bullying behavior is decreasing. Once implemented, the program must be continually improved and updated. The content and structure of the program will be adapted to the changing conditions and needs of the school dynamics. The long-term goal of the program is to reduce the incidence of aggression and bullying and to make the school environment more supportive and safe. The success of the program is measured through continuous monitoring, evaluation, and correction when deemed necessary (Olweus, 2005; Olweus & Limber, 2010).

"Steps to Respect" Intervention Program

The Steps to Respect intervention program was developed by an organization called Committee for Children. The goal of this program is to ensure that students communicate with each other in the school environment and to prevent peer bullying.

The first step of the program is to increase the knowledge of parents, teachers, and students about what peer bullying is, why it is important, and how to recognize it. This is followed by training on positive behaviors and anti-bullying strategies. Establish rules and policies that are adopted and accepted by the school community (these rules may include building empathy, anti-bullying, and respectful behavior).

Adults and students are encouraged to monitor and report bullying behaviors and incidents. This reporting helps to identify the prevalence of bullying and to intervene in bullying incidents. The program emphasizes the development of students' social skills. Students are taught conflict resolution, good communication, and friendship relationships. Families are encouraged to participate and support their child's learning in the program. Families can be very supportive of students as an important part of the program. It is necessary to continuously monitor and evaluate the implemented program for its effectiveness. If there are problems and deficiencies in some aspects of the applied situation, improvements can be made to the program (Frey et al., 2005; Hirschstein & Frey, 2006).

Kiva Anti-Bullying Program

The Kiva Anti-Bullying Program is a school-based intervention program developed in Finland to prevent bullying. The goal of the program is to enable students to build healthier relationships and reduce peer bullying. Kiva stands for "personal strength and camaraderie" and through this program, students are taught to develop friendships and friendship relationships and to increase their skills to resist bullying incidents by using their personal strength. Before the program is implemented, the school staff and administration hold a meeting during the preparation phase to determine the goals of the program and decide on the implementation of the Kiva program. The classes in which the program will be implemented are selected and the age groups are determined. Necessary trainings are given to the team members formed to implement the program. Training is given on important social skills such as empathy, strengthening friendships, dealing with bullying, and conflict resolution. Various trainings are organized to empower students to recognize, report, and intervene in bullying incidents. Teachers play an important role in this program. Teachers receive a series of trainings on how to successfully implement the Kiva Program, which are designed to help them learn the strategies necessary to identify, monitor, and intervene in bullying incidents. The Kiva program builds buddy support systems by fostering friendship relationships among students. Through these developed systems, it attempts to provide the necessary support to victims of bullying. Students are taught to support victims of bullying, to work together to fight bullying, and to report bullying incidents to the appropriate authorities. As part of the fight against bullying, teachers and school administrators monitor and record bullying incidents. Monitoring bullying incidents in the school environment is very important in order to evaluate the effects of the implemented program. Regular monitoring and evaluation of the program provides an opportunity to regulate and improve deficiencies and shortcomings (Herkama & Salmivalli, 2018; Salmivalli et al., 2011).

Bullying Prevention and Intervention Program (BPIP)

It is a program designed to prevent and intervene in bullying. The steps for implementing the program may vary from institution to institution. The first step to be taken before beginning the implementation of the program is to conduct a needs assessment to determine what type of problems exist in the school environment regarding peer bullying and in what areas improvements should be made to address these problems. This needs assessment; teacher and staff interviews are conducted using student surveys, statistical data, and other sources. As part of this program, a team should be established to manage the fight against bullying. This team may include teachers, parents, school administrators, guidance counselors, and local community leaders, as appropriate. With the selection of the Bullying Prevention and Interaction Program (BPIP); teachers, students, school staff and parents are trained to fight bullying and awareness training is provided. These trainings include definitions of bullying concepts, its symptoms, the harms caused by bullying, and how to prevent and intervene in bullying. School rules and policies against peer bullying are updated and clearly stated. This demonstrates the school's commitment and stance in the fight against bullying. Effective intervention strategies are developed to intervene with bullies, solve problems for victims, and provide support. It is important to continually monitor and evaluate the impact of the program. If the positive behavior in the school increases and the number of bullying incidents decreases, the program is considered successful and can be revised in some aspects if necessary (Faas, 2015).

Bernese Antibullying Program

The Bernese Program can be used to address bullying in preschool and elementary school settings. The program aims to train teachers to provide students in these settings with the skills to deal with bullying behaviors. Depending on this purpose, the skills that are thought to be acquired by the teachers are; identifying bullying behaviors, preventing bullying behaviors, changing the attitude of the class against bullying by holding meetings and discussions with children, and intervening when bullying behaviors occur. The target skills to be acquired through this program are delivered to teachers through peer mentoring. The program lasts approximately four months and consists of six sessions. Thus, awareness of bullying behaviors is raised with group sessions created for teachers, practices to address these behaviors are introduced, and problems related to practice are discussed after these practices are implemented in the classroom (Alsaker & Valkanover, 2012).

Schoolwide Positive Behaviour Support System

Between 2007 and 2009, the Schoolwide Positive Behavior Support System (SWPBS), which was implemented in a school in Canada, provided training to teachers at the school where students with special needs were placed. In addition, it is very important for this program to track student behavior by teachers. It focuses on consistent behavioral expectations in all areas of the school. The goal is to provide a more inclusive environment. SWPBS creates a common language for all students and staff in the school. Although individual student support for students with special needs varies according to need, there should be a common and inclusive language for everyone in the school environment. Thanks to SWPBS, it was seen that bullying behaviors in the 2007-2008 and 2008-2009 school years decreased by approximately 40% compared to the previous two years, and this situation was generally generalized in non-school environments (McIntosh & Bennett, 2011).

EVALUATING PREVENTION AND INTERVENTION STRATEGIES FOR STUDENTS WITH SPECIAL NEEDS

In reviewing peer bullying prevention and intervention studies, it is apparent that the majority of studies have examined typically developing students and extremely few studies have examined students with special needs. This section discusses peer bullying prevention and intervention studies for typically developing students and limited peer bullying prevention and intervention studies for students with special needs.

Houchins et al. (2016) found that there were very limited studies with strong research methodologies, and the authors identified and discussed only six studies on the pre-set criteria. (Espelage et al., 2015; Humphrey et al., 2013; Rahill & Teglasi, 2003; Ross & Horner, 2014; Saylor & Leach, 2009; Vessey & O'Neill, 2011). The included studies met five pre-set criteria: a-) an empirical evaluation of a bullying prevention or intervention program, b-) the intervention targeted bullying and/or victim behavior, c-) the authors reported outcomes specifically for individuals with special needs, d-) the studies were conducted in a school setting, e-) the research methods used were experimental, quasi-experimental, single-subject, or mixed methods. Although the authors of all six studies adhere to the context and setting standards, certain characteristics of the intervention site have changed to a great extent. One article (Humphrey et al., 2013) was conducted in the United Kingdom, and the remaining five studies were conducted in the United States. Results indicated that prevention and intervention programs have the potential to reduce the negative effects of bullying for students with special needs.

In another study, Gao (2020) examined prevention and intervention efforts targeting peer bullying among students with special needs. The research revealed that the first study was conducted in 2003, followed by a second study in 2009, indicating a 6-year gap between them. Subsequent studies were carried out at intervals of 1 to 2 years, demonstrating an increase in the frequency of high-quality research (e.g., 2009-2011, 2011-2013, 2013-2014, and 2014-2016). This trend is promising and suggests that the body of literature on bullying prevention and intervention for students with special needs has intensified. It is hoped that this progress continues.

The growing literature also identified two peer mentoring programs (Bradley, 2016; Sreckovic et al., 2017) that were based on increasing interactions between participants and general peer groups to help students with ASD gain self-esteem, social satisfaction, and reduce bullying victimization. It should be noted that the results of the study were extremely positive.

In addition, multimedia, which is an important element of communication, can become a facilitator or a barrier that affects children's development, depending on the information it provides. Multimedia tools were used to teach the participants about the ability to copy with the complaint of bullying. Two studies were conducted for the participants through distance learning and necessary training videos (Vessey & O'Neill, 2011; Rex et al., 2018). This method was found to be useful in increasing participants' self-confidence and reducing new bullying.

Parental involvement in the prevention of bullying of children with special needs has also been highlighted as an important factor in curbing bullying. Studies by Ganotz et al. (2023); Vessey and O'Neill (2011) collected parents' perceptions of their children. Similarly, in another study by Chu et al. (2015), a bullying program was implemented and parents' perceptions of participants were assessed both before and after the intervention. According to the results obtained, it was found that the attitudes and approaches of families and their commitment to the program positively influenced the results obtained. One study (Sreckovic et al., 2017) reported that two participants received extra help from the support staff. Thus, it was shown that professional staff also play an active role in prevention and intervention programs.

The literature has shown that different scales and tools have been used to assess participant performance in terms of outcomes, but the aspects of the outcomes they measure are similar. The most common outcome is learning coping skills to respond to bullying/victimization. According to the results, participants in all of the studies performed better after the intervention programs than they did before the treatment. The most positive outcomes were in the areas of increasing children's self-confidence, reducing bullying/victimization, and gaining information about bullying (Gao, 2020).

CONCLUSION

In this chapter, previous research studies were reviewed with the aim of providing the importance of understanding the effects of peer bullying on students with special needs and developing appropriate strategies while addressing peer bullying programs. The authors also tried to highlight strategies and suggestions on what should be done to create a positive and safe school environment with all stakeholders of the school, including students with special needs, students with typical development, families and communities of these students, teachers and school administration, which are considered as important elements of peer bullying prevention programs. It was emphasized that prevention and intervention programs should be prepared with the support of relevant literature, taking into account the nature of students included in inclusive settings, individual differences and disability groups, risk situations of students with special needs and the status of mainstreaming students according to some demographic variables. Finally, the review of international successful programs for the prevention of peer bullying was presented and information about the status of the very limited studies was provided.

Direction for Future Research

Bullying of children with special needs is still an area that needs further development. It is recommended that further experimental studies be designed to successfully prevent peer bullying of students with special educational needs. It is unfortunate that there is currently no widely used peer bullying and intervention program specifically designed to meet the individual needs of students with special educational needs. It is imperative that this study serves as a foundation for future research efforts and that students with special needs are included in the development of prevention and intervention programs. It is imperative that future studies adhere to the highest standards of evidence-based reliability and validity data. Expanding the number of evidence-based intervention programs targeting peer bullying among students with special needs, in addition to conducting experimental evaluations, would significantly contribute to the global pool of widely used bullying prevention and intervention strategies.

REFERENCES

Alsaker, F. D., & Valkanover, S. (2012). The Bernese program against victimization in kindergarten and elementary school. *New Directions for Youth Development*, 133(133), 15–28. DOI: 10.1002/yd.20004 PMID: 22504788

American Psychiatric Association. (2000). *Diagnostic and statistical manual of mental disorders* (4th ed.). American Psychological Association.

Bakker, J. T. A., & Bosman, A. M. T. (2003). Self-image and peer acceptance of Dutch students in regular and special education. *Learning Disability Quarterly*, 26(1), 5–14. DOI: 10.2307/1593680

Ball, L., Lieberman, L., Beach-Haibach, P., Perreault, M., & Tirone, K. (2021). Bullying in physical education of children and youth with visual impairments: A systematic review. *British Journal of Visual Impairment*, 40(3), 1–17. DOI: 10.1177/02646196211009927

Basilici, M. C., Palladino, B. E., & Menesini, E. (2022). Ethnic diversity and bullying in school: A systematic review. *Aggression and Violent Behavior*, 65, 1359–1789. DOI: 10.1016/j.avb.2022.101762

Black, L. I., & Zablotsky, B. (2018). *Chronic school absenteeism among children with selected developmental disabilities: National Health Interview Survey. 2014-2016* [National Health Statistics Reports. No. 118]. National Center for Health Statistics.

Blake, J. J., Zhou, Q., Kwok, O., & Benz, M. R. (2016). Predictors of bullying behavior, victimization, and bully-victim risk among high school. *Remedial and Special Education*, 37(5), 285–295. DOI: 10.1177/0741932516638860

Boske, C., & Osanloo, A. F. (2015). Conclusion-preparing all school community leaders to live their work. *Promoting Social Justice and Equity Work in Schools Around the World Advances in Educational Administration*, 23, 405–426. DOI: 10.1108/S1479-366020140000023032

Bourke, S., & Burgman, I. (2010). Coping with bullying in Australian schools: How children with disabilities experience support from friends, parents and teachers. *Disability & Society*, 25(3), 359–371. DOI: 10.1080/09687591003701264

Bradley, R. (2016). 'Why single me out?' Peer mentoring, autism and inclusion in mainstream secondary schools. *British Journal of Special Education*, 43(3), 272–288. DOI: 10.1111/1467-8578.12136

Bromand, Z., Temur-Erman, S., Yesil, R., Montesinos, A. H., Aichberger, M. C., Kleiber, D., Schouler-Ocak, M., Heinz, A., Kastrup, M. C., & Rapp, M. A. (2012). Mental health of Turkish women in Germany: Resilience and risk factors. *European Psychiatry*, 27, 17–21. DOI: 10.1016/S0924-9338(12)75703-6 PMID: 22863245

Campbell, M., Hwang, Y. S., Whiteford, C., Dillon-Wallace, J., Ashburner, J., Saggers, B., & Carrington, S. (2017). Bullying prevalence in students with Autism Spectrum Disorder. *Australasian Journal of Special Education*, 41(2), 101–122. DOI: 10.1017/jse.2017.5

Çetinkaya, S., Nur, N., Ayvaz, A., Özdemir, D., & Kavakcı, Ö. (2009). The relationship between peer bullying and depression and self-esteem levels in three primary school students with different socio-economic status. *Anatolian Journal of Psychiatry*, 10, 151–158.

Chalamandaris, A. G., & Piette, D. (2015). School-based anti-bullying interventions: Systematic review of the methodology to assess their effectivenes. *Aggression and Violent Behavior*, 24, 131–174. DOI: 10.1016/j.avb.2015.04.004

Chan, K. L., Lo, C. K. M., & Ip, P. (2018). Associating disabilities, school environments, and child victimization. *Child Abuse & Neglect*, 83, 21–30. DOI: 10.1016/j.chiabu.2018.07.001 PMID: 30016742

Chu, B. C., Hoffman, L., Johns, A., Reyes-Portillo, J., & Hansford, A. (2015). Transdiagnostic behavior therapy for bullying-related anxiety and depression: Initial development and pilot study. *Cognitive and Behavioral Practice*, 22(4), 415–429. DOI: 10.1016/j.cbpra.2014.06.007

Cincioğlu, Ş. (2023). *Peer Bullying Against Inclusion Students*, (Unpublished Ph.D. Thesis, Trakya University), Edirne.

Cincioğlu, Ş., & Ergin, D. Y. (2023a). Evaluation of peer bullying towards inclusion students by teachers. *Social Sciences Research Journal*, 12(15), 2017–2027.

Cincioğlu, Ş., & Ergin, D. Y. (2023b). Kaynaştırma öğrencilerine yönelik akran zorbalığının veli görüşlerine göre değerlendirilmesi. *Balkan and Near Eastern Journal of Social Sciences*, 9, 179–184.

Cook, L., & Friend, M. (2010). The state of the art of collaboration on behalf of students with disabilities. *Journal of Educational & Psychological Consultation*, 20(1), 1–8. DOI: 10.1080/10474410903535398

Diamanduros, T., Downs, E., & Jenkins, S. J. (2008). The role of school psychologists in the assessment, prevention, and intervention of cyberbullying. *Psychology in the Schools*, 45(8), 693–704. DOI: 10.1002/pits.20335

Dölek, N. (2002). *Investigation of Bullying Behaviors in Students and a Preventive Program Model*, (Unpublished Ph.D. Thesis, Marmara University), Istanbul.

Du, C., DeGuisto, K., Albrigh, J., & Alrehaili, S. (2018). Peer support as a mediator between bullying victimization and depression. *International Journal of Psychological Studies*, 10(1), 59–68. DOI: 10.5539/ijps.v10n1p59

Erdoğan, Y., Hammami, N., & Elgar, F. J. (2023). Bullying, family support, and life satisfaction in adolescents of single-parent households in 42 countries. *Child Indicators Research*, 16(2), 739–753. DOI: 10.1007/s12187-022-09996-4

Espelage, D. L., Rose, C. A., & Polanin, J. R. (2015). Socialemotional learning program to reduce bullying, fighting, and victimization among middle school students with disabilities. *Remedial and Special Education*, 36(5), 299–311. DOI: 10.1177/0741932514564564

Estell, D. B., Farmer, T. W., Irvin, M. J., Crowther, A., Akos, P., & Baudah, D. J. (2009). Students with exceptionalities and the peer group context of bullying and victimization in late elementary school. *Journal of Child and Family Studies*, 18(2), 136–150. DOI: 10.1007/s10826-008-9214-1

Evans, C. B. R., Fraser, M. W., & Cotter, K. L. (2014). The effectiveness of school-based bullying prevention programs: A systematic review. *Aggression and Violent Behavior*, 19(5), 532–544. DOI: 10.1016/j.avb.2014.07.004

Faas, Z. (2015). *Elementary School Psychologists' Experiences with School-Based Bullying Prevention and İntervention Efforts*, (New Hampshire University, Unpublished Ph.D. Thesis), New Hampshire, ABD.

Fleming, L. C., & Jacobsen, K. H. (2009). Bullying among middle-school students in low and middle income countries. *Health Promotion International*, 25(1), 73–84. DOI: 10.1093/heapro/dap046 PMID: 19884243

Forrest, D. L., Kroeger, R. A., & Stroope, S. (2019). Autism spectrum disorder symptoms and bullying victimization among children with Autism in the United States. *Journal of Autism and Developmental Disorders*, 50(2), 560–571. DOI: 10.1007/s10803-019-04282-9 PMID: 31691063

Fox, C. L., & Boulton, M. J. (2005). The social skills problems of bullying: Self, peer, and teacher perceptions. *The British Journal of Educational Psychology*, 75(2), 313–328. DOI: 10.1348/000709905X25517 PMID: 16033669

Frederickson, N., Simmonds, E., Evans, L., & Soulsby, C. (2007). Assessing the social and affective outcomes of inclusion. *British Journal of Special Education*, 34(2), 105–115. DOI: 10.1111/j.1467-8578.2007.00463.x

Frey, K., Edstrom, L. V. S., & Hirschstein, M. (2005). The steps to respect program uses a multilevel approach to reduce playground bullying and destructive bystander behaviors. the *National Conference of the Hamilton Fish Enstitute on School and Community Violence*, https://digitalcommons.georgefox.edu/cgi/viewcontent.cgi?article=1336&context=gscp_fac

Gage, N. A., & Larson, A. (2014). School climate and bullying victimization: A latent class growth model analysis. *School Psychology Quarterly*, 29(3), 256–271. DOI: 10.1037/spq0000064 PMID: 24933216

Ganotz, T., Schwab, S., & Lehofer, M. (2023). Bullying among primary school-aged students: Which factors could strengthen their tendency towards resilience? *International Journal of Inclusive Education*, 27(8), 890–903. DOI: 10.1080/13603116.2021.1879949

Gao, W. (2020). *Anti-bullying interventions for Children with special needs: A 2003-2020 Systematic Literature Review*, (Master Thesis, Jönköping University School of Education and Communication, Jönköping), Sweden.

Gökler, R. (2009). Peer bullying in schools. *International Journal of the Humanities*, 6(2), 511–537.

Good, C. P., Mcintosh, K., & Gietz, C. (2011). İntegrating bullying prevention into schoolwide positive behavior support. *Teaching Exceptional Children*, 44(1), 48–56. DOI: 10.1177/004005991104400106

Gottfried, M. A., & Kirksey, J. J. (2017). "When" students miss school: The role of timing of absenteeism on students' test performance. *Educational Researcher*, 46(3), 119–130. DOI: 10.3102/0013189X17703945

Grills-Taquechel, A. E., Fletcher, J. M., Vaughn, S. R., & Stuebing, K. K. (2012). Anxiety and reading difficulties in early elementary school: Evidence for uni-directional- or bidirectional relations? *Child Psychiatry and Human Development*, 43(1), 35–47. DOI: 10.1007/s10578-011-0246-1 PMID: 21822734

Hajdukova, E. B., Hornby, G., & Cushman, P. (2015). Bullying experiences of students with social, emotional and behavioural difficulties (SEBD). *Educational Review*, 68(2), 207–221. DOI: 10.1080/00131911.2015.1067880

Halliday, S., Gregory, T., Taylor, A., Digenis, C., & Turnbull, D. (2021). The impact of bullying victimization in early adolescence on subsequent psychosocial and academic outcomes across the adolescent period: A systematic review. *Journal of School Violence*, 20(3), 351–373. DOI: 10.1080/15388220.2021.1913598

Herkama, S., & Salmivalli, C. (2018). KiVa antibullying program, *Reducing Cyberbullying in Schools*, 125-134. https://doi.org/DOI: 10.1016/B978-0-12-811423-0.00009-2

Hirschstein, M., & Frey, K. S. (2006). Promoting behavior and beliefs that reduce bullying: The Steps to Respect Program. In Jimerson, S. R., & Furlong, M. (Eds.), *Handbook of school violence and school safety: From research to practice* (pp. 309–323). Lawrence Erlbaum Associates Publishers.

Hopkins, B. (2002). Restorative justice in schools. *Support for Learning*, 17(3), 144–149. DOI: 10.1111/1467-9604.00254

Horishna, N. M. (2022). Typology of social skills and their impairments in children with autism spectrum disorders. *Scientific Bulletin of Mukachevo State University. Series. Pedagogy and Psychology*, 8(3), 33–38. DOI: 10.52534/msu-pp.8(3).2022.33-38

Houchins, D. E., Oakes, W. P., & Johnson, Z. G. (2016). Bullying and students with disabilities: A systematic literature review of intervention studies. *Remedial and Special Education*, 37(5), 259–273. DOI: 10.1177/0741932516648678

Humphrey, N., Lendrum, A., Barlow, A., Wigelsworth, M., & Squires, G. (2013). Achievement for all: Improving psychosocial outcomes for students with special education needs and disabilities. *Research in Developmental Disabilities*, 24(4), 1210–1225. DOI: 10.1016/j.ridd.2012.12.008 PMID: 23380579

Humphrey, N., & Symes, W. (2011). Peer interaction patterns among adolescents with autistic spectrum disorders (ASDs) in mainstream school settings. *Autism*, 15(4), 397–419. DOI: 10.1177/1362361310387804 PMID: 21454385

Iyanda, A. E. (2022). Bullying victimization of children with mental, emotional, and developmental or behavioral (medb) disorders in the United States. *Journal of Child & Adolescent Trauma*, 15(2), 221–233. DOI: 10.1007/s40653-021-00368-8 PMID: 35600527

Kamran, M., & Siddiqui, S. (2024). Roots of resilience: Uncovering the secrets behind 25+ years of inclusive education sustainability. *Sustainability (Basel)*, 16(4), 1–23. DOI: 10.3390/su16114364

Karataş, H. (2011). *Investigation of the effect of the program developed for bullying in primary schools*. (Unpublished Ph.D. Thesis, Dokuz Eylül University), İzmir.

Karatas, H., & Ozturk, C. (2011). Relationship Between Bullying and Health Problems in Primary School Children. *Asian Nursing Research*, 5(2), 81–87. DOI: 10.1016/S1976-1317(11)60016-9 PMID: 25030257

Katic, B., Alba, L. A., & Johnson, A. H. (2020). A systematic evaluation of restorative justice practices: School violence prevention and response. *Journal of School Violence*, 19(4), 579–593. DOI: 10.1080/15388220.2020.1783670

Konishi, C., Hymel, S., Zumbo, B. D., & Li, Z. (2010). Do school bullying and student–teacher relationships matter for academic achievement? A multilevel analysis. *Canadian Journal of School Psychology*, 25(1), 19–39. DOI: 10.1177/0829573509357550

Kuhne, M., & Wiener, J. (2000). Stability of social status of children with and without learning disabilities. *Learning Disability Quarterly*, 23(1), 64–75. DOI: 10.2307/1511100

Laftman, S. B., Fransson, E., Modin, B., & Östberg, V. (2017). National data study showed that adolescents living in poorer households and with one parent were more likely to be bullied. *Acta Paediatrica (Oslo, Norway)*, 106(12), 2048–2054. DOI: 10.1111/apa.13997 PMID: 28727173

Lebrun-Harris, L. A., Sherman, L. J., Limber, S. P., Miller, B. D., & Edgerton, E. A. (2019). Bullying victimization and perpetration among U.S. children and adolescents: 2016 National survey of children's health. *Journal of Child and Family Studies*, 28(9), 2543–2557. DOI: 10.1007/s10826-018-1170-9

Li, Y., Chen, P. Y., Chen, F. L., & Chen, Y. L. (2017). Preventing school bullying: Investigation of the link between anti-bullying strategies, prevention ownership, prevention climate, and prevention leadership. *Applied Psychology*, 66(4), 577–598. DOI: 10.1111/apps.12107

Lindsay, S., & McPherson, A. C. (2012). Experiences of social exclusion and bullying at school among children and youth with cerebral palsy. *Disability and Rehabilitation*, 34(2), 101–109. DOI: 10.3109/09638288.2011.587086 PMID: 21870932

Lodi, E., Perrella, L., Lepri, G. L., Scarpa, M. L., & Patrizi, P. (2022). Use of restorative justice and restorative practices at school: A systematic literature review. *International Journal of Environmental Research and Public Health*, 19(1), 1–36. DOI: 10.3390/ijerph19010096 PMID: 35010355

Lösel, F., & Farrington, D. P. (2012). Direct protective and buffering protective factors in the development of youth violence. *American Journal of Preventive Medicine*, 43(2), 8–23. DOI: 10.1016/j.amepre.2012.04.029 PMID: 22789961

Luciano, S., & Savage, R. S. (2007). Bullying risk in children with learning difficulties in inclusive educational settings. *Canadian Journal of School Psychology*, 22(1), 14–31. DOI: 10.1177/0829573507301039

Malecki, C. K., Demaray, M. K., Smith, T. J., & Emmons, J. (2020). Disability, poverty, and other risk factors associated with involvement in bullying behaviors. *Journal of School Psychology*, 78, 115–132. DOI: 10.1016/j.jsp.2020.01.002 PMID: 32178807

McIntosh, K., Bennett, J. L., & Price, K. (2011). Evaluation of social and academic effects of school-wide positive behaviour support in a Canadian school district. *Exceptionality Education International*, 21(1), 46–60. DOI: 10.5206/eei.v21i1.7669

McNicholas, C. I., Orpinas, P., & Raczynski, K. (2017). Victimized for being different: Young adults with disabilities and peer victimization in middle and high school. *Journal of Interpersonal Violence*, 35(19-20), 3683–3709. DOI: 10.1177/0886260517710485 PMID: 29294765

Mynard, H., Joseph, S., & Alexandera, J. (2000). Peer-victimisation and posttraumatic stress in adolescents. *Personality and Individual Differences*, 29(5), 815–821. DOI: 10.1016/S0191-8869(99)00234-2

Nelson, J. M., & Harwood, H. (2011). Learning disabilities and anxiety: A meta-analysis. *Journal of Learning Disabilities*, 44(1), 3–17. DOI: 10.1177/0022219409359939 PMID: 20375288

Olweus, D. (1995). Peer abuse or bullying at school: Basic facts and a school-based intervention programme. *Current Directions in Psychological Science*, 4(6), 196–200. DOI: 10.1111/1467-8721.ep10772640

Olweus, D. (2005). A useful evaluation design, and effects of the Olweus Bullying Prevention Program. *Psychology, Crime & Law*, 11(4), 389–402. DOI: 10.1080/10683160500255471

Olweus, D., & Limber, S. P. (2010). Bullying in school: Evaluation and dissemination of the Olweus Bullying Prevention Program. *The American Journal of Orthopsychiatry*, 80(1), 124–134. DOI: 10.1111/j.1939-0025.2010.01015.x PMID: 20397997

Owens, M., Stevenson, J., Hadwin, J. A., & Norgate, R. (2012). Anxiety and depression in academic performance: An exploration of the mediating factors of worry and working memory. *School Psychology International*, 33(4), 433–449. DOI: 10.1177/0143034311427433

Özdemir, Ş. A. (2020) *A Comparative Investigation of Exposure to Peer Bullying of Mentally Handicapped Students Educated with the Inclusion Model and Students with Normal Development*, (Unpublished Master's Thesis, Necmettin Erbakan University), Konya.

Rahill, S. A., & Teglasi, H. (2003). Processes and outcomes of story-based and skill-based social competency programs for children with emotional disabilities. *Journal of School Psychology*, 41(6), 413–429. DOI: 10.1016/j.jsp.2003.08.001

Ramirez, I. (2017). The Effects of Bullying Among Adolescents with Special Needs, İnformation Age Publishing, p:167-194. United States Of America.

Rex, C., Charlop, M. H., & Spector, V. (2018). Using video modeling as an anti-bullying intervention for children with Autism Spectrum Disorder. *Journal of Autism and Developmental Disorders*, 48(8), 2701–2713. DOI: 10.1007/s10803-018-3527-8 PMID: 29516338

Rigby, K. (2002). *New Perspectives on Bullying*. Jessica Kingsley Publishers.

Rose, C. A., & Espelage, D. L. (2012). Risk and protective factors associated with the bullying ınvolvement of students with emotional and behavioral disorders. *Behavioral Disorders*, 37(3), 133–148. DOI: 10.1177/019874291203700302

Rose, C. A., Espelage, D. L., & Monda-Amaya, L. E. (2009). Bullying and victimisation rates among students in general and special education: A comperative analysis. *Educational Psychology*, 29(7), 761–776. DOI: 10.1080/01443410903254864

Rose, C. A., Monda-Amaya, L. E., & Espelage, D. L. (2010). Bullying perpetration and victimization in special education: A review of the literature. *Remedial and Special Education*, 32(2), 114–130. DOI: 10.1177/0741932510361247

Rose, C. A., Simpson, C. G., & Ellis, S. K. (2015). The relationship between school belonging, sibling aggression and bullying involvement: Implications for students with and without disabilities. *Educational Psychology*, 36(8), 1462–1486. DOI: 10.1080/01443410.2015.1066757

Ross, S. W., & Horner, R. H. (2014). Bully prevention in positive behavior support: Preliminary evaluation of third-fourth-, and fifth-grade attitudes toward bullying. *Journal of Emotional and Behavioral Disorders*, 22(4), 225–236. DOI: 10.1177/1063426613491429

Sabramani, V., Idris, I. B., Ismail, H., Nadarajaw, T., Zakaria, E., & Kamaluddin, M. R. (2021). Bullying and its associated individual, peer, family and school factors: Evidence from Malaysian national secondary school students. *International Journal of Environmental Research and Public Health*, 18(13), 2–28. DOI: 10.3390/ijerph18137208 PMID: 34281145

Sabuncuoğlu, O., Ekinci, Ö., Bahadır, T., Akyuva, Y., Altınöz, E., & Berkem, M. (2006). Peer abuse among adolescent students and ıts relationship with depression symptoms. *Annals of Clinical Psychiatry*, 9, 27–35.

Sacks, S. Z., & Wolffe, K. E. (2006). *Teaching Social Skills to Students with Virsual İmpairments*. From Theory to Practice.

Salmivalli, C., Karna, A., & Poskiparta, E. (2011). Counteracting bullying in Finland: The KiVa program and its effects on different forms of being bullied. *International Journal of Behavioral Development*, 35(5), 405–411. DOI: 10.1177/0165025411407457

Savage, R. (2005). Friendship bullying patterns in children attending in language base in mainstream school. *Educational Psychology in Practice*, 21(1), 23–36. DOI: 10.1080/02667360500035140

Saylor, C. F., & Leach, J. B. (2009). Percieved bullying and social support in students accessing special inclusion programming. *Journal of Developmental and Physical Disabilities*, 21(1), 69–80. DOI: 10.1007/s10882-008-9126-4

Shaheen, A. M., Hamdan, K. M., Albqoor, M., Othman, A. K., Amre, H. M., & Hazeem, M. N. A. (2019). Perceived social support from family and friends and bullying victimization among adolescents. *Children and Youth Services Review*, 107, 1–38. DOI: 10.1016/j.childyouth.2019.104503

Siddiqui, S., & Schultze-Krumbholz, A. (2023). The Sohanjana Antibullying Intervention: Pilot results of peer-training module in Pakistan. *Social Sciences (Basel, Switzerland)*, 12(7), 409. Advance online publication. DOI: 10.3390/socsci12070409

Sreckovic, M. A., Hume, K., & Able, H. (2017). Examining the efficacy of peer network interventions on the social interactions of high school students with autism spectrum disorder. *Journal of Autism and Developmental Disorders*, 47(8), 2556–2574. DOI: 10.1007/s10803-017-3171-8 PMID: 28567546

Svetaz, M. V., Ireland, M., & Blum, R. (2000). Adolescents with learning disabilities: Risk and protective factors associated with emotional well-being: Findings from the National Longitudinal Study of Adolescent Health. *The Journal of Adolescent Health*, 27(5), 340–348. DOI: 10.1016/S1054-139X(00)00170-1 PMID: 11044706

Swanson, S., & Howell, C. (1996). Test anxiety in adolescents with learning disabilities and behavior disorders. *Exceptional Children*, 62(5), 389–389. DOI: 10.1177/001440299606200501

Theobald, R., Goldhaber, D., Gratz, T., & Holden, K. (2017). Career and technical education, ınclusion and postsecondary outcomes for students with learning disabilities. *Journal of Learning Disabilities*, 52(2), 109–119. DOI: 10.1177/0022219418775121 PMID: 29790412

Ttofi, M. M., & Farrington, D. P. (2011). Effectiveness of school-based programs to reduce bullying: A systematic and meta-analytic review. *Journal of Experimental Criminology*, 7(1), 27–56. DOI: 10.1007/s11292-010-9109-1

U.S. Department of Education. (2016, June 7). 2013-2014 Civil rights data collection: A first look. https://www2.ed.gov/about/offices/list/ocr/docs/2013-14-first-look.pdf

Van Cleave, J., & Davis, M. M. (2006). Bullying and peer victimization among children with special health care needs. *Pediatrics*, 118(4), 1212–1219. DOI: 10.1542/peds.2005-3034 PMID: 17015509

Vessey, J. A., & O'Neill, K. M. (2011). Helping students with disabilities better address teasing and bullying situations: A MASNRN study. *The Journal of School Nursing: the Official Publication of the National Association of School Nurses*, 27(2), 139–148. DOI: 10.1177/1059840510386490 PMID: 20956579

Windsor, S., Maxwell, G., & Antonsen, Y. (2022). Incorporating sustainable development and inclusive education in teacher education for the Arctic. *Polar Geography*, 45(4), 246–259. DOI: 10.1080/1088937X.2022.2105970

Winters, R. R., Blake, J. J., & Chen, S. (2018). Bully victimization among children with attention-deficit/hyperactivity disorder: A longitudinal examination of behavioral phenotypes. *Journal of Emotional and Behavioral Disorders*, 28(2), 80–91. DOI: 10.1177/1063426618814724

Wood, C., & Orpinas, P. (2020). Victimization of children with disabilities: Coping strategies and protective factors. *Disability & Society*, 36(9), 1469–1488. DOI: 10.1080/09687599.2020.1802578

Woods, S., & Wolke, D. (2004). Direct and relational bullying among primary school children and academic achievement. *Journal of School Psychology*, 42(2), 135–155. DOI: 10.1016/j.jsp.2003.12.002

Wu, X., Zhen, R., Shen, L., Tan, R., & Zhou, X. (2023). Patterns of elementary school students' bullying victimization: Roles of family and individual factors. *Journal of Interpersonal Violence*, 38(4), 2410–2431. DOI: 10.1177/08862605221101190 PMID: 35576274

Young, J., Ne'eman, A., & Gelser, S. (2012). *Bullying and Students with Disabilities: A Briefing Paper from the National Council on Disability*. National Council on Disability.

Zablotsky, B., Bradshaw, C. P., Anderson, C. M., & Law, P. (2014). Risk factors for bullying among children with autism spectrum disorders. *Autism*, 18(4), 419–427. DOI: 10.1177/1362361313477920 PMID: 23901152

Chapter 9
Practical Interventions to Address Bullying and Support Students With Special Educational Needs

Afroditi Malisiova
https://orcid.org/0009-0005-0778-5028
Aristotle University of Thessaloniki, Greece

Vasiliki Folia
https://orcid.org/0000-0002-2159-7032
Aristotle University of Thessaloniki, Greece

ABSTRACT

The number of bullying incidents in school environments worldwide has increased rapidly over the past few decades undermining and obstructing the creation of inclusive classrooms in which all students feel appreciated, respected, and welcome. Despite increased awareness and efforts of the stakeholders, including educators, psychologists, parents, and students to combat and mitigate bullying, it remains a persistent problem, constantly deteriorating and seeking victims among whom students with Special Educational Needs (SEN) constitute the majority. The present chapter, drawing upon a narrative literature review, will delve into the various forms and expressions of bullying toward all students while focusing on children with SEN since they are more frequently victimized. It aims to highlight the underlying causes and the far-reaching effects and to suggest effective solutions, strategies, and antibullying interventions to address this critical problem by underscoring the

DOI: 10.4018/979-8-3693-5315-8.ch009

significance of school counseling in promoting respect, empathy, interaction, and collaboration among students.

INTRODUCTION

Bullying is a multifaceted and diverse issue impacting millions of individuals annually. School bullying constitutes a pervasive and miscellaneous issue that profoundly impacts the lives, psychology, and academic progress of the students involved. Its significance has spurred extensive research for over four decades, resulting in numerous scholarly articles on the subject (Menesini & Salmivalli, 2017; Olweus, 1978; Volk et al., 2014). Ongoing interdisciplinary research has yielded significant discoveries and conclusions about bullying in schools, recognizing it as a global issue that needs to be addressed by educators, parents, and legislators across national, regional, and international levels (Margevičiūtė, 2017).

Drawing upon existing literature, it has been estimated that 10% to 33% of students report being victimized by peers, whereas 5% to 13% admit to bullying others (Berchiatti et al., 2021; Hymel & Swearer, 2015). In a recent review, Juvonen and Graham (2014) indicate that about 20-25% of young people are directly involved in bullying, either as perpetrators, victims, or both (Menesini & Salmivalli, 2017). Additionally, extensive studies in Western countries indicate that 4-9% of youths frequently engage in bullying behaviors, while 9-25% of school-aged children are victims of bullying (Menesini & Salmivalli, 2017). A recent meta-analysis by Modecki et al. (2014) on the prevalence of bullying and cyberbullying, encompassing a sample of 335,519 adolescents aged 12-18 years, estimated a mean prevalence of 35% for traditional bullying (including both perpetrators and victims) and 15% for cyberbullying involvement (Menesini & Salmivalli, 2017). According to the National Center for Education Statistics (NCES), approximately one in five students in the United States experience some form of school bullying (Foon et al., 2020; Lessne & Yanez, 2018). Recent research has highlighted that bullying constitutes a worldwide phenomenon affecting the lives of millions of people whether they are victims, perpetrators, bystanders, or part of the family social environment of those involved in bullying incidents. Research first began in Scandinavia with Dan Olweus' influential book "Aggression in the Schools: Bullies and Whipping Boys" (Forskning om skolmobbning, 1973; English translation 1978) (Smith, 2016). In the East, Japan and South Korea have also conducted studies since the 1980s (Morita, 1985; Koo, 2007; Smith, 2016). Research on traditional bullying expanded internationally from the mid-1990s to the mid-2000s, with numerous surveys and interventions conducted across various countries (Smith, 1999, 2016; Smith et al., 2004). A significant methodological advancement was the identification of participant roles in bullying categorizing individuals as ringleaders, assistants, reinforcers, defenders, victims, bully/victims, or bystanders (Salmivalli et al., 2017; Smith, 2016).

Although school environments should be safe, creative, and supportive spaces for all students, whether those with special educational needs (SEN) or typically developing, based on an inclusive educational approach, bullying has infiltrated the school community, threatening, obstructing, and deteriorating the inclusion of students in the learning process, thereby hindering their progress, academic growth, and overall well-being (Malisiova & Folia, 2024). To this aim, the educational community and researchers worldwide have conducted systematic studies of school bullying to comprehend the causes, the repercussions, and the possible antibullying interventions. Their goal is to promote empathy, respect, and creative collaboration among students and teachers.

1. DEFINING BULLYING: FORMS, EXPRESSIONS, AND CAUSES

Bullying is generally defined as repeated, intentional aggressive behavior aimed at harming, causing discomfort, or intimidating others, manifesting in physical, verbal, relational/social, and cyber forms (Fink et al., 2015; Margevičiūtė, 2017; Olweus, 1994; Smith, 2016; Volk et al., 2014). It may even entail mobbing, harassment, pestering, silent treatment, ignoring, etc., aiming to cause negative feelings, annoyance, and distress to others (Margevičiūtė, 2017). Cyberbullying, which has grown with the rise of smartphones and social networking sites, is distinct in its anonymity, broader audience, and the lack of respite for victims, often occurring outside school yet involving classmates (Kowalski et al., 2014; Smith, 2016; Zych et al., 2015). Furthermore, school bullying typically thrives due to children's lack of knowledge, maturity, and empathy, leading to repeated negative behavior by students towards their peers (Foon et al., 2020; Power-Elliot & Harris, 2012). It involves bullies, victims, and bystanders, impacting the school climate and leading to unhealthy physical and mental development in affected students (Antwi et al., 2014; Foon et al., 2020; McCormac, 2014; Olweus, 1994). Notably, this phenomenon affects around 36% of children globally (Badger et al., 2023; Falla et al., 2021). Olweus (1991) highlights bullying's key characteristics: intentionality, repetition, and power imbalance, categorizing it into direct (overt attacks like physical or verbal abuse) and indirect (subtle actions like social exclusion) forms (Berchiatti et al., 2021; Menesini & Salmivalli, 2017; Smith, 2016). The complexity of bullying, especially in cases like social exclusion, along with cultural differences, complicates the establishment of a universally agreed-upon definition. However, some researchers argue that this lack of a universal definition allows for more adaptable and effective local prevention strategies (Batsche & Knoff, 1994; Davis & Davis, 2007; Margevičiūtė, 2017; Sanchez, 2008; Smith, 2016; Watkins & Wagner, 2000; Whitted & Dupper, 2005; Younan, 2019).

Peer dynamics play a crucial role in either promoting or preventing bullying, with some students displaying "pro-bullying" attitudes, often peaking during adolescence (Berchiatti et al., 2021; Rigby, 1997; Saracho & Spodek, 2007; Smith, 2016). School bullies usually exhibit unacceptable insulting behaviors and seek to assert power and dominance over their peers by intimidating, abusing, and threatening them (Fink et al., 2015). They capitalize on power disparities to impose prolonged harm on their victims (Falla et al., 2021). Additionally, the dominance hypothesis suggests that some children bully to achieve status within their peer groups, especially during adolescence when concerns about peer status and fear of rejection are heightened (Ellis et al., 2012; Salmivalli, 2010; Smith, 2016). Volk et al. (2012) suggest that bullying can be viewed as an evolutionary adaptation, providing short-term benefits to bullies (Smith, 2016). Some perpetrators are popular, possess strong social skills, and are adept at manipulating others (Smith, 2016). They often excel in the theory of mind tasks, allowing them to understand and effectively harm their victims, a concept known as "cold cognition" (Smith, 2016). Peeters et al. (2009) identified three types of bullies: popular and socially intelligent bullies, moderately popular bullies with average social intelligence, and unpopular bullies with lower social intelligence (Smith, 2016). Concerning bullies, significant predictors include externalizing behaviors such as defiance, disruption, and aggression (Smith, 2016). They also tend to exhibit lower levels of empathy, with some studies indicating that they have reduced affective empathy meaning their ability to share another's feelings but not necessarily lower cognitive empathy that is the ability to recognize another's feelings (Smith, 2016). Bullies often demonstrate high levels of moral disengagement, enabling them to sidestep the typical moral reasoning that prevents harming others (Gini et al., 2013; Smith, 2016). Finally, recent research has also highlighted the student-teacher relationship that may either prevent or promote bullying behaviors (Berchiatti et al., 2021; Longobardi et al., 2018; Sointu et al., 2016). Certain student-teacher relationships may potentially lead to increased disruption and coercion among students (Berchiatti et al., 2021; Jalón & Arias, 2013).

The phenomenon of school bullying has led to the emergence of a term known as "bullycide", introduced in 2001, which refers to the act of suicide committed by a student who finds it less painful than enduring continued bullying, taunting, and humiliation (Margevičiūtė, 2017; Marr & Field, 2001; Thodelius, 2022). This term highlights the severe consequences of prolonged bullying and its profound impact (Margevičiūtė, 2017; Marr & Field, 2001; Thodelius, 2022). Bullycides can be seen as a desperate solution to a dire situation when all other alternatives or options seem unavailable, thereby underscoring the urgent need for adequate and effective interventions (Thodelius, 2022).

2. CHILDREN WITH SPECIAL EDUCATIONAL NEEDS EXPERIENCING BULLYING

The present chapter focuses on students with Special Education Needs (SEN), as they are more likely to be bullied due to their diversity and the cognitive, emotional, and social difficulties they face (Badger et al., 2024). SEN is a term referring to learning difficulties, disabilities, or impairments that require students to receive additional support (UNESCO, 2017: 7). Although there are various definitions, SEN generally refers to children with physical and/or mental disabilities, as well as cognitive and/or educational impairments. The definition of children with SEN varies significantly across countries, as do the policies for their assessment (Barow & Östlund, 2020). Students with SEN are those who experience temporary or permanent difficulties due to socioeconomic, linguistic, cultural factors, or physical, and developmental disabilities/disorders (Kryszewska, 2017). They may encounter challenges in thinking, understanding, and learning, emotional and behavioral difficulties, speech, language, and communication disorders, or even physical and sensory disabilities affecting their learning such as visual or hearing impairments (Kryszewska, 2017). This broad category includes children with autism, speech, language, and communication needs; ADHD; physical disabilities; social and emotional mental health needs; and specific learning disabilities/difficulties (SLDs), such as deficits in reading, writing, and mathematics, which are among the most commonly diagnosed developmental disorders (Berchiatti et al., 2021; Cainelli & Bisiacchi, 2019; Malisiova et al., 2023).

Students with SEN are usually integrated into mainstream classrooms, where regular teachers, special educators, and psychologists provide pedagogical support to improve students' behavioral and academic outcomes (Malisiova & Folia, 2024). However, depending on the cognitive, emotional, and socialization difficulties these students face and on the state policies and laws of each country, they may oftentimes attend schools addressing special education needs. In such cases, they may be deprived of a general classroom and excluded from interacting with neurotypical students. Research indicates that children with SEN struggle with social skills (Freire et al., 2019). Compared to their peers, they exhibit less prosocial behaviors, face lower acceptance, and often have fewer or no friends (Banks et al., 2017; Broomhead, 2018; Dasioti & Kolaitis, 2018; Pinto et al., 2018). They also experience lower quality friendships, higher levels of conflict, more difficulties in repairing relationships, and less stable friendships than their classmates (Berchiatti et al., 2021; Wiener & Schneider, 2002). Additionally, they face challenges in maintaining close, conflict-free relationships with teachers and exhibit greater dependency and dissatisfaction with teacher relationships (Berchiatti et al., 2021; Freire et al., 2019; Murray & Greenberg, 2001; Pasta et al., 2017). They often feel a heightened sense of danger at school and exhibit internalizing and externalizing issues, such as emotional symptoms and hyperactivity, which are linked to bullying victimization (Berchiatti et al., 2021; Boyes et al., 2020; Dasioti & Kolaitis, 2018; Murray & Greenberg, 2001).

According to the World Health Organization's World Report on Disability more than 5% of children between the ages of 0 and 14 have disabilities, including autism spectrum disorders, developmental delays, conduct disorders, and learning difficulties (Falla et al., 2021). These children are especially susceptible to bullying due to inherent power imbalances, yet research focusing on this group remains limited compared to studies on nondisabled students (Badger et al., 2023; Falla et al., 2021). This research gap can be attributed to several factors: the emphasis on providing educational supports for better academic inclusion, the lack of specialized researchers in the area of bullying among disabled students, and the distinct challenges these students encounter in articulating behaviors (Falla et al., 2021). Although there are limited research findings regarding bullying and students with SEN, the data have indicated that these children are more likely to experience and perpetrate bullying compared to their peers (Berchiatti et al., 2021; Dasioti & Kolaitis, 2018; Falla et al., 2021; Rose & Gage, 2016). The trauma they endure is equally harmful on emotional, psychological, and social levels (Falla et al., 2021). Moreover, these children often struggle with having fewer friendships and may adopt aggressive behaviors as a coping strategy (Falla et al., 2021). A systematic review conducted by Badger et al. (2023) found that children with mild disabilities face lower levels of victimization compared to those with severe cognitive or physical disabilities (Falla et al., 2021). Additionally, students in special education classes or segregated schools tend to experience higher rates of victimization than those in inclusive settings (Falla et al., 2021). Subsequent research highlights that students with intellectual disabilities encounter increased rates of victimization, with varying experiences in perpetration (Falla et al., 2021). Furthermore, studies involving children with physical or sensory disabilities and chronic illnesses reveal heightened rates of both victimization and aggression (Falla et al., 2021). Research focusing on students with Autism Spectrum Disorder (ASD) points to a higher prevalence of bullying, though it also emphasizes the limited number of studies and their small sample sizes (Falla et al., 2021). Additionally, studies on cyberbullying among young people with developmental disorders indicate higher rates of prevalence, particularly in segregated educational settings and more so among girls (Falla et al., 2021).

Numerous studies indicate elevated rates of bullying among children with disabilities, particularly when compared to well-matched control groups (Smith, 2016). A Northern Ireland survey (Watters, 2011) revealed significantly higher victimization and perpetration rates among children with disabilities in both primary and post-primary schools (Smith, 2016). Several factors contribute to the increased involvement of children with SEN in bullying, either as victims or perpetrators. These factors include having fewer and lower-quality friendships and experiencing negative peer perceptions and social rejection due to their limited social skills, which do not help them to avoid or cope with bullying. Additionally, certain disability characteristics, such as clumsiness, stammering, or poor hearing, render them easy targets for bullies (Hugh-Jones & Smith, 1999; Mishna, 2003; Smith, 2016; van Roekel et al., 2009). Research also suggests that behavioral and emotional problems may predict bullying behaviors in children with SEN since they often report higher levels of behavioral issues compared to their typically developing peers (Dasioti & Kolaitis, 2018; Fink et al., 2015). On the other hand, students with SEN involving only SLDs, such as reading, writing, and math difficulties, which are less noticeable to their classmates, may experience fewer bullying incidents compared to those with visible or severe disabilities that cause more widespread impairment. Students with SEN have oftentimes reported high levels of behavioral issues, which can make their impairments more striking than the difficulties faced by children with SLDs (Dasioti & Kolaitis, 2018).

In the case of students with SEN being bullied, ignorance, lack of awareness, prejudice, and discrimination that already exist in society contribute to the constant victimization of these students by their classmates. Being perceived as different, weak, vulnerable, or even inferior by their peers leads to these students' social exclusion and targeted bullying (Berchiatti et al., 2021). The challenges they face in social participation and forming relationships with teachers and peers put them at a higher risk of victimization and isolation (Berchiatti et al., 2021; Boyes et al., 2020; Dasioti & Kolaitis, 2018; Freire et al., 2019). Due to their disability or specific learning difficulty, they are considered easy targets by bullies who intimidate, insult, and harm others to gain "respect" and "acceptance" out of fear and to establish their dominance in class as they perceive it. To conclude, former research findings have indicated that children with SEN face more difficulties in social participation and might be at higher risk of being bullied, compared with their classmates, thus, deteriorating their inclusion in the school environment and damaging their psychological state, self-esteem, relationships with peers, and consequently their socialization (Berchiatti et al., 2021).

3. IDENTIFYING THE NEGATIVE REPERCUSSIONS OF BULLYING

Previous research has documented the significant psychological impact of bullying on students, resulting in severe distress, including elevated levels of stress, anxiety, depression, and low self-esteem (Berchiatti et al., 2021; Menesini & Salmivalli, 2017). These psychological effects can cause students to feel unsafe, disillusioned, demotivated, unwilling to participate in class, and isolated. For students with SEN, the impact is even more profound due to their heightened vulnerability. The unique challenges associated with their conditions often make them frequent targets, exacerbating the negative consequences of bullying. School bullying leads to isolation, despair, poor academic performance, and reluctance to attend school, with particularly severe consequences for SEN students. These students may suffer more acutely from academic underachievement, disengagement from school, and absenteeism due to the compounded effects of bullying on their already challenging educational experiences (Fink et al., 2015).

Research findings have consistently shown that bullying leads to significant mental health issues in students, with similar patterns observed across countries (Foon et al., 2020; UNESCO, 2017; Zych et al., 2017). Moreover, the profound mental health effects caused by bullying can persist into adulthood, affecting both SEN students and their neurotypical peers (Foon et al., 2020). In recent years, there has been a rising incidence of suicide or suicidal ideation among teenagers and children due to bullying, further highlighting the critical need for intervention (Foon et al., 2020). Bullying particularly undermines students' mental health and academic performance, obstructing the development of inclusive learning environments essential for both SEN and neurotypical students. Victims of severe bullying, especially those with SEN, exhibit higher levels of depression, emotional symptoms, hyperactivity, and inattention, along with lower levels of school enjoyment and academic achievement compared to their uninvolved peers (Berchiatti et al., 2021; Konishi et al., 2010; Marengo et al., 2018; Stefanek et al., 2017).

Research on bullying has underscored the interplay between individual vulnerabilities, contextual factors, and experiences, suggesting that a social-ecological model is valuable for understanding bullying as a systemic issue that affects the environments in which such behaviors occur (Berchiatti et al., 2021; Hymel & Swearer, 2015). The severe repercussions of bullying on SEN students, as well as their neurotypical peers, highlight the urgent need for targeted interventions and strategies to address this pervasive issue effectively (Foon et al., 2020; Menesini & Salmivalli, 2017).

4. SOLUTIONS, STRATEGIES, AND INTERVENTIONS TO ADDRESS BULLYING

Mainstream anti-bullying interventions can reduce victimization in primary schools by 15-16% and bullying perpetration by 19-20% (Badger et al., 2023). However, there is limited research on interventions specifically tailored for pupils with SEN, even though these students are at least 2-4 times more likely to be involved in bullying (Badger et al., 2023). Research on school bullying identifies two crucial predictive factors: the relationship between students and teachers, and the students' social status among their peers (Berchiatti et al., 2021). Hence, addressing bullying demands both individual coping strategies adopted by the victims as well as the activation of the entire school community entailing teachers, students, parents, and school psychologists, who will promote respect, empathy, understanding, and collaboration among students while resolving bullying incidents, and preventing or addressing expressions of bullying that undermine the inclusion of students in the educational process.

4.1 Individual Coping Strategies

Pupils employ manifold coping strategies when facing bullying, with the effectiveness of these strategies often varying depending on the students' age and gender (Smith, 2016). Non-assertive strategies, such as crying tend to be less effective than strategies such as ignoring bullying or seeking help (Smith, 2016). Former studies reported that the most common coping strategies were talking to someone, ignoring or avoiding the bully, standing up for oneself, and making new friends (Smith, 2016; Smith et al., 2004). High-quality friendships serve as a protective factor against victimization (Fox & Boulton, 2006; Smith, 2016). Additionally, children with high popularity or peer status are often the most effective defenders and may assist victims in gaining their confidence and self-esteem (Caravita et al., 2009; Nickerson et al., 2008; Nickerson et al., 2016; Smith, 2016). Nonetheless, the most successful strategy appeared to be talking to someone, as 67% of those who ceased being victims had used this approach, compared to 46% of those who remained victims and 41% of those who became victims (Smith, 2016). According to Frisén et al. (2012), support from school staff, transitioning to a new school level, and changing coping strategies were the most effective solutions suggested by students to prevent being bullied (Smith, 2016). With cyberbullying, seeking help or support is also found to be effective. A longitudinal study, conducted by Machmutow et al. (2012) indicated that seeking support from peers and family was associated with reduced depression, whereas assertive coping strategies, like contacting the bully, correlated with increased depression (Smith, 2016). Finally, while all students, particularly those with SEN, are encouraged to inform their teachers about bullying, its effectiveness largely depends on the teachers' reactions and responses (Smith, 2016). Students may appear uncertain about teachers' ability to handle cyberbullying and support the victims, and therefore, they often turn to friends and family for guidance, relief, and assistance rather than teachers (Smith, 2016; Zhou et al., 2013).

4.2 Antibullying Interventions Based on Collaborative Approaches

Addressing bullying requires a comprehensive and collaborative approach involving educators, psychologists, parents, policymakers, and community stakeholders. Research and recent literature have suggested raising awareness by implementing educational and counseling programs that foster student empathy, understanding, respect, and acceptance of diversity (Foon et al., 2020). Over the past 30 years, numerous anti-bullying interventions have been developed in addition to promoting individual coping strategies (Smith, 2016). Creating and implementing a comprehensive anti-bullying policy at institutional and governmental levels could offer significant benefits by providing a framework that enables educators to address bullying effectively. Ministries of education, educators, school psychologists, and all stakeholders in educational policies need to promote a culture of inclusivity and zero-tolerance for bullying, with clear policies and procedures for promptly addressing incidents. Furthermore, students with SEN, or those who may differ in any way in terms of race, nationality, social/financial background, or gender, ought to be provided with the support and strategies needed to advocate for themselves (Verasammy & Cooper, 2021). To this aim, peer support programs may assist students in connecting with their peers and receiving guidance, support, and solidarity (Verasammy & Cooper, 2021). Raising awareness, empowering students being bullied, and most importantly eliminating bullying by helping bullies realize the harm they are causing, and the consequences of their actions may lead to the creation of an inclusive school environment (Foon et al., 2020).

To improve the effectiveness of school authorities in addressing bullying, many schools in the United States and Europe have implemented research-based prevention programs, such as the Olweus Bullying Prevention Program (OBBP), STAC ("Stealing the show, Turning it over, Accompanying others, and Coaching compassion"), and Steps to Respect (STR) (Brown et al., 2011; Foon et al., 2020; Midgett et al., 2015; Olweus, 1993). Based on the findings of Badger et al. (2023), several key interventions can be recommended to address bullying among students with SEN. These interventions include implementing programs that enhance social skills and peer networks through strategies such as buddy systems, peer mentoring, role-playing, and creating storyboards, integrated across the entire school to foster inclusivity and peer support (Badger et al., 2023). Anti-bullying programs should utilize clear, accessible language, person-first terminology, and concrete examples of bullying, ensuring materials are relatable and understandable to SEN students (Badger et al., 2023; Raskauskas & Modell, 2011; Walton, 2012). A whole-school approach is essential, with mainstream programs like KiVa adapted to include SEN-specific elements, involving the entire school community, staff, students, and parents, in unified anti-bullying efforts (Badger et al., 2023; Salmivalli et al., 2012). Increasing supervision in high-risk areas and providing individualized support can help SEN students navigate social situations and report bullying more effectively (Badger et al., 2023; Heinrichs, 2003). Incorporating interactive methods, such as video modeling and movement opportunities, can engage SEN students and provide practical strategies for addressing bullying (Badger et al., 2023; McNamara, 2017). Finally, adapting evidence-based programs like Second Step or the Olweus Bullying Prevention Program (OBPP) to meet the unique needs of SEN students ensures that they fully benefit from the interventions (Badger et al., 2023; Espelage et al., 2015; Sullivan et al., 2015). Implementing these strategies can create a safer, more inclusive environment for SEN students, thereby reducing bullying and improving their overall school experience (Badger et al., 2023).

However, such programs are implemented in certain countries and schools, whereas the majority of schools struggle to cope with bullying incidents without the support of counselors or the potential to apply evidence-based prevention programs that could provide them with guidelines assisting them to combat bullying. The limited number of counselors and the lack of institutional support hinder the implementation of these programs that could prove most beneficial (Foon et al., 2020; Midgett et al., 2017; Power-Elliot & Harris, 2012). School counselors could support students' behavior, emotions, and cognition, ensure a safe learning environment, and play a crucial role in this process (ASCA, 2003; Foon et al., 2020). Nevertheless, they cannot address bullying alone and need to collaborate with principals, district administrators, teachers, and parents to identify suitable prevention programs for students' welfare. Addressing the complex issue of school bullying requires specialized skills for effective intervention. Consequently, counselors have become central figures in managing bullying and leading the implementation of anti-bullying programs (Foon et al., 2020; Midgett et al., 2015). However, there is a notable shortage of certified counselors with the necessary training in anti-bullying strategies. As a result, teachers are often required to develop counseling skills while identifying and implementing appropriate prevention programs (American School Counselor Association "ASCA", 2003; Foon et al., 2020). Oftentimes, there are no specific national programs for bullying prevention, and schools typically employ their own methods to address bullying incidents (Foon et al., 2020; Fadzlina & Li, 2018). Consequently, most prevention programs are designed by school authorities in cooperation with counselors (Fadzlina & Li, 2018). Regrettably, it has been reported that most bullying cases go unreported (Foon et al., 2020). Studies suggest that victims have little trust in counselors or doubt the effectiveness of the school's prevention programs, primarily due to fear of retaliation (Foon et al., 2020; McCormac, 2014). This fear must be addressed to enhance students' confidence in reporting bullying incidents.

4.3 The Role of the Teacher-Counselor

The particularly demanding role of the teacher-counselor entails counseling skills, interpersonal interactions, and the building of trusting and honest relationships among teachers and students. Since most schools worldwide are deprived of the presence of a counselor, teachers are expected to adopt and undertake this intricate role along with the assistance and support of school psychologists, whenever they both have sufficient time, due to their heavy workload and insufficient staffing (Malisiova & Folia, 2024). The teacher's role in addressing bullying is of utmost importance, as they are responsible for creating a friendly and collaborative classroom atmosphere, offering protection, guidance, and understanding to students, and implementing school counseling with the guidance provided by psychologists (Iotti et al., 2020; Longobardi et al., 2019; Foon et al., 2020). Although it is essential for teachers to receive training through educational psychology and counseling programs, such training is not always provided, making this task extremely challenging (Kottler & Kottler, 2006). The counseling process mandates the educator to demonstrate empathy, respect, and understanding by sharing personal feelings and experiences, reflecting and identifying the thoughts, emotions, and reactions of the students, and building a mutual relationship of trust with the students (Carlozzi et al., 2002; Malikiosi-Loizou, 2011; Thwaites & Bennett-Levy, 2007).

Educators frequently encounter negative reactions, bullying incidents, psychological fluctuations, hostile behaviors, and various other behavioral issues from students. It is essential that they adopt and implement appropriate counseling approaches and methods to meet the continuously evolving needs of students and conduct an effective counseling process (Hornby, 2003). Building a relationship of trust between students and the educator can be a lengthy process requiring patience, persistence, tolerance, understanding, and empathy from the educator (Hornby et al., 2003). Educators need to possess good listening skills, be devoid of critical, dogmatic, and judgmental comments, and refrain from imposing personal opinions or beliefs on others. Instead by posing open-ended questions followed by clarifying questions teachers may allow students to express themselves and become aware of the problem. They should aim to assist students in approaching, addressing, and resolving issues by encouraging free expression and showing genuine interest in the student's life, thoughts, and feelings (Hornby et al., 2003; Malikiosi-Loizou, 2011). Thus, it becomes necessary for teachers to receive training in counseling, and to be supported by educational institutions and collaborate with specialists, such as school psychologists (Brouzos et al., 2015).

As recent research has suggested a warm and close student-teacher relationship can serve as a protective factor against bullying (Berchiatti et al., 2021; Iotti et al., 2020). This type of relationship is especially crucial during the early school years since it significantly influences students' future adaptation and development (Wanders et al., 2020). The attitude of teacher-counselors regarding the school environment plays a crucial role in resolving bullying incidents. Teachers who exhibit enthusiasm are more inclined to provide counseling and engage other adults, such as principals, staff, and parents, thereby bolstering the efficacy of prevention programs (Power-Elliot & Harris, 2012). This comprehensive collaboration promotes a consensus-driven approach to managing bullying, tailored to the severity of the incidents (Foon et al., 2020). Apart from being alert to bullying expressions and incidents at school, teachers are also responsible for educating parents about recognizing bullying signs in their children (Arcuri, 2018; McCormac, 2014). Furthermore, Bagley et al. (2001) emphasize the importance of parental involvement in bullying cases, especially those involving students with SEN (Begotti et al., 2018). To this aim, teachers should build effective alliances with parents to facilitate their cooperation, help, and support in addressing bullying incidents among students. Parental understanding and cooperation provide a foundation for more effective anti-bullying interventions when necessary (Begotti et al., 2018).

Classroom-based interventions can serve as an early approach by promoting and integrating bullying prevention campaigns within the regular classroom schedule (Midgett et al., 2017; Tawalbeh et al., 2015). Teachers should be encouraged and supported to tailor programs that fit the specific needs of their schools while collaborating with principals, administrators, school psychologists, and staff, as such modifications often yield more positive results (Lund et al., 2012; McCormac, 2014; Midgett et al., 2017; Power-Elliot & Harris, 2012). Additionally, designing tailored programs allows teachers to address the unique bullying phenomena within their schools, considering the school environment and peer relationships to better tackle bullying based on the school climate (Acuri, 2018; Lund et al., 2012). However, formal training in this area is crucial for teachers to implement antibullying programs efficiently and successfully (Acuri, 2018; Cornell & Huang, 2014). Educators also need to consistently implement awareness campaigns within the school community since research has indicated that the level of awareness regarding bullying prevention programs is frequently low among students, partly due to some schools not prioritizing anti-bullying initiatives (Foon et al., 2020; McCormac, 2014). To address this, teachers need to consistently implement awareness campaigns within the school community to enhance targeting both students and teachers (Foon et al., 2020; McElearney et al., 2012; Uzunboylu et al., 2017). Furthermore, they should be adequately trained to recognize victims, perpetrators, and bystanders for appropriate counseling interventions while fostering self-respect, promoting positive values, and encouraging respect for the rights of others (Foon et al., 2020). Students, particularly victims and bystanders, frequently fear retaliation. Thus, it is crucial to establish a secure reporting mechanism to safeguard these students (Cornell & Huang, 2014; Tawalbeh et al., 2015). Implementing a safe reporting system can mitigate the stigma associated with reporting bullying and encourage a larger proportion of students to come forward (Foon et al., 2020).

Consequently, teachers play a pivotal role in addressing bullying, particularly involving students with SEN, and require specific training in both pre-service and in-service contexts to intervene effectively. This training should encompass both overt and covert forms of bullying, enabling teachers to distinguish these behaviors from other forms of aggression that are not repetitive, imbalanced, or intentional (Begotti et al., 2018). Effective training should include examples of successful interventions for both bullies and victims and employ techniques such as videos and role plays to aid in understanding theories and applying intervention strategies in simulated scenarios (Bauman & Del Rio, 2005; Begotti et al., 2018). Additionally, training should enhance teachers' abilities to promote empathy and pro-social skills throughout the classroom, not just among bullies and victims, thereby disrupting the bully-victim dynamic and influencing children's attitudes towards bullying and bystander behavior (Begotti et al., 2018). This is especially crucial for SEN students who are particularly vulnerable and require an accommodating classroom environment (Begotti et al., 2018). Specific university courses can further enhance teachers' capacities for effective intervention by addressing the nature and causes of bullying, the roles of those involved, and the unique challenges posed by bullying of SEN students, ultimately helping to stop and prevent bullying incidents and, thus, benefiting victims, perpetrators, the classroom community, and teachers' well-being (Nicolaides et al., 2002; Begotti et al., 2018).

4.4 School Counseling as a Framework for Addressing Bullying

School counseling could offer the most efficient framework for addressing bullying, by guiding students, including both bullies and victims, through a process of recognizing, accepting, and overcoming their negative behaviors, feelings, difficulties, and stressful or traumatic experiences. Bullying cannot be effectively prevented or eliminated unless educational policies emphasize the implementation of school counseling programs to provide guidance and support to all students since bullying harms not only the victim but also the perpetrator and all stakeholders (Foon et al.,

2020). School counseling is defined as an approach applied by teachers, guided by school psychologists, to provide psychological support to students whenever there is a need or concern (Malikiosi-Loizou, 2011). The benefits of counseling are manifold. At the classroom level, it addresses problems in interpersonal relationships and interactions among students, resolves conflicts, and fosters a positive atmosphere in the school classroom, thereby promoting participation, cooperation, and academic progress among students (Malikiosi-Loizou, 2011). On an individual level, counseling assists students in achieving better psychological balance, managing difficult or unpleasant situations more effectively, and generally evolving and progressing as mentally healthy and creative individuals who respect themselves and others (Malikiosi-Loizou, 2011).

The utilization and implementation of the humanistic counseling model involve three stages, as shown in Table 1 (Malikiosi-Loizou, 2011). The first stage, "exploration," involves understanding the concerns of the students receiving counseling, who express their thoughts and feelings and gain self-awareness about their issues (Malikiosi-Loizou, 2011). At this preliminary stage, the educator's role is crucial in building a trusting relationship with the students by approaching them with understanding and empathy, and encouraging them to express themselves without hesitation or fear of criticism (Fahlevi, 2020; Malikiosi-Loizou, 2011). The middle stage referred to as "insight" is that of self-exploration (Fahlevi, 2020). It involves students comprehending their emotions, capabilities, and behaviors while considering alternative perspectives provided by the counselor-educator, who helps broaden the students' thinking, especially when emotions hinder the problem-solving process (Fahlevi, 2020; Malikiosi-Loizou, 2011). In this stage, the counselor may use techniques such as active listening and open-ended questions, paraphrasing, and reflecting emotions, "challenge", "interpretation", and "self-disclosure" techniques (Malikiosi-Loizou, 2011). The final stage, "actualization", encompasses the students addressing and resolving the problem by making decisions and demonstrating new behaviors and reactions (Fahlevi, 2020; Hill, 2020; Malikiosi-Loizou, 2011). The educator's role remains significant, guiding the student with alternative approaches and suggestions regarding problem-solving, future behaviors, and actions (Malikiosi-Loizou, 2011).

Table 1. Humanistic counseling model

Humanistic Counseling Model	Key Components	Educator's Role	Techniques Used
Stage 1: Exploration	- Understanding student concerns - Students express thoughts and feelings - Gaining self-awareness	- Build a trusting relationship - Approach with understanding and empathy - Encourage expression without fear	- Active Listening - Empathy - Open-ended questions
Stage 2: Insight	- Self-exploration - Understanding emotions, capabilities, behaviors - Broadening perspectives with counselor's help	- Facilitate deeper self-exploration - Broaden students' thinking, especially in emotional contexts	- Active Listening - Open-ended questions - Paraphrasing - Reflecting emotions - Challenge - Interpretation - Self-disclosure
Stage 3: Actualization	- Addressing and making decisions - Demonstrating new behaviors	- Guide problem-solving approaches - Suggest future behaviors and actions	- Decision-Making support - Guidance on problem-solving

Correspondingly counseling psychology delineates five stages in the counseling process, closely aligning with the humanistic counseling model (Table 2). Initially, the educator establishes a relationship of trust, respect, and cooperation with the students, explaining the counseling process and fostering positive feelings and attitudes toward each other and the process itself (Hardy et al., 2007; Malikiosi-Loizou, 2011). The counseling relationship is multidimensional, requiring a "working alliance", an agreement between counselor and students on the goals and methods of the counseling process (Malikiosi-Loizou, 2011). It is also a "transference" relationship, where the educator becomes the recipient of the students' emotions, perceptions, and behaviors (Malikiosi-Loizou, 2011). All these aspects necessitate the creation of a "genuine" and sincere relationship (Stalikas & Mertika, 2004; Malikiosi-Loizou, 2011). Once such a relationship is established, the students' concerns are identified, whether they are difficulties, worries, sadness, doubts, or anything that causes negative emotions, anxiety, and distress (Malikiosi-Loizou, 2011). Having understood and clarified the problem in the students' minds, students set the goals they wish to achieve (Malikiosi-Loizou, 2011). It is essential that these goals are achievable, realistic, and feasible based on the students' capabilities, allowing them to feel confident and secure, and dismissing fears, doubts, and reservations (Malikiosi-Loizou, 2011). In the fourth stage, students examine alternative solutions and proposals they can adopt and implement to solve the problem. The educator proposes, guides, and assists students in finding the best solution (Fatchurahman et al., 2020; Malikiosi-Loizou, 2011). If this proves difficult, the educator uses techniques such as brainstorming, summarizing concerns, "interpretation", and "self-disclosure" (Egan, 2009). In the final stage, known as "generalization", students apply their new behavior and attitude in practice with the support and guidance of the counselor, which is combined with planning future behaviors and reactions, reinforced by family or group counseling, and continuous monitoring (Malikiosi-Loizou, 2011).

Table 2. Counseling process in counseling psychology

Stage in Counseling Process	Description	Educator's Role	Techniques Used
Stage 1: Relationship Building	- Establish trust, respect, and cooperation - Explain the counseling process - Foster positive feelings and attitudes	- Build a multidimensional relationship - Create a "working alliance" and "transference" relationship	- Active listening - Empathy - Positive reinforcement
Stage 2: Problem Identification	- Identify students' concerns - Understand and clarify the problem	- Encourage students to express concerns - Help students articulate their issues	- Open-ended questions - Reflective listening - Paraphrasing
Stage 3: Goal Setting	- Set achievable, realistic, and feasible goals - Ensure goals align with students' capabilities	- Guide students in setting appropriate goals - Boost students' confidence and security	- Goal-setting strategies - Encouragement - Clarification
Stage 4: Exploring Solutions	- Examine alternative solutions - Propose, guide, and assist in finding the best solution	- Support students in exploring and evaluating options - Facilitate decision-making	- Brainstorming - Summarizing - Interpretation - Self-disclosure
Stage 5: Generalization	- Apply new behavior and attitude in practice - Plan future behaviors and reactions - Continuous monitoring and reinforcement	- Provide ongoing support - Reinforce learning through family/group counseling	- Follow-up sessions - Continuous monitoring - Planning and reinforcement strategies

By implementing school counseling, whether for individual students or groups involved in bullying incidents, all participants could benefit by gaining insight into their feelings, behaviors, and actions and, consequently, their impact on others. During the counseling process, students, whether victims or bullies, must comprehend the causes and effects of their actions. Bullies attending counseling sessions will have the opportunity to listen to their victims' perspectives, understand the challenges they face in their daily lives, and comprehend the emotional toll of bullying. Through interaction with students with SEN, bullies may gain insight into their victims' experiences and the impact of bullying on them. Consequently, this awareness of their actions and the expression of both parties' emotions, will pave the way for conflict resolution.

5. DISCUSSION

Recent research findings have proven valuable for teachers and educational researchers by highlighting the specific needs and challenges of SEN students concerning bullying. Despite the international focus on bullying, research on this topic remains limited, particularly concerning specific populations (Berchiatti et al., 2021). Badger et al. (2023) emphasize the significant need for high-quality randomized controlled trials to establish an evidence base for anti-bullying programs tailored to SEN students. Additionally, further research is needed to understand the unique aspects of bullying and reporting within the SEN population. With better-designed, evidence-based anti-bullying programs, SEN students can receive more effective support globally, offering an opportunity to reconsider pedagogical strategies to address bullying and promote social inclusion (Berchiatti et al., 2021).

For educational researchers, the findings contribute to the understanding of the links between bullying, student-teacher relationships, and peer status in children. Therefore, drawing upon existing literature, addressing bullying requires a multifaceted approach that targets its root causes, mitigates its detrimental effects, and promotes a culture of respect and inclusiveness. Inclusive classrooms must support all students and advocate for the inclusion of those who are victimized due to their SEN or any form of differentiation, as well as those students who engage in bullying behavior, potentially stemming from their own traumas and difficulties. An essential prerequisite for creating such a constructive, supportive, and creative school environment is recognizing behavioral problems and bullying and the implementation of counseling by teachers and other stakeholders, whenever deemed necessary.

The teacher's role in this context appears most demanding, as educators must remain vigilant and approach students with empathy, respect, and understanding. They are tasked with managing the intricate societal issue of bullying under significant expectations from school authorities and parents. Their responsibilities include implementing successful prevention programs, organizing awareness activities and campaigns, collaborating with the involved parties, encouraging student reporting, and personally addressing individual cases (Foon et al., 2020). These demands can be challenging to meet without sufficient assistance and institutional support. Most importantly, educators and students should jointly address behavioral and bullying issues. Open and honest dialogue, interaction, and communication facilitated through school counseling and educational policies aimed at addressing bullying could therefore contribute to creating inclusive, safe, and nurturing classroom environments (Verasammy & Cooper, 2021).

Furthermore, it is essential to remind students of the continuous support available from the school, empowering them to assertively address bullying. This approach may foster a love for learning, promote progress and collaboration, and cultivate an environment of trust, acceptance, and support among all stakeholders (Foon et al., 2020). In conclusion, an effective bullying prevention strategy necessitates comprehensive programs, committed school stakeholders, and the dedicated efforts of educators to promote healthier physical and mental development among students affected by bullying incidents (Foon et al., 2020). The necessary knowledge of counseling and the expected support by all members of the school community, including principals, school psychologists, and parents, will enable educators to resolve continually emerging problems, support, and guide students, and, thus, create a climate of cooperative learning in the classroom, aiming for the inclusion of all students and the establishment of an optimal educational environment (Athanasiadou, 2011).

REFERENCES

American School Counselor Association. (n.d.). *(2003). The ASCA national model: A framework for school counselling programs.* Author.

Antwi, H. A., Yiranbon, E., Lulin, Z., Maxwell, B. A., Agebase, A. J., Yaw, N. E., & Vakalalabure, T. T. (2014). Innovation Diffusion Among Healthcare Workforce: Analysis of adoption and use of medical ICT in Ghanaian tertiary hospitals. *International Journal of Academic Research in Business & Social Sciences*, 4(7). Advance online publication. DOI: 10.6007/IJARBSS/v4-i7/987

Arcuri, N. M. (2018). Counseling Relationship Experiences for K-12 School Counselors Who Also Fulfill the Role of Anti-Bullying Specialist. *Journal of School Counseling*, 16(5), n5.

Athanasiadou, C. (2011). Counseling psychology in the school context. *Hellenic Journal of Psychology*, 8, 289–308.

Badger, J. R., Nisar, A., & Hastings, R. P. (2023). School-based anti-bullying approaches for children and young people with special educational needs and disabilities: A systematic review and synthesis. *Journal of Research in Special Educational Needs*, 24(3), 742–757. DOI: 10.1111/1471-3802.12665

Bagley, C., Woods, P. A., & Woods, G. (2001). Implementation of School Choice Policy: Interpretation and response by parents of students with special educational needs. *British Educational Research Journal*, 27(3), 287–311. DOI: 10.1080/01411920120048313

Banks, J., McCoy, S., & Frawley, D. (2017). One of the gang? peer relations among students with special educational needs in Irish mainstream primary schools. *European Journal of Special Needs Education*, 33(3), 396–411. DOI: 10.1080/08856257.2017.1327397

Barow, T., & Östlund, D. (2020). Stuck in failure: Comparing special education needs assessment policies and practices in Sweden and Germany. *Nordic Journal of Studies in Educational Policy*, 6(1), 37–46. DOI: 10.1080/20020317.2020.1729521

Batsche, G. M., & Knoff, H. M. (1994). Bullies and their victims: Understanding a pervasive problem in the schools. *School Psychology Review*, 23(2), 165–174. DOI: 10.1080/02796015.1994.12085704

Bauman, S., & Del Rio, A. (2005). Knowledge and beliefs about bullying in schools. *School Psychology International*, 26(4), 428–442. DOI: 10.1177/0143034305059019

Begotti, T., Tirassa, M., & Acquadro Maran, D. (2018). Pre-service teachers' intervention in school bullying episodes with special education needs students: A research in Italian and Greek samples. *International Journal of Environmental Research and Public Health*, 15(9), 1908. DOI: 10.3390/ijerph15091908 PMID: 30200541

Berchiatti, M., Ferrer, A., Galiana, L., Badenes-Ribera, L., & Longobardi, C. (2021). Bullying in students with special education needs and learning difficulties: The role of the student–teacher relationship quality and students' social status in the Peer Group. *Child &amp. Child and Youth Care Forum*, 51(3), 515–537. DOI: 10.1007/s10566-021-09640-2

Boyes, M. E., Leitão, S., Claessen, M., Badcock, N. A., & Nayton, M. (2020). Correlates of externalising and internalising problems in children with dyslexia: An analysis of data from clinical casefiles. *Australian Psychologist*, 55(1), 62–72. DOI: 10.1111/ap.12409

Broomhead, K. E. (2018). Acceptance or rejection? the social experiences of children with special educational needs and disabilities within a mainstream primary school. *Education 3-13*, 47(8), 877–888. DOI: 10.1080/03004279.2018.1535610

Brouzos, A., Vassilopoulos, S., Korfiati, A., & Baourda, V. (2015). Secondary school students' perceptions of their counselling needs in an era of global financial crisis: An exploratory study in Greece. *International Journal for the Advancement of Counseling*, 37(2), 168–178. DOI: 10.1007/s10447-015-9235-6

Brown, E. C., Low, S., Smith, B. H., & Haggerty, K. P. (2011). Outcomes from a school-randomized controlled trial of steps to respect: A bullying prevention program. *School Psychology Review*, 40(3), 423–443. DOI: 10.1080/02796015.2011.12087707

Cainelli, E., & Bisiacchi, P. S. (2019a). Diagnosis and treatment of developmental dyslexia and specific learning disabilities: Primum Non Nocere. *Journal of Developmental &amp. Journal of Developmental and Behavioral Pediatrics*, 40(7), 558–562. DOI: 10.1097/DBP.0000000000000702 PMID: 31259753

Caravita, S. C., Di Blasio, P., & Salmivalli, C. (2009). Unique and interactive effects of empathy and social status on involvement in bullying. *Social Development*, 18(1), 140–163. DOI: 10.1111/j.1467-9507.2008.00465.x

Carlozzi, A. F., Bull, K. S., Stein, L. B., Ray, K., & Barnes, L. (2002). Empathy theory and practice: A survey of psychologists and counselors. *The Journal of Psychology*, 136(2), 161–170. DOI: 10.1080/00223980209604147 PMID: 12081091

Cornell, D., & Huang, F. (2014). School counselor use of peer nominations to identify victims of bullying. *Professional School Counseling*, 18(1), 191–205. DOI: 10.5330/2156-759X-18.1.191

Dasioti, & Kolaitis, G. (2018). Bullying and the mental health of schoolchildren with special educational needs in primary education. *Psychiatriki*, 29(2), 149–159. DOI: 10.22365/jpsych.2018.292.149

Davis, S., & Davis, J. (2007). *Schools where everyone belongs: Practical strategies for reducing bullying*. Research Press.

Egan, G. (2009). *The skilled helper. A problem management and opportunity approach to helping*. Brooks Cole.

Ellis, B. J., Del Giudice, M., Dishion, T. J., Figueredo, A. J., Gray, P., Griskevicius, V., Hawley, P. H., Jacobs, W. J., James, J., Volk, A. A., & Wilson, D. S. (2012). The evolutionary basis of risky adolescent behavior: Implications for science, policy, and practice. *Developmental Psychology*, 48(3), 598–623. DOI: 10.1037/a0026220 PMID: 22122473

Espelage, D. L., Rose, C. A., & Polanin, J. R. (2015). Social-emotional learning program to reduce bullying, fighting, and victimization among middle school students with disabilities. *Remedial and Special Education*, 36(5), 299–311. DOI: 10.1177/0741932514564564

Fadzlina, H. S. L. A. N., & Li, N. L. P. (2018). Counseling To Understand and Intervene School Bullying. *Social Science Learning Education Journal*, 3(1). Advance online publication. DOI: 10.15520/sslej.v3i1.58

Fahlevi, R. (2020). The human and existential approach to improve students' emotional intelligence in school counseling program. *Konselor*, 9(1), 29–35. DOI: 10.24036/0202091105961-0-00

Falla, D., Sánchez, S., & Casas, J. A. (2021). What do we know about bullying in schoolchildren with disabilities? A systematic review of recent work. *Sustainability (Basel)*, 13(1), 416. DOI: 10.3390/su13010416

Fatchurahman, M., Karyanti, K., Setiawan, M. A., & Habsy, B. A. (2020). Development of Guidance Counselling for Increased Engagement and Empathy of Middle School Bullies. *International Journal of Innovation* [IJICC]. *Creativity and Change*, 13(10), 1366–1385.

Fink, E., Deighton, J., Humphrey, N., & Wolpert, M. (2015). Assessing the bullying and victimisation experiences of children with special educational needs in mainstream schools: Development and validation of the bullying behaviour and experience scale. *Research in Developmental Disabilities*, 36, 611–619. DOI: 10.1016/j.ridd.2014.10.048 PMID: 25462521

Foon, L. W., Hassan, S. A., & Nordin, M. H. (2020). Counselling intervention to address school bullying: A systematic review of literature. *International Journal of Academic Research in Business & Social Sciences*, 10(16). Advance online publication. DOI: 10.6007/IJARBSS/v10-i16/8301

Fox, C. L., & Boulton, M. J. (2006). Friendship as a moderator of the relationship between social skills problems and peer victimisation. *Aggressive Behavior*, 32(2), 110–121. DOI: 10.1002/ab.20114

Freire, S., Pipa, J., Aguiar, C., Vaz da Silva, F., & Moreira, S. (2019). Student–teacher closeness and conflict in students with and without special educational needs. *British Educational Research Journal*, 46(3), 480–499. DOI: 10.1002/berj.3588

Frisén, A., Hasselblad, T., & Holmqvist, K. (2012). What actually makes bullying stop? reports from former victims. *Journal of Adolescence*, 35(4), 981–990. DOI: 10.1016/j.adolescence.2012.02.001 PMID: 22475445

Gini, G., Pozzoli, T., & Hymel, S. (2013). Moral disengagement among children and youth: A Meta-analytic review of links to aggressive behavior. *Aggressive Behavior*, 40(1), 56–68. DOI: 10.1002/ab.21502 PMID: 24037754

Hardy, G., Cahill, J., & Barkham, M. (2007). Active ingredients of the therapeutic relationship that promote client change. In Gilbert, P., & Leahy, R. (Eds.), *The therapeutic relationship in the cognitive behavioral psychotherapies* (pp. 24–42). Routledge., DOI: 10.4324/9780203099995

Heinrichs, R. R. (2003). A whole-school approach to bullying: Special considerations for children with exceptionalities. *Intervention in School and Clinic*, 38(4), 195–204. DOI: 10.1177/105345120303800401

Hill, C. E. (2020). *Helping skills: Facilitating exploration, insight, and action.* American Psychological Association. DOI: 10.1037/0000147-000

Hornby, G. (2003). A model for counselling in schools. In *Counselling pupils in schools* (pp. 24–34). Routledge.

Hornby, G., Hall, C., & Hall, E. (2003). *Counselling pupils in schools*. RoutledgeFalmer., DOI: 10.4324/9780203182772

Hugh-Jones, S., & Smith, P. K. (1999). Self-reports of short- and long-term effects of bullying on children who stammer. *The British Journal of Educational Psychology*, 69(2), 141–158. DOI: 10.1348/000709999157626 PMID: 10405616

Hymel, S., & Swearer, S. M. (2015). Four decades of research on school bullying: An introduction. *The American Psychologist*, 70(4), 293–299. DOI: 10.1037/a0038928 PMID: 25961310

Iotti, N. O., Thornberg, R., Longobardi, C., & Jungert, T. (2020). Early adolescents' emotional and behavioral difficulties, student–teacher relationships, and motivation to defend in bullying incidents. In *Child & Youth Care Forum* (Vol. 49, pp. 59–75). Springer US., DOI: 10.1007/s10566-019-09519-3

Jalón, M. J. D. A., & Arias, R. M. (2013). Peer bullying and disruption-coercion escalations in student-teacher relationship. *Psicothema*, 25(2), 206–213. DOI: 10.7334/psicothema2012.312 PMID: 23628535

Juvonen, J., & Graham, S. (2014). Bullying in schools: The power of bullies and the plight of victims. *Annual Review of Psychology*, 65(1), 159–185. DOI: 10.1146/annurev-psych-010213-115030 PMID: 23937767

Konishi, C., Hymel, S., Zumbo, B. D., & Li, Z. (2010). Do school bullying and student—Teacher relationships matter for academic achievement? A multilevel analysis. *Canadian Journal of School Psychology*, 25(1), 19–39. DOI: 10.1177/0829573509357550

Koo, H. (2007). A time line of the evolution of school bullying in differing social contexts. *Asia Pacific Education Review*, 8(1), 107–116. DOI: 10.1007/BF03025837

Kottler, J. A., & Kottler, E. (2006). *Counseling skills for teachers*. Corwin Press.

Kowalski, R. M., Giumetti, G. W., Schroeder, A. N., & Lattanner, M. R. (2014). Bullying in the digital age: A critical review and meta-analysis of cyberbullying research among youth. *Psychological Bulletin*, 140(4), 1073–1137. DOI: 10.1037/a0035618 PMID: 24512111

Kryszewska, H. (2017). Teaching students with special needs in inclusive classrooms special educational needs. *ELT Journal*, 71(4), 525–528. DOI: 10.1093/elt/ccx042

Lessne, D., & Yanez, C. (2018). *Repetition and Power Imbalance in Bullying Victimization at School. Data Point. NCES 2018-093*. National Center for Education Statistics.

Longobardi, C., Badenes-Ribera, L., Gastaldi, F. G., & Prino, L. E. (2018). The student–teacher relationship quality in children with selective mutism. *Psychology in the Schools*, 56(1), 32–41. DOI: 10.1002/pits.22175

Longobardi, C., Settanni, M., Prino, L. E., Fabris, M. A., & Marengo, D. (2019). Students' psychological adjustment in normative school transitions from kindergarten to high school: Investigating the role of teacher-student relationship quality. *Frontiers in Psychology*, 10, 1238. Advance online publication. DOI: 10.3389/fpsyg.2019.01238 PMID: 31191415

Lund, E. M., Blake, J. J., Ewing, H. K., & Banks, C. S. (2012). School counselors' and school psychologists' bullying prevention and intervention strategies: A look into real-world practices. *Journal of School Violence*, 11(3), 246–265. DOI: 10.1080/15388220.2012.682005

Machmutow, K., Perren, S., Sticca, F., & Alsaker, F. D. (2012). Peer victimisation and depressive symptoms: Can specific coping strategies buffer the negative impact of cybervictimisation? *Emotional & Behavioural Difficulties*, 17(3–4), 403–420. DOI: 10.1080/13632752.2012.704310

Malikiosi-Loizou, M. (2011). *Counseling Psychology in Education*. Pedio.

Malisiova, A., & Folia, V. (2024). Educational Challenges and Perspectives in Developmental Dyslexia. In *Childhood Developmental Language Disorders: Role of Inclusion, Families, and Professionals* (pp. 49-64). IGI Global. DOI: 10.4018/979-8-3693-1982-6.ch004

Malisiova, A., Kougioumtzis, G. A., Tsitsas, G., Koundourou, C., & Mitraras, A. (2023). Implementing inclusive education in mixed-ability classrooms by employing differentiated instruction. In Perspectives of cognitive, psychosocial, and learning difficulties from childhood to adulthood: Practical counseling strategies (pp. 155–178). IGI Global., 1-6684-8203-2.ch009.DOI: 10.4018/978-1-6684-8203-2.ch009

Marengo, D., Jungert, T., Iotti, N. O., Settanni, M., Thornberg, R., & Longobardi, C. (2018). Conflictual student–teacher relationship, emotional and behavioral problems, prosocial behavior, and their associations with bullies, victims, and bullies/victims. *Educational Psychology*, 38(9), 1201–1217. DOI: 10.1080/01443410.2018.1481199

Margevičiūtė, A. (2017). The definition of bullying in compulsory education: From a general to a legal perspective. *Baltic Journal of Law &amp. Politics*, 10(1), 205–229. DOI: 10.1515/bjlp-2017-0008

Marr, N., & Field, T. (2001). *Bullycide: Death at playtime*. Success Unlimited.

McCormac, M. (2014). Preventing and responding to bullying: An elementary school's 4-Year journey. *Professional School Counseling*, 18(1), 1–14. DOI: 10.5330/prsc.18.1.55607227n4428tkp

McElearney, A., Adamson, G., Shevlin, M., & Bunting, B. (2012). Impact evaluation of a school-based counselling intervention in Northern Ireland: Is it effective for pupils who have been bullied? *Child Care in Practice*, 19(1), 4–22. DOI: 10.1080/13575279.2012.732557

McNamara, B. E. (2017). Practices That Address Bullying of Students with Disabilities. *Journal for Leadership and Instruction*, 16(2), 31–35.

Menesini, E., & Salmivalli, C. (2017). Bullying in schools: The state of knowledge and effective interventions. *Psychology, Health & Medicine, 22*(sup1), 240–253. DOI: 10.1080/13548506.2017.1279740

Midgett, A., Doumas, D., Sears, D., Lundquist, A., & Hausheer, R. (2015). A bystander bullying psychoeducation program with middle school students: A preliminary report. *The Professional Counselor*, 5(4), 486–500. DOI: 10.15241/am.5.4.486

Midgett, A., Doumas, D. M., Johnston, A., Trull, R., & Miller, R. (2017). Rethinking bullying interventions for high school students: A qualitative study. *Journal of Child and Adolescent Counseling*, 4(2), 146–163. DOI: 10.1080/23727810.2017.1381932

Mishna, F. (2003). Learning disabilities and bullying. *Journal of Learning Disabilities*, 36(4), 336–347. DOI: 10.1177/00222194030360040501 PMID: 15490906

Modecki, K. L., Minchin, J., Harbaugh, A. G., Guerra, N. G., & Runions, K. C. (2014). Bullying prevalence across contexts: A meta-analysis measuring cyber and traditional bullying. *The Journal of Adolescent Health*, 55(5), 602–611. DOI: 10.1016/j.jadohealth.2014.06.007 PMID: 25168105

Morita, Y. (1985). *Sociological study on the structure of bullying group*. Department of Sociology, Osaka City University.

Murray, C., & Greenberg, M. T. (2001). Relationships with teachers and bonds with school: Social Emotional adjustment correlates for children with and without disabilities. *Psychology in the Schools*, 38(1), 25–41. DOI: 10.1002/1520-6807(200101)38:1<25::AID-PITS4>3.0.CO;2-C

Nickerson, A. B., Feeley, T. H., & Tsay-Vogel, M. (2016). Applying mass communication theory to bystander intervention in bullying. *Adolescent Research Review*, 2(1), 37–48. DOI: 10.1007/s40894-016-0030-3

Nickerson, A. B., Mele, D., & Princiotta, D. (2008). Attachment and empathy as predictors of roles as defenders or outsiders in bullying interactions. *Journal of School Psychology*, 46(6), 687–703. DOI: 10.1016/j.jsp.2008.06.002 PMID: 19083379

Nicolaides, S., Toda, Y., & Smith, P. K. (2002). Knowledge and attitudes about school bullying in trainee teachers. *The British Journal of Educational Psychology*, 72(1), 105–118. DOI: 10.1348/000709902158793 PMID: 11916467

Olweus, D. (1978). *Aggression in the schools: Bullies and whipping boys*. Hemisphere.

Olweus, D. (1991). Chapter 3 victimization among school children. *Advances in Psychology*, 76, 45–102. DOI: 10.1016/S0166-4115(08)61056-0

Olweus, D. (1993). *Bullying at school: What we know and what we can do*. Blackwell Publishing.

Olweus, D. (1994). Bullying at school. *Promotion &amp. Education*, 1(4), 27–31. DOI: 10.1177/102538239400100414 PMID: 7820380

Pasta, T., Mendola, M., Longobardi, C., Prino, L. E., & Gastaldi, F. G. (2017). Attributional style of children with and without specific learning disability. *Electronic Journal of Research in Educational Psychology*, 11(31), 649–664. DOI: 10.14204/ejrep.31.13064

Peeters, M., Cillessen, A. H., & Scholte, R. H. (2009). Clueless or powerful? identifying subtypes of bullies in adolescence. *Journal of Youth and Adolescence*, 39(9), 1041–1052. DOI: 10.1007/s10964-009-9478-9 PMID: 20625880

Pinto, C., Baines, E., & Bakopoulou, I. (2018). The peer relations of pupils with special educational needs in mainstream primary schools: The importance of meaningful contact and interaction with peers. *The British Journal of Educational Psychology*, 89(4), 818–837. DOI: 10.1111/bjep.12262 PMID: 30580444

Power-Elliott, M., & Harris, G. E. (2012). Guidance counsellor strategies for handling bullying. British Journal of Guidance &amp. *British Journal of Guidance & Counselling*, 40(1), 83–98. DOI: 10.1080/03069885.2011.646947

Raskauskas, J., & Modell, S. (2011). Modifying anti-bullying programs to include students with disabilities. *Teaching Exceptional Children*, 44(1), 60–67. DOI: 10.1177/004005991104400107

Rigby, K. (1997). Attitudes and beliefs about bullying among Australian school children. *The Irish Journal of Psychology*, 18(2), 202–220. DOI: 10.1080/03033910.1997.10558140

Rose, C. A., & Gage, N. A. (2016). Exploring the involvement of bullying among students with disabilities over time. *Exceptional Children*, 83(3), 298–314. DOI: 10.1177/0014402916667587

Salmivalli, C. (2010). Bullying and the Peer Group: A Review. *Aggression and Violent Behavior*, 15(2), 112–120. DOI: 10.1016/j.avb.2009.08.007

Salmivalli, C., Kärnä, A., & Poskiparta, E. (2012). Development, evaluation, and diffusion of a national anti-bullying program, KiVa. In *Handbook of youth prevention science* (pp. 238–252). Routledge.

Salmivalli, C., Lagerspetz, K., Björkqvist, K., Österman, K., & Kaukiainen, A. (2017). Bullying as a group process: Participant roles and their relations to social status within the group. *Interpersonal Development*, 233–247. DOI: 10.4324/9781351153683-13

Sanchez, J. (2008). 2007-2008 Survey of Florida Public Employment Law. *Nova Law Review*, 33, 169.

Saracho, O., & Spodek, B. (Eds.). (2007). *Contemporary perspectives on socialization and social development in early childhood education*. IAP.

Smith, P. K. (Ed.). (1999). *The nature of school bullying: A cross-national perspective*. Psychology Press.

Smith, P. K. (2016). Bullying: Definition, types, causes, consequences and intervention. *Social and Personality Psychology Compass*, 10(9), 519–532. DOI: 10.1111/spc3.12266

Smith, P. K., Talamelli, L., Cowie, H., Naylor, P., & Chauhan, P. (2004). Profiles of non-victims, escaped victims, continuing victims and new victims of school bullying. *The British Journal of Educational Psychology*, 74(4), 565–581. DOI: 10.1348/0007099042376427 PMID: 15530202

Sointu, E. T., Savolainen, H., Lappalainen, K., & Lambert, M. C. (2016). Longitudinal associations of student–teacher relationships and behavioural and emotional strengths on academic achievement. *Educational Psychology*, 37(4), 457–467. DOI: 10.1080/01443410.2016.1165796

Stalikas, A., & Mertika, A. (2004). *The Therapeutic Alliance*. Ellinika Grammata.

Stefanek, E., Strohmeier, D., & Yanagida, T. (2017). Depression in groups of bullies and victims: Evidence for the differential importance of peer status, reciprocal friends, school liking, academic self-efficacy, school motivation and academic achievement. *International Journal of Developmental Science*, 11(1–2), 31–43. DOI: 10.3233/DEV-160214

Sullivan, T. N., Sutherland, K. S., Farrell, A. D., & Taylor, K. A. (2015). An evaluation of Second Step. *Remedial and Special Education*, 36(5), 286–298. DOI: 10.1177/0741932515575616

Tawalbeh, A. H., Abueita, J. D., Mahasneh, A., & Shammout, N. (2015). Effectiveness of a counseling program to improve self-concept and achievement in bully-victims. *Review of European Studies*, 7(7). Advance online publication. DOI: 10.5539/res.v7n7p36

Thodelius, C. (2022). Re-framing and exploring online suicidal games as a specific form of cyberbullying. *International Journal of Criminology and Sociology*, 9, 231–240. DOI: 10.6000/1929-4409.2020.09.21

Thwaites, R., & Bennett-Levy, J. (2007). Conceptualizing empathy in cognitive behaviour therapy: Making the implicit explicit. *Behavioural and Cognitive Psychotherapy*, 35(05), 591–612. DOI: 10.1017/S1352465807003785

UNESCO. (2017). *A guide for ensuring inclusion and equity in education*. Author.

Uzunboylu, H., Baglama, B., özer, N., Kucuktamer, T., & Kuimova, M. V. (2017). Opinions of school counselors about bullying in Turkish high schools. *Social Behavior and Personality*, 45(6), 1043–1055. DOI: 10.2224/sbp.6632

van Roekel, E., Scholte, R. H., & Didden, R. (2009). Bullying among adolescents with autism spectrum disorders: Prevalence and perception. *Journal of Autism and Developmental Disorders*, 40(1), 63–73. DOI: 10.1007/s10803-009-0832-2 PMID: 19669402

Verasammy, K.-J., & Cooper, M. (2021). Helpful aspects of counselling for young people who have experienced bullying: A thematic analysis. *British Journal of Guidance &amp. British Journal of Guidance & Counselling*, 49(3), 468–479. DOI: 10.1080/03069885.2021.1900777

Volk, A. A., Camilleri, J. A., Dane, A. V., & Marini, Z. A. (2012). Is adolescent bullying an evolutionary adaptation? *Aggressive Behavior*, 38(3), 222–238. DOI: 10.1002/ab.21418 PMID: 22331629

Volk, A. A., Dane, A. V., & Marini, Z. A. (2014). What is bullying? A theoretical redefinition. *Developmental Review*, 34(4), 327–343. DOI: 10.1016/j.dr.2014.09.001

Walton, E. (2012). Using literature as a strategy to promote inclusivity in high school classrooms. *Intervention in School and Clinic*, 47(4), 224–233. DOI: 10.1177/1053451211424604

Wanders, F. H., van der Veen, I., Dijkstra, A. B., & Maslowski, R. (2019). The influence of teacher-student and student-student relationships on societal involvement in Dutch primary and secondary schools. *Theory &amp. Theory and Research in Social Education*, 48(1), 101–119. DOI: 10.1080/00933104.2019.1651682

Watkins, C., & Wagner, P. (2000). *Improving school behaviour*. SAGE Publications Ltd., DOI: 10.4135/9781446219096

Watters, R. M. (2011). *The nature and extent of pupil bullying in schools in the North of Ireland*. Department of Education for Northern Ireland.

Whitted, K. S., & Dupper, D. R. (2005). Best practices for preventing or reducing bullying in schools. *Children &amp. Children & Schools*, 27(3), 167–175. DOI: 10.1093/cs/27.3.167

Wiener, J., & Schneider, B. H. (2002). A multisource exploration of the friendship patterns of children with and without learning disabilities. *Journal of Abnormal Child Psychology*, 30(2), 127–141. DOI: 10.1023/A:1014701215315 PMID: 12002394

Younan, B. (2019). A systematic review of bullying definitions: How definition and format affect study outcome. *Journal of Aggression, Conflict and Peace Research*, 11(2), 109–115. DOI: 10.1108/JACPR-02-2018-0347

Zhou, Z., Tang, H., Tian, Y., Wei, H., Zhang, F., & Morrison, C. M. (2013). Cyberbullying and its risk factors among Chinese high school students. *School Psychology International*, 34(6), 630–647. DOI: 10.1177/0143034313479692

Zych, I., Farrington, D. P., Llorent, V. J., & Ttofi, M. M. (2017). School bullying in different countries: Prevalence, risk factors, and short-term outcomes. *SpringerBriefs in Psychology*, 5–22. DOI: 10.1007/978-3-319-53028-4_2

Zych, I., Ortega-Ruiz, R., & Del Rey, R. (2015). Scientific research on bullying and cyberbullying: Where have we been and where are we going. *Aggression and Violent Behavior*, 24, 188–198. DOI: 10.1016/j.avb.2015.05.015

Chapter 10
Relations Among Perceived Peer Acceptance, Fear of Missing Out, and Cyberbullying:
A Comparative Study Between Elementary School Students Without and With High Functioning ASD

Thanos Touloupis
https://orcid.org/0009-0008-8310-306X
University of the Aegean, Greece

Anastasia Alevriadou
https://orcid.org/0000-0001-7022-5537
Aristotle University of Thessaloniki, Greece

Asimenia Papoulidi
University of West Attica, Greece

ABSTRACT

The present chapter presents a study which investigated comparatively cyberbullying (as victims/bullies) between students without and with high functioning ASD. Also, the contributing role of perceived peer acceptance and FoMO was examined.

DOI: 10.4018/979-8-3693-5315-8.ch010

Overall, 252 students without (53% boys) and 239 students with high functioning ASD (63% boys) of fifth and sixth grades of Greek elementary schools completed a related self-report scales. The results showed that both male and female students with high functioning ASD engage in cyberbullying (as victims/bullies) to a greater extent than their typically developing peers. Additionally, in the relationship between perceived peer acceptance and cyberbullying involvement FoMO proved a full mediator for typically developing students and a partial mediator for students with high functioning ASD. The findings imply the intensification of cyberbullying prevention actions in elementary education, especially for students with ASD, which could be enriched with experiential activities aimed at strengthening face to face peer relationships.

INTRODUCTION

The present study investigated comparatively cyberbullying involvement (as victims/bullies) between elementary school students without and with high functioning Autistic Spectrum Disorder (ASD). At the same time, within the framework of the social cognitive theory (SCT; Bandura, 2002), the contributing role of perceived peer acceptance and Fear of Missing Out (FoMO) in cyberbullying involvement was examined for each student subgroup.

Cyberbullying is defined as "an aggressive, intentional act carried out by a group of individuals or an individual, using electronic means of communication, repeatedly and over time, against a victim who he cannot easily defend himself/herself" (Smith et al., 2008, p. 376). Today, due the rapid increase of social media use by youths, cyberbullying concerns not only adolescents but elementary school children as well (Arslan et al., 2012; Barlett, 2023; Evangelio et al., 2022; Mehari et al., 2023; Monks et al., 2012; Olenik-Shemesh & Heiman, 2014; Rodríguez-Álvarez et al., 2021; Sezer et al., 2013; Tian et al., 2023). However, the studies on elementary school students reveal a wide range of rates of cyber-victims (from 19% to 27%) and cyberbullies (from 5% to 18%) implying an unclear research picture regarding the real extent of this phenomenon in this age group. Therefore, future related studies are needed to offer more evidence for possible intensification of related prevention actions in elementary education. This is of high importance considering that elementary school years is an optimal time period to introduce prevention and awareness initiatives (Sprague & Walker, 2021).

Furthermore, international findings reveal that students with ASD, due to their difficulties in their interpersonal relationships and the subsequent stigmatization issues usually arise at school (Aubé et al., 2021; Mazumder & Thompson-Hodgetts, 2019) engage as bullies/victims not only in face to face but also in online arguments/

fights, indicative of cyberbullying (Beckman et al., 2020; Begara Iglesias et al., 2019; Holfeld et al., 2019; Hu et al., 2019; Kowalski & Fedina, 2011; Lin et al., 2023; Liu et al., 2021). Nevertheless, most of these studies have been conducted exclusively on secondary education (Begara Iglesias et al., 2019; Hu et al., 2019; Liu et al., 2021) or in a mixed sample of both elementary and secondary school students (Holfeld et al., 2019; Kowalski & Fedina, 2011; Lin et al., 2023). Consequently, we are not allowed to draw safe conclusions about autistic elementary school students' involvement in cyberbullying. Related findings could highlight the necessity to expand the school prevention programs against this phenomenon to other vulnerable student groups, such as elementary school children with ASD. Additionally, according to the authors' knowledge, only two studies have examined comparatively cyberbullying in elementary education between students without and with ASD leading, however, to inconsistent findings. For example, Begara Iglesias et al. (2019) found that that there are no significant differences in cyberbullying frequency between secondary school students without and with Asperger syndrome (high functioning ASD), while more recently Touloupis and Athanasiades (2022) concluded that elementary school students with Asperger syndrome engage as victims/bullies in this phenomenon to a greater extent, compared to their peers of typical development. It is, therefore, an imperative need future comparative studies to offer more evidence concerning the possibly greater vulnerability of any of these target groups in elementary education (children with/without ASD) towards cyberbullying. In this way, cyberbullying school prevention actions may be oriented mainly to specific student groups.

Regarding the gender-based profile of elementary school students who tend to engage in cyberbullying episodes (as victims/bullies), the studies also reveal conflicted findings. On the one hand, it is mentioned that among students of typical development boys tend to engage more frequently as bullies while girls more often as victims (Arslan et al., 2012; Delgado & Escortell Sánchez, 2018; Deniz, 2015; Evangelio et al., 2022; Jiménez, 2019; Sorrentino et al., 2019), while, on the other hand, other studies conclude no gender differences (Monks et al., 2012; Touloupis & Athanasiades, 2014). Accordingly, regarding findings from elementary school students with ASD (Asperger syndrome), systematic reviews show girls' over-involvement in cyberbullying (Beckman et al., 2020), while other studies do not highlight gender as a significant differentiating factor (Touloupis & Athanasiades, 2022). Therefore, the above research picture reflects an ambiguous gender-based profile of students without and with ASD at risk for experiencing (as victims/bullies) cyberbullying. Clarifying whether male or female students tend to be more prone to the involvement in cyberbullying (as victim/bully) could highlight the necessity of intensifying related school prevention actions and their content based on students' gender.

Except for identifying student groups vulnerable to cyberbullying, it is important possible contributors to be highlighted. In this way, prevention actions could aim not only to raise awareness of cyberbullying but also to strengthen or weaken protective and risk factors, respectively. In this context, socio-ecological framework proposed by the SCT (Bandura, 2002) could be utilized. Based on the SCT, the manifestation of a human behavior (e.g., cyberbullying incidence) could be explained more holistically and realistically by an interplay between context-related and intrapersonal variables.

Considering that cyberbullying incidents usually occur between classmates (Touloupis & Athanasiades, 2014, 2022) the contributing role of peers and mainly of perceived peer acceptance could be examined. This is of higher importance for students with ASD, given the stigmatizing behaviors from classmates they often experience in school (Aubé et al., 2021; Mazumder & Thompson-Hodgetts, 2019). Perceived peer acceptance concerns students' sense of classmates with whom students have social interactions at school but not necessarily close/friendly relationships (Hall, 2019; Parks, 2007). Since peer acceptance reflects students' sense of being accepted by classmates (perceived peer acceptance) in the school context, it could be viewed as a perceived school context-related variable. According to international literature, only few partially related studies are identified. For example, it is mentioned that high deviant peer affiliation, negative peer group status and peer support for sexual violence positively contribute to adolescents' involvement in cyberbullying (Collibee et al., 2021; Ding et al., 2020; Vanden Abeele & De Cock, 2013). Also, adolescents' perceived peer norms as well as their interaction with deviant peers seem to predict their involvement in cyberbullying (Maftei & Măirean, 2023; Wang et al., 2023). These contributors, although somehow related to peers, do not reflect the exact content of the concept of peer acceptance and concern only secondary school students. Thus, there is no clear research evidence about the contributing role of perceived peer acceptance in cyberbullying, and primarily for elementary school students without and with ASD. Identifying for each student subgroup the contribution of perceived peer acceptance to cyberbullying engagement could imply the extent to which peers should have a decisive role in school prevention programs against cyberbullying among students without and with ASD.

As far as the intrapersonal contributors to cyberbullying, FoMO could be considered one such under-investigated variable that appears to have a positive predictive value for cyberbullying involvement. FoMO, which is considered a personal trait, is defined as individuals' general anxiety about missing out on others' information, events, experiences, or life decisions posted on social media (Przybylski et al., 2013; Sun et al., 2022). Based on the theory of "Use and Satisfy" (Ferris et al., 2021; Kircaburun et al., 2018) individuals' lack of basic psychological needs triggers FoMO, which in turn makes them use social media platforms excessively in an effort to acquire, maintain or strengthen interpersonal relationships and feel psychologically autonomous and competent. Within this context, individuals are likely to end up engaging in unpleasant online experiences indicative of cyberbullying. The latter is supported by limited studies on secondary school and university students, which reveal that individuals characterized by FoMO tend to be more vulnerable to engage in problematic/addictive use of social media and cyberbullying incidents (Brailovskaia & Margraf, 2024; Hosseini Sfidvadjani et al., 2023; Sun et al., 2022).

Except for the above conclusions about the contributing role of perceived peer acceptance and FoMO in cyberbullying involvement (as victims/bullies), a recent study highlighted a more complex interplay among similar variables. Specifically, Kostić et al. (2022) found that late adolescents' perceived peer support (as a variable partially related to perceived peer acceptance) contributes to social media use not only directly but also indirectly via the mediating role of FoMO. This finding along with the framework of the SCT described above (Bandura, 2002) could imply that perceived peer acceptance (as a perceived context-related factor) may hinder (as a negative contributor to) cyberbullying (as a negative way of social media use). At the same time, perceived peer acceptance may interact with FoMO (as an intrapersonal underlying psychological mechanism) and explain in a multidimensional way cyberbullying involvement. Nevertheless, this proposed pattern of relationships has never been tested empirically for the variables of perceived peer acceptance and cyberbullying, as well as for the under-investigated target groups of elementary school students without and with ASD. Testing this pattern of relationships via a proposed mediation model, separately for students without and with ASD, may reveal the kind of variables (perceived context-related, intrapersonal) with a dominant contribution to cyberbullying involvement of each student subgroup. Therefore, possibly differentiated variables should be considered when planning cyberbullying school prevention programs for students of typical development or with ASD.

Considering the above literature review, the present study investigated comparatively cyberbullying involvement (as victims/bullies) between elementary school students without and with high functioning ASD. Additionally, within the framework of the SCT the contributing role of perceived peer acceptance and FoMO in cyberbullying involvement was tested for each student subgroup.

Specifically, the research goals were to investigate:

(a) The effect of the presence/absence of high functioning ASD on the extent of students' involvement in cyberbullying (as victims/bullies)
(b) Gender-based differences in the extent of cyberbullying involvement (as victims/bullies) for both student subgroups.
(c) The pattern of the relationships among the variables under study (perceived peer acceptance, FoMO, cyberbullying) which explains cyberbullying involvement (as victims/bullies) for both student subgroups.

According to the available literature, the hypothesized connection model of the variables involved is reflected in Figure 1.

Figure 1. Hypothetical structural model of the relationships among variables

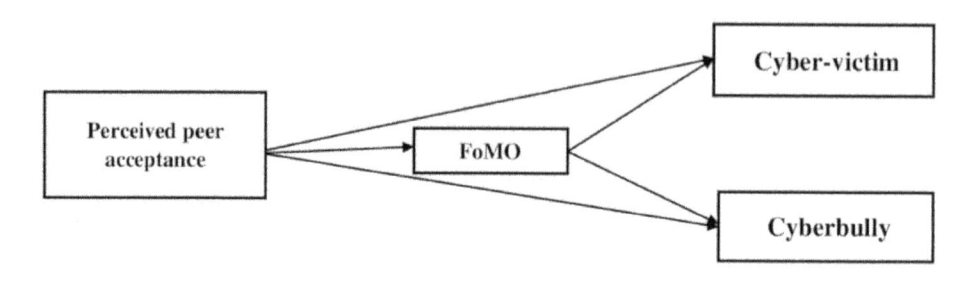

The corresponding research hypotheses were the following:

Hypothesis 1: Students with high functioning ASD involve in cyberbullying (as victims/bullies) to a greater extent, compared to their peers of typical development (Touloupis & Athanasiades, 2022).
Hypothesis 2: For both student subgroups boys are involved mainly as bullies and girls as victims in cyberbullying (Evangelio et al., 2022; Sorrentino et al., 2019; Touloupis & Athanasiades, 2022).
Hypothesis 3: For students of typical development perceived peer acceptance negatively contributes to cyberbullying involvement (as victims/bullies), not only directly (Hypothesis 3a), but also indirectly through the negative mediating role of FoMO (Hypothesis 3b) (Kostić et al., 2022). A corresponding hypothesis for students with high functioning ASD was not formulated due to the lack of related findings.

METHOD

Sample

Based on the results of the G*Power analysis (see Data Analysis Plan), the sample included 252 students of typical development (53% boys) and 239 students with high functioning ASD (63% boys). All students made use of social media platforms (e.g., Facebook, Instagram, Twitter, TikTok) through their own or others' digital devices. Students attended fifth and sixth grades[1] of randomly selected Greek elementary schools (response rate: 39%) in mainstream education in Thessaloniki and Athens, which are the two largest cities with students that are representative of the whole Greek student population (Pan-Hellenic School Network, n.d.). All schools had an integration class, namely a class where students with mild special educational needs such as high functioning ASD are supported some hours per day by a special education teacher (Ministry of Education, 2018). For both student subgroups ages ranged from 11 to 13 years (students of typical development: M_{age} = 11.9, SD = .93, students with high functioning ASD: M_{age} = 12.4, SD = 1.02). Students with high functioning ASD had been diagnosed in the past by officially institutionalized educational diagnostic centers under the auspices of the Greek Ministry of Education. Finally, the pilot sample, which was not incorporated into the final sample, included 32 students of typical development (48% boys) and 30 students with high functioning ASD (60% boys).

Measures

The self-report questionnaire, except for the demographic questions (gender, age), included the following three main parts:

Cyberbullying: Students' involvement in cyberbullying was investigated via a short version of the "Cyberbullying Questionnaire" (Smith et al., 2006), which has been previously used in Greek elementary school students without and with high functioning ASD with good psychometric properties (Touloupis & Athanasiades, 2022). The questionnaire includes 8 questions regarding different ways of cyberbullying involvement as a victim (4 questions; e.g., "Have you received on social media (e.g., Facebook, Instagram, Twitter), in the last year, offensive photos/images or videos?") and as a bully (4 questions; e.g., "Have you spread, in the last year, negative rumors or comments about someone on social media (e.g., Facebook, Instagram, Twitter) to make him/her feel bad/sad/upset?"), reflecting the dimensions of cyber-victim and cyberbully, respectively. The questions refer to the last year so that even earlier cyberbullying incidents to be mentioned. Responses are given on a five-point scale as follows: 1 = *I have not done anything similar / Nothing similar has ever happened to me*, 2 = *I have done it/It has happened to me 1 or 2 times*, 3 = *I have done it/It has happened to me 2 or 3 times a month*, 4 = *I do it/It happens to me about once a week*, and 5 = *I do it/It happens to me several times a week*. Higher mean scores in each dimension reflect higher involvement in cyberbullying as victim and bully, respectively.

Testing the questionnaire's factorial validity, a principal component analysis was applied using the Varimax-type rotation for the total sample (KMO = .901, Bartlett Chi-square = 2398.032, $p < .001$), as well as separately for students without (KMO = .895, Bartlett Chi-square = 1959.109, $p < .001$) and with high functioning ASD

(KMO = .881, Bartlett Chi-square = 1803.182, $p < .001$) to ensure the same factorial structure in each case. Two factors emerged in each case with eigenvalue > 1.0 and significant interpretive values: Total sample (Factor 1 = Cyber-victim, explaining 34.29% of the total variance with loading from .588 to .792, Factor 2 = Cyberbully, explaining 33.81% of the total variance with loading from .683 to .724), Students of typical development (Factor 1 = Cyber-victim, explaining 37.18% of the total variance with loading from .531 to .609, Factor 2 = Cyberbully, explaining 35.02% of the total variance with loading from .502 to .708), Students with high functioning ASD (Factor 1 = Cyber-victim, explaining 32.05% of the total variance with loading from .499 to .582, Factor 2 = Cyberbully, explaining 31.21% of the total variance with loading from .412 to .604). The internal consistency indexes in each case were the following: Total sample (Factor 1 [$\alpha = .902$], Factor 2 [$\alpha = .883$]), Students of typical development (Factor 1 [$\alpha = .894$], Factor 2 [$\alpha = .859$]), Students with high functioning ASD (Factor 1 [$\alpha = .852$], Factor 2 [$\alpha = .841$]).

Peer acceptance: Students' perceived peer acceptance was investigated via the Greek version (using the back-and-forth translation method) of the peer acceptance subscale of the Classmate Social Isolation Questionnaire for adolescents (CSIQ-A; Cavicchiolo et al., 2019). The subscale includes 4 questions about students' sense of classmates with whom they have social interactions at school but not necessarily close/friendly relationships (e.g., "How many of your classmates do you get along with?", "How many of your classmates do you have a chat with?"). Responses are given on a five-point Likert scale (from 1 = *None* to 5 = *All*). Higher mean scores show higher sense of peer acceptance.

Testing the scale' factorial validity, a principal component analysis was applied using the Varimax-type rotation for the total sample (KMO = .884, Bartlett Chi-square = 1873.019, $p < .001$), as well as separately for students without (KMO = .859, Bartlett Chi-square = 1408.908, $p < .001$) and with high functioning ASD (KMO = .828, Bartlett Chi-square = 1730.104, $p < .001$) to ensure the same factorial structure in each case. One factor emerged in each case with eigenvalue > 1.0 and significant interpretive values: Total sample (Factor 1 = Perceived peer acceptance, explaining 66.83% of the total variance with loading from .505 to .611), Students of typical development (Factor 1 = Perceived peer acceptance, explaining 64.02% of the total variance with loading from .482 to .552), Students with high functioning ASD (Factor 1 = Perceived peer acceptance, explaining 62.85% of the total variance with loading from .435 to .591). The internal consistency indexes in each case were the following: Total sample (Factor 1 [$\alpha = .876$]), Students of typical development (Factor 1 [$\alpha = .848$]), Students with high functioning ASD (Factor 1 [$\alpha = .833$]).

FoMO: Students' FoMO was investigated via the Greek version (using the back-and-forth translation method) of the Fear of Missing Out Scale by Przybylski et al. (2013). The scale includes 10 statements reflecting one dimension that concerns students' sense of missing out on others' important information, events, or experiences (e.g., "I fear my friends have more rewarding experiences than me."). Responses are given on a five-point Likert scale (from 1 = *Not at all true of me* to 5 = *Extremely true of me*). Higher mean scores show higher FoMO.

Testing the scale' factorial validity, a principal component analysis was applied using the Varimax-type rotation for the total sample (KMO = .831, Bartlett Chi-square = 1382.022, $p < .001$), as well as separately for students without (KMO = .838, Bartlett Chi-square = 1539.301, $p < .001$) and with high functioning ASD (KMO = .821, Bartlett Chi-square = 1402.039, $p < .001$) to ensure the same factorial structure in each case. One factor emerged in each case with eigenvalue > 1.0 and significant interpretive values: Total sample (Factor 1 = FoMO, explaining 69.02% of the total variance with loading from .514 to .629), Students of typical development (Factor 1 = FoMO, explaining 65.11% of the total variance with loading from .501 to .694), Students with high functioning ASD (Factor 1 = FoMO, explaining 63.04% of the total variance with loading from .509 to .632). The internal consistency indexes in each case were the following: Total sample (Factor 1 [α = .889]), Students of typical development (Factor 1 [α = .857]), Students with high functioning ASD (Factor 1 [α = .824]).

Procedure

Upon obtaining approval for the study by the Greek Institute of Educational Policy (Φ22/2298/Δ1, 28/08/2023), the researchers emailed the randomly selected schools describing all the necessary information about the study and attaching the research approval. In case of a positive response from school principals, the researchers forwarded the consent form through email, asking school principals to deliver it to parents/guardians of students who attended fifth and sixth grade. Parents/guardians via the consent form were informed about the study and were asked to mention if their child had been diagnosed in the past with high functioning ASD by an official educational diagnostic center. After the return of the signed consent forms, and upon consultation with the teachers of the fifth and sixth grades of the participating schools, the researchers were invited to administer the questionnaire to students whose parents/guardians had consented (November 2023 - February 2024). Before completing the questionnaire, students were asked if they make use of social media platforms through their own or others' digital devices. Only 9 students replied negatively and they were excluded from the sample. Students' filled in the questionnaire in the classroom in about 15 minutes in the presence of the researchers in case of questions. The above procedure was also applied to the pilot study (October 2023). The study was conducted fully in line with the ethical rules of anonymity and confidentiality.

Data Analysis Plan

Without any missing cases different statistical tests were applied to the study. For each analysis an a priori power analysis of sample size was performed, using G*Power 3.1 (Faul et al., 2007), with power (1-β) of 85%, medium effect ($f = .05$), and an alpha error of probability $\alpha = .05$. The effect of the presence/absence of high functioning ASD on the extent of students' involvement in cyberbullying (Hypothesis 1) was investigated via a multivariate analysis of variance-MANOVA (Noncentrality parameter $\delta = 2.79$, Critical t = 1.63, df = 52, Actual power: .85, required sample per group: $N = 203$). Accordingly, the effect of gender on the extent of students' involvement in cyberbullying (Hypothesis 2) was tested through a MANOVA (Non-centrality parameter $\delta = 3.22$, Critical t = 1.43, df = 48, Actual power: .84, required sample per group: $N = 211$). To examined the bivariate relationships among the variables involved Pearson (Pearson r) correlations were performed (Noncentrality parameter $\delta = 3.82$, Critical t = 2.19, df = 59, Actual power: .85, required sample: $N = 205$). Furthermore, to explore the pattern of the relationships among the variables under study (Hypotheses 3), a path model was tested (based on the Mplus program with the Maximum Likelihood method). Firstly, preliminary multiple regressions were performed to investigate the predictive relationships per two variables at a time (Noncentrality parameter $\delta = 2.47$, Critical t = 2.85, df = 51, Actual power: .85, required sample: $N = 201$). Secondarily, the mediating role of FoMO was checked for the path model (Noncentrality parameter $\delta = 3.14$, Critical t = 2.91, df = 54, Actual power: .84, required sample: $N = 209$). The assumptions of normality were met, since the skewness and kurtosis values of the variables were lower than |3| and lower than |10|, respectively (Kline 2004).

RESULTS

Cyberbullying Involvement (as Victims/Bullies) Between Students Without and With High Functioning ASD

According to the results, the absence/existence of high functioning ASD affected significantly the extent of students' involvement in cyberbullying, Pillai's trace = .542, $F(4, 487) = 4.018$, $p = .000$, partial $\eta^2 = .49$. Applying Bonferroni correction ($p < .025$), the above effect proved significant for both roles, cyber-victim: $F(2, 489) = 3.115$, $p = .002$, partial $\eta^2 = .41$ and cyberbully: $F(2, 489) = 3.834$, $p = .003$, partial $\eta^2 = .44$. Specifically, according to Chart 1, students with high functioning ASD reported that they are involved in cyberbullying as cyber-victims ($Mean = 3.11$, $SD = .89$) and cyberbullies ($Mean = 2.98$, $SD = .81$) to a greater extent, compared to their peers of typical development (*Mean* = 2.61, *SD* = .49 and *Mean* = 2.54, *SD* = .53, respectively). However, it should be mentioned that, based on the 5-point answering scale of "Cyberbullying Questionnaire", cyberbullying involvement (as victims/bullies) is considered above average for students with high functioning ASD and slightly above average for students of typical development.

Table 1. Cyber-victimization and cyberbullying between students without (N = 252) and with high functioning ASD (N = 239)

Gender and Cyberbullying Involvement (as Victims/Bullies)

According to the results, gender did not seem to affect significantly the extent of involvement in cyberbullying for both, students of typical development, Pillai's trace = .288, $F(4, 487) = 2.301$, $p = .214$, and students with high functioning ASD, Pillai's trace = .109, $F(4, 487) = 2.123$, $p = .321$. Therefore, both students of typical development and with high functioning ASD, regardless of their gender, are involved in cyberbullying incidents (as victims/bullies). As a result, gender was not inserted in the path models for the two student subgroups.

Correlations Among the Variables

Correlational analyses were run for the total sample and separately for students of typical development and with high functioning ASD, to ensure the same pattern of correlations among the variables under examination in each case. In each case, the following correlations were observed: positive correlations between the roles of cyber-victim and cyberbully (from $r = .492$ to $r = .612$, $p < .01$), namely being a cyber-victim may trigger being a cyberbully and vice versa, negative correlations between perceived peer acceptance, on the one hand, and the roles of cyber-victim and cyberbully, on the other hand (from $r = -.121$, $p < .05$ to $r = -.612$, $p < .01$), namely the higher the sense of peer acceptance the lower involvement in cyberbullying, negative correlations between perceived peer acceptance, on the one hand, and FoMO, on the other hand (from $r = -.348$ to $r = -.502$, $p < .01$), namely the higher the sense of peer acceptance the lower FoMO, and finally positive correlations between FoMO, on the one hand, and the roles of cyber-victim and cyberbully, on the other hand (from $r = .314$ to $r = .523$, $p < .01$), namely the higher the FoMO the higher the involvement in cyberbullying.

The Structure of the Relationships Among the Variables

The results showed good fit indexes for path models for both student subgroups: students of typical development, $\chi^2(61, N = 252) = 19.104$, $p < .01$ (CFI = .982, TLI = .937, RMSEA = .051, SRMR = .052) explaining 51% of the variance of cyberbullying involvement, students with high functioning ASD, $\chi^2(81, N = 239) = 15.032$, $p < .01$ (CFI = .966, TLI = .961, RMSEA = .048, SRMR = .043) explaining 54% of the variance of cyberbullying involvement (Figure 2). To test the validity of these two mediation models, the bootstrapping method was used. This non-parametric method was chosen for its ability to produce accurate confidence intervals (CI) for the indirect effect, without the need for assumptions about the normality of the data distribution.

Based on the bootstrapping analysis for the mediation model for students of typical development, the indirect effects were statistically significant, with a 95% confidence interval that did not include zero (CI: .27, .44). This implies that the mediating role of FoMO is significant in the relationship between perceived peer acceptance and cyberbullying involvement (as victims/bullies). When FoMO (as a mediator) entered the relationship between perceived peer acceptance and cyberbullying involvement (as victims/bullies), the negative direct contribution of perceived peer acceptance to being a cyber-victim ($\beta = -.14$, $p > .05$) and a cyberbully ($\beta = -.11$, $p > .05$) was non-significant. Therefore, is it suggested that FoMO acts as a full mediator between perceived peer acceptance and cyberbullying involvement (as victims/bullies). The estimated size of all the indirect effects of FoMO, based on the mean of 5,000 bootstrap re-samples, ranged between .26 and .44, which implies the statistical significance of the full mediation process. In other words, it seemed that perceived peer acceptance contributed negatively to being a cyber-victim ($Z^2 = -3.11$, $p = .001$) and a cyberbully ($Z = -3.94$, $p = .000$) only indirectly, through the negative mediating role of FoMO. This means that students' perceived peer acceptance may decreases primarily their FoMO and subsequently the possibility of their involvement in cyberbullying (as victims/bullies).

According to the bootstrapping analysis for the mediation model reflected in Figure 2 for students with high functioning ASD, the indirect effects were statistically significant, with a 95% confidence interval that did not include zero (CI: .21, .38). This implies that the mediating role of FoMO is significant in the relationship between perceived peer acceptance and cyberbullying involvement (as victims/bullies). When FoMO (as a mediator) entered the relationship between perceived peer acceptance and cyberbullying involvement (as victims/bullies), the negative direct contribution of perceived peer acceptance to being a cyber-victim ($\beta = -.42$, $p < .01$) and a cyberbully ($\beta = -.39$, $p < .01$) were still significant. Therefore, is it suggested that FoMO acts as a partial mediator between perceived peer acceptance and cyberbullying involvement (as victims/bullies). The estimated size of all the indirect effects of FoMO, based on the mean of 5,000 bootstrap re-samples, ranged between .21 and .35, which implies the statistical significance of the partial mediation process. Consequently, according to Figure 2, it seemed that perceived peer acceptance contributed to being a cyber-victim and a cyberbully, not only directly, but also indirectly, through the negative mediating role of FoMO ($Z = -4.08$, $p = .000$ and $Z = -4.31$, $p = .000$, respectively). In other words, it seems that students' perceived peer acceptance may directly decreases the likelihood of being involved in cyberbullying (as victims/bullies). At the same time, students' perceived peer acceptance may decreases primarily their FoMO and subsequently the possibility of their involvement in cyberbullying (as victims/bullies).

Figure 2. Schematic representation of the path model for cyberbullying involvement (as victims/bullies) for students with high functioning ASD (N = 239)

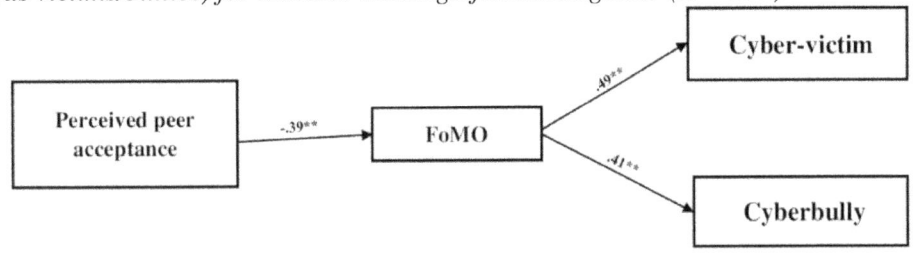

Note 1: The values on the arrows are standardized coefficients of the model.
Note 2: ** $p < .01$

DISCUSSION

The present study investigated comparatively cyberbullying involvement (as victims/bullies) between elementary school students without and with high functioning ASD. Additionally, within the framework of the SCT the contributing role of perceived peer acceptance and FoMO in cyberbullying involvement was tested for each student subgroup.

According to the findings, students with high functioning ASD mentioned that they engage in cyberbullying (as victims/bullies) to a greater extent, compared to their peers of typical development. This aligns with Hypothesis 1 and confirms related findings from limited comparative studies conducted on elementary school students without and with Asperger syndrome (Touloupis & Athanasiades, 2022). The social deficits of students with ASD along with the stigmatization issues they often experience at school (Aubé et al., 2021; Mazumder & Thompson-Hodgetts, 2019), could make (close) face to face social interactions a challenge for these students. In contrast, the online environment of social media platforms could be viewed by students with ASD as a safer context for approaching and communicating with others (e.g., peers). However, the social and sometimes cognitive difficulties of students with ASD (American Psychiatric Association, n.d.) could make less easy for them to perceive the possibly metaphorical use of language and/or choose the appropriate words/responses during an online conversation. Subsequently, students with ASD could be viewed as more vulnerable to engage in an online conversation (e.g., via Facebook, Instagram) ineffectively, resulting in unpleasant experiences, such as sending or receiving insulting messages, reflecting cyberbullying incidents. Furthermore, it is worth mentioning that even typically developing elementary school students' involvement in cyberbullying (as victims/bullies) seemed to be slightly above average (based on the 5-point answering system of the related scale), which is in line with previous studies conducted on elementary school students of typical development (e.g., Barlett, 2023; Evangelio et al., 2022; Mehari et al., 2023; Tian et al., 2023). This implies the general necessity for implementation of school prevention actions against cyberbullying in mainstream elementary education, perhaps with a more intensified effort for specific student groups such as those with high functioning ASD. Furthermore, considering the positive correlation between the roles of cyber-victim and cyberbully, as it was described in the correlations results, it seems that there is an overlap of cyber-victimization and cyberbullying experiences for both students without and with ASD. Namely, being a cyber-victim may trigger being a cyberbully and vice versa.

Additionally, it was found that both boys and girls without and with high functioning ASD reported their engagement in cyberbullying as bullies and victims. This finding confirms to a great extent Hypothesis 2 and related studies, which mention that boys are involved in this phenomenon mainly as bullies and girls primarily as victims (Evangelio et al., 2022; Sorrentino et al., 2019). The fact that the penetration of digital devices at young ages (e.g., school age) is getting stronger every year (Fong et al., 2021; Sriandila & Suryana, 2023) probably intensifies the familiarity of both sexes with the use of social media platforms and their often violent content (Bender et al., 2018; Busching et al., 2016). In this way, both boys and girls could be considered almost equally prone to receiving (as victims) and/or sending (as bullies) violent instant messages indicative of cyberbullying.

Also, the path analyses results regarding the pattern of relationships among the variables involved revealed similarities and differentiations between the two student subgroups. A common finding was the fact that FoMO proved a negative mediator between perceived peer acceptance and cyberbullying involvement (as victims/bullies). In general, this is in line with Hypothesis 3b regarding the negative mediating role of FoMO in the relationship between peer acceptance and cyberbullying involvement (as victims/bullies), not only for students of typical development (as hypothesized) but also for students with high functioning ASD. It seems that students' anxious sense of missing out on others' important posted information on social media (Przybylski et al., 2013; Sun et al., 2022) could act as a general underlying psychological mechanism, which burdens the influence of perceived peer acceptance on students' involvement in cyberbullying (as victims/bullies). In other words, students' perceived peer acceptance, although it could act as a protective filter against cyberbullying involvement (as victims/bullies), when interacting with FoMO could possibly make students' prone to excessive social media use (Kostić et al., 2022) in the context of which they may victimize or be victimized. This finding reflects the general theoretical framework of the SCT (Bandura, 2002), according to which the interaction between a (perceived) context-related (perceived peer acceptance) and an intrapersonal factor (FoMO) could explain in a multidimensional but probably more realistic way a human behavior (cyberbullying). Additionally, the above path analyses results reflect the findings of other studies which, although they do not utilize a mediation model, however highlight the contributing role of FoMO in cyberbullying involvement and problematic social media use in general (Brailovskaia & Margraf, 2024; Hosseini Sfidvadjani et al., 2023; Sun et al., 2022).

Regarding the differentiations of the two path models, it was found that in the relationship between perceived peer acceptance and cyberbullying involvement (as victims/bullies) FoMO proved a full mediator for students of typical development and a partial mediator for students with high functioning ASD. This implies that only for students with high functioning ASD perceived peer acceptance had the potential to influence not only indirectly (through FoMO) but also directly their involvement in cyberbullying (as victims/bullies). This finding is in contrast with Hypothesis 3a regarding the direct contribution of perceived peer acceptance to cyberbullying involvement (as victims/bullies) for students of typical development (as hypothesized), but it does for students with high functioning ASD. Given the discrimination and stigmatization issues that students with ASD usually experience by peers at school (Aubé et al., 2021; Mazumder & Thompson-Hodgetts, 2019), it could be suggested that perceived peer acceptance is of great importance for students with ASD and has the potential to influence significantly the quality of their off-line and online social interactions. This could somehow explain the direct positive contribution of perceived peer acceptance to cyberbullying involvement (as an ineffective interaction with peers) and, therefore, the partial mediating role of FoMO. In contrast, for students of typical development perceived peer acceptance does not seem to have a decisive (direct) contribution to the quality of their online interactions (e.g., cyberbullying episodes), as is has been highlighted by other studies conducted on typically developing students (e.g., Maftei & Măirean, 2023; Wang et al., 2023). It is likely that today's typically developing students' psychological mechanisms related to their digital daily life (FoMO) seem to gradually overshadow to some extent the role of peers at school (perceived peer acceptance). Therefore, only the interaction between their perceived peer acceptance and FoMO could constitute a strong contributor to their involvement in cyberbullying incidents (as victims/bullies). Undoubtedly, future examination of the proposed path model could confirm or not the differentiated patterns of relationships among the variables involved for the two student subgroups.

The above findings should be interpreted with caution due to specific limitations, such as the possibly socially acceptable responses, the restriction to a Greek student sample and to the quantitative methodology, as well as the cross-sectional research design of the study. These limitations could have influenced the validity and the generalizability of the results. Furthermore, the use of the specific Cyberbullying Questionnaire and the subsequent focus of the study only on the two distinct roles of cyber-victim and cyberbully does not allow us to draw conclusions about the intermediary role of victim-bully in cyberspace, which could highlight for each student subgroup if their previous possible experience of cyber-victimization may contribute to being a cyberbully. Nevertheless, the findings contribute to both a theoretical and an applied level. Theoretically, they offer comparative research evidence about the extent of cyberbullying in the under-investigated target group of elementary school students and especially those with high functioning ASD. Also, the findings propose an unexplored explanatory mediation model, which reflecting the SCT could better capture the reason for students' cyberbullying involvement. At an applied level, the findings could awake the school community regarding the necessity to intensify school prevention programs in mainstream elementary education against cyberbullying, primarily for risk groups such as students with ASD. Finally, within these programs school stakeholders (e.g., teachers, school psychologists) could implement experiential activities aimed at strengthening face to face peer relationships (especially for students with ASD), which may act protectively against cyberbullying.

FUTURE RESEARCH DIRECTIONS

Within the general scope of the book "Preventing Bullying Among Children With Special Educational Needs" and the more specific framework of the present chapter, future research directions emerge in this research field. For example, future related studies, conducted on a geographically and numerically more representative sample, could follow a longitudinal research design to allow safer conclusions regarding the relationships among the variables involved and, therefore, more generalizable results. Furthermore, supplementary qualitative data, via semi-structured interviews with students of both subgroups, may highlight new aspects of the issue. Additionally, it is important future studies to enrich the proposed mediation model by co-examining more context-related variables (e.g., variables related to the family/school context) and other intrapersonal characteristics to offer a more multidimensional explanation of contributors to students' engagement in cyberbullying. Finally, the above research enrichments (e.g., mixed research method, multidimensional mediation model) could also highlight a more in-depth explanation of being a victim-bully in cyberspace.

CONCLUSION

Summing up, the present chapter concludes that cyberbullying involvement (as victims/bullies) concerns both male and female elementary school students, and mainly those with high functioning ASD. Furthermore, adopting the framework of the SCT, a mediation model was proposed which explains students' involvement in cyberbullying. Based on this model, it seems that both perceived school context-related variables, such as perceived peer acceptance, and intrapersonal characteristics, such as FoMO, interact with each other and contribute in a more multifaceted way to students' tendency to engage in cyberbullying (as victims/bullies). Specifically, it was found that the above interaction between perceived peer acceptance and FoMO constitutes a strong contributor to cyberbullying involvement of typically developing students. Regarding students with high functioning ASD, it seemed that their perceived peer acceptance proved not only an indirect (via FoMO) but also a decisive (direct) contributor to their cyberbullying involvement.

REFERENCES

American Psychiatric Association. (n.d.). *Diagnostic and Statistical Manual of Mental Disorders (DSM-5-TR)*. Retrieved from https://www.psychiatry.org/psychiatrists/practice/dsm

Arslan, S., Savaser, S., Hallett, V., & Balci, S. (2012). Cyberbullying among primary school students in Turkey: Self-reported prevalence and associations with home and school life. *Cyberpsychology, Behavior, and Social Networking*, 15(10), 527–533. DOI: 10.1089/cyber.2012.0207 PMID: 23002988

Aubé, B., Follenfant, A., Goudeau, S., & Derguy, C. (2021). Public stigma of autism spectrum disorder at school: Implicit attitudes matter. *Journal of Autism and Developmental Disorders*, 51(5), 1584–1597. DOI: 10.1007/s10803-020-04635-9 PMID: 32780195

Bandura, A. (2002). Social cognitive theory in cultural context. *Applied Psychology*, 51(2), 269–290. DOI: 10.1111/1464-0597.00092

Barlett, C. P. (2023). Predicting cyberbullying perpetration in US elementary school children. *International Journal of Environmental Research and Public Health*, 20(15), 6442. DOI: 10.3390/ijerph20156442 PMID: 37568984

Beckman, L., Hellström, L., & von Kobyletzki, L. (2020). Cyber bullying among children with neurodevelopmental disorders: A systematic review. *Scandinavian Journal of Psychology*, 61(1), 54–67. DOI: 10.1111/sjop.12525 PMID: 30820957

Begara Iglesias, O., Gómez Sánchez, L. E., & Alcedo Rodríguez, M. D. L. Á. (2019). Do young people with Asperger syndrome or intellectual disability use social media and are they cyberbullied or cyberbullies in the same way as their peers? *Psicothema*, 31(1), 30–37. DOI: 10.7334/psicothema2018.243 PMID: 30664408

Bender, P. K., Plante, C., & Gentile, D. A. (2018). The effects of violent media content on aggression. *Current Opinion in Psychology*, 19, 104–108. DOI: 10.1016/j.copsyc.2017.04.003 PMID: 29279205

Brailovskaia, J., & Margraf, J. (2024). From fear of missing out (FoMO) to addictive social media use: The role of social media flow and mindfulness. *Computers in Human Behavior*, 150, 107984. DOI: 10.1016/j.chb.2023.107984

Busching, R., Allen, J. J., & Anderson, C. A. (2016). *Violent media content and effects*. Oxford research encyclopedia of communication. DOI: 10.1093/acrefore/9780190228613.013.1

Cavicchiolo, E., Girelli, L., Lucidi, F., Manganelli, S., & Alivernini, F. (2019). The Classmates Social Isolation Questionnaire for Adolescents (CSIQ-A): Validation and invariance across immigrant background, gender and socioeconomic level. *Journal of Educational. Cultural and Psychological Studies*, 19(19), 163–174. DOI: 10.7358/ecps-2019-019-cavi

Collibee, C., Rizzo, C., Bleiweiss, K., & Orchowski, L. M. (2021). The influence of peer support for violence and peer acceptance of rape myths on multiple forms of interpersonal violence among youth. *Journal of Interpersonal Violence*, 36(15-16), 7185–7201. DOI: 10.1177/0886260519832925 PMID: 30832526

Delgado, B., & Escortell Sánchez, R. (2018). Sex and grade differences in cyberbullying of Spanish students of 5th and 6th grade of Primary Education. *Anales de Psicología / Annals of Psychology,*. 34(3), 472-481. DOI: 10.6018/analesps.34.3.283871

Deniz, M. (2015). A study on primary school students' being cyber bullies and victims according to gender, grade, and socioeconomic status. *Croatian Journal of Education*, 17(3), 659–680. DOI: 10.15516/cje.v17i3.835

Ding, Y., Li, D., Li, X., Xiao, J., Zhang, H., & Wang, Y. (2020). Profiles of adolescent traditional and cyber bullying and victimization: The role of demographic, individual, family, school, and peer factors. *Computers in Human Behavior*, 111, 106439. DOI: 10.1016/j.chb.2020.106439

Evangelio, C., Rodriguez-Gonzalez, P., Fernandez-Rio, J., & Gonzalez-Villora, S. (2022). Cyberbullying in elementary and middle school students: A systematic review. *Computers & Education*, 176, 104356. DOI: 10.1016/j.compedu.2021.104356

Faul, F., Erdfelder, E., Lang, A.-G., & Buchner, A. (2007). G*Power 3: A flexible statistical power analysis program for the social, behavioral, and biomedical sciences. *Behavior Research Methods*, 39(2), 175–191. DOI: 10.3758/BF03193146 PMID: 17695343

Ferris, A. L., Hollenbaugh, E. E., & Sommer, P. A. (2021). Applying the uses and gratifications model to examine consequences of social media addiction. *Social Media + Society*, 7(2), 20563051211019003. DOI: 10.1177/20563051211019003

Fong, F. T., Imuta, K., Redshaw, J., & Nielsen, M. (2021). The digital social partner: Preschool children display stronger imitative tendency in screen-based than live learning. *Human Behavior and Emerging Technologies*, 3(4), 585–594. DOI: 10.1002/hbe2.280

Hall, J. A. (2019). How many hours does it take to make a friend? *Journal of Social and Personal Relationships*, 36(4), 1278–1296. DOI: 10.1177/0265407518761225

Holfeld, B., Stoesz, B., & Montgomery, J. (2019). Traditional and cyber bullying and victimization among youth with autism spectrum disorder: An investigation of the frequency, characteristics, and psychosocial correlates. *Journal on Developmental Disabilities*, 24(2), 61–76.

Hosseini Sfidvadjani, M., Ghorban Jahromi, R., Dortaj, F., & Hosseini, S. B. (2023). Negative emotions, fear of missing out, victim of cyberbullying: A structural equation modeling for adolescents. *Social Psychological Review*, 13(49), 91–101. DOI: 10.22034/spr.2023.375154.1799

Hu, H. F., Liu, T. L., Hsiao, R. C., Ni, H. C., Liang, S. H. Y., Lin, C. F., Chan, H.-L., Hsieh, Y.-H., Wang, L.-J., Lee, M.-J., Chou, W.-J., & Yen, C. F. (2019). Cyberbullying victimization and perpetration in adolescents with high-functioning autism spectrum disorder: Correlations with depression, anxiety, and suicidality. *Journal of Autism and Developmental Disorders*, 49(10), 4170–4180. DOI: 10.1007/s10803-019-04060-7 PMID: 31267285

Kircaburun, K., Alhabash, S., Tosuntaş, Ş. B., & Griffiths, M. D. (2020). Uses and gratifications of problematic social media use among university students: A simultaneous examination of the Big Five of personality traits, social media platforms, and social media use motives. *International Journal of Mental Health and Addiction*, 18(3), 525–547. DOI: 10.1007/s11469-018-9940-6

Kline, R. B. (2004). *Principles and practice of structural equation modeling*. The Guilford Press.

Kostić, J. O., Pedović, I., & Stošić, M. (2022). Predicting social media use intensity in late adolescence: The role of attachment to friends and fear of missing out. *Acta Psychologica*, 229, 103667. DOI: 10.1016/j.actpsy.2022.103667 PMID: 35841690

Kowalski, R. M., & Fedina, C. (2011). Cyber bullying in ADHD and Asperger Syndrome populations. *Research in Autism Spectrum Disorders*, 5(3), 1201–1208. DOI: 10.1016/j.rasd.2011.01.007

Lin, H. T., Tai, Y. M., & Gau, S. S. F. (2023). Autistic traits and cyberbullying involvement mediated by psychopathologies and school functions in a nationally representative child sample. *Cyberpsychology, Behavior, and Social Networking*, 26(9), 706–716. DOI: 10.1089/cyber.2022.0309 PMID: 37477877

Liu, T. L., Hsiao, R. C., Chou, W. J., & Yen, C. F. (2021). Social anxiety in victimization and perpetration of cyberbullying and traditional bullying in adolescents with autism spectrum disorder and attention-deficit/hyperactivity disorder. *International Journal of Environmental Research and Public Health*, 18(11), 5728. DOI: 10.3390/ijerph18115728 PMID: 34073617

Maftei, A., & Măirean, C. (2023). Not so funny after all! Humor, parents, peers, and their link with cyberbullying experiences. *Computers in Human Behavior*, 138, 107448. DOI: 10.1016/j.chb.2022.107448

Mazumder, R., & Thompson-Hodgetts, S. (2019). Stigmatization of children and adolescents with autism spectrum disorders and their families: A scoping study. *Review Journal of Autism and Developmental Disorders*, 6(1), 96–107. DOI: 10.1007/s40489-018-00156-5

Mehari, K. R., Beulah, B., Paskewich, B., Leff, S. S., & Waasdorp, T. E. (2023). Cyberbullying and empathy among late-elementary school children. *International Journal of Bullying Prevention : an Official Publication of the International Bullying Prevention Association*, 5(1), 79–87. DOI: 10.1007/s42380-022-00119-9 PMID: 37066126

Ministry of Education. (2018) Ministerial decision (N. 4547/2018, ΦΕΚ 102/12-6-2018). *Reorganization of the support structures of the primary and secondary education and other provisions* [in Greek]. Retrieved from https://www.esos.gr/arthra/57432/fek-toy-n-454718-gia-tis-domes-ekpaideysis-anadiorganosi-ton-domon-ypostirixis-tis

Ministry of Education. (n.d.). *Primary Schools* [in Greek]. Retrieved from https://www.minedu.gov.gr/dimotiko-2/to-thema-dimotiko

Monks, C. P., Robinson, S., & Worlidge, P. (2012). The emergence of cyberbullying: A survey of primary school pupils' perceptions and experiences. *School Psychology International*, 33(5), 477–491. DOI: 10.1177/0143034312445242

Olenik-Shemesh, D., & Heiman, T. (2014). Exploring cyberbullying among primary children in relation to social support, loneliness, self-efficacy, and well-being. *Child Welfare*, 93(5), 27–46.

Pan-Hellenic School Network. (n.d.). Retrieved from https://www.sch.gr/

Parks, M. R. (2007). *LEA's series on personal relationships: Personal relationships and personal networks*. Lawrence Erlbaum Associates.

Przybylski, A. K., Murayama, K., DeHaan, C. R., & Gladwell, V. (2013). Motivational, emotional, and behavioral correlates of fear of missing out. *Computers in Human Behavior*, 29(4), 1841–1848. DOI: 10.1016/j.chb.2013.02.014

Rodríguez-Álvarez, J. M., Yubero, S., Navarro, R., & Larrañaga, E. (2021). Relationship between socio-emotional competencies and the overlap of bullying and cyberbullying behaviors in primary school students. *European Journal of Investigation in Health, Psychology and Education*, 11(3), 686–696. DOI: 10.3390/ejihpe11030049 PMID: 34563062

Sezer, M., Sahin, I., & Akturk, A. O. (2013). Cyber Bullying Victimization of Elementary School Students and Their Reflections on the Victimization. *Online Submission*, 7(12), 1942–1945.

Smith, P. K., Mahdavi, J., Carvalho, M., Fisher, S., Russell, S., & Tippett, N. (2008). Cyberbullying: Its nature and impact in secondary school pupils. *Journal of Child Psychology and Psychiatry, and Allied Disciplines*, 49(4), 376–385. DOI: 10.1111/j.1469-7610.2007.01846.x PMID: 18363945

Sorrentino, A., Baldry, A. C., Farrington, D. P., & Blaya, C. (2019). Epidemiology of cyberbullying across europe: Differences between countries and genders. *Educational Sciences: Theory & Practice*, 19(2), 74–91. DOI: 10.12738/estp.2019.2.005

Sprague, J. R., & Walker, H. M. (2021). *Safe and healthy schools: Practical prevention strategies*. Guilford Publications.

Sriandila, R., & Suryana, D. (2023). Exploring the Impact of Digital Devices on Social Development in Young Children. *AL-ISHLAH: Jurnal Pendidikan*, 15(2), 2230–2239. DOI: 10.35445/alishlah.v15i2.3735

Sun, C., Sun, B., Lin, Y., & Zhou, H. (2022). Problematic mobile phone use increases with the fear of missing out among college students: The effects of self-control, perceived social support and future orientation. *Psychology Research and Behavior Management*, 15, 1–8. DOI: 10.2147/PRBM.S345650 PMID: 35018126

Tian, L., Huang, J., & Huebner, E. S. (2023). Profiles and transitions of cyberbullying perpetration and victimization from childhood to early adolescence: Multi-contextual risk and protective factors. *Journal of Youth and Adolescence*, 52(2), 434–448. DOI: 10.1007/s10964-022-01633-1 PMID: 35648261

Touloupis, T., & Athanasiades, C. (2014). The Risky Use of New Technology among Elementary School Students: Internet Addiction and Cyberbullying [in Greek]. *Hellenic Journal of Psychology*, 11, 83–110.

Touloupis, T., & Athanasiades, C. (2022). Cyberbullying and empathy among elementary school students: Do special educational needs make a difference? *Scandinavian Journal of Psychology*, 63(6), 609–623. DOI: 10.1111/sjop.12838 PMID: 35698831

Vanden Abeele, M., & De Cock, R. (2013). Cyberbullying by mobile phone among adolescents: The role of gender and peer group status. *Communications*, 38(1), 107–118. DOI: 10.1515/commun-2013-0006

Wang, X., Wang, S., & Zeng, X. (2023). Does deviant peer affiliation accelerate adolescents' cyberbullying perpetration? Roles of moral disengagement and self-control. *Psychology in the Schools*, 60(12), 5025–5040. DOI: 10.1002/pits.23037

ADDITIONAL READING

Betts, L. R., Spenser, K. A., & Gardner, S. E. (2017). Adolescents' involvement in cyber bullying and perceptions of school: The importance of perceived peer acceptance for female adolescents. *Sex Roles*, 77(7-8), 471–481. DOI: 10.1007/s11199-017-0742-2 PMID: 28979061

Burton, K. A., Florell, D., & Wygant, D. B. (2013). The role of peer attachment and normative beliefs about aggression on traditional bullying and cyberbullying. *Psychology in the Schools*, 50(2), 103–115. DOI: 10.1002/pits.21663

D'Lima, P., & Higgins, A. (2021). Social media engagement and Fear of Missing Out (FOMO) in primary school children. *Educational Psychology in Practice*, 37(3), 320–338. DOI: 10.1080/02667363.2021.1947200

Festl, R., Scharkow, M., & Quandt, T. (2013). Peer influence, internet use and cyberbullying: A comparison of different context effects among German adolescents. *Journal of Children and Media*, 7(4), 446–462. DOI: 10.1080/17482798.2013.781514

Gosain, P., & Yadav, K. (2020). A study on social media usage and fear of missing out (FOMO) among youngsters. *Journal of Studies in Social Sciences and Humanities*, 6(2), 76–87.

Hefner, D., Knop, K., & Vorderer, P. (2018, January). "I Wanna be in the Loop!"– The Role of Fear of Missing Out (FoMO) for the Quantity and Quality of Young Adolescents' Mobile Phone Use. In *Youth and Media* (pp. 39-54). Nomos Verlagsgesellschaft mbH & Co. KG.

Liu, T. L., Chen, Y. L., Hsiao, R. C., Ni, H. C., Liang, S. H. Y., Lin, C. F., Chan, H.-L., Hsieh, Y.-H., Wang, L.-J., Lee, M.-J., Chou, W.-J., & Yen, C. F. (2023). Adolescent–Caregiver Agreement Regarding the School Bullying and Cyberbullying Involvement Experiences of Adolescents with Autism Spectrum Disorder. *International Journal of Environmental Research and Public Health*, 20(4), 3733. DOI: 10.3390/ijerph20043733 PMID: 36834428

Shahzadi, M., Zahid, H., Rafiq, A., & Bibi, M. (2024). Cyberbullying, Fear of Missing Out and Self-Perception in Adolescents. *Jahan-e-Tahqeeq*, 7(1), 561–576.

Tomczyk, Ł., & Szotkowski, R. (2023). Sexting, fear of missing out (FOMO), and problematic social network use among adolescents. *Human Technology*, 19(2), 283–301. DOI: 10.14254/1795-6889.2023.19-2.8

Triantafyllopoulou, P., Clark-Hughes, C., & Langdon, P. E. (2022). Social media and cyber-bullying in autistic adults. *Journal of Autism and Developmental Disorders*, 52(11), 4966–4974. DOI: 10.1007/s10803-021-05361-6 PMID: 34799787

KEY TERMS AND DEFINITIONS

Comparative Study: A study that is based on research techniques and strategies for drawing inferences about causation and/or association of factors that are similar or different between two or more subjects/objects.
Cyberbullying: The use of new technology to harass, threaten, embarrass, or target another person.
Elementary Education: The first stage traditionally found in formal education, beginning at about age 6 to 7 and ending at about age 11 to 13.
FoMO: A worried feeling that you may miss exciting events that other people are going to, especially caused by things you see on social media.
High Functioning ASD: An informal term that some people use when they talk about people with autism spectrum disorder, or ASD, who can speak, read, write, and handle basic life skills like eating and getting dressed.
Peer Acceptance: It is distinct from friendship in that it refers to the degree to which individuals are liked or not liked by classmates in a setting such as a classroom or school grad.

ENDNOTES

[1]   In Greece elementary education last six years (Ministry of Education, n.d.).

[2] Z = standardized normal distribution value

Compilation of References

Abdullah, M. (2024, March). The Impact of Bullying in an Inclusive Classroom Among Students of ASD and Peers in Social Development and Academic Performance in UAE. In *BUiD Doctoral Research Conference 2023: Multidisciplinary Studies* (pp. 49-58). Cham: Springer Nature Switzerland. DOI: 10.1007/978-3-031-56121-4_5

Academy of Science of South Africa (ASSAf). (2022). *Webinar on Mental Health and Bullying*. http://dx.doi.org/.DOI: 10.17159/assaf.2022/0085

Acar, S., Chen, C. I., & Xie, H. (2021). Parental involvement in developmental disabilities across three cultures: A systematic review. *Research in Developmental Disabilities*, 110, 103861. DOI: 10.1016/j.ridd.2021.103861 PMID: 33482560

Accardo, A. L., Neely, L. C., Pontes, N. M. H., & Pontes, M. C. F. (2024). Bullying victimization is associated with heightened rates of anxiety and depression among Autistic and ADHD youth: National Survey of Children's Health 2016–2020. *Journal of Autism and Developmental Disorders*. Advance online publication. DOI: 10.1007/s10803-024-06479-z PMID: 39034347

ACER's National Bullying Prevention Center. (2021). *Bullying and students with disabilities*. Retrieved from https://www.pacer.org/bullying/info/students-with-disabilities/

Affairs, U. N. O. O. (1989). The Law of the Sea: Navigation on the High Seas: Legislative History of Part VII, Section I (Articles 87, 89, 90-94, 96-98) of the United Nations Convention on the Law of the Sea (Vol. 18). New York: United Nations.

Ahmad, S. S., & Koncsol, S. W. (2022). Cultural factors influencing mental health stigma: Perceptions of mental illness (POMI) in Pakistani emerging adults. *Religions*, 13(5), 1–21. DOI: 10.3390/rel13050401

Ahmad, S., & Yousaf, M. (2011). Special education in Pakistan: In the perspectives of educational policies and plans. *Academic Research International*, 1(2), 228.

Ahmed, B., Yousaf, F. N., Ahmad, A., Zohra, T., & Ullah, W. (2023). Bullying in educational institutions: College students' experiences. *Psychology Health and Medicine*, 28(9), 2713–2719. DOI: 10.1080/13548506.2022.2067338 PMID: 35440249

Ainscow, M., Booth, T., & Dyson, A. (2004). Understanding and developing inclusive practices in schools: A collaborative action research network. *International Journal of Inclusive Education*, 8(2), 125–139. DOI: 10.1080/1360311032000158015

Akram, B., & Munawar, A. (2016). Bullying victimization: A risk factor of health problems among adolescents with hearing impairment. *JPMA. The Journal of the Pakistan Medical Association*, 66(1), 13–17. PMID: 26712172

Ali, F., & Shah, A. (2020). Cultural influences on peer victimization in Pakistani schools. *Journal of Social Sciences*, 15(3), 78–90.

Alizadeh Maralani, F., Mirnasab, M. M., & Hashemi, T. (2019). The Predictive Role of Maternal Parenting and Stress on Pupils' Bullying involvement. *Journal of Interpersonal Violence*, 34(17), 3691–3710. DOI: 10.1177/0886260516672053 PMID: 27701082

Alsaker, F. D., & Valkanover, S. (2012). The Bernese program against victimization in kindergarten and elementary school. *New Directions for Youth Development*, 133(133), 15–28. DOI: 10.1002/yd.20004 PMID: 22504788

Álvarez-Guerrero, G., García-Carrión, R., Khalfaoui, A., Santiago-Garabieta, M., & Flecha, R. (2023). Preventing bullying of students with special educational needs through dialogic gatherings: A case study in elementary education. *Humanities & Social Sciences Communications*, 10(1), 1–9. DOI: 10.1057/s41599-023-02470-8

American Psychiatric Association. (2013). *Diagnostic and statistical manual of mental disorders* (5th ed.). American Psychiatric Publishing.

American Psychiatric Association. (n.d.). *Diagnostic and Statistical Manual of Mental Disorders (DSM-5-TR)*. Retrieved from https://www.psychiatry.org/psychiatrists/practice/dsm

American Psychological Association [APA]. (2024). *Bullying*. APA. Retrieved April 22, 2024, from https://www.apa.org/topics/bullying

American School Counselor Association. (n.d.). *(2003). The ASCA national model: A framework for school counselling programs*. Author.

Americans with Disabilities Act of 1990, 42 U.S.C. § 12101 et seq. (1990).

Amiola, A. J., Zia, A., Gangadharan, S. K., & Alexander, R. T. (2023). *Intellectual disability services in the Indian subcontinent.* Psychiatry of Intellectual Disability Across Cultures.

Amjad, A. I., & Malik, M. A. (2024). Interviewing students with special needs: Developing ethical considerations and interviewing protocols. *Journal of Research in Special Educational Needs*, 24(4), 1161–1174. Advance online publication. DOI: 10.1111/1471-3802.12702

Anderson, D. W. (2006). Inclusion and interdependence: Students with special needs in the regular classroom. *Journal of Education & Christian Belief*, 10(1), 43–59. DOI: 10.1177/205699710601000105

Anderson, M., & Jiang, J. (2018). *Teens, Social Media & Technology 2018*. Pew Research Center.

Andreou, E., Didaskalou, E., & Vlachou, A. (2015). Bully/victim problems among Greek pupils with special educational needs: Associations with loneliness and self-efficacy for peer interactions. *Journal of Research in Special Educational Needs*, 15(4), 235–246. DOI: 10.1111/1471-3802.12028

Anna, L., & Angharad, E. B. (2021). The social and human rights models of disability: Towards a complementarity thesis. *The International Journal of Human Rights*, 25(2), 348-379. https://doi.org/DOI: 10.1080/13642987.2020.1783533

Antwi, H. A., Yiranbon, E., Lulin, Z., Maxwell, B. A., Agebase, A. J., Yaw, N. E., & Vakalalabure, T. T. (2014). Innovation Diffusion Among Healthcare Workforce: Analysis of adoption and use of medical ICT in Ghanaian tertiary hospitals. *International Journal of Academic Research in Business & Social Sciences*, 4(7). Advance online publication. DOI: 10.6007/IJARBSS/v4-i7/987

Anuruddhika, B. (2018). Teachers' instructional behaviors towards inclusion of children with visual impairment in the teaching learning process. *European Journal of Special Education Research*, 3(3), 164–182. DOI: 10.5281/zenodo.1246950

Arcuri, N. M. (2018). Counseling Relationship Experiences for K-12 School Counselors Who Also Fulfill the Role of Anti-Bullying Specialist. *Journal of School Counseling*, 16(5), n5.

Armitage. (2021). Bullying in children: impact on child health. *National Library of Medicine* .

Arslan, M., & Zaman, R. (2014). Unemployment and its determinants: A study of Pakistan economy (1999-2010). *Journal of Economics and Sustainable Development*, 5(13), 20–24.

Arslan, S., Savaser, S., Hallett, V., & Balci, S. (2012). Cyberbullying among primary school students in Turkey: Self-reported prevalence and associations with home and school life. *Cyberpsychology, Behavior, and Social Networking*, 15(10), 527–533. DOI: 10.1089/cyber.2012.0207 PMID: 23002988

Aruma. (2020, August 24). *Disability stereotypes in the media*. Aruma. Retrieved August 29, 2024, from https://www.aruma.com.au/about-us/blog/run-forest-run-disability-stereotypes-in-the-media/

Asghar, I., Cang, S., & Yu, H. (2017). Assistive technology for people with dementia: An overview and bibliometric study. *Health Information and Libraries Journal*, 34(1), 5–19. DOI: 10.1111/hir.12173 PMID: 28191727

Ashfaq, U., Waqas, A., & Naveed, S. (2018). Bullying prevention programs in the developing world: Way forward for Pakistan. *Pakistan Journal of Public Health*, 8(4), 174–175. DOI: 10.32413/pjph.v8i4.239

Assistant Secretary for Public Affairs (ASPA). (2021, Novemeber 10). *Warning Signs for Bullying*. StopBullying.gov. https://www.stopbullying.gov/bullying/warning-signs

Assistant Secretary for Public Affairs (ASPA). (2022, May 27). *Kid Videos*. StopBullying.gov. https://www.stopbullying.gov/kids/kid-videos

Assistant Secretary for Public Affairs [ASPA]. (2020). *Bullying and youth with disabilities and special health needs*. StopBullying.gov. Retrieved April 22, 2024, from https://www.stopbullying.gov/bullying/special-needs

Astor, R. A., Meyer, H. A., & Pitner, R. O. (2001). Elementary and middle school students' perceptions of safety: An examination of violence-prone school sub-context. *The Elementary School Journal*, 101, 511–528. DOI: 10.1086/499685

Athanasiadou, C. (2011). Counseling psychology in the school context. *Hellenic Journal of Psychology*, 8, 289–308.

Aubé, B., Follenfant, A., Goudeau, S., & Derguy, C. (2021). Public stigma of autism spectrum disorder at school: Implicit attitudes matter. *Journal of Autism and Developmental Disorders*, 51(5), 1584–1597. DOI: 10.1007/s10803-020-04635-9 PMID: 32780195

Azad, T. (2016). *Exploring inclusive practice: The beliefs and practices of classroom teachers in two mainstream primary schools in Karachi* [Unpublished doctoral dissertation, King's College London, University of London] London.

Babarro, J. M., & Árias, R. M. (2008). Socio Program for the Prevention of School Bullying. *Educational Psychology: Journal of Educational Psychologists*, 14(2), 129–146.

Badger, J. R., Nisar, A., & Hastings, R. P. (2023). School-based anti-bullying approaches for children and young people with special educational needs and disabilities: A systematic review and synthesis. *Journal of Research in Special Educational Needs*, 24(3), 742–757. DOI: 10.1111/1471-3802.12665

Bagley, C., Woods, P. A., & Woods, G. (2001). Implementation of School Choice Policy: Interpretation and response by parents of students with special educational needs. *British Educational Research Journal*, 27(3), 287–311. DOI: 10.1080/01411920120048313

Baker, K., & Donelly, M. (2010). The social experiences of children with disability and the influence of environment: A framework for intervention. *Disability & Society*, 16(1), 71–85. DOI: 10.1080/713662029

Bakker, J. T. A., & Bosman, A. M. T. (2003). Self-image and peer acceptance of Dutch students in regular and special education. *Learning Disability Quarterly*, 26(1), 5–14. DOI: 10.2307/1593680

Ball, L. E., & Zhu, X. (2023). Brief report prevalence of bullying among autistic adolescents in the United States: Impact of disability severity status. *Journal of Autism and Developmental Disorders*. Advance online publication. DOI: 10.1007/s10803-023-06041-3 PMID: 37380848

Ball, L., Lieberman, L., Haibach-Beach, P., Perreault, M., & Tirone, K. (2022). Bullying in physical education of children and youth with visual impairments: A systematic review. *British Journal of Visual Impairment*, 40(3), 513–529. DOI: 10.1177/02646196211009927

Bandura, A. (2002). Social cognitive theory in cultural context. *Applied Psychology*, 51(2), 269–290. DOI: 10.1111/1464-0597.00092

Banks, J., McCoy, S., & Frawley, D. (2017). One of the gang? peer relations among students with special educational needs in Irish mainstream primary schools. *European Journal of Special Needs Education*, 33(3), 396–411. DOI: 10.1080/08856257.2017.1327397

Barlett, C. P. (2023). Predicting cyberbullying perpetration in US elementary school children. *International Journal of Environmental Research and Public Health*, 20(15), 6442. DOI: 10.3390/ijerph20156442 PMID: 37568984

Barnes, C. (1992). Disabling imagery and the media. *An Exploration of the Principles for Media Representations of Disabled People. The First in a Series of Reports. Halifax.*

Barow, T., & Östlund, D. (2020). Stuck in failure: Comparing special education needs assessment policies and practices in Sweden and Germany. *Nordic Journal of Studies in Educational Policy*, 6(1), 37–46. DOI: 10.1080/20020317.2020.1729521

Bartlett, D. J., Macnab, J., Macarthur, C., Mandich, A., Magill-Evans, J., Young, N. L., Beal, D., Conti-Becker, A., & Polatajko, H. J. (2006). Advancing rehabilitation research: An interactionist perspective to guide question and design. *Disability and Rehabilitation*, 28(19), 1169–1176. DOI: 10.1080/09638280600551567 PMID: 17005478

Bashir, S., & Ahsan, H. (2023). *Educational Exclusion of Children with Special Needs* (No. 2023: 109). Pakistan Institute of Development Economics.

Basilici, M. C., Palladino, B. E., & Menesini, E. (2022). Ethnic diversity and bullying in school: A systematic review. *Aggression and Violent Behavior*, 65, 1359–1789. DOI: 10.1016/j.avb.2022.101762

Batsche, G. M., & Knoff, H. M. (1994). Bullies and their victims: Understanding a pervasive problem in the schools. *School Psychology Review*, 23(2), 165–174. DOI: 10.1080/02796015.1994.12085704

Bauman, S., & Del Rio, A. (2005). Knowledge and beliefs about bullying in schools. *School Psychology International*, 26(4), 428–442. DOI: 10.1177/0143034305059019

Bauman, S., & Del Rio, A. (2006). Preservice teachers' responses to bullying scenarios: Comparing physical, verbal, and relational bullying. *Journal of Educational Psychology*, 98(1), 219–231. DOI: 10.1037/0022-0663.98.1.219

Beckman, L., Hellström, L., & von Kobyletzki, L. (2020). Cyber bullying among children with neurodevelopmental disorders: A systematic review. *Scandinavian Journal of Psychology*, 61(1), 54–67. DOI: 10.1111/sjop.12525 PMID: 30820957

Begara Iglesias, O., Gómez Sánchez, L. E., & Alcedo Rodríguez, M. D. L. Á. (2019). Do young people with Asperger syndrome or intellectual disability use social media and are they cyberbullied or cyberbullies in the same way as their peers? *Psicothema*, 31(1), 30–37. DOI: 10.7334/psicothema2018.243 PMID: 30664408

Begotti, T., Tirassa, M., & Acquadro Maran, D. (2018). Pre-service teachers' intervention in school bullying episodes with special education needs students: A research in Italian and Greek samples. *International Journal of Environmental Research and Public Health*, 15(9), 1908. DOI: 10.3390/ijerph15091908 PMID: 30200541

Begum, M., & Nair, S. (2023). Understanding bullying experiences among SEN students: A parental perspective. *Asia Pacific Journal of Developmental Differences*, 10(2), 249–288.

Bejerot, S., Plenty, S., Humble, A., & Humble, M. B. (2013). Poor motor skills: A risk marker for bully victimization. *Aggressive Behavior*, 39(6), 453–461. DOI: 10.1002/ab.21489 PMID: 23784933

Bellini, S., & Akullian, J. (2007). A meta-analysis of video modeling and video self-modeling interventions for children and adolescents with autism spectrum disorders. *Exceptional Children*, 73(3), 264–287. DOI: 10.1177/001440290707300301

Bender, P. K., Plante, C., & Gentile, D. A. (2018). The effects of violent media content on aggression. *Current Opinion in Psychology*, 19, 104–108. DOI: 10.1016/j.copsyc.2017.04.003 PMID: 29279205

Berchiatti, M., Ferrer, A., Galiana, L., Badenes-Ribera, L., & Longobardi, C. (2021). Bullying in Students with Special Education Needs and Learning Difficulties: The Role of the Student–Teacher Relationship Quality and Students' Social Status in the Peer Group. *Child and Youth Care Forum*, 51(3), 515–537. DOI: 10.1007/s10566-021-09640-2

Berchiatti, M., Ferrer, A., Galiana, L., Badenes-Ribera, L., & Longobardi, C. (2021). Bullying in students with special education needs and learning difficulties: The role of the student–teacher relationship quality and students' social status in the peer group. In *Child & Youth Care Forum* (pp. 1–23). Springer US.

Berkowitz, R., Moore, H., Astor, R. A., & Benbenishty, R. (2017). A research synthesis of the associations between socioeconomic background, inequality, school climate, and academic achievement. *Review of Educational Research*, 87(2), 425–469. DOI: 10.3102/0034654316669821

Bhargava, D. (2015). Balanced Timetable Key to Student Engagement. Retrieved from https://www.carsonst.wa.edu.au/wp-content/uploads/2012/11/Balanced-Timetable-Manual-1.pdf

Bibi, T. (2018). Article 25th A: Implications of free and compulsory secondary education. *VFAST Transactions on Education and Social Sciences*, 6(1), 57–63.

Biggs, M. J., Simpson, C. G., & Gaus, M. D. (2009). A case of bullying: Bringing together the disciplines. *Children & Schools*, 31(1), 39–42. DOI: 10.1093/cs/31.1.39

Biswas, T., Scott, J. G., Munir, K., Thomas, H. J., Huda, M. M., Hasan, M. M., de Vries, T. D., Baxter, J., & Mamun, A. A. (2020). Global variation in the prevalence of bullying victimisation amongst adolescents: Role of peer and parental supports. *EClinicalMedicine*, 20, 1–8. DOI: 10.1016/j.eclinm.2020.100276 PMID: 32300737

Bjereld, Y. (2018). The challenging process of disclosing bullying victimization: A grounded theory study from the victim's point of view. *Journal of Health Psychology*, 23(8), 1110–1118. DOI: 10.1177/1359105316644973 PMID: 27153857

Black, L. I., & Zablotsky, B. (2018). *Chronic school absenteeism among children with selected developmental disabilities: National Health Interview Survey. 2014-2016* [National Health Statistics Reports. No. 118]. National Center for Health Statistics.

Black, S., Weinles, D., & Washington, E. (2010). Victim strategies to stop bullying. *Youth Violence and Juvenile Justice*, 8(2), 138–147. DOI: 10.1177/1541204009349401

Blake, J. J., Lund, E. M., Zhou, Q., Kwok, O. M., & Benz, M. R. (2012). National prevalence rates of bully victimization among students with disabilities in the United States. *School Psychology Quarterly*, 27(4), 210–222. DOI: 10.1037/spq0000008 PMID: 23294235

Blake, J. J., Zhou, Q., Kwok, O., & Benz, M. R. (2016). Predictors of bullying behavior, victimization, and bully-victim risk among high school. *Remedial and Special Education*, 37(5), 285–295. DOI: 10.1177/0741932516638860

Boden, J. M., Horwood, L. J., & Fergusson, D. M. (2007). Exposure to childhood sexual and physical abuse and subsequent educational achievement outcomes. *Child Abuse & Neglect*, 31(10), 1101–1114. DOI: 10.1016/j.chiabu.2007.03.022 PMID: 17996302

Boruah, A. S. (2022). Problems faced by the teachers in educating the physically challenged children in special schools. *Towards Excellence*, 14(4), 78–93. DOI: 10.37867/TE140409

Boske, C., & Osanloo, A. F. (2015). Conclusion-preparing all school community leaders to live their work. *Promoting Social Justice and Equity Work in Schools Around the World Advances in Educational Administration*, 23, 405–426. DOI: 10.1108/S1479-366020140000023032

Bouldin, E., Patel, S. R., Tey, C. S., White, M., Alfonso, K. P., & Govil, N. (2021). Bullying and children who are deaf or hard-of-hearing: A Scoping Review. *The Laryngoscope*, 131(8), 1884–1892. DOI: 10.1002/lary.29388 PMID: 33438758

Bourke, S., & Burgman, I. (2010). Coping with bullying in Australian schools: How children with disabilities experience support from friends, parents and teachers. *Disability & Society*, 25(3), 359–371. DOI: 10.1080/09687591003701264

Boyes, M. E., Leitão, S., Claessen, M., Badcock, N. A., & Nayton, M. (2020). Correlates of externalising and internalising problems in children with dyslexia: An analysis of data from clinical casefiles. *Australian Psychologist*, 55(1), 62–72. DOI: 10.1111/ap.12409

Bradley, R. (2016). 'Why single me out?' Peer mentoring, autism and inclusion in mainstream secondary schools. *British Journal of Special Education*, 43(3), 272–288. DOI: 10.1111/1467-8578.12136

Bradshaw, C. P., Waasdorp, T. E., & Leaf, P. J. (2012). Effects of school-wide positive behavioral interventions and supports on child behavior problems. *Pediatrics*, 130(5), e1136–e1145. DOI: 10.1542/peds.2012-0243 PMID: 23071207

Bradshaw, C. P., Waasdorp, T. E., O'Brennan, L. M., & Gulemetova, M. (2013). Teachers' and education support professionals' perspectives on bullying and prevention: Findings from a National Education Association study. *School Psychology Review*, 42(3), 280–297. DOI: 10.1080/02796015.2013.12087474 PMID: 25414539

Bradshaw, C., Sawyer, A., & O'Brennan, L. (2007). Bullying and peer victimization at school: Perceptual differences between students and school staff. *School Psychology Review*, 36(3), 361–382. DOI: 10.1080/02796015.2007.12087929

Brailovskaia, J., & Margraf, J. (2024). From fear of missing out (FoMO) to addictive social media use: The role of social media flow and mindfulness. *Computers in Human Behavior*, 150, 107984. DOI: 10.1016/j.chb.2023.107984

Braun, V., & Clarke, V. (2006). Using thematic analysis in psychology. *Qualitative Research in Psychology*, 3(2), 77–101. DOI: 10.1191/1478088706qp063oa

Bromand, Z., Temur-Erman, S., Yesil, R., Montesinos, A. H., Aichberger, M. C., Kleiber, D., Schouler-Ocak, M., Heinz, A., Kastrup, M. C., & Rapp, M. A. (2012). Mental health of Turkish women in Germany: Resilience and risk factors. *European Psychiatry*, 27, 17–21. DOI: 10.1016/S0924-9338(12)75703-6 PMID: 22863245

Brooks, R., TeRiele, K., & Maguire, M. (2014). *Ethics and Education Research*. Sage. DOI: 10.4135/9781473909762

Broomhead, K. E. (2018). Acceptance or rejection? the social experiences of children with special educational needs and disabilities within a mainstream primary school. *Education 3-13*, 47(8), 877–888. DOI: 10.1080/03004279.2018.1535610

Brouzos, A., Vassilopoulos, S., Korfiati, A., & Baourda, V. (2015). Secondary school students' perceptions of their counselling needs in an era of global financial crisis: An exploratory study in Greece. *International Journal for the Advancement of Counseling*, 37(2), 168–178. DOI: 10.1007/s10447-015-9235-6

Brown, E. C., Low, S., Smith, B. H., & Haggerty, K. P. (2011). Outcomes from a school-randomized controlled trial of steps to respect: A bullying prevention program. *School Psychology Review*, 40(3), 423–443. DOI: 10.1080/02796015.2011.12087707

Buchanan, R., & Clark, M. (2017). Understanding parent–school communication for students with emotional and behavioral disorders. *The Open Family Studies Journal, 9* (Suppl 1 M5), 122. https://doi.org/DOI: 0.2174/1874922401709010122

Buchanan, R., Nese, R. N., Palinkas, L. A., & Ruppert, T. (2015). Refining an intervention for students with emotional disturbance using qualitative parent and teacher data. *Children and Youth Services Review*, 58, 41–49. DOI: 10.1016/j.childyouth.2015.08.014 PMID: 28966422

Bunnett, E. R. (2021). Bullying in pre-adolescents: Prevalence, emotional intelligence, aggression and resilience. *Issues in Educational Research*, 31(4), 1049–1066.

Burger, C., Strohmeier, D., & Kollerová, L. (2022). Teachers can make a difference in bullying: Effects of teacher interventions on students' adoption of bully, victim, bully-victim or defender roles across time. *Journal of Youth and Adolescence*, 51(12), 2312–2327. DOI: 10.1007/s10964-022-01674-6 PMID: 36053439

Burger, C., Strohmeier, D., Spröber, N., Bauman, S., & Rigby, K. (2015). How teachers respond to school bullying: An examination of self-reported intervention strategy use, moderator effects, and concurrent use of multiple strategies. *Teaching and Teacher Education*, 51, 191–202. DOI: 10.1016/j.tate.2015.07.004

Burkhart, K., & Keder, R. D. (2020). Bullying: The role of the clinician in prevention and intervention. In *Clinician's Toolkit for Children's Behavioral Health* (pp. 143-173). Academic Press.

Busching, R., Allen, J. J., & Anderson, C. A. (2016). *Violent media content and effects*. Oxford research encyclopedia of communication. DOI: 10.1093/acrefore/9780190228613.013.1

Bussey, K. (2023). The contribution of social cognitive theory to school bullying research and practice. *Theory into Practice*, 62(3), 293–305. DOI: 10.1080/00405841.2023.2226549

Buttimer, J., & Tierney, E. (2005). Patterns of leisure participation among adolescents with a mild intellectual disability. *Journal of Intellectual Disabilities*, 9(1), 25–42. DOI: 10.1177/1744629505049728 PMID: 15757870

Cainelli, E., & Bisiacchi, P. S. (2019a). Diagnosis and treatment of developmental dyslexia and specific learning disabilities: Primum Non Nocere. *Journal of Developmental &amp. Journal of Developmental and Behavioral Pediatrics*, 40(7), 558–562. DOI: 10.1097/DBP.0000000000000702 PMID: 31259753

Campbell, M., Hwang, Y. S., Whiteford, C., Dillon-Wallace, J., Ashburner, J., Saggers, B., & Carrington, S. (2017). Bullying prevalence in students with Autism Spectrum Disorder. *Australasian Journal of Special Education*, 41(2), 101–122. DOI: 10.1017/jse.2017.5

Canales, M. U.Miguel Urra Canales. (2023). Bullying. Description of the roles of victim, bully, peer group, school, family and society. *Influence: International Journal of Science Review*, 5(2), 184–194. DOI: 10.54783/influencejournal.v5i2.148

Cappadocia, M. C., Weiss, J. A., & Pepler, D. (2012). Bullying experiences among children and youth with Autism Spectrum Disorders. *Journal of Autism and Developmental Disorders*, 42(2), 266–277. DOI: 10.1007/s10803-011-1241-x PMID: 21499672

Caravita, S. C., Di Blasio, P., & Salmivalli, C. (2009). Unique and interactive effects of empathy and social status on involvement in bullying. *Social Development*, 18(1), 140–163. DOI: 10.1111/j.1467-9507.2008.00465.x

Card, N. A., & Hodges, E. V. (2008). Peer victimization among schoolchildren: Correlations, causes, consequences, and considerations in assessment and intervention. *School Psychology Quarterly*, 23(4), 451–461. DOI: 10.1037/a0012769

Carlozzi, A. F., Bull, K. S., Stein, L. B., Ray, K., & Barnes, L. (2002). Empathy theory and practice: A survey of psychologists and counselors. *The Journal of Psychology*, 136(2), 161–170. DOI: 10.1080/00223980209604147 PMID: 12081091

Carter, B., & Spencer, V. G. (2006). The fear factor: Bullying and students with disabilities. *International Journal of Special Education*, 21, 11–23.

Carter, E. W., Cushing, L. S., & Kennedy, C. H. (2009). Peer support strategies for improving the social interactions and job skills of adolescents with disabilities. *Education and Training in Autism and Developmental Disabilities*, 44(4), 440–450.

Carter, E. W., Lane, K. L., Cooney, M., Weir, K., Moss, C. K., & Machalicek, W. (2013). Self-determination among transition-age youth with autism or intellectual disability: Parent perspectives. *Research and Practice for Persons with Severe Disabilities: the Journal of TASH*, 38(3), 129–138. DOI: 10.1177/154079691303800301

Carter, S. (2009). Bullying of students with asperger syndrome. *Issues in Comprehensive Pediatric Nursing*, 32(3), 145–154. DOI: 10.1080/01460860903062782 PMID: 21992104

Cavicchiolo, E., Girelli, L., Lucidi, F., Manganelli, S., & Alivernini, F. (2019). The Classmates Social Isolation Questionnaire for Adolescents (CSIQ-A): Validation and invariance across immigrant background, gender and socioeconomic level. *Journal of Educational. Cultural and Psychological Studies*, 19(19), 163–174. DOI: 10.7358/ecps-2019-019-cavi

Center for Disease Control and Prevention [CDC]. (2023). *Fast facts: Preventing bullying*. CDC. Retrieved April 22, 2024 from, https://www.cdc.gov/violenceprevention/youthviolence/ bullyingresearch/fastfact.html

Cerda, G. A., Salazar, Y. S., Guzmán, C. E., & Narváez, G. (2018). Impact of the school coexistence on academic performance according to perception of typically developing and special educational needs students. *Journal of Educational Psychology-Propositos y Representaciones*, 6(1), 275–300.

Cerf, C., Gantwerk, B., Martz, S., Hespe, D., & Vermeire, G. (2012, September). *Guidance for parents on the anti-bullying bill of rights act*. https://www.nj.gov/education/safety/sandp/hib/docs/ParentGuide.pdf

Cerna, L., Mezzanotte, C., Rutigliano, A., Brussino, O., Santiago, P., Borgonovi, F., & Guthrie, C. (2021). Promoting inclusive education for diverse societies: A conceptual framework. *OECD Education Working Papers*, No. 260, OECD Publishing, Paris. https://doi.org/DOI: 10.1787/19939019

Çetinkaya, S., Nur, N., Ayvaz, A., Özdemir, D., & Kavakcı, Ö. (2009). The relationship between peer bullying and depression and self-esteem levels in three primary school students with different socio-economic status. *Anatolian Journal of Psychiatry*, 10, 151–158.

Chae, S., Park, E. Y., & Shin, M. (2019). School-based interventions for improving disability awareness and attitudes towards disability of students without disabilities: A meta-analysis. *International Journal of Disability Development and Education*, 66(4), 343–361. DOI: 10.1080/1034912X.2018.1439572

Chalamandaris, A. G., & Piette, D. (2015). School-based anti-bullying interventions: Systematic review of the methodology to assess their effectivenes. *Aggression and Violent Behavior*, 24, 131–174. DOI: 10.1016/j.avb.2015.04.004

Chan, K. L., Lo, C. K. M., & Ip, P. (2018). Associating disabilities, school environments, and child victimization. *Child Abuse & Neglect*, 83, 21–30. DOI: 10.1016/j.chiabu.2018.07.001 PMID: 30016742

Chen, Q., Zhu, Y., & Chui, W. H. (2021). A meta-analysis on effects of parenting programs on bullying prevention. *Trauma, Violence & Abuse*, 22(5), 1209–1220. DOI: 10.1177/1524838020915619 PMID: 32242506

Cheshire, L. (2022). *School Violence and Bullying of Children with Disabilities in the Eastern and Southern African Region: A Needs Assessment*. Retrieved August 2, 2024, from https://www.leonardcheshire.org/sites/default/files/2022-03/Leonard-Cheshire-SVB-report-foreword.pdf

Chisala, M., Ndhlovu, D., & Mandyata, J.M. (2023). Child protection measures on bullying in special education schools. *European Journal of Special Education Research, 9(3)*, 57-77. https://doi.org/Cincioğlu, Ş., Ergin, D. Y. (2023). Evaluation of peer bullying towards inclusion students by teachers. *Social Sciences Research Journal, 12*(15), 2017-2027. DOI: 10.46827/ejse.v9i3.4964

Chou, W. J., Hsiao, R. C., Ni, H. C., Liang, S. H. Y., Lin, C. F., Chan, H. L., Hsieh, Y. H., Wang, L. J., Lee, M. J., Hu, H. F., & Yen, C. F. (2019). Self-reported and parent-reported school bullying in adolescents with high functioning autism spectrum disorder: The roles of autistic social impairment, attention-deficit/hyperactivity and oppositional defiant disorder symptoms. *International Journal of Environmental Research and Public Health*, 16(7), 1117. Advance online publication. DOI: 10.3390/ijerph16071117 PMID: 30925769

Chou, W. J., Wang, P. W., Hsiao, R. C., Hu, H. F., & Yen, C. F. (2020). Role of school bullying involvement in depression, anxiety, suicidality, and low self-esteem among adolescents with high-functioning autism spectrum disorder. *Frontiers in Psychiatry*, 11(9), 9. Advance online publication. DOI: 10.3389/fpsyt.2020.00009 PMID: 32082201

Christensen, L., Fraynt, R. J., Neece, C. L., & Baker, B. L. (2012). Bullying adolescents with intellectual disability. *Journal of Mental Health Research in Intellectual Disabilities*, 5(1), 49–65. DOI: 10.1080/19315864.2011.637660

Chu, B. C., Hoffman, L., Johns, A., Reyes-Portillo, J., & Hansford, A. (2015). Transdiagnostic behavior therapy for bullying-related anxiety and depression: Initial development and pilot study. *Cognitive and Behavioral Practice*, 22(4), 415–429. DOI: 10.1016/j.cbpra.2014.06.007

Chu, S. Y. (2018). Family voices: Promoting foundation skills of self-determination for young children with disabilities in Taiwan. *Asia Pacific Education Review*, 19(1), 91–101. DOI: 10.1007/s12564-018-9519-8

Cincioğlu, Ş. (2023). *Peer Bullying Against Inclusion Students*, (Unpublished Ph.D. Thesis, Trakya University), Edirne.

Cincioğlu, Ş., & Ergin, D. Y. (2023a). Evaluation of peer bullying towards inclusion students by teachers. *Social Sciences Research Journal*, 12(15), 2017–2027.

Cincioğlu, Ş., & Ergin, D. Y. (2023b). Kaynaştırma öğrencilerine yönelik akran zorbalığının veli görüşlerine göre değerlendirilmesi. *Balkan and Near Eastern Journal of Social Sciences*, 9, 179–184.

Clair, M. (2018). *Stigma: Forthcoming in Core Concepts in Sociology*. Scholars Harvard.

Class, E. (2021, August 30). *Inclusive Perspectives in Primary Education*. Pressbooks.pub; Pressbooks. https://pressbooks.pub/inclusiveperspectives/

Climaco, M. (2020, February 25). *Confronting shame—and accepting my disability—with Judy Heumann - Ford Foundation*. Ford Foundation. Retrieved August 4, 2024, from https://www.fordfoundation.org/news-and-stories/stories/confronting-shame-and-accepting-my-disability-with-judy-heumann/

Collaborative for Academic, Social, and Emotional Learning (CASEL). (2021). *What is SEL?* Retrieved from https://casel.org/what-is-sel/

Collibee, C., Rizzo, C., Bleiweiss, K., & Orchowski, L. M. (2021). The influence of peer support for violence and peer acceptance of rape myths on multiple forms of interpersonal violence among youth. *Journal of Interpersonal Violence*, 36(15-16), 7185–7201. DOI: 10.1177/0886260519832925 PMID: 30832526

Columbia Mailman School of Public Health. (2022, March 23). *One in Three Children With Disabilities Has Experienced Violence: Global Study*. Columbia University Mailman School of Public Health. Retrieved July 24, 2024, from https://www.publichealth.columbia.edu/news/one-three-children-disabilities-has-experienced-violence-global-study

Colver, A. (2005). A shared framework and language for childhood disability. *Developmental Medicine and Child Neurology*, 47(11), 780–784. DOI: 10.1111/j.1469-8749.2005.tb01078.x PMID: 16225744

Combs-Jones, W. L. (2021). An Investigation of Teachers' Descriptions, Understandings, and Perceptions of Intervention and Prevention Tactics Addressing Students with Disabilities: A Collective Case Study [Doctoral Dissertation, University of Liberty]

Compas, B. E., Connor-Smith, J. K., Saltzman, H., Thomsen, A. H., & Wadsworth, M. E. (2001). Coping with stress during childhood and adolescence: Problems, progress, and potential in theory and research. *Psychological Bulletin*, 127(1), 87–127. DOI: 10.1037/0033-2909.127.1.87 PMID: 11271757

Conners-Burrow, N. A., Johnson, D. L., Whiteside-Mansell, L., McKelvey, L., & Gargus, R. A. (2009). Adults matter: Protecting children from the negative impacts of bullying. *Psychology in the Schools*, 46(7), 593–604. DOI: 10.1002/pits.20400

Conti-Becker, A. (2003). Between the ideal and the real: Reconsidering the international classification of functioning, disability and health. *Disability and Rehabilitation*, 25(31), 2125–2129. DOI: 10.3109/09638280902912509 PMID: 19888843

Convention on the Rights of Persons with Disabilities. (2007). Resolution/Adopted by the General Assembly, 24 January 2007, A/RES/61/106. Available online: https://www.refworld.org/docid/45f973632.html

Cook, C. R., Williams, K. R., Guerra, N. G., Kim, T. E., & Sadek, S. (2010). Predictors of bullying and victimization and childhood and adolescents: A meta-analytic investigation. *School Psychology Quarterly*, 25(2), 65–83. DOI: 10.1037/a0020149

Cook, L., & Friend, M. (2010). The state of the art of collaboration on behalf of students with disabilities. *Journal of Educational & Psychological Consultation*, 20(1), 1–8. DOI: 10.1080/10474410903535398

Cooper, L., & Nickerson, A. (2013). Parent retrospective recollections of bullying and current views, concerns, and strategies to cope with children's bullying. *Journal of Child and Family Studies*, 22(4), 526–540. DOI: 10.1007/s10826-012-9606-0

Corboz, J., Hemat, O., Siddiq, W., & Jewkes, R. (2018). Children's peer violence perpetration and victimization: Prevalence and associated factors among school children in Afghanistan. *PLoS One*, 13(2), e0192768. Advance online publication. DOI: 10.1371/journal.pone.0192768 PMID: 29438396

Corcoran, L., Mc Guckin, C., & Prentice, G. (2015). Cyberbullying or cyber aggression?: A review of existing definitions of cyber-based peer-to-peer aggression. *Societies (Basel, Switzerland)*, 5(2), 245–255. DOI: 10.3390/soc5020245

Cornell, D., Gregory, A., Huang, F., & Fan, X. (2013). Perceived prevalence of teasing and bullying predicts high school dropout rates. *Journal of Educational Psychology*, 105(1), 138–149. DOI: 10.1037/a0030416

Cornell, D., & Huang, F. (2014). School counselor use of peer nominations to identify victims of bullying. *Professional School Counseling*, 18(1), 191–205. DOI: 10.5330/2156-759X-18.1.191

Cowden, P. A. (2010). Social anxiety in children with disabilities. *Journal of Instructional Psychology*, 37(4), 301–305.

Craig, W. M., & Pepler, D. J. (2003). Identifying and targeting risk for involvement in bullying and victimization. *Canadian Journal of Psychiatry*, 48(9), 577–582. DOI: 10.1177/070674370304800903 PMID: 14631877

Creswell, J. W. (2007). *Qualitative Inquiry and Research Design: Choosing Among Five Traditions* (2nd ed.). Sage Publications.

Cross, D., Runions, K. C., & Pearce, N. (2021). Friendly schools' bullying prevention research: Implications for school counsellors. *Journal of Psychologists and Counsellors in Schools*, 31(2), 146–158. DOI: 10.1017/jgc.2021.19

Crowe, T. K., VanLeit, B., & Berghmans, K. K. (2000). Mothers' perceptions of child care assistance: The impact of a child's disability. *The American Journal of Occupational Therapy*, 54(1), 52–58. DOI: 10.5014/ajot.54.1.52 PMID: 10686627

Cullinane, M. (2020). An exploration of the sense of belonging of students with special educational needs. *REACH: Journal of Inclusive Education in Ireland*, 33(1), 2–12.

Dasioti, & Kolaitis, G. (2018). Bullying and the mental health of schoolchildren with special educational needs in primary education. *Psychiatriki*, 29(2), 149–159. DOI: 10.22365/jpsych.2018.292.149

Dasioti, M., & Kolaitis, G. (2018). Bullying and victimization of children and adolescents with disabilities. In Costello, M. (Ed.), *Handbook of bullying in schools: An international perspective* (pp. 85–97). Routledge.

Davis, S., & Nixon, C. (2010). Preliminary results from the Youth Voice Research Project: Victimization & Strategies. Retrieved from http://www.youthvoiceproject.com/YVPMarch2010.pdf

Davis, S., & Davis, J. (2007). *Schools where everyone belongs: Practical strategies for reducing bullying*. Research Press.

Davis, S., & Nixon, C. (2010). *The youth voice project: Preliminary results from the youth voice project: victimization and strategies*. Research Press Publishers.

Dawkins, J. L. (1996). Bullying, physical disability, and the pediatric patient. *Developmental Medicine and Child Neurology*, 38(7), 603–612. DOI: 10.1111/j.1469-8749.1996.tb12125.x PMID: 8674911

Dedousis-Wallace, A., & Shute, R. H. (2009). Indirect bullying: Predictors of teacher intervention, and outcome of a pilot educational presentation about impact on adolescent mental health. *Australian Journal of Educational & Developmental Psychology*, 9, 2–17.

deLara, E. W. (2019). *Bullying scars: The impact on adult life and relationships.* Oxford University Press.

Delgado, B., & Escortell Sánchez, R. (2018). Sex and grade differences in cyberbullying of Spanish students of 5th and 6th grade of Primary Education. *Anales de Psicología/Annals of Psychology,. 34*(3), 472-481. DOI: 10.6018/analesps.34.3.283871

Demaray, M. K., Malecki, C. K., Secord, S. M., & Lyell, K. M. (2013). Agreement among students', teachers', and parents' perceptions of victimization by bullying. *Children and Youth Services Review*, 35(12), 2091–2100. DOI: 10.1016/j.childyouth.2013.10.018

Dema, T., Tripathy, J. P., Thinley, S., Rani, M., Dhendup, T., Laxmeshwar, C., Tenzin, K., Gurung, M. S., Tshering, T., Subba, D. K., Penjore, T., & Lhazeen, K. (2019). Suicidal ideation and attempt among school going adolescents in Bhutan–A secondary analysis of a global school-based student health survey in Bhutan 2016. *BMC Public Health*, 19(1), 1–12. DOI: 10.1186/s12889-019-7791-0 PMID: 31791280

Deniz, M. (2015). A study on primary school students' being cyber bullies and victims according to gender, grade, and socioeconomic status. *Croatian Journal of Education*, 17(3), 659–680. DOI: 10.15516/cje.v17i3.835

Department of Education (ED). (2014). *Guiding principles: A resource guide for improving school climate and discipline.* ERIC Clearinghouse.

Diamanduros, T., Downs, E., & Jenkins, S. J. (2008). The role of school psychologists in the assessment, prevention, and intervention of cyberbullying. *Psychology in the Schools*, 45(8), 693–704. DOI: 10.1002/pits.20335

Didaskalou, E., Andreou, E., & Vlachou, A. (2009). Bullying and victimization in children with special educational needs: Implications for inclusive practices. *Revista Interacções*, 13(1), 249–274.

Didaskalou, E., Andreou, E., & Vlachou, A. (2009). Bullying and victimization in children with special educational needs: Implications for inclusive practices. *Revista Interacções, 13,* 249-274. https://doi.org/DOI: 10.25755/INT.406

Ding, J. L., Lv, N., Wu, Y. F., Chen, I. H., & Yan, W. J. (2024). The hidden curves of risk: A nonlinear model of cumulative risk and school bullying victimization among adolescents with autism spectrum disorder. *Child and Adolescent Psychiatry and Mental Health*, 18(1), 1–13. DOI: 10.1186/s13034-023-00694-9 PMID: 38282053

Ding, Y., Li, D., Li, X., Xiao, J., Zhang, H., & Wang, Y. (2020). Profiles of adolescent traditional and cyber bullying and victimization: The role of demographic, individual, family, school, and peer factors. *Computers in Human Behavior*, 111, 106439. DOI: 10.1016/j.chb.2020.106439

DiPerna, J. C., Lei, P., Bellinger, J., & Cheng, W. (2015). Efficacy of the social skills improvement system classwide intervention program (SSIS-CIP) primary version. *School Psychology Quarterly*, 30(1), 123–141. DOI: 10.1037/spq0000079 PMID: 25111465

Dölek, N. (2002). *Investigation of Bullying Behaviors in Students and a Preventive Program Model*, (Unpublished Ph.D. Thesis, Marmara University), Istanbul.

Du, C., DeGuisto, K., Albrigh, J., & Alrehaili, S. (2018). Peer support as a mediator between bullying victimization and depression. *International Journal of Psychological Studies*, 10(1), 59–68. DOI: 10.5539/ijps.v10n1p59

Dunst, C. J. (2014). Meta-analysis of the effects of puppet shows on attitudes toward and knowledge of individuals with disabilities. *Exceptional Children*, 80(2), 136–148. DOI: 10.1177/001440291408000201

Durlak, J. A., Weissberg, R. P., Dymnicki, A. B., Taylor, R. D., & Schellinger, K. B. (2011). The impact of enhancing students' social and emotional learning: A meta-analysis of school-based universal interventions. *Child Development*, 82(1), 405–432. DOI: 10.1111/j.1467-8624.2010.01564.x PMID: 21291449

Earnshaw, V. A., Reisner, S. L., Menino, D. D., Poteat, V. P., Bogart, L. M., Barnes, T. N., & Schuster, M. A. (2018). Stigma-based bullying interventions: A systematic review. *Developmental Review*, 48, 178–200. DOI: 10.1016/j.dr.2018.02.001 PMID: 30220766

Ebersold, S., & Meijer, C. (2016). Financing inclusive education: Policy challenges, issues and trends, implementing inclusive education: Issues in bridging the policy-practice gap. *International Perspectives on Inclusive Education*, 8, 37–62. DOI: 10.1108/S1479-363620160000008004

Education (2004). The Salamanca statement and framework for action on special needs education. Special Educational Needs and Inclusive Education: Systems and contexts, 1, 382.

Egan, G. (2009). *The skilled helper. A problem management and opportunity approach to helping.* Brooks Cole.

Ehsan, M. (2018). Inclusive education in primary and secondary Schools of Pakistan: Role of teachers. *American Academic Scientific Research Journal for Engineering, Technology, and Sciences, 40*(1), 40–61. Retrieved from https://asrjetsjournal.org/index.php/American_Scientific_Journal/article/view/3684

Eilts, J., & Koglin, U. (2022). Bullying and victimization in students with emotional and behavioural disabilities: A systematic review and meta-analysis of prevalence rates, risk and protective factors. *Emotional & Behavioural Difficulties, 27*(2), 133–151. DOI: 10.1080/13632752.2022.2092055

Ellery, F., Kassam, N., & Bazan, C. (2010). *Prevention pays: The economic benefits of ending violence in schools.* Plan International.

Ellis, B. J., Del Giudice, M., Dishion, T. J., Figueredo, A. J., Gray, P., Griskevicius, V., Hawley, P. H., Jacobs, W. J., James, J., Volk, A. A., & Wilson, D. S. (2012). The evolutionary basis of risky adolescent behavior: Implications for science, policy, and practice. *Developmental Psychology, 48*(3), 598–623. DOI: 10.1037/a0026220 PMID: 22122473

Engelbrecht, P., Swart, E., & Eloff, I. (2016). Stress and coping skills of teachers with a learner with Down's syndrome in inclusive classrooms. *South African Journal of Education, 21*(4), 256–259.

Erdoğan, Y., Hammami, N., & Elgar, F. J. (2023). Bullying, family support, and life satisfaction in adolescents of single-parent households in 42 countries. *Child Indicators Research, 16*(2), 739–753. DOI: 10.1007/s12187-022-09996-4

Eroglu, M., & Kılıç, B. G. (2020). Peer bullying among children with autism spectrum disorder in formal education settings: Data from Turkey. *Research in Autism Spectrum Disorders, 75*, 101572. DOI: 10.1016/j.rasd.2020.101572

Espelage, D. L., Forber-Pratt, A., Rose, C. A., Graves, K. A., Hanebutt, R. A., Sheikh, A. E., Woolswaever, A., Milarsky, T. K., Ingram, M. K., Robinson, L., Gomez, A. M., Chalfant, P. K., Salama, C., & Poekert, P. (2024). Development of online professional development for teachers: Understanding, recognizing and responding to bullying for students with disabilities. *Education and Urban Society, 56*(5), 601–623. DOI: 10.1177/00131245231187370

Espelage, D. L., Green, H. D., & Polanin, J. (2012). Willingness to intervene in bullying episodes among middle school students: Individual and peer group influences. *The Journal of Early Adolescence*, 32(6), 776–801. Advance online publication. DOI: 10.1177/0272431611423017

Espelage, D. L., Rose, C. A., & Polanin, J. R. (2015). Social-emotional learning program to reduce bullying, fighting, and victimization among middle school students with disabilities. *Remedial and Special Education*, 36(5), 299–311. DOI: 10.1177/0741932514564564

Estell, D. B., Farmer, T. W., Irvin, M. J., Crowther, A., Akos, P., & Boudah, D. J. (2009). Students with exceptionalities and the peer group context of bullying and victimization in late elementary school. *Journal of Child and Family Studies*, 18(2), 136–150. DOI: 10.1007/s10826-008-9214-1

Evangelio, C., Rodriguez-Gonzalez, P., Fernandez-Rio, J., & Gonzalez-Villora, S. (2022). Cyberbullying in elementary and middle school students: A systematic review. *Computers & Education*, 176, 104356. DOI: 10.1016/j.compedu.2021.104356

Evans, C. B. R., Fraser, M. W., & Cotter, K. L. (2014). The effectiveness of school-based bullying prevention programs: A systematic review. *Aggression and Violent Behavior*, 19(5), 532–544. DOI: 10.1016/j.avb.2014.07.004

Faas, Z. (2015). *Elementary School Psychologists' Experiences with School-Based Bullying Prevention and İntervention Efforts*, (New Hampshire University, Unpublished Ph.D. Thesis), New Hampshire, ABD.

Factor, P. I., Rosen, P. J., & Reyes, R. A. (2016). The relation of poor emotional awareness and externalizing behavior among children with ADHD. *Journal of Attention Disorders*, 20(2), 168–177. DOI: 10.1177/1087054713494005 PMID: 23839724

Fadzlina, H. S. L. A. N., & Li, N. L. P. (2018). Counseling To Understand and Intervene School Bullying. *Social Science Learning Education Journal*, 3(1). Advance online publication. DOI: 10.15520/sslej.v3i1.58

Fahlevi, R. (2020). The human and existential approach to improve students' emotional intelligence in school counseling program. *Konselor*, 9(1), 29–35. DOI: 10.24036/0202091105961-0-00

Faith, M. A., Reed, G., Heppner, C. E., Hamill, L. C., Tarkenton, T. R., & Donewar, C. W. (2015). Bullying in medically fragile youth: A review of risks, protective factors, and recommendations for medical providers. *Journal of Developmental and Behavioral Pediatrics*, 36(4), 285–301. DOI: 10.1097/DBP.0000000000000155 PMID: 25923529

Falla, D., Sánchez, S., & Casas, J. A. (2021). What do we know about bullying in schoolchildren with disabilities? A systematic review of recent work. *Sustainability (Basel)*, 13(1), 416. DOI: 10.3390/su13010416

Fang, Z., Cerna-Turoff, I., Zhang, C., Lu, M., Lachman, J. M., & Barlow, J. (2022). Global estimates of violence against children with disabilities: An updated systematic review and meta-analysis. *The Lancet. Child & Adolescent Health*, 6(5), 313–323. DOI: 10.1016/S2352-4642(22)00033-5 PMID: 35305703

Farmer, T. W., Petrin, R., Brooks, D. S., Hamm, J. V., Lambert, K., & Gravelle, M. (2012). Bullying involvement and the school adjustment of rural students with and without disabilities. *Journal of Emotional and Behavioral Disorders*, 20(1), 19–37. DOI: 10.1177/1063426610392039

Farrington, C. A., Roderick, M., Allensworth, E., Nagaoka, J., Keyes, T. S., Johnson, D. W., & Beechum, N. O. (2012). *Teaching Adolescents to Become Learners: The Role of Noncognitive Factors in Shaping School Performance—A Critical Literature Review*. University of Chicago Consortium on Chicago School Research.

Fatchurahman, M., Karyanti, K., Setiawan, M. A., & Habsy, B. A. (2020). Development of Guidance Counselling for Increased Engagement and Empathy of Middle School Bullies. *International Journal of Innovation* [IJICC]. *Creativity and Change*, 13(10), 1366–1385.

Fattore, T., & Mason, J. (2020). Humiliation, resistance and state violence: Using the sociology of emotions to understand institutional violence against women and girls and their acts of resistance. *International Journal for Crime. Justice and Social Democracy*, 9(4), 104–117. DOI: 10.5204/ijcjsd.1693

Faul, F., Erdfelder, E., Lang, A.-G., & Buchner, A. (2007). G*Power 3: A flexible statistical power analysis program for the social, behavioral, and biomedical sciences. *Behavior Research Methods*, 39(2), 175–191. DOI: 10.3758/BF03193146 PMID: 17695343

Ferrara, P., Franceschini, G., Villani, A., & Corsello, G. (2019). Physical psychological and social impact of school violence on children. *Italian Journal of Pediatrics*, 45(1), 76. DOI: 10.1186/s13052-019-0669-z PMID: 31248434

Ferrer-Cascales, R., Albaladejo-Blázquez, N., Sánchez-SanSegundo, M., Portilla-Tamarit, I., Lordan, O., & Ruiz-Robledillo, N. (2019). Effectiveness of the TEI program for bullying and cyberbullying reduction and school climate improvement. *International Journal of Environmental Research and Public Health*, 16(4), 580. DOI: 10.3390/ijerph16040580 PMID: 30781543

Ferris, A. L., Hollenbaugh, E. E., & Sommer, P. A. (2021). Applying the uses and gratifications model to examine consequences of social media addiction. *Social Media + Society*, 7(2), 20563051211019003. DOI: 10.1177/20563051211019003

Finardi, G., Paleari, F. G., & Fincham, F. D. (2022). Parenting a child with learning disabilities: Mothers' self-forgiveness, well-being, and parental behaviors. *Journal of Child and Family Studies*, 31(9), 2454–2471. DOI: 10.1007/s10826-022-02395-x

Fink, E., Deighton, J., Humphrey, N., & Wolpert, M. (2015). Assessing the bullying and victimisation experiences of children with special educational needs in mainstream schools: Development and validation of the Bullying Behaviour and Experience Scale. *Research in Developmental Disabilities*, 36, 611–619. DOI: 10.1016/j.ridd.2014.10.048 PMID: 25462521

Fite, P. J., Evans, S. C., Cooley, J. L., & Rubens, S. L. (2014). Further evaluation of associations between attention-deficit/hyperactivity and oppositional defiant disorder symptoms and bullying-victimization in adolescence. *Child Psychiatry and Human Development*, 45(1), 32–41. DOI: 10.1007/s10578-013-0376-8 PMID: 23516013

Fleming, L. C., & Jacobsen, K. H. (2009). Bullying among middle-school students in low and middle income countries. *Health Promotion International*, 25(1), 73–84. DOI: 10.1093/heapro/dap046 PMID: 19884243

Fogleman, N. D., McQuade, J. D., Mehari, K. R., & Becker, S. P. (2021). In-person victimization, cyber victimization, and polyvictimization in relation to internalizing symptoms and self-esteem in adolescents with attention-deficit/hyperactivity disorder. *Child: Care, Health and Development*, 47(6), 805–815. DOI: 10.1111/cch.12888 PMID: 34155671

Fong, F. T., Imuta, K., Redshaw, J., & Nielsen, M. (2021). The digital social partner: Preschool children display stronger imitative tendency in screen-based than live learning. *Human Behavior and Emerging Technologies*, 3(4), 585–594. DOI: 10.1002/hbe2.280

Foon, L. W., Hassan, S. A., & Nordin, M. H. (2020). Counselling intervention to address school bullying: A systematic review of literature. *International Journal of Academic Research in Business & Social Sciences*, 10(16). Advance online publication. DOI: 10.6007/IJARBSS/v10-i16/8301

Forrest, D. L., Kroeger, R. A., & Stroope, S. (2019). Autism spectrum disorder symptoms and bullying victimization among children with Autism in the United States. *Journal of Autism and Developmental Disorders*, 50(2), 560–571. DOI: 10.1007/s10803-019-04282-9 PMID: 31691063

Fox, C. L., & Boulton, M. J. (2005). The social skills problems of bullying: Self, peer, and teacher perceptions. *The British Journal of Educational Psychology*, 75(2), 313–328. DOI: 10.1348/000709905X25517 PMID: 16033669

Fox, C., & Boulton, M. (2006). Friendship as a moderator of the relationship between social skills problems and peer victimization. *Aggressive Behavior*, 32(2), 110–121. DOI: 10.1002/ab.20114

Frederickson, N. L., & Furnham, A. F. (2004). Peer-assessed behavioral characteristics and sociometric rejection: Differences between pupils who have moderate learning difficulties and their mainstream peers. *The British Journal of Educational Psychology*, 74(3), 391–410. DOI: 10.1348/0007099041552305 PMID: 15296547

Frederickson, N., Simmonds, E., Evans, L., & Soulsby, C. (2007). Assessing the social and affective outcomes of inclusion. *British Journal of Special Education*, 34(2), 105–115. DOI: 10.1111/j.1467-8578.2007.00463.x

Fredrick, S. S., Nickerson, A. B., Sun, L., Rodgers, J. D., Thomeer, M. L., Lopata, C., & Todd, F. (2023). ASD symptoms, social skills, and comorbidity: Predictors of bullying perpetration. *Journal of Autism and Developmental Disorders*, 53(8), 3092–3102. DOI: 10.1007/s10803-022-05612-0 PMID: 35678945

Freeman, J. A., & Kirksey, J. (2023). Linking IEP status to parental involvement for high school students of first-generation and native-born families. *Exceptional Children*, 89(2), 197–215. DOI: 10.1177/00144029221108402

Freire, S., Pipa, J., Aguiar, C., Vaz da Silva, F., & Moreira, S. (2019). Student–teacher closeness and conflict in students with and without special educational needs. *British Educational Research Journal*, 46(3), 480–499. DOI: 10.1002/berj.3588

Frey, K., Edstrom, L. V. S., & Hirschstein, M. (2005). The steps to respect program uses a multilevel approach to reduce playground bullying and destructive bystander behaviors. the *National Conference of the Hamilton Fish Enstitute on School and Community Violence*, https://digitalcommons.georgefox.edu/cgi/viewcontent.cgi?article=1336&context=gscp_fac

Frisén, A., Hasselblad, T., & Holmqvist, K. (2012). What actually makes bullying stop? reports from former victims. *Journal of Adolescence*, 35(4), 981–990. DOI: 10.1016/j.adolescence.2012.02.001 PMID: 22475445

Frith, U., & Hill, E. (2003). *Autism: Mind and brain*. Oxford University Press.

Gaffney, H., Ttofi, M. M., & Farrington, D. P. (2021). What works in anti-bullying programs? Analysis of effective intervention components. *Journal of School Psychology*, 85, 37–56. DOI: 10.1016/j.jsp.2020.12.002 PMID: 33715780

Gage, N. A., Katsiyannis, A., Rose, C., & Adams, S. E. (2021). Disproportionate bullying victimization and perpetration by disability status, race, and gender: A national analysis. *Advances in Neurodevelopmental Disorders*, 5(3), 256–268. DOI: 10.1007/s41252-021-00200-2

Gage, N. A., & Larson, A. (2014). School climate and bullying victimization: A latent class growth model analysis. *School Psychology Quarterly*, 29(3), 256–271. DOI: 10.1037/spq0000064 PMID: 24933216

Ganotz, T., Schwab, S., & Lehofer, M. (2023). Bullying among primary school-aged students: Which factors could strengthen their tendency towards resilience? *International Journal of Inclusive Education*, 27(8), 890–903. DOI: 10.1080/13603116.2021.1879949

Gansle, K. A. (2005). The effectiveness of school-based anger interventions and programs: A meta-analysis. *Journal of School Psychology*, 43(4), 321–341. DOI: 10.1016/j.jsp.2005.07.002

Gao, W. (2020). *Anti-bullying interventions for Children with special needs: A 2003-2020 Systematic Literature Review*, (Master Thesis, Jönköping University School of Education and Communication, Jönköping), Sweden.

Gau, S. S. F., Liu, L. T., Wu, Y. Y., Chiu, Y. N., & Tsai, W. C. (2013). Psychometric properties of the Chinese version of the social responsiveness scale. *Research in Autism Spectrum Disorders*, 7(2), 349–360. DOI: 10.1016/j.rasd.2012.10.004

Genc, Z., Babieva, N. S., Zarembo, G. V., Lobanova, E. V., & Malakhova, V. Y. (2021). The views of special education department students on the use of assistive technologies in special education. [iJET]. *International Journal of Emerging Technologies in Learning*, 16(19), 69–80. DOI: 10.3991/ijet.v16i19.26025

Geng, C. (2024, May). *What are the different types of bullying?* Medicalnewstoday.com; Medical News Today. Retrieved August 25, 2024, from https://www.medicalnewstoday.com/articles/types-of-bullying#summary

Georgiadi, M., Kalyva, E., Kourkoutas, E., & Tsakiris, V. (2012). Young children's attitudes toward peers with intellectual disabilities: Effect of the type of school. *Journal of Applied Research in Intellectual Disabilities*, 25(6), 531–541. DOI: 10.1111/j.1468-3148.2012.00699.x PMID: 23055287

Gibson, C. L. (2012). An investigation of neighborhood disadvantage, low self-control, and violent victimization among youth. *Youth Violence and Juvenile Justice*, 10(1), 41–63. DOI: 10.1177/1541204011423767

Gibson, C. L., Fagan, A. A., & Antle, K. (2014). Avoiding violent victimization among youths in urban neighborhoods: The importance of street efficacy. *American Journal of Public Health*, 104(2), 154–161. DOI: 10.2105/AJPH.2013.301571 PMID: 24328615

Gini, G., Pozzoli, T., & Hymel, S. (2013). Moral disengagement among children and youth: A Meta-analytic review of links to aggressive behavior. *Aggressive Behavior*, 40(1), 56–68. DOI: 10.1002/ab.21502 PMID: 24037754

Gladden, M. R., Vivolo-Kantor, A. M., Hamburger, M. E., & Lumpkin, C. D. (2014). *Bullying surveillance among youths: uniform definitions for public health and recommended data elements, Version 1.0*. National Center for Injury Prevention and Control, (U.S.). Division of Violence Prevention. https://stacks.cdc.gov/view/cdc/21596

Gladden, R. M., Vivolo-Kantor, A. M., Hamburger, M. E., & Lumpkin, C. D. (2014). Bullying surveillance among youths: Uniform definitions for public health and recommended data elements, version 1.0.

Goffman, E. (1963). *Stigma. Notes on the Management of Spoiled Identity*. Simon & Schuster.

Gökler, R. (2009). Peer bullying in schools. *International Journal of the Humanities*, 6(2), 511–537.

Gomes, A., Martins, M. C., Silva, B., Ferreira, E., Nunes, O., & Caldas, A. C. (2022). How different are girls and boys as bullies and victims? Comparative perspectives on gender and age in the bullying dynamics. *International Journal of Educational Psychology*, 11(3), 237–260. DOI: 10.17583/ijep.9310

Gómez-Ortiz, O., Apolinario, C., Romera, E. M., & Ortega-Ruiz, R. (2019). The role of family in bullying and cyberbullying involvement: Examining a new typology of parental education management based on adolescents' view of their parents. *Social Sciences (Basel, Switzerland)*, 8(1), 25. Advance online publication. DOI: 10.3390/socsci8010025

González Contreras, A. I., Pérez-Jorge, D., Rodríguez-Jiménez, M. D. C., & Bernadette-Lupson, K. (2021). Peer bullying in students aged 11 to 13 with and without special educational needs in Extremadura (Spain). *Education 3-13, 49*(8), 945-956.

González-Calatayud, V., Roman-García, M., & Prendes-Espinosa, P. (2021). Knowledge about bullying by young adults with special educational needs with or without disabilities (SEN/D). *Frontiers in Psychology*, 11, 622517. DOI: 10.3389/fpsyg.2020.622517 PMID: 33488487

Good, J. M., McIntosh, K., & Gietz, C. (2011). Integrating bullying prevention into schoolwide positive behavior support. *Teaching Exceptional Children*, 44(1), 48–56. DOI: 10.1177/004005991104400106

GoP. (2009). National Education Policy Islamabad: Government of Pakistan. http://itacec.org/document/2015/7/National_Education_Policy_2009.pdf

Gottfried, M. A., & Kirksey, J. J. (2017). "When" students miss school: The role of timing of absenteeism on students' test performance. *Educational Researcher*, 46(3), 119–130. DOI: 10.3102/0013189X17703945

Goudie, A., Narcisse, M. R., Hall, D. E., & Kuo, D. Z. (2014). Financial and psychological stressors associated with caring for children with disability. *Families, Systems & Health*, 32(3), 280–290. DOI: 10.1037/fsh0000027 PMID: 24707826

Graybill, E. C., Vinoski, E., Black, M., Varjas, K., Henrich, C., & Meyers, J. (2016, March). Examining the Outcomes of Including Students With Disabilities in a Bullying/Victimization Intervention. *School Psychology Forum*, 10(1), •••.

Greeff, A. P., & Van den Berg, E. (2013). Resilience in families in which a child is bullied. *British Journal of Guidance & Counselling*, 41(5), 504–517. DOI: 10.1080/03069885.2012.757692

Grills-Taquechel, A. E., Fletcher, J. M., Vaughn, S. R., & Stuebing, K. K. (2012). Anxiety and reading difficulties in early elementary school: Evidence for unidirectional- or bidirectional relations? *Child Psychiatry and Human Development*, 43(1), 35–47. DOI: 10.1007/s10578-011-0246-1 PMID: 21822734

Gusfre, S. A. (2022). Bullying by teachers towards atudents—A scoping review. *International Journal of Bullying Prevention*, 5(4), 331-347.Hussain, S., Alam, A., & Ullah, S. (2022). Challenges to persons with disabilities in Pakistan: A review of literature. *Journal of Social Sciences Review*, 2(3), 35–42.

Haataja, A., Sainio, M., Turtonen, M., & Salmivalli, C. (2016). Implementing the KiVa antibullying program: Recognition of stable victims. *Educational Psychology*, 36(3), 595–611. DOI: 10.1080/01443410.2015.1066758

Hahn, G. (2023). Bullying: Violência na linguagem e sua dimensão perlocucionária/Language violence and its perlocutionary dimension. *Revista Linguagem em Foco/Language in Focus Journal*, 15(1), 152-176.

Hajdukova, E. B., Hornby, G., & Cushman, P. (2015). Bullying experiences of students with social, emotional and behavioural difficulties (SEBD). *Educational Review*, 68(2), 207–221. DOI: 10.1080/00131911.2015.1067880

Hakim, F., & Shah, S. A. (2017). Investigation of bullying controlling strategies by primary school teachers at district Haripur. [PJPBS]. *Peshawar Journal of Psychology and Behavioral Sciences*, 3(2), 165–174.

Halliday, S., Gregory, T., Taylor, A., Digenis, C., & Turnbull, D. (2021). The impact of bullying victimization in early adolescence on subsequent psychosocial and academic outcomes across the adolescent period: A systematic review. *Journal of School Violence*, 20(3), 351–373. DOI: 10.1080/15388220.2021.1913598

Hall, J. A. (2019). How many hours does it take to make a friend? *Journal of Social and Personal Relationships*, 36(4), 1278–1296. DOI: 10.1177/0265407518761225

Hameed, A., & Manzoor, A. (2019). Similar agenda, diverse strategies: A review of inclusive education reforms in the Subcontinent. *Bulletin of Education and Research*, 41(2), 53–66.

Hardy, G., Cahill, J., & Barkham, M. (2007). Active ingredients of the therapeutic relationship that promote client change. In Gilbert, P., & Leahy, R. (Eds.), *The therapeutic relationship in the cognitive behavioral psychotherapies* (pp. 24–42). Routledge., DOI: 10.4324/9780203099995

Harper, K. M. (2015). *Teacher perceptions of the use of school-wide positive behavior interventions and supports at reducing the presence of bullying in middle schools*. The University of Southern Mississippi.

Hartley, M. T., Bauman, S., Nixon, C. L., & Davis, S. (2015). Comparative study of bullying victimization among students in general and special education. *Exceptional Children*, 81(2), 176–193. DOI: 10.1177/0014402914551741

Hartley, M. T., Bauman, S., Nixon, C. L., & Davis, S. (2017). Responding to bullying victimization: Comparative analysis of victimized students in general and special education. *Journal of Disability Policy Studies*, 28(2), 77–89. DOI: 10.1177/1044207317710700

Haru, E. (2022). Perilaku bullying di kalangan pelajar/ Bullying behavior among students. *Jurnal Alternatif Wacanal lmiah Interkultural/ Journal of Alternative Intercultural Academic Discourse*, *11*(2), 59-71.

Hassan, B. A. R., & Mohammed, A. H. (2023). Overview of bullying. *Studies in Social Science & Humanities*, 2(4), 69–71. DOI: 10.56397/SSSH.2023.04.07

Hawker, D. S., & Boulton, M. J. (2000). Twenty years' research on peer victimization and psychosocial maladjustment: A meta-analytic review of cross-sectional studies. *Journal of Child Psychology and Psychiatry, and Allied Disciplines*, 41(4), 441–455. DOI: 10.1111/1469-7610.00629 PMID: 10836674

Hayes, S. A., & Watson, S. L. (2013). The impact of parenting stress: A meta-analysis of studies comparing the experience of parenting stress in parents of children with and without autism spectrum disorder. *Journal of Autism and Developmental Disorders*, 43(3), 629–642. DOI: 10.1007/s10803-012-1604-y PMID: 22790429

Haynie, D. L., Nansel, T., Eitel, P., Crump, A. D., Saylor, K., Yu, K., & Simons-Morton, B. (2001). Bullies, victims, and bully/victims: Distinct groups of at-risk youth. *The Journal of Early Adolescence*, 21(1), 29–49. DOI: 10.1177/0272431601021001002

Heiman, T., & Olenik Shemesh, D. (2018). Predictors of cyber-victimization of higher-education students with and without learning disabilities. *Journal of Youth Studies*, 22(2), 205–222. DOI: 10.1080/13676261.2018.1492103

Heiman, T., & Olenik-Shemesh, D. (2020). Social-emotional profile of children with and without learning disabilities: The relationships with perceived loneliness, self-efficacy and well-being. *International Journal of Environmental Research and Public Health*, 17(20), 7358. DOI: 10.3390/ijerph17207358 PMID: 33050221

Heinrichs, R. R. (2003). A whole-school approach to bullying: Special considerations for children with exceptionalities. *Intervention in School and Clinic*, 38(4), 195–204. DOI: 10.1177/105345120303800401

Henson, M. (2012). *Issues of crime and school safety: Zero tolerance policies and children with disabilities* [Master's Thesis, University of Central Florida]

Herkama, S., & Salmivalli, C. (2018). KiVa antibullying program, *Reducing Cyberbullying in Schools*, 125-134. https://doi.org/DOI: 10.1016/B978-0-12-811423-0.00009-2

Heyne, D., Sauter, F. M., & Maynard, B. R. (2011). School refusal and truancy. In Shackelford, T. K., & Weekes-Shackelford, V. A. (Eds.), *Encyclopedia of Evolutionary Psychological Science*. Springer.

Hill, C. E. (2020). *Helping skills: Facilitating exploration, insight, and action*. American Psychological Association. DOI: 10.1037/0000147-000

Hirschstein, M., & Frey, K. S. (2006). Promoting behavior and beliefs that reduce bullying: The Steps to Respect Program. In Jimerson, S. R., & Furlong, M. (Eds.), *Handbook of school violence and school safety: From research to practice* (pp. 309–323). Lawrence Erlbaum Associates Publishers.

Holfeld, B., Stoesz, B., & Montgomery, J. (2019). Traditional and cyber bullying and victimization among youth with autism spectrum disorder: An investigation of the frequency, characteristics, and psychosocial correlates. *Journal on Developmental Disabilities*, 24(2), 61–76.

Hong, J. S., & Espelage, D. L. (2012). A review of research on bullying and peer victimization in school: An ecological system analysis. *Aggression and Violent Behavior*, 17(4), 311–322. DOI: 10.1016/j.avb.2012.03.003

Hopkins, B. (2002). Restorative justice in schools. *Support for Learning*, 17(3), 144–149. DOI: 10.1111/1467-9604.00254

Horishna, N. M. (2022). Typology of social skills and their impairments in children with autism spectrum disorders. *Scientific Bulletin of Mukachevo State University. Series. Pedagogy and Psychology*, 8(3), 33–38. DOI: 10.52534/msu-pp.8(3).2022.33-38

Hornby, G. (2003). A model for counselling in schools. In *Counselling pupils in schools* (pp. 24–34). Routledge.

Hosseini Sfidvadjani, M., Ghorban Jahromi, R., Dortaj, F., & Hosseini, S. B. (2023). Negative emotions, fear of missing out, victim of cyberbullying: A structural equation modeling for adolescents. *Social Psychological Review*, 13(49), 91–101. DOI: 10.22034/spr.2023.375154.1799

Houchins, D. E., Oakes, W. P., & Johnson, Z. G. (2016). Bullying and students with disabilities: A systematic literature review of intervention studies. *Remedial and Special Education*, 37(5), 259–273. DOI: 10.1177/0741932516648678

Hugh-Jones, S., & Smith, P. K. (1999). Self-reports of short- and long-term effects of bullying on children who stammer. *The British Journal of Educational Psychology*, 69(2), 141–158. DOI: 10.1348/000709999157626 PMID: 10405616

Hu, H. F., Liu, T. L., Hsiao, R. C., Ni, H. C., Liang, S. H. Y., Lin, C. F., Chan, H. L., Hsieh, Y. H., Wang, L. J., Lee, M. J., Chou, W. J., & Yen, C. F. (2019). Cyberbullying victimization and perpetration in adolescents with high-functioning autism spectrum disorder: Correlations with depression, anxiety, and suicidality. *Journal of Autism and Developmental Disorders*, 49(10), 4170–4180. DOI: 10.1007/s10803-019-04060-7 PMID: 31267285

Humphrey, N., Lendrum, A., Barlow, A., Wigelsworth, M., & Squires, G. (2013). Achievement for All: Improving psychosocial outcomes for students with special educational needs and disabilities. *Research in Developmental Disabilities*, 34(4), 1210–1225. DOI: 10.1016/j.ridd.2012.12.008 PMID: 23380579

Humphrey, N., & Symes, W. (2011). Peer interaction patterns among adolescents with autistic spectrum disorders (ASDs) in mainstream school settings. *Autism*, 15(4), 397–419. DOI: 10.1177/1362361310387804 PMID: 21454385

Hussein, M. H. (2013). The social and emotional skills of bullies, victims, and bully-victims of Egyptian primary school children. *International Journal of Psychology*, 48(5), 910–921. DOI: 10.1080/00207594.2012.702908 PMID: 22853459

Hwang, S., Kim, Y. S., Koh, Y. J., & Leventhal, B. L. (2018). Autism spectrum disorder and school bullying: Who is the victim? Who is the perpetrator? *Journal of Autism and Developmental Disorders*, 48(1), 225–238. DOI: 10.1007/s10803-017-3285-z PMID: 28936640

Hymel, S., & Swearer, S. M. (2015). Four decades of research on school bullying: An introduction. *The American Psychologist*, 70(4), 293–299. DOI: 10.1037/a0038928 PMID: 25961310

Ian, H., & Stuart, W. (2015). Inclusive education policies: Discourses of difference, diversity and deficit. *International Journal of Inclusive Education*, 19(2), 141–164. DOI: 10.1080/13603116.2014.908965

Imran, S. (2014). Students' perception of cyber bullying : A comparative analysis in Sweden and Pakistan (Dissertation). Retrieved from https://urn.kb.se/resolve?urn=urn:nbn:se:kau:diva-31937

Individuals with disabilities education act (IDEA; 2017). Sec. 300.8 (c) (4). https://sites.ed.gov/idea/regs/b/a/300.8/c/4

Iqbal, F., Senin, M. S., Nordin, M. N. B., & Hasyim, M. (2021). A qualitative study: Impact of bullying on children with special needs. *Linguistica Antverpiensia*, 2, 1639–1643.

Irish, A., & Murshid, N. S. (2020). Suicide ideation, plan, and attempt among youth in Bangladesh: Incidence and risk factors. *Children and Youth Services Review*, 116, 105215. DOI: 10.1016/j.childyouth.2020.105215

Ison, N., McIntyre, S., Rothery, S., Smithers-Sheedy, H., Goldsmith, S., Parsonage, S., & Foy, L. (2010). 'just like you': A disability awareness programme for children that enhanced knowledge, attitudes and acceptance: Pilot study findings. *Developmental Neurorehabilitation*, 13(5), 360–368. DOI: 10.3109/17518423.2010.496764 PMID: 20828333

Iyanda, A. E. (2021). Bullying Victimization of Children with Mental, Emotional, and Developmental or Behavioral (MEDB) Disorders in the United States. *Journal of Child & Adolescent Trauma*, 15(2), 221–233. DOI: 10.1007/s40653-021-00368-8 PMID: 35600527

Jahanzaib, M., Fatima, G., & Shoaib, M. (2021). Review of policy documents in perspective of rehabilitation of persons with special needs in Pakistan. *Journal of ISOSS*, 7(4), 419–432.

Jalón, M. J. D. A., & Arias, R. M. (2013). Peer bullying and disruption-coercion escalations in student-teacher relationship. *Psicothema*, 25(2), 206–213. DOI: 10.7334/psicothema2012.312 PMID: 23628535

Javed, K., Malik, S., Younus, W., & Shahid, A. (2023). Confronting the destructive impact of Bullying: The harmful consequences and laws for anti-bullying initiatives. *Journal of Social Sciences Review*, 3(2), 666–675. DOI: 10.54183/jssr.v3i2.309

Jones, S. (2019). *Bullying in schools: A shared understanding* (Doctoral dissertation, Cardiff University).

Jones, A., & Brown, B. (2019). Developmental Theory: Understanding the emergence of bullying behavior. *Child Development Perspectives*, 13(4), 321–335.

Jordan, K., & Austin, J. (2012). A review of the literature on bullying in US schools and how a parent–educator partnership can be an effective way to handle bullying. *Journal of Aggression, Maltreatment & Trauma*, 21(4), 440–458. DOI: 10.1080/10926771.2012.675420

Juvonen, J., & Graham, S. (2014). Bullying in schools: The power of bullies and the plight of victims. *Annual Review of Psychology*, 65(1), 159–185. DOI: 10.1146/annurev-psych-010213-115030 PMID: 23937767

Kaltsas, E. P., & Kaltsas, J. (2023). Combatting bullying in school and its consequences. In *Research Highlights in Language, Literature and Education* (Vol. 6, pp. 28-35). B P International. ISBN 978-81-19217-91-5. DOI: 10.9734/bpi/rhlle/v6/9918F

Kamran, & Siddiqui, S. (2024). Roots of resilience: Uncovering the secrets behind 25+ years of inclusive education sustainability. *Sustainability 16*(11), 4364. https://doi.org/DOI: 10.3390/su16114364

Kamran, M., & Bano, N. (2023). A systematic review of literature on inclusive education with special emphasis on children with disability in Pakistan. *International Journal of Inclusive Education*, •••, 1–19. DOI: 10.1080/13603116.2023.2256321

Kamran, M., & Siddiqui, S. (2023). Assistive technology integration: Promoting inclusion and achieving sustainable development goals. In Escudeiro, P., Escudeiro, N., & Bernardes, O. (Eds.), *Handbook of research on advancing equity and inclusion through educational technology* (pp. 1–25). IGI Global., DOI: 10.4018/978-1-6684-6868-5.ch001

Kamran, M., Siddiqui, S., & Adil, M. S. (2023). Breaking barriers: The influence of teachers' attitudes on inclusive education for students with mild learning disabilities (MLD). *Education Sciences*, 13(6), 606. Advance online publication. DOI: 10.3390/educsci13060606

Kamran, M., Thomas, M., & Siddiqui, S. (2022). Teachers' opinions about promoting inclusive classroom settings: An investigation regarding the presence of special needs assistants. *The Government: Research Journal of Political Science*, 11, 57–71.

Karataş, H. (2011). *Investigation of the effect of the program developed for bullying in primary schools.* (Unpublished Ph.D. Thesis, Dokuz Eylül University), İzmir.

Karatas, H., & Ozturk, C. (2011). Relationship Between Bullying and Health Problems in Primary School Children. *Asian Nursing Research*, 5(2), 81–87. DOI: 10.1016/S1976-1317(11)60016-9 PMID: 25030257

Karmaliani, R., McFarlane, J., Khuwaja, H. M. A., Somani, Y., Bhamani, S. S., Saeed Ali, T., Asad, N., Chirwa, E. D., & Jewkes, R. (2020). Right To Play's intervention to reduce peer violence among children in public schools in Pakistan: A cluster-randomized controlled trial. *Global Health Action*, 13(1), 1836604. DOI: 10.1080/16549716.2020.1836604 PMID: 33138740

Karmaliani, R., Mcfarlane, J., Somani, R., Khuwaja, H. M., Bhamani, S. S., Ali, T. S., Gulzar, S., Somani, Y., Chirwa, E. D., & Jewkes, R. (2017). Peer violence perpetration and victimization: Prevalence, associated factors and pathways among 1752 sixth grade boys and girls in schools in Pakistan. *PLoS One*, 12(8), e0180833. DOI: 10.1371/journal.pone.0180833 PMID: 28817565

Kartika, A., Suminar, D. R., Tairas, M. M., & Hendriani, W. (2017). *Individualized education program (IEP) paperwork: A narrative review.* In: Asia International Multidisciplinary Conference 2017, 1-2 May, 2017, Universiti Teknologi Malaysia, Johor Bahru, Malaysia.

Katic, B., Alba, L. A., & Johnson, A. H. (2020). A systematic evaluation of restorative justice practices: School violence prevention and response. *Journal of School Violence*, 19(4), 579–593. DOI: 10.1080/15388220.2020.1783670

Kazimi, A. B., & Kazmi, S. W. (2018). Developing Inclusive education approaches among stakeholders in Pakistan. *Journal of Education & Social Sciences*, 6(1), 86–95. DOI: 10.20547/jess0611806106

Kearney, C. A., & Albano, A. M. (2004). The functional profiles of school refusal behavior: Diagnostic aspects. *Behavior Modification*, 28(1), 147–161. DOI: 10.1177/0145445503259263 PMID: 14710711

Kearney, C. A., Lemos, A., & Silverman, J. (2004). The functional assessment of school refusal behavior. *The Behavior Analyst Today*, 5(3), 275–283. DOI: 10.1037/h0100040

Kelly, E. V., Newton, N. C., Stapinski, L. A., Slade, T., Barrett, E. L., Conrod, P. J., & Teesson, M. (2015). Suicidality, internalizing problems and externalizing problems among adolescent bullies, victims and bully-victims. *Preventive Medicine*, 73, 100–105. DOI: 10.1016/j.ypmed.2015.01.020 PMID: 25657168

Kennedy, T. D., Russom, A. G., & Kevorkian, M. M. (2012). Teacher and administrator perceptions of bullying in schools. *International Journal of Education Policy and Leadership*, 7(5), 1–12. DOI: 10.22230/ijepl.2012v7n5a395

Khalil, H., & Tricco, A. C. (2022). Differentiating between mapping reviews and scoping reviews in the evidence synthesis ecosystem. *Journal of Clinical Epidemiology*, 149, 175–182. DOI: 10.1016/j.jclinepi.2022.05.012 PMID: 35636593

Khan, M., & Khan, S. (2019). Socioeconomic factors in school bullying: A Pakistani perspective. *International Journal of Educational Research*, 28(1), 45–57.

Khasawneh, M. A. S. (2023). Social attitude of children with special needs in the learning process. *Acta Scientiae. Journal of Science*, 24(6), 32–43.

Khawar, R., & Malik, F. (2016). Bullying behavior of Pakistani pre-adolescents: Findings based on Olweus questionnaire. *Pakistan Journal of Psychological Research*, 31(1), 23–43.

Killen, M., & Rutland, A. (2022). Promoting fair and just school environments: Developing inclusive youth. *Policy Insights from the Behavioral and Brain Sciences*, 9(1), 81–89. DOI: 10.1177/23727322211073795 PMID: 35402700

Kim, S. (2022). The role of social capital in the onset of victimization against children. *Child Indicators Research*, 15(1), 67–86. DOI: 10.1007/s12187-021-09859-4

Kircaburun, K., Alhabash, S., Tosuntaş, Ş. B., & Griffiths, M. D. (2020). Uses and gratifications of problematic social media use among university students: A simultaneous examination of the Big Five of personality traits, social media platforms, and social media use motives. *International Journal of Mental Health and Addiction*, 18(3), 525–547. DOI: 10.1007/s11469-018-9940-6

Kirksey, J. J., Gottfried, M. A., & Freeman, J. A. (2022). Does parental involvement change after schools assign students an IEP? *Peabody Journal of Education*, 97(1), 18–31. DOI: 10.1080/0161956X.2022.2026717

Kirst, S., Bögl, K., Gross, V. L., Diehm, R., Poustka, L., & Dziobek, I. (2022). Subtypes of aggressive behavior in children with autism in the context of emotion recognition, hostile attribution bias, and dysfunctional emotion regulation. *Journal of Autism and Developmental Disorders*, 52(12), 5367–5382. DOI: 10.1007/s10803-021-05387-w PMID: 34931277

Klenk, C., Albrecht, J., & Nagel, S. (2019). Social participation of people with disabilities in organized community sport: A systematic review. *German Journal of Exercise and Sport Research*, 49(4), 365–380. DOI: 10.1007/s12662-019-00584-3

Kline, R. B. (2004). *Principles and practice of structural equation modeling*. The Guilford Press.

Knox, E., & Conti-Ramsden, G. (2007). Bullying in young people with a history of specific language impairment (SLI). *Educational and Child Psychology*, 24(4), 130–141. DOI: 10.53841/bpsecp.2007.24.4.130

Kochenderfer-Ladd, B. (2004). Peer victimization: The role of emotions in adaptive and maladaptive coping. *Social Development*, 13(3), 329–349. DOI: 10.1111/j.1467-9507.2004.00271.x

Kok, F. M., Groen, Y., Fuermaier, A. B., & Tucha, O. (2016). Problematic peer functioning in girls with ADHD: A systematic literature review. *PLoS One*, 11(11), e0165119. DOI: 10.1371/journal.pone.0165119 PMID: 27870862

Konishi, C., Hymel, S., Zumbo, B. D., & Li, Z. (2010). Do school bullying and student–teacher relationships matter for academic achievement? A multilevel analysis. *Canadian Journal of School Psychology*, 25(1), 19–39. DOI: 10.1177/0829573509357550

Koo, H. (2007). A time line of the evolution of school bullying in differing social contexts. *Asia Pacific Education Review*, 8(1), 107–116. DOI: 10.1007/BF03025837

Koo, H., Kwak, K., & Smith, P. K. (2008). Victimization in Korean schools: The nature, incidence, and distinctive features of Korean bullying or wang-ta. *Journal of School Violence*, 7(4), 119–139. DOI: 10.1080/15388220801974084

Kostić, J. O., Pedović, I., & Stošić, M. (2022). Predicting social media use intensity in late adolescence: The role of attachment to friends and fear of missing out. *Acta Psychologica*, 229, 103667. DOI: 10.1016/j.actpsy.2022.103667 PMID: 35841690

Kottler, J. A., & Kottler, E. (2006). *Counseling skills for teachers*. Corwin Press.

Kowalski, R. M., & Fedina, C. (2011). Cyber bullying in ADHD and Asperger Syndrome populations. *Research in Autism Spectrum Disorders*, 5(3), 1201–1208. DOI: 10.1016/j.rasd.2011.01.007

Kowalski, R. M., Giumetti, G. W., Schroeder, A. N., & Lattanner, M. R. (2014). Bullying in the digital age: A critical review and meta-analysis of cyberbullying research among youth. *Psychological Bulletin*, 140(4), 1073–1137. DOI: 10.1037/a0035618 PMID: 24512111

Kowalski, R. M., & Toth, A. (2018). Cyberbullying among youth with and without disabilities. *Journal of Child & Adolescent Trauma*, 11(1), 7–15. DOI: 10.1007/s40653-017-0139-y PMID: 32318133

Kozleski, E. B., & Choi, J. H. (2018). Leadership for equity and inclusivity in schools: The cultural work of inclusive schools. *Inclusion (Washington, D.C.)*, 6(1), 33–34. DOI: 10.1352/2326-6988-6.1.33

Kryszewska, H. (2017). Teaching students with special needs in inclusive classrooms special educational needs. *ELT Journal*, 71(4), 525–528. DOI: 10.1093/elt/ccx042

Kuhne, M., & Wiener, J. (2000). Stability of social status of children with and without learning disabilities. *Learning Disability Quarterly*, 23(1), 64–75. DOI: 10.2307/1511100

Kuriakose, V., Bishwas, S. K., & Mohandas, N. P. (2023). Does bullying among students hamper their well-being? Roles of helplessness and psychological capital. *International Journal of Educational Management*, 37(5), 1104–1123. DOI: 10.1108/IJEM-10-2022-0437

Laftman, S. B., Fransson, E., Modin, B., & Östberg, V. (2017). National data study showed that adolescents living in poorer households and with one parent were more likely to be bullied. *Acta Paediatrica (Oslo, Norway)*, 106(12), 2048–2054. DOI: 10.1111/apa.13997 PMID: 28727173

Lang, J., Wylie, G., Haig, C., Gillberg, C., & Minnis, H. (2024). Towards system redesign: An exploratory analysis of neurodivergent traits in a childhood population referred for autism assessment. *PLoS One*, 19(1), e0296077. DOI: 10.1371/journal.pone.0296077 PMID: 38198484

Laugeson, E. A., Frankel, F., Mogil, C., & Dillon, A. R. (2009). Parent-assisted social skills training to improve friendships in teens with autism spectrum disorders. *Journal of Autism and Developmental Disorders*, 39(4), 596–606. DOI: 10.1007/s10803-008-0664-5 PMID: 19015968

Lebrón-Cruz, A., & Orvell, A. (2023). I am what I am: The role of essentialist beliefs and neurodivergent identification on individuals' self-efficacy. *Journal of Experimental Psychology. General*, 152(11), 2995–3001. DOI: 10.1037/xge0001457 PMID: 37498695

Lebrun-Harris, L. A., Sherman, L. J., Limber, S. P., Miller, B. D., & Edgerton, E. A. (2018). Bullying victimization and perpetration among U.S. children and adolescents: 2016 national survey of children's health. *Journal of Child and Family Studies*, 28(9), 2543–2557. DOI: 10.1007/s10826-018-1170-9

Leijen, A., Arcidiacono, F., & Baucal, A. (2021). The dilemma of inclusive education: Inclusion for some or inclusion for all. *Frontiers in Psychology*, 12, 633066. DOI: 10.3389/fpsyg.2021.633066 PMID: 34566742

Lepley, C. (2023). *Bullying in Schools: Teacher Perceptions on Effectiveness of the Current Bullying Program*. Immaculata University.

Lessne, D., & Yanez, C. (2018). *Repetition and Power Imbalance in Bullying Victimization at School. Data Point. NCES 2018-093*. National Center for Education Statistics.

Lhamon, C. E. (2014, October 21). Dear colleague letter: Responding to bullying of students with disabilities from the assistant secretary for civil rights. https://www2.ed.gov/about/offices/list/ocr/letters/colleague-bullying-201410.pdf

Lieberman, L. J., & Houston-Wilson, C. (2018). *Strategies for inclusion: physical education for everyone* (3rd ed.). Human Kinetics.

Lightfoot, J., Wright, S., & Sloper, P. (1999). Supporting pupils in mainstream school with an illness or disability: Young people's views. *Child: Care, Health and Development*, 25(4), 267–284. DOI: 10.1046/j.1365-2214.1999.00112.x PMID: 10399032

Limber, S. P., Kowalkski, R. M., Agatston, P. W., & Huynh, H. V. (2016). Bullying and children with disabilities. In Saracho, O. (Ed.), *Contemporary Perspectives on Research on Bullying and Victimization in Early Childhood Education* (pp. 129–155). Information Age Publishing.

Lin, C. W., Lee, K. H., Hsiao, R. C., Chou, W. J., & Yen, C. F. (2021). Relationship between bullying victimization and quality of life in adolescents with attention-deficit/hyperactivity disorder (ADHD) in Taiwan: Mediation of the effects of emotional problems and ADHD and oppositional defiant symptoms. *International Journal of Environmental Research and Public Health*, 18(18), 9470. Advance online publication. DOI: 10.3390/ijerph18189470 PMID: 34574409

Lincoln, Y. S., & Guba, E. G. (1985). *Naturalistic inquiry*. Sage. DOI: 10.1016/0147-1767(85)90062-8

Lindsay, S., & McPherson, A. C. (2012). Experiences of social exclusion and bullying at school among children and youth with cerebral palsy. *Disability and Rehabilitation*, 34(2), 101–109. DOI: 10.3109/09638288.2011.587086 PMID: 21870932

Lindstrom Johnson, S., Waasdorp, T. E., Gaias, L. M., & Bradshaw, C. P. (2019). Parental responses to bullying: Understanding the role of school policies and practices. *Journal of Educational Psychology*, 111(3), 475–487. DOI: 10.1037/edu0000295

Lin, H. T., Tai, Y. M., & Gau, S. S. F. (2023). Autistic traits and cyberbullying involvement mediated by psychopathologies and school functions in a nationally representative child sample. *Cyberpsychology, Behavior, and Social Networking*, 26(9), 706–716. DOI: 10.1089/cyber.2022.0309 PMID: 37477877

Little, L. (2002). Middle-class mothers' perceptions of peer and sibling victimization among children with asperger's syndrome and nonverbal learning disorders. *Issues in Comprehensive Pediatric Nursing*, 25(1), 43–57. DOI: 10.1080/014608602753504847 PMID: 11934121

Liu, T. L., Chen, Y. L., Hsiao, R. C., Ni, H. C., Liang, S. H. Y., Lin, C. F., Chan, H. L., Hsieh, Y. H., Wang, L. J., Lee, M. J., Chou, W. J., & Yen, C. F. (2023). Adolescent–caregiver agreement regarding the school bullying and cyberbullying involvement experiences of adolescents with autism spectrum disorder. *International Journal of Environmental Research and Public Health*, 20(4), 3733. Advance online publication. DOI: 10.3390/ijerph20043733 PMID: 36834428

Liu, T. L., Hsiao, R. C., Chou, W. J., & Yen, C. F. (2021a). Perpetration of and victimization in cyberbullying and traditional bullying in adolescents with attention-deficit/hyperactivity disorder: Roles of impulsivity, frustration intolerance, and hostility. *International Journal of Environmental Research and Public Health*, 18(13), 6872. Advance online publication. DOI: 10.3390/ijerph18136872 PMID: 34206834

Liu, T. L., Hsiao, R. C., Chou, W. J., & Yen, C. F. (2021b). Self-reported depressive symptoms and suicidality in adolescents with attention-deficit/hyperactivity disorder: Roles of bullying involvement, frustration intolerance, and hostility. *International Journal of Environmental Research and Public Health*, 18(15), 7829. Advance online publication. DOI: 10.3390/ijerph18157829 PMID: 34360120

Liu, T. L., Hsiao, R. C., Chou, W. J., & Yen, C. F. (2021c). Social anxiety in victimization and perpetration of cyberbullying and traditional bullying in adolescents with autism spectrum disorder and attention-deficit/hyperactivity disorder. *International Journal of Environmental Research and Public Health*, 18(11), 5728. Advance online publication. DOI: 10.3390/ijerph18115728 PMID: 34073617

Li, Y., Chen, P. Y., Chen, F. L., & Chen, Y. L. (2017). Preventing school bullying: Investigation of the link between anti-bullying strategies, prevention ownership, prevention climate, and prevention leadership. *Applied Psychology*, 66(4), 577–598. DOI: 10.1111/apps.12107

Lochman, J. E., & Wells, K. C. (2002). The Coping Power program at the middle-school transition: Universal and indicated prevention effects. *Psychology of Addictive Behaviors*, 16(4, Suppl, 4S), S40–S54. DOI: 10.1037/0893-164X.16.4S.S40 PMID: 12502276

Lodhi, S. K., Thaver, D., Akhtar, I. N., Javaid, H., Masoor, M., Bano, S., Malik, F. N., Iqbal, M. R., Hashmi, H. R., Siddiqullah, S., & Saleem, S. (2016). Assessing the knowledge, attitudes and practices of school teachers regarding dyslexia, attention-deficit/ hyperactivity and autistic spectrum disorders in Karachi, Pakistan. *Journal of Ayub Medical College, Abbottabad: JAMC*, 28(1), 99–104. PMID: 27323572

Lodi, E., Perrella, L., Lepri, G. L., Scarpa, M. L., & Patrizi, P. (2022). Use of restorative justice and restorative practices at school: A systematic literature review. *International Journal of Environmental Research and Public Health*, 19(1), 1–36. DOI: 10.3390/ijerph19010096 PMID: 35010355

Lo, L. L. H., Suen, Y. N., Chan, S. K. W., Sum, M. Y., Charlton, C., Hui, C. L. M., Chang, W. C., & Chen, E. Y. H. (2021). Sociodemographic correlates of public stigma about mental illness: A population study on Hong Kong's Chinese population. *BMC Psychiatry*, 21(1), 1–8. DOI: 10.1186/s12888-021-03301-3 PMID: 34051783

Longobardi, C., Badenes-Ribera, L., Gastaldi, F. G., & Prino, L. E. (2018). The student–teacher relationship quality in children with selective mutism. *Psychology in the Schools*, 56(1), 32–41. DOI: 10.1002/pits.22175

Longobardi, C., Settanni, M., Prino, L. E., Fabris, M. A., & Marengo, D. (2019). Students' psychological adjustment in normative school transitions from kindergarten to high school: Investigating the role of teacher-student relationship quality. *Frontiers in Psychology*, 10, 1238. Advance online publication. DOI: 10.3389/fpsyg.2019.01238 PMID: 31191415

Lösel, F., & Farrington, D. P. (2012). Direct protective and buffering protective factors in the development of youth violence. *American Journal of Preventive Medicine*, 43(2), 8–23. DOI: 10.1016/j.amepre.2012.04.029 PMID: 22789961

Lovegrove, P. J., Bellmore, A. D., Green, J. G., Jens, K., & Ostrov, J. M. (2013). "My voice is not going to be silent": What can parents do about children's bullying? *Journal of School Violence*, 12(3), 253–267. DOI: 10.1080/15388220.2013.792270

Lubna, Abid, M., & Qamreen (2022). The trends of verbal bullying among university students: A sociolinguistic analysis. *International Journal of Linguistics and Culture*. https://doi.org/DOI: 10.52700/ijlc.v3i2.123

Lucas-Molina, B., Pérez-Albéniz, A., Solbes-Canales, I., Ortuño-Sierra, J., & Fonseca-Pedrero, E. (2022). Bullying, cyberbullying and mental health: The role of student connectedness as a school protective factor. *Psychosocial Intervention*, 31(1), 33–41. DOI: 10.5093/pi2022a1 PMID: 37362615

Luciano, S., & Savage, R. S. (2007). Bullying risk in children with learning difficulties in inclusive educational settings. *Canadian Journal of School Psychology*, 22(1), 14–31. DOI: 10.1177/0829573507301039

Lund, E. M., Blake, J. J., Ewing, H. K., & Banks, C. S. (2012). School counselors' and school psychologists' bullying prevention and intervention strategies: A look into real-world practices. *Journal of School Violence*, 11(3), 246–265. DOI: 10.1080/15388220.2012.682005

Lung, F. W., Shu, B. C., Chiang, T. L., & Lin, S. J. (2019). Prevalence of bullying and perceived happiness in adolescents with learning disability, intellectual disability, ADHD, and autism spectrum disorder. *Medicine*, 98(6), e14483. DOI: 10.1097/MD.0000000000014483 PMID: 30732217

Lu, W. H., Chou, W. J., Hsiao, R. C., Hu, H. F., & Yen, C. F. (2019). Correlations of internet addiction severity with reinforcement sensitivity and frustration intolerance in adolescents with attention-deficit/hyperactivity disorder: The moderating effect of medications. *Frontiers in Psychiatry*, 10, 268. DOI: 10.3389/fpsyt.2019.00268 PMID: 31105605

Lydecker, J. A., Winschel, J., Gilbert, K., & Cotter, E. W. (2023). School absenteeism and impairment associated with weight bullying. *Journal of Adolescence*, 95(7), 1478–1487. DOI: 10.1002/jad.12220 PMID: 37487590

Maag, J. W., & Katsiyannis, A. (2012). Bullying and students with disabilities: Legal and practice considerations. *Behavioral Disorders*, 37(2), 78–86. DOI: 10.1177/019874291203700202

Machmutow, K., Perren, S., Sticca, F., & Alsaker, F. D. (2012). Peer victimisation and depressive symptoms: Can specific coping strategies buffer the negative impact of cybervictimisation? *Emotional & Behavioural Difficulties*, 17(3–4), 403–420. DOI: 10.1080/13632752.2012.704310

Macionis, J. J. (2012). *Sociology*. Pearson. Fourteen Edition

Maftei, A., & Măirean, C. (2023). Not so funny after all! Humor, parents, peers, and their link with cyberbullying experiences. *Computers in Human Behavior*, 138, 107448. DOI: 10.1016/j.chb.2022.107448

Mahady Wilton, M. M., Craig, W. M., & Pepler, D. J. (2000). Emotional regulation and display in classroom victims of bullying: Characteristic expressions of affect, coping styles and relevant contextual factors. *Social Development*, 9(2), 226–245. DOI: 10.1111/1467-9507.00121

Mahjoob, M., Paul, T., Carbone, J., Bokadia, H., Cardy, R. E., Kassam, S., Anagnastou, E., Andrade, B. F., Penner, M., & Kushi, A. (2024). Predictors of health-related quality of life in neurodivergent children: A systematic review. *Clinical Child and Family Psychology Review*, 27(1), 91–129. DOI: 10.1007/s10567-023-00462-3 PMID: 38070100

Mahmoudi, M., & Keashly, L. (2021). Filling the space: A framework for coordinated global actions to diminish academic bullying. *Angewandte Chemie/Applied Chemistry, 133*(7), 3378-3384.

Maiano, C., Normand, C. L., Salvas, M. C., Moullec, G., & Aime, A. (2016). Prevalence of school bullying among youth with autism spectrum disorders: A systematic review and meta-analysis. *Autism Research*, 9(6), 601–615. DOI: 10.1002/aur.1568 PMID: 26451871

Malecki, C. K., Demaray, M. K., Smith, T. J., & Emmons, J. (2020). Disability, poverty, and other risk factors associated with involvement in bullying behaviors. *Journal of School Psychology*, 78, 115–132. DOI: 10.1016/j.jsp.2020.01.002 PMID: 32178807

Malik, A., & Abdullah, N. A. (2017). Level of aggression among college teachers and students in Pakistan: An analysis. *Pakistan Journal of Social Sciences*, 37(2), 343–353.

Malikiosi-Loizou, M. (2011). *Counseling Psychology in Education*. Pedio.

Malisiova, A., & Folia, V. (2024). Educational Challenges and Perspectives in Developmental Dyslexia. In *Childhood Developmental Language Disorders: Role of Inclusion, Families, and Professionals* (pp. 49-64). IGI Global. DOI: 10.4018/979-8-3693-1982-6.ch004

Malisiova, A., Kougioumtzis, G. A., Tsitsas, G., Koundourou, C., & Mitraras, A. (2023). Implementing inclusive education in mixed-ability classrooms by employing differentiated instruction. In Perspectives of cognitive, psychosocial, and learning difficulties from childhood to adulthood: Practical counseling strategies (pp. 155–178). IGI Global., 1-6684-8203-2.ch009.DOI: 10.4018/978-1-6684-8203-2.ch009

Mandelberg, J., Laugeson, E. A., Cunningham, T. D., Ellingsen, R., Bates, S., & Frankel, F. (2014). Long-term treatment outcomes for parent-assisted social skills training for adolescents with autism spectrum disorders: The UCLA PEERS program. *Journal of Mental Health Research in Intellectual Disabilities*, 7(1), 45–73. DOI: 10.1080/19315864.2012.730600

Marengo, D., Jungert, T., Iotti, N. O., Settanni, M., Thornberg, R., & Longobardi, C. (2018). Conflictual student–teacher relationship, emotional and behavioral problems, prosocial behavior, and their associations with bullies, victims, and bullies/victims. *Educational Psychology*, 38(9), 1201–1217. DOI: 10.1080/01443410.2018.1481199

Margevičiūtė, A. (2017). The definition of bullying in compulsory education: From a general to a legal perspective. *Baltic Journal of Law &amp. Politics*, 10(1), 205–229. DOI: 10.1515/bjlp-2017-0008

Marlina, M., & Sakinah, D. N. (2019). Bullying at students with special needs in inclusive schools: Implication for role of special teachers. In: *3rd International Conference on Special Education (ICSE 2019)*, 2019 DOI: 10.31227/osf.io/9q7cw

Marr, N., & Field, T. (2001). *Bullycide: Death at playtime*. Success Unlimited.

Marshall, S. A., & Allison, M. K. (2017). Midwestern misfits. *Youth & Society*, 51(3), 318–338. DOI: 10.1177/0044118X17697885

Maryam, U., & Ijaz, T. (2018). Efficacy of a school based intervention plan for victims of bullying. *e-Academia Journal, 8*, 206-216.

Mazumder, R., & Thompson-Hodgetts, S. (2019). Stigmatization of children and adolescents with autism spectrum disorders and their families: A scoping study. *Review Journal of Autism and Developmental Disorders*, 6(1), 96–107. DOI: 10.1007/s40489-018-00156-5

Mbah, R. M. (2020). *The perception of students about school bullying and how it affects academic performance in Cameroon* (Doctoral dissertation, Memorial University of Newfoundland). https://doi.org/DOI: 10.48336/6KA2-2F62

McCormac, M. (2014). Preventing and responding to bullying: An elementary school's 4-Year journey. *Professional School Counseling*, 18(1), 1–14. DOI: 10.5330/prsc.18.1.55607227n4428tkp

McElearney, A., Adamson, G., Shevlin, M., & Bunting, B. (2012). Impact evaluation of a school-based counselling intervention in Northern Ireland: Is it effective for pupils who have been bullied? *Child Care in Practice*, 19(1), 4–22. DOI: 10.1080/13575279.2012.732557

McEvoy, A. (2013). *Abuse of Power*. Learning for Justice. Retrieved April 22, 2024 from, https://www.learningforjustice.org/magazine/fall-2014/abuse-of-power

McFarlane, J., Karmaliani, R., Khuwaja, H. M. A., Gulzar, S., Somani, R., Ali, T. S., Somani, Y. H., Bhamani, S. S., Krone, R. D., Paulson, R. M., Muhammad, A., & Jewkes, R. (2017). Preventing peer violence against children: Methods and baseline data of a cluster randomized controlled trial in Pakistan. *Global Health, Science and Practice*, 5(1), 115–137. DOI: 10.9745/GHSP-D-16-00215 PMID: 28351880

McIntosh, K., Bennett, J. L., & Price, K. (2011). Evaluation of social and academic effects of school-wide positive behaviour support in a Canadian school district. *Exceptionality Education International*, 21(1), 46–60. DOI: 10.5206/eei.v21i1.7669

McKenna, J. W., Muething, C., Flower, A., Bryant, D. P., & Bryant, B. (2015). Use and relationships among effective practices in co-taught inclusive high school classrooms. *International Journal of Inclusive Education*, 19(1), 53–70. DOI: 10.1080/13603116.2014.906665

McNamara, B. E. (2013). *Bullying and students with disabilities: strategies and techniques to create a safe learning environment for all*. Corwin.

McNamara, B. E. (2017). Practices That Address Bullying of Students with Disabilities. *Journal for Leadership and Instruction*, 16(2), 31–35.

McNicholas, C. I., Orpinas, P., & Raczynski, K. (2017). Victimized for being different: Young adults with disabilities and peer victimization in middle and high school. *Journal of Interpersonal Violence*, 35(19-20), 3683–3709. DOI: 10.1177/0886260517710485 PMID: 29294765

McWood, L. M., Frosch, C. A., Wienke Garrison, C. M., Erath, S. A., & Troop-Gordon, W. (2023). "But There's Only So Much You Can Do…" Parent support-giving within the context of peer victimization. *The Journal of Early Adolescence*, 43(4), 455–489. DOI: 10.1177/02724316221105587

Meadan, H., & Monda-Amaya, L. (2008). Collaboration to promote social competence for students with mild disabilities in the general classroom: A structure for providing social support. *Intervention in School and Clinic*, 43(3), 158–167. DOI: 10.1177/1053451207311617

Mehari, K. R., Beulah, B., Paskewich, B., Leff, S. S., & Waasdorp, T. E. (2023). Cyberbullying and empathy among late-elementary school children. *International Journal of Bullying Prevention : an Official Publication of the International Bullying Prevention Association*, 5(1), 79–87. DOI: 10.1007/s42380-022-00119-9 PMID: 37066126

Mehmood, M. U., & Parveen, Z. (2021). Explore areas of needed support, competencies, attitudes, and concerns of elementary school teachers for inclusion of CWDS in elementary schools of Punjab. *Global Educational Studies Review, VI*, 6(III), 109–120. DOI: 10.31703/gesr.2021(VI-III).12

Mehta, S. B. (2011). *School climate and the assessment of bullying* (Order No. 3501727). Available from ProQuest Dissertations & Theses Global. (929145544). Retrieved April 22, 2024 from, https://www.proquest.com/dissertations-theses/school-climate-assessment-bullying/docview/929145544/se-2

Menesini, E. (2017). Bullying in schools: The state of knowledge and effective interventions. *Psicologia Educativa*, 23(2), 61–71. DOI: 10.1016/j.pse.2017.04.002 PMID: 28114811

Menesini, E., & Salmivalli, C. (2017). Bullying in schools: The state of knowledge and effective interventions. *Psychology Health and Medicine*, 22(sup1), 240–253. DOI: 10.1080/13548506.2017.1279740 PMID: 28114811

Merriam, S. B. (2009). *Qualitative Research: A Guide to Design and Implementation*. Jossey-Bass.

Merten, D. E. (1996). Visibility and vulnerability: Responses to rejection by non-aggressive junior high school boys. *The Journal of Early Adolescence*, 16(1), 5–26. DOI: 10.1177/0272431696016001001

Midgett, A., Doumas, D. M., Johnston, A., Trull, R., & Miller, R. (2017). Rethinking bullying interventions for high school students: A qualitative study. *Journal of Child and Adolescent Counseling*, 4(2), 146–163. DOI: 10.1080/23727810.2017.1381932

Midgett, A., Doumas, D., Sears, D., Lundquist, A., & Hausheer, R. (2015). A bystander bullying psychoeducation program with middle school students: A preliminary report. *The Professional Counselor*, 5(4), 486–500. DOI: 10.15241/am.5.4.486

Miles, M. B., & Huberman, A. M. (1994). Qualitative data analysis: An expanded sourcebook. *Sage (Atlanta, Ga.)*.

Ministry of Education. (2018) Ministerial decision (N. 4547/2018, ΦΕΚ 102/12-6-2018). *Reorganization of the support structures of the primary and secondary education and other provisions* [in Greek]. Retrieved from https://www.esos.gr/arthra/57432/fek-toy-n-454718-gia-tis-domes-ekpaideysis-anadiorganosi-ton-domon-ypostirixis-tis

Ministry of Education. (n.d.). *Primary Schools* [in Greek]. Retrieved from https://www.minedu.gov.gr/dimotiko-2/to-thema-dimotiko

Mishna, F. (2003). Learning disabilities and bullying: Double jeopardy. *Journal of Learning Disabilities*, 36(4), 1–15. DOI: 10.1177/00222194030360040501 PMID: 15490906

Mishna, F., Scarcello, I., Pepler, D., & Wiener, J. (2005). Teachers' understanding of bullying. *Revue canadienne de l'éducation. Canadian Journal of Education*, 28(4), 718–738. DOI: 10.2307/4126452

Mittleman, J. (2022). Homophobic bullying as gender policing: Population-based evidence. *Gender & Society*, 37(1), 5–31. DOI: 10.1177/08912432221138091

Mobarki, A. A., Morsi, N. M. A., & Hamouda, G. M. (2020). *Teachers' Perception Regarding Bullying Behavior in Elementary Schools at Jizan City* (Doctoral dissertation, King Abdul Aziz University, Jeddah).

Modecki, K. L., Minchin, J., Harbaugh, A. G., Guerra, N. G., & Runions, K. C. (2014). Bullying prevalence across contexts: A meta-analysis measuring cyber and traditional bullying. *The Journal of Adolescent Health*, 55(5), 602–611. DOI: 10.1016/j.jadohealth.2014.06.007 PMID: 25168105

Monks, C. P., Robinson, S., & Worlidge, P. (2012). The emergence of cyberbullying: A survey of primary school pupils' perceptions and experiences. *School Psychology International*, 33(5), 477–491. DOI: 10.1177/0143034312445242

Moola, S., Munn, Z., Tufunaru, C., Aromataris, E., Sears, K., Sfetc, R., Currie, M., Lisy, K., Qureshi, R., Mattis, P., & Mu, P. F. (2024). Systematic reviews of Aetiology and risk. In E. Aromataris, C. Lockwood, K. Porritt, B. Pilla, & Z. Jordan (Eds.), *JBI Manual for Evidence Synthesis*. JBI. https://doi.org/DOI: 10.46658/JBIMES-24-06

Morita, Y. (1985). *Sociological study on the structure of bullying group*. Department of Sociology, Osaka City University.

Morton, H. E., Bottini, S. B., McVey, A. J., Magnus, B. E., Gillis, J. M., & Romanczyk, R. G. (2024). The Assessment of Bullying Experiences Questionnaire (ABE) for neurodivergent youth: Establishing scoring criteria and clinical thresholds. *International Journal of Bullying Prevention : an Official Publication of the International Bullying Prevention Association*, 6(2), 138–148. DOI: 10.1007/s42380-022-00151-9

Morton, H. E., Gillis, J. M., Zale, E. L., Brimhall, K. C., & Romanczyk, R. G. (2022). Development and validation of the Assessment of Bullying Experiences Questionnaire for neurodivergent youth. *Journal of Autism and Developmental Disorders*, 52(11), 4651–4664. DOI: 10.1007/s10803-021-05330-z PMID: 34713376

Murray, J. (1999). An Inclusive School Library for the 21st Century: Fostering Independence.

Murray, A. L., Zych, I., Ribeaud, D., & Eisner, M. (2021). Developmental relations between ADHD symptoms and bullying perpetration and victimization in adolescence. *Aggressive Behavior*, 47(1), 58–68. DOI: 10.1002/ab.21930 PMID: 32895934

Murray, C., & Greenberg, M. T. (2001). Relationships with teachers and bonds with school: Social Emotional adjustment correlates for children with and without disabilities. *Psychology in the Schools*, 38(1), 25–41. DOI: 10.1002/1520-6807(200101)38:1<25::AID-PITS4>3.0.CO;2-C

Mynard, H., Joseph, S., & Alexandera, J. (2000). Peer-victimisation and posttraumatic stress in adolescents. *Personality and Individual Differences*, 29(5), 815–821. DOI: 10.1016/S0191-8869(99)00234-2

Myszograj, M. (2023). Representation of people with disabilities in children's media. Retrieved August 4, 2024, from https://www.researchgate.net/publication/371044792_Representation_of_people_with_disabilities_in_children's_media

Nabuzoka, D. (2003). Teacher ratings and peer nominations of bullying and other behavior of children with and without learning disabilities. *Educational Psychology*, 23(3), 307–321. DOI: 10.1080/0144341032000060147

Najdowski, A. C., Gharapetian, L., & Jewett, V. (2021). Toward the development of antiracist and multicultural graduate training programs in behavior analysis. *Behavior Analysis in Practice*, 14(2), 462–477. DOI: 10.1007/s40617-020-00504-0 PMID: 34150459

Nation, T. (2019, December 2). *Special Education Policy 2019*. The Nation; The Nation. Retrieved July 22, 2024, from https://www.nation.com.pk/03-Dec-2019/special-education-policy-2019

National Academies of Science, Engineering, and Medicine. (2016). *Preventing bullying through science, policy, and practice*. National Academies Press. Retrieved April 22, 2024 from, https://www.sciencedirect.com.proxy.library.nyu.edu/science/article/pii/S0273229717300138?via%3Dihub#b0440

National Autistic Society. (2017). Bullying: A guide for parents. Retrieved from http:// researchautism.net

National Center for Education Statistics. (2019, July). *Student reports of bullying results from the 2017 school crime supplement to the national crime victimization survey*. https://nces.ed.gov/pubs2019/2019054.pdf

National Center for Education Statistics. (2023). *Students with Disabilities*. Condition of Education. U.S. Department of Education, Institute of Education Sciences. https://nces.ed.gov/programs/coe/indicator/cgg

National Center for Educational Statistics [NCES] (2019). The Condition of Education 2019. NCES 2019-144. *National Center for Education Statistics*.

National Center for Injury Prevention and Control (U.S). (2014). *The relationship between bullying and suicide: What we know and what it means for schools*. Centers for Disease Control and Prevention. https://stacks.cdc.gov/view/cdc/34163

National Education Association. (2020). *How to identify bullying*. NEA. Retrieved April 22,2024 from https://www.nea.org/professional-excellence/student-engagement/tools-tips/how-identify-bullying

National Education Policy. (2017). Ministry of Federal Education and Professional Training Government of Pakistan. Available online: https://dgse.gov.pk/SiteImage/Downloads/National%20Policy%20for%20Persons%20with%20Disability.pdf (accessed on 5 February 2023)

Nations, U. (2015). Transforming our world: The 2030 agenda for sustainable development. New York: United Nations, Department of Economic and Social Affairs, 1, 41.

Nations, U. (2007). Convention on the Rights of Persons with Disabilities. *European Journal of Health Law*, 14(3), 281–298. PMID: 18348362

Naveed, S., Waqas, A., Shah, Z. A., Ahmad, W., Wasim, M., Rasheed, J., & Afzaal, T. (2020). Trends in bullying and emotional and behavioral difficulties among Pakistani schoolchildren: A cross-sectional survey of seven cities. *Frontiers in Psychiatry*, 10, 976. Advance online publication. DOI: 10.3389/fpsyt.2019.00976 PMID: 32009998

Ncontsa, V. N., & Shumba, A. (2013). The nature, causes and effects of school violence in South African high schools. *South African Journal of Education*, 33(3), 15. DOI: 10.15700/201503070802

Nelson, H. J., Burns, S. K., Kendall, G. E., & Schonert-Reichl, K. A. (2019). Preadolescent children's perception of power imbalance in bullying: A thematic analysis. *PLoS One*, 14(3), e0211124. Advance online publication. DOI: 10.1371/journal.pone.0211124 PMID: 30849078

Nelson, J. M., & Harwood, H. (2011). Learning disabilities and anxiety: A meta-analysis. *Journal of Learning Disabilities*, 44(1), 3–17. DOI: 10.1177/0022219409359939 PMID: 20375288

Neupane, T., Pandey, A. R., Bista, B., & Chalise, B. (2020). Correlates of bullying victimization among school adolescents in Nepal: Findings from 2015 global school-based student health survey Nepal. *PLoS ONE, 15*(8), 1-13. e0237406. DOI: 10.1371/journal.pone.0237406

Nickerson, A. B., Feeley, T. H., & Tsay-Vogel, M. (2016). Applying mass communication theory to bystander intervention in bullying. *Adolescent Research Review*, 2(1), 37–48. DOI: 10.1007/s40894-016-0030-3

Nickerson, A. B., Guttman, D., & Cook, E. (2017). Prevention and early intervention efforts for targets of bullying and youth who bully. In Bradshaw, C. P. (Ed.), *Handbook on bullying prevention: A life course perspective*. NASW Press.

Nickerson, A. B., Mele, D., & Princiotta, D. (2008). Attachment and empathy as predictors of roles as defenders or outsiders in bullying interactions. *Journal of School Psychology*, 46(6), 687–703. DOI: 10.1016/j.jsp.2008.06.002 PMID: 19083379

Nicolaides, S., Toda, Y., & Smith, P. K. (2002). Knowledge and attitudes about school bullying in trainee teachers. *The British Journal of Educational Psychology*, 72(1), 105–118. DOI: 10.1348/000709902158793 PMID: 11916467

Nikopoulous, C. K., & Keenan, M. (2004). Effects of video modeling on social initiations by children with autism. *Journal of Applied Behavior Analysis*, 37(1), 93–96. DOI: 10.1901/jaba.2004.37-93 PMID: 15154221

Nixon, C. L., Jairam, D., Davis, S., Linkie, C. A., Chatters, S., & Hodge, J. J. (2020). Effects of students' grade level, gender, and form of bullying victimization on coping strategy effectiveness. *International Journal of Bullying Prevention : an Official Publication of the International Bullying Prevention Association*, 2(3), 190–204. DOI: 10.1007/s42380-019-00027-5

Njelesani, J., Lai, J., Gigante, C. M., & Trelles, J. (2021). Will you protect me or make the situation worse?: Teachers' responses to school violence against students with disabilities. *Journal of Interpersonal Violence*, 37(23-24), NP21723–NP21748. DOI: 10.1177/08862605211062996 PMID: 34937449

Noor, W. (2022). Choose not to place 'Dis' in my ability. *Pakistan Journal of Rehabilitation*, 11(1), 5–7. DOI: 10.36283/pjr.zu.11.1/002

Norwich, B., & Kelly, N. (2004). Pupils' views on inclusion: Moderate learning difficulties and bullying in mainstream and special schools. *British Educational Research Journal*, 30(1), 43–65. DOI: 10.1080/01411920310001629965

Nwankwo, I. U., & Nnatu, S. O. (2018). Exploring inclusive education strategy for optimization of learning capacity and access to health information among children with disabilities (CWD) in Nigeria. *International Journal of Academic Research in Business & Social Sciences*, 8(9), 1147–1163. DOI: 10.6007/IJARBSS/v8-i9/4687

O'Connor, E. (2016). The use of 'Circle of Friends' strategy to improve social interactions and social acceptance: A case study of a child with Asperger's Syndrome and other associated needs. *Support for Learning*, 31(2), 138–147. DOI: 10.1111/1467-9604.12122

O'moore, M., & Kirkham, C. (2001). Self-esteem and its relationship to bullying behaviour. *Aggressive Behavior*, 27(4), 269–283. DOI: 10.1002/ab.1010

Ochi, M., Kawabe, K., Ochi, S., Miyama, T., Horiuchi, F., & Ueno, S. I. (2020). School refusal and bullying in children with autism spectrum disorder. *Child and Adolescent Psychiatry and Mental Health*, 14(1), 1–7. DOI: 10.1186/s13034-020-00325-7 PMID: 32419839

Odom, S. L., Zercher, C., Li, S., Marquart, J. M., Sandall, S., & Brown, W. H. (2006). Social acceptance and rejection of preschool children with disabilities: A mixed-method analysis. *Journal of Educational Psychology*, 98(4), 807–823. DOI: 10.1037/0022-0663.98.4.807

Office of Special Education and Rehabilitation Services [OSERS]. (2013). *OSERS August 20, 2013 dear colleague letter to educators*. United State Department of Education [USDOE]. Retrieved April 22, 2024 from, https://sites.ed.gov/idea/files/bullyingdcl-8-20-13.pdf

Olenik-Shemesh, D., & Heiman, T. (2014). Exploring cyberbullying among primary children in relation to social support, loneliness, self-efficacy, and well-being. *Child Welfare*, 93(5), 27–46.

Olweus, D. (2023). *Olweus bullying prevention program*. Olweus bullying prevention program, Clemson University. Retrieved April 22, 2024 from, https://olweus.sites.clemson.edu/olweusinfo.php

Olweus, D. (1978). *Aggression in the schools: Bullies and whipping boys*. Hemisphere.

Olweus, D. (1991). Chapter 3 victimization among school children. *Advances in Psychology*, 76, 45–102. DOI: 10.1016/S0166-4115(08)61056-0

Olweus, D. (1993). *Bullying at school: What we know and what we can do*. Blackwell Publishing.

Olweus, D. (1994). Bullying at school. *Promotion &amp. Education*, 1(4), 27–31. DOI: 10.1177/102538239400100414 PMID: 7820380

Olweus, D. (1994). Bullying at school: Long-term outcomes for the victims and an effective school-based intervention program. In *Aggressive behavior: Current perspectives* (pp. 97–130). Springer US. DOI: 10.1007/978-1-4757-9116-7_5

Olweus, D. (1995). Peer abuse or bullying at school: Basic facts and a school-based intervention programme. *Current Directions in Psychological Science*, 4(6), 196–200. DOI: 10.1111/1467-8721.ep10772640

Olweus, D. (2005). A useful evaluation design, and effects of the Olweus Bullying Prevention Program. *Psychology, Crime & Law*, 11(4), 389–402. DOI: 10.1080/10683160500255471

Olweus, D. (2011). Bullying at school and later criminality: Findings from three Swedish community samples of males. *Criminal Behaviour and Mental Health*, 21(2), 151–156. DOI: 10.1002/cbm.806 PMID: 21370301

Olweus, D. (2013). School bullying: Development and some important challenges. *Annual Review of Clinical Psychology*, 9(1), 751–780. DOI: 10.1146/annurev-clinpsy-050212-185516 PMID: 23297789

Olweus, D. (2014). Victimization by peers: Antecedents and long-term outcomes. In *Social withdrawal, inhibition, and shyness in childhood* (pp. 315–341). Psychology Press.

Olweus, D., & Limber, S. P. (2010). Bullying in school: Evaluation and dissemination of the Olweus Bullying Prevention Program. *The American Journal of Orthopsychiatry*, 80(1), 124–134. DOI: 10.1111/j.1939-0025.2010.01015.x PMID: 20397997

Ordonez, M. A. (2006). *Prevalence of bullying among elementary school children as a function of the comprehensiveness of anti-bullying policies and programs in the school* [Doctoral dissertation, Ball State University].

Organisation for Economic Cooperation and Development (OECD). (2008). 21st century learning: Research, innovation and policy directions from recent OECD analyses. Retrieved on the 19th of January 2015, from www.oecd.org/dataoecd/39/8/40554299.pdf

Orpinas, P., Horne, A. M., & Staniszewski, D. (2003). School bullying: Changing the problem by changing the school. *School Psychology Review*, 32(3), 431–444. DOI: 10.1080/02796015.2003.12086210

Ouzzani, M., Hammady, H., Fedorowicz, Z., & Elmagarmid, A. (2016). Rayyan-a web and mobile app for systematic reviews. *Systematic Reviews*, 5(1), 210. DOI: 10.1186/s13643-016-0384-4 PMID: 27919275

Owens, M., Stevenson, J., Hadwin, J. A., & Norgate, R. (2012). Anxiety and depression in academic performance: An exploration of the mediating factors of worry and working memory. *School Psychology International*, 33(4), 433–449. DOI: 10.1177/0143034311427433

Özdemir, Ş. A. (2020) *A Comparative Investigation of Exposure to Peer Bullying of Mentally Handicapped Students Educated with the Inclusion Model and Students with Normal Development*, (Unpublished Master's Thesis, Necmettin Erbakan University), Konya.

PACER National Bullying Prevention Center. (2024). *What is bullying?* PACER. Retrieved April 22, 2024 from, https://www.pacerkidsagainstbullying.org/what-is-bullying/

PACER's National Bullying Prevention Center. (2019). *Working with the school-What parents should know about bullying*. https://www.pacer.org/bullying/parents/working-with-school.asp

Pakistan. (1982). *The Constitution of Islamic Republic of Pakistan, with the Provisional Constitution Order, 1981: As amended up-to-date.* Lahore: All Pakistan Legal Decision.

Pan, B., Zhang, L., Ji, L., Garandeau, C. F., Salmivalli, C., & Zhang, W. (2020). Classroom status hierarchy moderates the association between social dominance goals and bullying behavior in middle childhood and early adolescence. *Journal of Youth and Adolescence*, 49(11), 2285–2297. DOI: 10.1007/s10964-020-01285-z PMID: 32661845

Pan-Hellenic School Network. (n.d.). Retrieved from https://www.sch.gr/

Parada, R. H. (2022). Bullying prevention and prosocial skill development in school settings. In *School-Wide Positive Behaviour Support* (pp. 170–188). Routledge. DOI: 10.4324/9781003186236-9

Paranti, S. M., & Hudiyana, J. (2022). Current Social Domination Theory: Is it still relevant. *Psikostudia: Jurnal Psikologi Psychostudia. The Journal of Psychology*, 11(2), 324–340.

Park, I., Gong, J., Lyons, G. L., Hirota, T., Takahashi, M., Kim, B., Lee, S. Y., Kim, Y. S., Lee, J., & Leventhal, B. L. (2020). Prevalence of and factors associated with school bullying in students with Autism Spectrum Disorder: A cross-cultural meta-analysis. *Yonsei Medical Journal*, 61(11), 909–922. DOI: 10.3349/ymj.2020.61.11.909 PMID: 33107234

Parks, M. R. (2007). *LEA's series on personal relationships: Personal relationships and personal networks*. Lawrence Erlbaum Associates.

Pasta, T., Mendola, M., Longobardi, C., Prino, L. E., & Gastaldi, F. G. (2017). Attributional style of children with and without specific learning disability. *Electronic Journal of Research in Educational Psychology*, 11(31), 649–664. DOI: 10.14204/ejrep.31.13064

Patton, M. Q. (1999). Enhancing the quality and credibility of qualitative analysis. *Health Services Research*, 34(5), 1189–1208. PMID: 10591279

Pearce, N., Monks, H., Alderman, N., Hearn, L., Burns, S., Runions, K., Francis, J., & Cross, D. (2024). 'It's all about context': Building school capacity to implement a whole-school approach to bullying. *International Journal of Bullying Prevention : an Official Publication of the International Bullying Prevention Association*, 6(1), 53–68. DOI: 10.1007/s42380-022-00138-6

Peeters, M., Cillessen, A. H., & Scholte, R. H. (2009). Clueless or powerful? identifying subtypes of bullies in adolescence. *Journal of Youth and Adolescence*, 39(9), 1041–1052. DOI: 10.1007/s10964-009-9478-9 PMID: 20625880

Peguero, A. A., & Hong, J. S. (2020). Bullying and Youth with Disabilities and Special Health Needs: Victimizing Students with Physical, Emotional/Behavioral, and Learning Disorders. In *School Bullying. Springer Series on Child and Family Studies* (pp. 85–98). Springer., DOI: 10.1007/978-3-030-64367-6_7

Perales-Hidalgo, P., Voltas, N., & Canals, J. (2024). Self-perceived bullying victimization in pre-adolescents on the autism spectrum: EPINED study. *Autism*, 28(11), 2848–2857. Advance online publication. DOI: 10.1177/13623613241244875 PMID: 38623050

Peskin, M. F., Tortolero, S. R., & Markham, C. M. (2006). Bullying and victimization among Black and Hispanic adolescents. *Adolescence*, 41(163), 467–484. PMID: 17225662

Peterson, A. M. (2020). *Teaching young adults with intellectual and developmental disabilities how to recognize and respond to coworker victimization scenarios.* [Master's Thesis, Michigan State University].

Piek, J. P., Barrett, N. C., Allen, L. S., Jones, A., & Louise, M. (2005). The relationship between bullying and self-worth in children with movement coordination problems. *The British Journal of Educational Psychology*, 75(3), 453–463. DOI: 10.1348/000709904X24573 PMID: 16238876

Pimm, C. (2012). The perspectives of parents, carers. and families. In C., McLaughlin, Colleen., R. Byers, & C. Oliver (Ed.), *Perspectives on bullying and difference supporting young people with special educational needs and/or disabilities in school* (1st ed., pp. 54-65). National Children's Bureau.

Pinquart, M. (2018). Parenting stress in caregivers of children with chronic physical condition—A meta-analysis. *Stress and Health*, 34(2), 197–207. DOI: 10.1002/smi.2780 PMID: 28834111

Pinto, C., Baines, E., & Bakopoulou, I. (2018). The peer relations of pupils with special educational needs in mainstream primary schools: The importance of meaningful contact and interaction with peers. *The British Journal of Educational Psychology*, 89(4), 818–837. DOI: 10.1111/bjep.12262 PMID: 30580444

Plant, K. M., & Sanders, M. R. (2007). Predictors of care-giver stress in families of preschool-aged children with developmental disabilities. *Journal of Intellectual Disability Research*, 51(2), 109–124. DOI: 10.1111/j.1365-2788.2006.00829.x PMID: 17217475

Policy, N. (2010). *National Education Policy*. Ministry of Education.

Pollock, D., Peters, M. D. J., Khalil, H., McInerney, P., Alexander, L., Tricco, A. C., Evans, C., de Moraes, É. B., Godfrey, C. M., Pieper, D., Saran, A., Stern, C., & Munn, Z. (2023). Recommendations for the extraction, analysis, and presentation of results in scoping reviews. *JBI Evidence Synthesis*, 21(3), 520–532. DOI: 10.11124/JBIES-22-00123 PMID: 36081365

Pongparadorn, W., Pityaratstian, N., Buathong, N., & Prasartpornsirichoke, J. (2021). School bullying behavior in attention-deficit hyperactivity disorder patients with and without comorbid autism spectrum disorder at King Chulalongkorn Memorial Hospital. *Chulalongkorn Medical Journal*, 65(4), 459–465. DOI: 10.58837/CHULA.CMJ.65.4.13

Potard, C., Kubiszewski, V., Combes, C., Henry, A., Pochon, R., & Roy, A. (2022). How adolescents cope with bullying at school: Exploring differences between pure victim and bully-victim roles. *International Journal of Bullying Prevention : an Official Publication of the International Bullying Prevention Association*, 4(2), 144–159. DOI: 10.1007/s42380-021-00095-6

Power-Elliott, M., & Harris, G. E. (2012). Guidance counsellor strategies for handling bullying. British Journal of Guidance &amp. *British Journal of Guidance & Counselling*, 40(1), 83–98. DOI: 10.1080/03069885.2011.646947

Prasartpornsirichoke, J., Pityaratstian, N., & Pongparadorn, W. (2022). School bullying behaviors and victimization in Thai children and adolescents with comorbid attention deficit hyperactivity disorder, anxiety disorders, and oppositional defiant disorder. *Chulalongkorn Medical Journal*, 66(3), 293–300. DOI: 10.58837/CHULA.CMJ.66.3.6

Prevnet. (2024). *Types of Bullying | PREVNet*. Prevnet.ca. Retrieved August 15, 2024, from https://www.prevnet.ca/bullying/types

Prinstein, M. J., Boergers, J., & Vernberg, E. M. (2001). Overt and relational aggression in adolescents: Social-psychological adjustment of aggressors and victims. *Journal of Clinical Child Psychology*, 30(4), 479–491. DOI: 10.1207/S15374424JCCP3004_05 PMID: 11708236

Przybylski, A. K., Murayama, K., DeHaan, C. R., & Gladwell, V. (2013). Motivational, emotional, and behavioral correlates of fear of missing out. *Computers in Human Behavior*, 29(4), 1841–1848. DOI: 10.1016/j.chb.2013.02.014

Qayyum, A., Lasi, S., & Rafique, G. (2013). Perceptions of primary caregivers of children with disabilities in two communities from Sindh and Balochistan, Pakistan. *Disability, CBR and Inclusive Development*, 24(1), 130–142. DOI: 10.5463/dcid.v24i1.193

Quintana-Orts, C., Mc Guckin, C., Del Rey, R., & Mora-Merchán, J. A. (2022). Overcoming bullying in education. *Overcoming Adversity in Education*, 1, 102–113. DOI: 10.4324/9781003180029-10

Qureshi, R., & Razzaq, F. (2019). I am not against Inclusive education but': Teachers' Voices from Pakistan. *Journal of Inclusive Education*, 3(1).

Ragusa, A., Caggiano, V., Obregón-Cuesta, A. I., González-Bernal, J. J., Fernández-Solana, J., Mínguez-Mínguez, L. A., León-del-Barco, B., Mendo-Lázaro, S., Di Petrillo, E., & González-Santos, J. (2023). The influence of bullying on positive emotions and their effect as mediators between controllable attributions of success and academic performance. *Children (Basel, Switzerland)*, 10(6), 929. DOI: 10.3390/children10060929 PMID: 37371161

Rahill, S. A., & Teglasi, H. (2003). Processes and outcomes of story-based and skill-based social competency programs for children with emotional disabilities. *Journal of School Psychology*, 41(6), 413–429. DOI: 10.1016/j.jsp.2003.08.001

Rahma, A., Istima, F., Addinullah, M. A., & Nihayah, U. (2022). Konseling interpersonal dalam menumbuhkan kesehatan mental korban bullying/ Interpersonal counseling in promoting the mental health of bullying victims. *Nosipakabelo: Jurnal Bimbingan Dan Konseling Islam/ Journal of Islamic Guidance and Counseling*, 3(2), 68-84.

Ralph, N. (2018). *Risk and Protective Factors for Bullying and Peer Victimisation of Children with and Without Special Educational Needs and Disability (SEND)* (Doctoral dissertation, Keele University). https://keele-repository.worktribe.com/OutputFile/463478

Ramirez, I. (2017). The Effects of Bullying Among Adolescents with Special Needs, İnformation Age Publishing, p:167-194. United States Of America.

Rapp, H. (2023). *An Exploratory Mixed Methods Study Considering Parents of Adolescents with Developmental Disabilities as Secondary Victims of Bullying Abuse*. [Doctoral Dissertation, The University of Wisconsin-Madison].

Raskauskas, J., & Modell, S. (2011). Modifying anti-bullying programs to include students with disabilities. *Teaching Exceptional Children*, 44(1), 60–67. DOI: 10.1177/004005991104400107

Reed, K. P., Nugent, W. R., & Cooper, R. L. (2015). The relationship between bullying and suicide: What we know and what it means for schools. *Adolescent Research Review*, 1(2), 133–146. DOI: 10.1007/s40894-015-0012-8

Rehman, A., Jingdong, L., & Hussain, I. (2015). The province-wise literacy rate in Pakistan and its impact on the economy. *Pacific Science Review B. Humanities and Social Sciences*, 1(3), 140–144.

Reicher, H. (2010). Building inclusive education on social and emotional learning: Challenges and perspectives–A review. *International Journal of Inclusive Education*, 14(3), 213–246. DOI: 10.1080/13603110802504218

Rex, C. (2014). An Anti-Bullying Intervention for Children with Autism Spectrum Disorder. https://scholarship.claremont.edu/cmc_theses/803

Rex, C., Charlop, M. H., & Spector, V. (2018). Using video modeling as an anti-bullying intervention for children with Autism Spectrum Disorder. *Journal of Autism and Developmental Disorders*, 48(8), 2701–2713. DOI: 10.1007/s10803-018-3527-8 PMID: 29516338

Reyes-Rodríguez, A. C., Valdés-Cuervo, A. A., Vera-Noriega, J. A., & Parra-Pérez, L. G. (2021). Principal's practices and school's collective efficacy to preventing bullying: The mediating role of school climate. *SAGE Open*, 11(4), 215824402110525. DOI: 10.1177/21582440211052551

Richards, K. A. R., Eberline, A. D., Padaruth, S., & Templin, T. J. (2015). Experiential learning through a physical activity program for children with disabilities. *Journal of Teaching in Physical Education*, 34(2), 165–188. DOI: 10.1123/jtpe.2014-0015

Rigby, K. (1997). Attitudes and beliefs about bullying among Australian school children. *The Irish Journal of Psychology*, 18(2), 202–220. DOI: 10.1080/03033910.1997.10558140

Rigby, K. (2002). *New Perspectives on Bullying*. Jessica Kingsley Publishers.

Rigby, K. (2014). How teachers address cases of bullying in schools: A comparison of five reactive approaches. *Educational Psychology in Practice*, 30(4), 409–419. DOI: 10.1080/02667363.2014.949629

Rigby, K. (2020). How teachers deal with cases of bullying at school: What victims say. *International Journal of Environmental Research and Public Health*, 17(7), 1–11. DOI: 10.3390/ijerph17072338 PMID: 32235651

Rigby, K. (2024). Theoretical perspectives and two explanatory models of school bullying. *International Journal of Bullying Prevention : an Official Publication of the International Bullying Prevention Association*, 6(2), 101–109. DOI: 10.1007/s42380-022-00141-x

Rillotta, F., & Nettlebeck, T. (2007). Effects of an awareness program on attitudes of students without an intellectual disability towards persons with an intellectual disability. *Journal of Intellectual & Developmental Disability*, 32(1), 19–27. DOI: 10.1080/13668250701194042 PMID: 17365364

Robertson, K., Chamberlain, B., & Kasari, C. (2003). General education teachers' relationships with included students with special educational autism. *Journal of Autism and Developmental Disorders*, 33(2), 123–130. DOI: 10.1023/A:1022979108096 PMID: 12757351

Robinson, L. E., Clements, G., Drescher, A., El Sheikh, A., Milarsky, T. K., Hanebutt, R., Graves, K., Delgado, A. V., Espelage, D. L., & Rose, C. A. (2023). Developing a multi-tiered system of support-based plan for bullying prevention among students with disabilities: Perspectives from general and special education teachers during professional development. *School Mental Health*, 15(3), 826–838. DOI: 10.1007/s12310-023-09589-8 PMID: 37359153

Rodríguez-Álvarez, J. M., Yubero, S., Navarro, R., & Larrañaga, E. (2021). Relationship between socio-emotional competencies and the overlap of bullying and cyberbullying behaviors in primary school students. *European Journal of Investigation in Health, Psychology and Education*, 11(3), 686–696. DOI: 10.3390/ejihpe11030049 PMID: 34563062

Rodríguez-Hidalgo, A. J., Alcívar, A., & Herrera-López, M. (2019). Traditional bullying and discriminatory bullying around special educational needs: Psychometric properties of two instruments to measure it. *International Journal of Environmental Research and Public Health*, 16(1), 142–150. DOI: 10.3390/ijerph16010142 PMID: 30621091

Roekel, E., Scholte, R. H., & Didden, R. (2010). Bullying among adolescents with autism spectrum disorders: Prevalence and perception. *Journal of Autism and Developmental Disorders*, 40(1), 63–73. DOI: 10.1007/s10803-009-0832-2 PMID: 19669402

Rogojan, L., & Turda, E. (2023). Educational Intervention Program for the Prevention of Bullying Behaviour in Primary School. In I. Albulescu, & C. Stan (Eds.), Education, Reflection, Development - ERD 2022, vol 6. European Proceedings of Educational Sciences (pp. 464-475). European Publisher. https://doi.org/DOI: 10.15405/epes.23056.42

Rose, C. A., Allison, S., & Simpson, C. G. (2012). Addressing bullying among students with disabilities within a multi-tier educational environment. In D. Hollar (Ed.), *Handbook of children with special health care needs* (pp. 383–397). Springer Science + Business Media. https://doi.org/DOI: 10.1007/978-1-4614-2335-5_20

Rose, C. A. (2010). Bullying among students with disabilities: Impact and implications. In *Bullying in North American schools* (pp. 54–64). Routledge.

Rose, C. A., & Espelage, D. L. (2012). Risk and protective factors associated with the bullying involvement of students with emotional and behavioral disorders. *Behavioral Disorders*, 37(3), 133–148. DOI: 10.1177/019874291203700302

Rose, C. A., Espelage, D. L., Aragon, S. R., & Elliot, J. (2011). Bullying and victimization among students and special education in general education curriculum. *Exceptionality Education International*, 21(3), 2–14. DOI: 10.5206/eei.v21i3.7679

Rose, C. A., Espelage, D. L., & Monda-Amaya, L. E. (2009). Bullying and victimization rates among students in general and special education: A comparative analysis. *Educational Psychology*, 29(7), 761–776. DOI: 10.1080/01443410903254864

Rose, C. A., & Gage, N. A. (2017). Exploring the involvement of bullying among students with disabilities over time. *Exceptional Children*, 83(3), 298–314. DOI: 10.1177/0014402916667587

Rose, C. A., & Monda-Amaya, L. E. (2012). Bullying and victimization among students with disabilities: Effective strategies for classroom teachers. *Intervention in School and Clinic*, 48(2), 99–107. DOI: 10.1177/1053451211430119

Rose, C. A., Monda-Amaya, L. E., & Espelage, D. L. (2011). Bullying perpetration and victimization in special education: A review of the literature. *Remedial and Special Education*, 32(2), 114–130. DOI: 10.1177/0741932510361247

Rose, C. A., Simpson, C. G., & Ellis, S. K. (2015). The relationship between school belonging, sibling aggression and bullying involvement: Implications for students with and without disabilities. *Educational Psychology*, 36(8), 1462–1486. DOI: 10.1080/01443410.2015.1066757

Rose, C. A., Simpson, C. G., & Moss, A. (2015). The bullying dynamic: Prevalence of involvement among a large-scale sample of middle and high school youth with and without disabilities. *Psychology in the Schools*, 52(5), 515–531. DOI: 10.1002/pits.21840

Rose, C. A., Stormont, M. A., Wang, Z., Simpson, C. G., Preast, J. L., & Green, A. L. (2015). Bullying and students with disabilities: Examination of disability status and educational placement. *School Psychology Review*, 44(4), 425–444. DOI: 10.17105/spr-15-0080.1

Rose, C. A., Swearer, S. M., & Espelage, D. L. (2012). Bullying and students with disabilities: The untold narrative. *Focus on Exceptional Children*, 45(2), 1–10. DOI: 10.17161/foec.v45i2.6682

Ross, S. W., & Horner, R. H. (2014). Bully prevention in positive behavior support: Preliminary evaluation of third-fourth-, and fifth-grade attitudes toward bullying. *Journal of Emotional and Behavioral Disorders*, 22(4), 225–236. DOI: 10.1177/1063426613491429

Rowbotham, M., Carroll, A., & Cuskelly, M. (2011). Mothers' and fathers' roles in caring for an adult child with an intellectual disability. *International Journal of Disability Development and Education*, 58(3), 223–240. DOI: 10.1080/1034912X.2011.598396

Rowley, E., Chandler, S., Baird, G., Simonoff, E., Pickles, A., Loucas, T., & Charman, T. (2012). The experience of friendship, victimization and bullying in children with an autism spectrum disorder: Associations with child characteristics and school placement. *Research in Autism Spectrum Disorders*, 6(3), 1126–1134. DOI: 10.1016/j.rasd.2012.03.004

Sabramani, V., Idris, I. B., Ismail, H., Nadarajaw, T., Zakaria, E., & Kamaluddin, M. R. (2021). Bullying and its associated individual, peer, family and school factors: Evidence from Malaysian national secondary school students. *International Journal of Environmental Research and Public Health*, 18(13), 2–28. DOI: 10.3390/ijerph18137208 PMID: 34281145

Sabuncuoğlu, O., Ekinci, Ö., Bahadır, T., Akyuva, Y., Altınöz, E., & Berkem, M. (2006). Peer abuse among adolescent students and its relationship with depression symptoms. *Annals of Clinical Psychiatry*, 9, 27–35.

Sacks, S. Z., & Wolffe, K. E. (2006). *Teaching Social Skills to Students with Visual Impairments*. From Theory to Practice.

Saeed Ali, T., Karmaliani, R., Mcfarlane, J., Khuwaja, H. M. A., Somani, Y., Chirwa, E. D., & Jewkes, R. (2017). Attitude towards gender roles and violence against women and girls (VAWG): Baseline findings from an RCT of 1752 youths in Pakistan. *Global Health Action*, 10(1), 1342454. DOI: 10.1080/16549716.2017.1342454 PMID: 28758882

Saeed, M., Rizvi, M., Saleem, S., & Li, C. (2019). Disasters of cyber world - A question on mental health. *Clinical Research in Psychology*, 2(1), 1–6. DOI: 10.33309/2639-9113.020102

Saleem, S., Khan, N. F., & Zafar, S. (2021). Prevalence of cyberbullying victimization among Pakistani youth. *Technology in Society*, 65, 101577. DOI: 10.1016/j.techsoc.2021.101577

Salmivalli, C., Lagerspetz, K., Björkqvist, K., Österman, K., & Kaukiainen, A. (2017). Bullying as a group process: Participant roles and their relations to social status within the group. *Interpersonal Development*, 233–247. DOI: 10.4324/9781351153683-13

Salmivalli, C. (2010). Bullying and the Peer Group: A Review. *Aggression and Violent Behavior*, 15(2), 112–120. DOI: 10.1016/j.avb.2009.08.007

Salmivalli, C., Karna, A., & Poskiparta, E. (2011). Counteracting bullying in Finland: The KiVa program and its effects on different forms of being bullied. *International Journal of Behavioral Development*, 35(5), 405–411. DOI: 10.1177/0165025411407457

Salmivalli, C., Kärnä, A., & Poskiparta, E. (2012). Development, evaluation, and diffusion of a national anti-bullying program, KiVa. In *Handbook of youth prevention science* (pp. 238–252). Routledge.

Sanchez, J. (2008). 2007-2008 Survey of Florida Public Employment Law. *Nova Law Review*, 33, 169.

Sancho, K., Sidener, T. M., Reeve, S. A., & Sidener, D. W. (2010). Two variations of video modeling interventions for teaching play skills to children with autism. *Education & Treatment of Children*, 33(3), 421–442. DOI: 10.1353/etc.0.0097

Sapouna, M., & Wolke, D. (2013). Resilience to bullying victimization: The role of individual, family, and peer characteristics. *Child Abuse & Neglect*, 37(11), 997–1006. DOI: 10.1016/j.chiabu.2013.05.009 PMID: 23809169

Saracho, O., & Spodek, B. (Eds.). (2007). *Contemporary perspectives on socialization and social development in early childhood education*. IAP.

Savage, R. (2005). Friendship bullying patterns in children attending in language base in mainstream school. *Educational Psychology in Practice*, 21(1), 23–36. DOI: 10.1080/02667360500035140

Saylor, C. F., & Leach, J. B. (2009). Perceived bullying and social support in students accessing special inclusion programming. *Journal of Developmental and Physical Disabilities*, 21(1), 69–80. DOI: 10.1007/s10882-008-9126-4

Schroeder, J. H., Cappadocia, M. C., Bebko, J. M., Pepler, D. J., & Weiss, J. A. (2014). Shedding light on a pervasive problem: A review of research on bullying experiences among children with Autism Spectrum Disorders. *Journal of Autism and Developmental Disorders*, 44(7), 1520–1534. DOI: 10.1007/s10803-013-2011-8 PMID: 24464616

Schuelka, M. J., Johnstone, C. J., Thomas, G., & Artiles, A. J. (2019). *The sage handbook of inclusion and diversity in education*. Sage Publications. DOI: 10.4135/9781526470430

Section 504 of the Rehabilitation Act of 1973, 29 U.S.C § 794 et seq. (1973).

Segura, B. P. (2012). *The superheroes social skills program: a study examining an evidence-based program for elementary-aged students with autism spectrum disorders who are frequently bullied*. [Doctoral dissertation. University of Utah].

Sentenac, M., Gavin, A., Arnaud, C., Molcho, M., Godeau, E., & Gabhainn, S. N. (2011). Victims of bullying among students with a disability or chronic illness and their peers: A cross-national study between Ireland and France. *The Journal of Adolescent Health*, 48(5), 461–466. DOI: 10.1016/j.jadohealth.2010.07.031 PMID: 21501804

Sentenac, M., Gavin, A., Gabhainn, S. N., Molcho, M., Due, P., Ravens-Sieberer, U., Gaspar de Matos, M., Malkowska-Szkutnik, A., Gobina, I., Vollebergh, W., Arnaud, C., Emmanuelle, G., & Godeau, E. (2013). Peer victimization and subjective health among students reporting disability or chronic illness in 11 Western countries. *European Journal of Public Health*, 23(3), 421–426. DOI: 10.1093/eurpub/cks073 PMID: 22930742

Sezer, M., Sahin, I., & Akturk, A. O. (2013). Cyber Bullying Victimization of Elementary School Students and Their Reflections on the Victimization. *Online Submission*, 7(12), 1942–1945.

Shaheen, A. M., Hamdan, K. M., Albqoor, M., Othman, A. K., Amre, H. M., & Hazeem, M. N. A. (2019). Perceived social support from family and friends and bullying victimization among adolescents. *Children and Youth Services Review*, 107, 1–38. DOI: 10.1016/j.childyouth.2019.104503

Shahid, M., Rauf, U., Sarwar, U., & Asif, S. (2022). Impact of bullying behavior on mental health and quality of life among pre-adolescents and adolescents in Sialkot-Pakistan. Pakistan. *Journal of the Humanities and Social Sciences*, 10(1), 324–331. DOI: 10.52131/pjhss.2022.1001.0200

Shah, S. S., Ali, N., Anwer, M., & Jaffar, A. (2015). Nurturing sustainable teachers' leadership culture: Possibilities, challenges, stakeholders' behavior analysis in the context of Pakistan. [IJR]. *International Journal of Research*, 2(3), 593–600.

Shaikh, M. A., Abio, A., Celedonia, K. L., & Lowery Wilson, M. (2019). Physical fighting among school-attending adolescents in Pakistan: Associated factors and contextual influences. *International Journal of Environmental Research and Public Health*, 16(24), 5039. DOI: 10.3390/ijerph16245039 PMID: 31835671

Sharma, U., Simi, J., & Forlin, C. (2015). Preparedness of pre service teachers for inclusive education in the Solomon Islands. *The Australian Journal of Teacher Education*, 40(5). Advance online publication. https://ro.ecu.edu.au/ajte/vol40/iss5/6. DOI: 10.14221/ajte.2015v40n5.6

Shaukat, S. (2023). Challenges for education of children with disabilities in Pakistan. *Intervention in School and Clinic*, 59(1), 75–80. DOI: 10.1177/10534512221130082

Sheehy, K. (Ed.). (2005). *Ethics and research in inclusive education: Values into practice*. Psychology Press.

Shigri, N. (2018). *The importance of disability awareness: Home and school*. Medium. Retrieved April 22, 2024 from, https://medium.com/arise-impact/the-importance-of-disability-awareness-home-and-school-eead2276f349

Shinde, S., Weiss, H. A., Varghese, B., Khandeparkar, P., Pereira, B., Sharma, A., Gupta, R., Ross, D. A., Patton, G., & Patel, V. (2018). Promoting school climate and health outcomes with the SEHER multi-component secondary school intervention in Bihar, India: A cluster-randomised controlled trial. *Lancet*, 392(10163), 2465–2477. DOI: 10.1016/S0140-6736(18)31615-5 PMID: 30473365

Shochet, I. M., Dadds, M. R., Ham, D., & Montague, R. (2006). School connectedness is an underemphasized parameter in adolescent mental health: Results of a community prediction study. *Journal of Clinical Child and Adolescent Psychology*, 35(2), 170–179. DOI: 10.1207/s15374424jccp3502_1 PMID: 16597213

Shujja, S., Atta, M., & Shujjat, J. M. (2014). Prevalence of bullying and victimization among sixth graders with reference to gender, socio-economic status and type of schools. *Journal of Social Sciences*, 38(2), 159–165. DOI: 10.1080/09718923.2014.11893246

Siddiqui, S., & Schultze-Krumbholz, A. (2023). Bullying prevalence in Pakistan's educational institutes: Preclusion to the framework for a teacher-led antibullying intervention. *PLoS One*, 18(4), e0284864. Advance online publication. DOI: 10.1371/journal.pone.0284864 PMID: 37104391

Siddiqui, S., & Schultze-Krumbholz, A. (2023). The Sohanjana Antibullying Intervention: Pilot results of a peer-training module in Pakistan. *Social Sciences (Basel, Switzerland)*, 12(7), 409. DOI: 10.3390/socsci12070409

Siddiqui, S., Schultze-Krumbholz, A., & Hinduja, P. (2023a). Practices for dealing with bullying by educators in Pakistan: Results from a study using the handling bullying questionnaire. *Cogent Education*, 10(2), 2236442. Advance online publication. DOI: 10.1080/2331186X.2023.2236442

Siddiqui, S., Schultze-Krumbholz, A., & Kamran, M. (2023b). Sohanjana antibullying intervention: Culturally and socially targeted intervention for teachers in Pakistan to take actions against bullying. *European Journal of Educational Research*, 12(3), 1523–1538. DOI: 10.12973/eu-jer.12.3.1523

Sigurdson, J. F., Undheim, A. M., Wallander, J. L., Lydersen, S., & Sund, A. M. (2015). The long-term effects of being bullied or a bully in adolescence on externalizing and internalizing mental health problems in adulthood. *Child and Adolescent Psychiatry and Mental Health*, 9(1), 1–13. DOI: 10.1186/s13034-015-0075-2 PMID: 26300969

Singal, N. (2019). Challenges and opportunities in efforts towards inclusive education: Reflections from India. *International Journal of Inclusive Education*, 23(7-8), 827–840. DOI: 10.1080/13603116.2019.1624845

Singal, N., Sabates, R., Aslam, M., & Saeed, S. (2018). School enrolment and learning outcomes for children with disabilities: Findings from a household survey in Pakistan. *International Journal of Inclusive Education*, 24(13), 1410–1430. DOI: 10.1080/13603116.2018.1531944

Singh, A., Mattoo, S. K., & Grover, S. (2016). Stigma associated with mental illness: Conceptual issues and focus on stigma perceived by the patients with schizophrenia and their caregivers. *Indian Journal of Social Psychiatry*, 32(2), 134–142. DOI: 10.4103/0971-9962.181095

Skinner, E. A., & Zimmer-Gembeck, M. J. (2007). The development of coping. *Annual Review of Psychology*, 58(1), 119–144. DOI: 10.1146/annurev.psych.58.110405.085705 PMID: 16903804

Smith, P. K., Thompson, F., Craig, W., Hong, I., Slee, P., Sullivan, K., & Green, V. A. (2016). Actions to prevent bullying in western countries. In P. K. Smith, K. Kwak, & Y. Toda (Eds.), *School Bullying in Different Cultures: Eastern and Western Perspectives* (pp. 301–333). chapter, Cambridge: Cambridge University Press. DOI: 10.1017/CBO9781139410878.018

Smith, B. H., & Low, S. (2013). The role of social-emotional learning in bullying prevention efforts. *Theory into Practice*, 52(4), 280–287. DOI: 10.1080/00405841.2013.829731

Smith, J. (2018). Organizational Cultural Theory and bullying behavior: Implications for educational institutions. *Journal of School Psychology*, 40(3), 211–225.

Smith, P. K. (2016). Bullying: Definition, types, causes, consequences and intervention. *Social and Personality Psychology Compass*, 10(9), 519–532. DOI: 10.1111/spc3.12266

Smith, P. K. (Ed.). (1999). *The nature of school bullying: A cross-national perspective*. Psychology Press.

Smith, P. K., Mahdavi, J., Carvalho, M., Fisher, S., Russell, S., & Tippett, N. (2008). Cyberbullying: Its nature and impact in secondary school pupils. *Journal of Child Psychology and Psychiatry, and Allied Disciplines*, 49(4), 376–385. DOI: 10.1111/j.1469-7610.2007.01846.x PMID: 18363945

Smith, P. K., Talamelli, L., Cowie, H., Naylor, P., & Chauhan, P. (2004). Profiles of non-victims, escaped victims, continuing victims and new victims of school bullying. *The British Journal of Educational Psychology*, 74(4), 565–581. DOI: 10.1348/0007099042376427 PMID: 15530202

Smith, P. K., Thompson, F., Craig, W., Hong, I., Slee, P., Sullivan, K., & Green, V. A. (2016). *15 Actions to prevent bullying in western countries. School Bullying in Different Cultures: Eastern and Western Perspectives*. Cambridge University Press. DOI: 10.1017/CBO9781139410878

Smith, T. B., Oliver, M. N., & Innocenti, M. S. (2001). Parenting stress in families of children with disabilities. *The American Journal of Orthopsychiatry*, 71(2), 257–261. DOI: 10.1037/0002-9432.71.2.257 PMID: 11347367

Sointu, E. T., Savolainen, H., Lappalainen, K., & Lambert, M. C. (2016). Longitudinal associations of student–teacher relationships and behavioural and emotional strengths on academic achievement. *Educational Psychology*, 37(4), 457–467. DOI: 10.1080/01443410.2016.1165796

Somani, R., Corboz, J., Karmaliani, R., Chirwa, E. D., Mcfarlane, J., Khuwaja, H. M., Asad, N., Somani, Y., van der Heijden, I., & Jewkes, R. (2020). Peer victimization and experiences of violence at school and at home among school age children with disabilities in Pakistan and Afghanistan. *Global Health Action*, 14(1), 1857084. DOI: 10.1080/16549716.2020.1857084 PMID: 33357165

Søndergaard, D. M. (2014). Social exclusion anxiety: Bullying and the forces that contribute to bullying amongst children at school. *School Bullying*, 47–80. DOI: 10.1017/CBO9781139226707.005

Sorrentino, A., Baldry, A. C., Farrington, D. P., & Blaya, C. (2019). Epidemiology of cyberbullying across europe: Differences between countries and genders. *Educational Sciences: Theory & Practice*, 19(2), 74–91. DOI: 10.12738/estp.2019.2.005

Special Need Alliance. (2015, March 24). *Bullying of the Special Needs Child and What Parents Can Do*. Special Needs Alliance. https://www.specialneedsalliance.org/the-voice/william-king-self-jr-cela-9/ (Accessed July 20, 2024).

Sprague, J. R., & Walker, H. M. (2021). *Safe and healthy schools: Practical prevention strategies*. Guilford Publications.

Sreckovic, M. A., Hume, K., & Able, H. (2017). Examining the efficacy of peer network interventions on the social interactions of high school students with autism spectrum disorder. *Journal of Autism and Developmental Disorders*, 47(8), 2556–2574. DOI: 10.1007/s10803-017-3171-8 PMID: 28567546

Sriandila, R., & Suryana, D. (2023). Exploring the Impact of Digital Devices on Social Development in Young Children. *AL-ISHLAH: Jurnal Pendidikan*, 15(2), 2230–2239. DOI: 10.35445/alishlah.v15i2.3735

St. Pierre, E. (2000). Post structural feminism in education: An overview. *International Journal of Qualitative Studies in Education : QSE*, 13(5), 477–515. DOI: 10.1080/09518390050156422

Stalikas, A., & Mertika, A. (2004). *The Therapeutic Alliance*. Ellinika Grammata.

Stannis, R. L., Crosland, K. A., Miltenberger, R., & Valbuena, D. (2019). Response to bullying (RTB): Behavioral skills and in situ training for individuals diagnosed with intellectual disabilities. *Journal of Applied Behavior Analysis*, 52(1), 73–83. DOI: 10.1002/jaba.501 PMID: 30168600

Stefanek, E., Strohmeier, D., & Yanagida, T. (2017). Depression in groups of bullies and victims: Evidence for the differential importance of peer status, reciprocal friends, school liking, academic self-efficacy, school motivation and academic achievement. *International Journal of Developmental Science*, 11(1–2), 31–43. DOI: 10.3233/DEV-160214

Sterzing, P. R., Shattuck, P. T., Narendorf, S. C., Wagner, M., & Cooper, B. P. (2012). Bullying involvement and autism spectrum disorders: Prevalence and correlates of bullying involvement among adolescents with an autism spectrum disorder. *Archives of Pediatrics & Adolescent Medicine*, 166(11), 1058–1064. DOI: 10.1001/archpediatrics.2012.790 PMID: 22945284

Stewart, J., & Bernard, M. E. (2023). Empowering the victims of bullying: the 'Bullying: The Power to Cope' program. *Journal of Evidence-Based Psychotherapies*, 23(2), 147–172. DOI: 10.24193/jebp.2023.2.15

Stickl Haugen, J., Sutter, C. C., Tinstman Jones, J. L., & Campbell, L. O. (2019). School district anti-bullying policies: A state-wide content analysis. *International Journal of Bullying Prevention : an Official Publication of the International Bullying Prevention Association*, 2(4), 309–323. DOI: 10.1007/s42380-019-00055-1

Stives, K. L., May, D. C., Mack, M., & Bethel, C. L. (2021, May). Understanding responses to bullying from the parent perspective. In Frontiers in Education (Vol. 6). Frontiers Media SA. https://doi.org/DOI: 10.3389/feduc.2021.642367

StopBullying.gov. (2023). *Bullying and youth with disabilities and special health needs*. StopBullying.gov. Retrieved April 22, 2024 from, https://www.stopbullying.gov/bullying/special-needs

STOPit Solutions. (2024). *STOPit: Anonymous Reporting System*. Retrieved from https://www.stopitsolutions.com

Strobel Education. (2024). *Climate culture in schools: Understanding the difference*. Retrieved April 22, 2024 from, https://strobeleducation.com/blog/climate-culture-in-schools-understanding-the- difference/

Strohmeier, D., Hoffmann, C., Schiller, E. M., Stefanek, E., & Spiel, C. (2012). ViSC social competence program. *New Directions for Youth Development*, 2012(133), 71–84. DOI: 10.1002/yd.20008 PMID: 22504792

Stuart-Cassel, V., Bell, A., & Springer, J. F. (2011). *Analysis of state bullying laws and policies*. U.S. Department of Education, Office of Planning, Evaluation and Policy Development, Policy and Program Studies Service., https://www2.ed.gov/rschstat/eval/bullying/state-bullying-laws/state-bullying-laws.pdf

Sullivan, T. N., Sutherland, K. S., Farrell, A. D., & Taylor, K. A. (2015). An evaluation of Second Step: What are the benefits for youth with and without disabilities? *Remedial and Special Education*, 36(5), 286–298. DOI: 10.1177/0741932515575616

Sun, C., Sun, B., Lin, Y., & Zhou, H. (2022). Problematic mobile phone use increases with the fear of missing out among college students: The effects of self-control, perceived social support and future orientation. *Psychology Research and Behavior Management*, 15, 1–8. DOI: 10.2147/PRBM.S345650 PMID: 35018126

Svetaz, M. V., Ireland, M., & Blum, R. (2000). Adolescents with learning disabilities: Risk and protective factors associated with emotional well-being: Findings from the National Longitudinal Study of Adolescent Health. *The Journal of Adolescent Health*, 27(5), 340–348. DOI: 10.1016/S1054-139X(00)00170-1 PMID: 11044706

Swanson, S., & Howell, C. (1996). Test anxiety in adolescents with learning disabilities and behavior disorders. *Exceptional Children*, 62(5), 389–389. DOI: 10.1177/001440299606200501

Swearer, S. M., & Givens, J. E. (2006). Designing an alternative to suspension for middle school bullies. Paper presented at the annual convention of the National Association of School Psychologists, Anaheim, CA.

Swearer, S. M., Espelage, D. L., & Napolitano, S. A. (2009). *Bullying prevention and intervention: Realistic strategies for schools*. Guilford.

Swearer, S. M., Wang, C., Maag, J. W., Siebecker, A. B., & Frerichs, L. J. (2012). Understanding the bullying dynamic among students in special and general education. *Journal of School Psychology*, 50(4), 503–520. DOI: 10.1016/j.jsp.2012.04.001 PMID: 22710018

Tahirkheli, H. (2022). *Special Education in Pakistan: Hope for Children with Special Needs | socialprotection.org*. Socialprotection.org. Retrieved September 3, 2024, from https://socialprotection.org/discover/blog/special-education-pakistan-hope-children-special-needs-0

Tawalbeh, A. H., Abueita, J. D., Mahasneh, A., & Shammout, N. (2015). Effectiveness of a counseling program to improve self-concept and achievement in bully-victims. *Review of European Studies*, 7(7). Advance online publication. DOI: 10.5539/res.v7n7p36

Taylor, D. (2022). *Bullying in Special Education: What it is and How to help*. Spero.academy. Retrieved September 2, 2024, from https://www.spero.academy/news/01gg8h7ys8dqvya21rbs5gxkrk/bullying-in-special-education-what-it-is-and-how-to-help

The Bully Project. (n.d.). *Tools for Parents*. https://www.thebullyproject.com/parents

Theobald, R., Goldhaber, D., Gratz, T., & Holden, K. (2017). Career and technical education, inclusion and postsecondary outcomes for students with learning disabilities. *Journal of Learning Disabilities*, 52(2), 109–119. DOI: 10.1177/0022219418775121 PMID: 29790412

Thodelius, C. (2022). Re-framing and exploring online suicidal games as a specific form of cyberbullying. *International Journal of Criminology and Sociology*, 9, 231–240. DOI: 10.6000/1929-4409.2020.09.21

Thompson, D., Whitney, I., & Smith, P. (2007). Bullying of children with special needs in mainstream schools. *Support for Learning*, 9(3), 103–106. DOI: 10.1111/j.1467-9604.1994.tb00168.x

Thornberg, R. (2015). The social dynamics of school bullying: The necessary dialogue between the blind men around the elephant and the possible meeting point at the social-ecological square. *Confero: Essays on Education. Philosophie Politique*, 3(2), 161–203. DOI: 10.3384/confero.2001-4562.1506245

Thornberg, R., Halldin, K., Bolmsjö, N., & Petersson, A. (2013). Victimising of school bullying: A grounded theory. *Research Papers in Education*, 28(3), 309–329. DOI: 10.1080/02671522.2011.641999

Thwaites, R., & Bennett-Levy, J. (2007). Conceptualizing empathy in cognitive behaviour therapy: Making the implicit explicit. *Behavioural and Cognitive Psychotherapy*, 35(05), 591–612. DOI: 10.1017/S1352465807003785

Tian, L., Huang, J., & Huebner, E. S. (2023). Profiles and transitions of cyberbullying perpetration and victimization from childhood to early adolescence: Multi-contextual risk and protective factors. *Journal of Youth and Adolescence*, 52(2), 434–448. DOI: 10.1007/s10964-022-01633-1 PMID: 35648261

Tippett, N., & Wolke, D. (2014). Socioeconomic status and bullying: A meta-analysis. *American Journal of Public Health*, 104(6), 48–59. DOI: 10.2105/AJPH.2014.301960 PMID: 24825231

Touloupis, T., & Athanasiades, C. (2014). The Risky Use of New Technology among Elementary School Students: Internet Addiction and Cyberbullying [in Greek]. *Hellenic Journal of Psychology*, 11, 83–110.

Touloupis, T., & Athanasiades, C. (2022). Cyberbullying and empathy among elementary school students: Do special educational needs make a difference? *Scandinavian Journal of Psychology*, 63(6), 609–623. DOI: 10.1111/sjop.12838 PMID: 35698831

Tripathi, I., Estabillo, J. A., Moody, C. T., & Laugeson, E. A. (2022). Long-term treatment outcomes of PEERS® for preschoolers: A parent-mediated social skills training program for children with autism spectrum disorder. *Journal of Autism and Developmental Disorders*, 52(6), 1–17. DOI: 10.1007/s10803-021-05147-w PMID: 34302574

Troop-Gordon, W., & Ladd, G. W. (2015). Teachers' victimization-related beliefs and strategies: Associations with students' aggressive behavior and peer victimization. *Journal of Abnormal Child Psychology*, 43(1), 45–60. DOI: 10.1007/s10802-013-9840-y PMID: 24362767

Ttofi, M. M., & Farrington, D. P. (2011). Effectiveness of school-based programs to reduce bullying: A systematic and meta-analytic review. *Journal of Experimental Criminology*, 7(1), 27–56. DOI: 10.1007/s11292-010-9109-1

Ttofi, M. M., Farrington, D. P., Losel, F., & Loeber, R. (2011). Do the victims of school bullies tend to become depressed later in life? A systematic review and meta-analysis of longitudinal studies. *Journal of Aggression, Conflict and Peace Research*, 3(2), 63–73. DOI: 10.1108/17596591111132873

Twemlow, S. W., & Fonagy, P. (2005). The prevalence of teachers who bully students in schools with differing levels of behavior problems. *The American Journal of Psychiatry*, 16(12), 2387–2389. DOI: 10.1176/appi.ajp.162.12.2387 PMID: 16330608

Twyman, K. A., Saylor, C. F., Saia, D., Macias, M. M., Taylor, L. A., & Spratt, E. (2010). Bullying and ostracism experiences in children with special health care needs. *Journal of Developmental and Behavioral Pediatrics*, 31(1), 1–8. DOI: 10.1097/DBP.0b013e3181c828c8 PMID: 20081430

Tzani-Pepelasi, C., Ioannou, M., Synnott, J., & McDonnell, D. (2019). Peer support at schools: The buddy approach as a prevention and intervention strategy for school bullying. *International Journal of Bullying Prevention : an Official Publication of the International Bullying Prevention Association*, 1(2), 111–123. DOI: 10.1007/s42380-019-00011-z

U.S. Department of Education [USDOE]. (2019). Student reports of bullying results from the 2017 school crime supplement to the national crime victimization survey. National Center for Educational Statistics [NCES]. Retrieved April 22, 2024, from https://nces.ed.gov/pubs2019/2019054.pdf

U.S. Department of Education [USDOE]. (2020). *Dear colleague letter regarding disability harassment*. Office of Civil Rights [OCR]. Retrieved April 22, 2024, from https://www2.ed.gov/about/offices/list/ocr/docs/disabharassltr.html

U.S. Department of Education. (2016, June 7). 2013-2014 Civil rights data collection: A first look. https://www2.ed.gov/about/offices/list/ocr/docs/2013-14-first-look.pdf

UNESCO. (2017). *A guide for ensuring inclusion and equity in education.* Author.

UNESCO. (2019, November 18). *Behind the numbers: Ending school violence and bullying.* Retrieved November 18, 2024, from https://www.unicef.org/media/66496/file/Behind-the-Numbers.pdf

UNESCO. (2020). *Pakistan is Using Innovative Approaches for Inclusive Education: GEM Report 2020.* Unesco.org. Retrieved July 25, 2024, from https://www.unesco.org/en/articles/pakistan-using-innovative-approaches-inclusive-education-gem-report-2020

UNESCO. (2023a). *Bullying rates higher for children with disabilities.* Unesco.org. Retrieved July 25, 2024, from https://www.unesco.org/en/articles/bullying-rates-higher-children-disabilities

UNESCO. (2023b). *School violence and bullying a major global issue, new UNESCO publication finds.* Retrieved July 29, 2024, from Unesco.org. https://www.unesco.org/en/articles/school-violence-and-bullying-major-global-issue-new-unesco-publication-finds

UNICEF. (2003). *Examples of Inclusive Education in Pakistan.* The United Nations Children's Fund.

UNICEF. (2023). *Bullying: What is it and how to stop it.* Unicef.org. Retrieved August 5, 2024, from https://www.unicef.org/parenting/child-care/bullying#understand

United Nations Educational & Organization. (2009). Policy guidelines on inclusion in education. In: UNESCO Paris.

United Nations. (2022). *Culture, Beliefs, and Disability.* Retrieved August 1, 2024, from https://www.un.org/esa/socdev/documents/disability/Toolkit/Cultures-Beliefs-Disability.pdf

Unnever, J. D., & Cornell, D. G. (2003). Bullying, self-control, and ADHD. *Journal of Interpersonal Violence*, 18(2), 129–147. DOI: 10.1177/0886260502238731

Unnever, J. D., & Cornell, D. G. (2004). Middle school victims of bullying: Who reports being bullied? *Aggressive Behavior*, 30(5), 373–388. DOI: 10.1002/ab.20030

Uzunboylu, H., Baglama, B., özer, N., Kucuktamer, T., & Kuimova, M. V. (2017). Opinions of school counselors about bullying in Turkish high schools. *Social Behavior and Personality*, 45(6), 1043–1055. DOI: 10.2224/sbp.6632

Van Cleave, J., & Davis, M. M. (2006). Bullying and peer victimization among children with special health care needs. *Pediatrics*, 118(4), e1212–e1219. DOI: 10.1542/peds.2005-3034 PMID: 17015509

Van Geel, M., Vedder, P., & Tanilon, J. (2014). Relationship between peer victimization, cyberbullying, and suicide in children and adolescents: A meta-analysis. *JAMA Pediatrics*, 168(5), 435–442. DOI: 10.1001/jamapediatrics.2013.4143 PMID: 24615300

Vanden Abeele, M., & De Cock, R. (2013). Cyberbullying by mobile phone among adolescents: The role of gender and peer group status. *Communications*, 38(1), 107–118. DOI: 10.1515/commun-2013-0006

Vasylenko, O., Chaikovskyi, M., Dobrovitska, O., Ostrovska, N., Kondratyuk, S., & Luchko, Y. (2022). Peculiarities of adaptive and rehabilitation processes of children with special educational needs. *Broad Research in Artificial Intelligence and Neuroscience*, 13(4), 398–420. DOI: 10.18662/brain/13.4/395

Verasammy, K.-J., & Cooper, M. (2021). Helpful aspects of counselling for young people who have experienced bullying: A thematic analysis. *British Journal of Guidance &amp. British Journal of Guidance & Counselling*, 49(3), 468–479. DOI: 10.1080/03069885.2021.1900777

Vessey, J. A., & O'Neill, K. M. (2011). Helping students with disabilities better address teasing and bullying situations: A MASNRN study. *The Journal of School Nursing: the Official Publication of the National Association of School Nurses*, 27(2), 139–148. DOI: 10.1177/1059840510386490 PMID: 20956579

Vilaseca, R., Rivero, M., Leiva, D., & Ferrer, F. (2023). Mothers' and fathers' parenting and other family context variables linked to developmental outcomes in young children with intellectual disability: A two-wave longitudinal study. *Journal of Developmental and Physical Disabilities*, 35(3), 387–416. DOI: 10.1007/s10882-022-09856-7

Vissing, Y. (2023). Children's Lives Are Different Today: More Reasons for Building a Children's Human Rights Framework. In *Children's Human Rights in the USA: Challenges and Opportunities* (pp. 147–178). Springer International Publishing. DOI: 10.1007/978-3-031-30848-2_7

Vlazan, A., & Pintea, S. (2021). The relationship between parenting styles, perceived social support and bullying: A cross-sectional retrospective study upon a sample of romanian students. *The Journal of School and University Medicine*. DOI: 10.51546/JSUM.2021.8101

Volk, A. A., Camilleri, J. A., Dane, A. V., & Marini, Z. A. (2012). Is adolescent bullying an evolutionary adaptation? *Aggressive Behavior*, 38(3), 222–238. DOI: 10.1002/ab.21418 PMID: 22331629

Volk, A. A., Dane, A. V., & Marini, Z. A. (2014). What is bullying? A theoretical redefinition. *Developmental Review*, 34(4), 327–343. DOI: 10.1016/j.dr.2014.09.001

Waasdorp, T. E., Bradshaw, C. P., & Leaf, P. J. (2012). The impact of schoolwide positive behavioral interventions and supports on bullying and peer rejection: A randomized controlled effectiveness trial. *Archives of Pediatrics & Adolescent Medicine*, 166(2), 149–156. DOI: 10.1001/archpediatrics.2011.755 PMID: 22312173

Wagner, H. R. (1983). *Phenomenology of Consciousness and Sociology of the Lifeworld: An Introductory Study*. The University of Alberta Press.

Walton, E. (2012). Using literature as a strategy to promote inclusivity in high school classrooms. *Intervention in School and Clinic*, 47(4), 224–233. DOI: 10.1177/1053451211424604

Walton, K. M., & Tiede, G. (2020). Brief report: Does "healthy" family functioning look different for families who have a child with autism? *Research in Autism Spectrum Disorders*, 72, 101527. Advance online publication. DOI: 10.1016/j.rasd.2020.101527 PMID: 32123539

Wanders, F. H., van der Veen, I., Dijkstra, A. B., & Maslowski, R. (2019). The influence of teacher-student and student-student relationships on societal involvement in Dutch primary and secondary schools. *Theory &amp. Theory and Research in Social Education*, 48(1), 101–119. DOI: 10.1080/00933104.2019.1651682

Wang, J. (2023). The Impacts and Interventions of School Bullying. In *SHS Web of Conferences* (Vol. 157, p. 04023). EDP Sciences. DOI: 10.1051/shsconf/202315704023

Wang, M. T., & Eccles, J. S. (2012). Social support matters: Longitudinal effects of social support on three dimensions of school engagement from middle to high school. *Child Development*, 83(3), 877–895. DOI: 10.1111/j.1467-8624.2012.01745.x PMID: 22506836

Wang, X., Wang, S., & Zeng, X. (2023). Does deviant peer affiliation accelerate adolescents' cyberbullying perpetration? Roles of moral disengagement and self-control. *Psychology in the Schools*, 60(12), 5025–5040. DOI: 10.1002/pits.23037

Wanti, L. P., Romadloni, A., Somantri, O., Sari, L., Prasetya, N. W. A., & Johanna, A. (2023). English learning assistance using interactive media for children with special needs to improve growth and development. *Pengabdian: JurnalAbdimas/Devotion. Journal of Community Service*, 1(2), 46–58.

Ward, B. R. (1995). The school's role in the prevention of youth suicide. *Social Work in Education*, 17(2), 92–100. DOI: 10.1093/cs/17.2.92

Ward, M. J. (2005). An historical perspective of self-determination in special education: Accomplishments and challenges. *Research and Practice for Persons with Severe Disabilities : the Journal of TASH*, 30(3), 108–112. DOI: 10.2511/rpsd.30.3.108

Waseem, M., & Nickerson, A. B. (2017). *Identifying and addressing bullying*. In StatPearls. StatPearls Publishing. https://www.ncbi.nlm.nih.gov/books/NBK441907/ (PMID: 28722959).

Watkins, C., & Wagner, P. (2000). *Improving school behaviour*. SAGE Publications Ltd., DOI: 10.4135/9781446219096

Watters, R. M. (2011). *The nature and extent of pupil bullying in schools in the North of Ireland*. Department of Education for Northern Ireland.

Werth, J. M. (2017). *Parent Perceptions of Social Vulnerability of Students with Disabilities: Experience of and Coping with Victimization*. [Doctoral Dissertation, State University of New York at Buffalo].

Whitted, K. S., & Dupper, D. R. (2005). Best practices for preventing or reducing bullying in schools. *Children &amp. Children & Schools*, 27(3), 167–175. DOI: 10.1093/cs/27.3.167

Wiener, J., & Mak, M. (2009). Peer victimization in children with attention-deficit/hyperactivity disorder. *Psychology in the Schools*, 46(2), 116–131. DOI: 10.1002/pits.20358

Wiener, J., & Schneider, B. H. (2002). A multisource exploration of the friendship patterns of children with and without learning disabilities. *Journal of Abnormal Child Psychology*, 30(2), 127–141. DOI: 10.1023/A:1014701215315 PMID: 12002394

Wiener, M. T., Day, S. J., & Galvan, D. (2013). Deaf and hard of hearing students' perspective on bullying and school climate. *American Annals of the Deaf*, 158(3), 324–343. DOI: 10.1353/aad.2013.0029

Windsor, S., Maxwell, G., & Antonsen, Y. (2022). Incorporating sustainable development and inclusive education in teacher education for the Arctic. *Polar Geography*, 45(4), 246–259. DOI: 10.1080/1088937X.2022.2105970

Winters, R. R., Blake, J. J., & Chen, S. (2018). Bully victimization among children with attention-deficit/hyperactivity disorder: A longitudinal examination of behavioral phenotypes. *Journal of Emotional and Behavioral Disorders*, 28(2), 80–91. DOI: 10.1177/1063426618814724

Wolke, D., Copeland, W. E., Angold, A. C., & Costello, E. (2013). Impact of bullying in on adult health, wealth, crime, and social outcomes. *Psychological Science*, 24(10), 1958–1970. DOI: 10.1177/0956797613481608 PMID: 23959952

Wolke, D., Woods, S., Bloomfield, L., & Karstadt, L. (2000). The association between direct and relational bullying and behaviour problems among primary school children. *Journal of Child Psychology and Psychiatry, and Allied Disciplines*, 41(8), 989–1002. DOI: 10.1111/1469-7610.00687 PMID: 11099116

Wood, C., & Orpinas, P. (2020). Victimization of children with disabilities: Coping strategies and protective factors. *Disability & Society*, 36(9), 1469–1488. DOI: 10.1080/09687599.2020.1802578

Woods, S., & Wolke, D. (2003). Does the content of anti-bullying policies inform us about the prevalence of direct and relational bullying behaviour in primary schools? *Educational Psychology*, 23(4), 381–401. DOI: 10.1080/01443410303215

Woods, S., & Wolke, D. (2004). Direct and relational bullying among primary school children and academic achievement. *Journal of School Psychology*, 42(2), 135–155. DOI: 10.1016/j.jsp.2003.12.002

World Health Organization. (1980). *International classification of impairments, disabilities, and handicaps: a manual of classification relating to the consequences of disease, published in accordance with resolution WHA29. 35 of the Twenty-ninth World Health Assembly, May 1976*. World Health Organization.

World Health Organization. (2001). World Health Organization. (2001). International Classification of Functioning, Disability and Health (ICF). Geneva: World Health Organisation. *Int Classif*.

Wright, M. F. (2020). *School Bullying and Students with Intellectual Disabilities*. Accessibility and Diversity in Education., DOI: 10.4018/978-1-7998-1213-5.ch019

Wu, X., Zhen, R., Shen, L., Tan, R., & Zhou, X. (2023). Patterns of elementary school students' bullying victimization: Roles of family and individual factors. *Journal of Interpersonal Violence*, 38(4), 2410–2431. DOI: 10.1177/08862605221101190 PMID: 35576274

Yeager, D. S., & Dweck, C. S. (2012). Mindsets that promote resilience: When students believe that personal characteristics can be developed. *Educational Psychologist*, 47(4), 302–314. DOI: 10.1080/00461520.2012.722805

Yen, C. F., Yang, P., Wang, P. W., Lin, H. C., Liu, T. L., Wu, Y. Y., & Tang, T. C. (2014). Association between school bullying levels/types and mental health problems among Taiwanese adolescents. *Comprehensive Psychiatry*, 55(3), 405–413. DOI: 10.1016/j.comppsych.2013.06.001 PMID: 24529472

Yeung, R., & Leadbeater, B. (2010). Adults make a difference: The protective effects of parent and teacher emotional support on emotional and behavioral problems of peer-victimized adolescents. *Journal of Community Psychology*, 38(1), 80–98. DOI: 10.1002/jcop.20353

Yoon, J. S. (2004). Predicting teacher interventions in bullying situations. *Education & Treatment of Children*, 27(1), 37–45.

Yoon, J. S., & Kerber, K. (2003). Bullying: Elementary teachers' attitudes and intervention strategies. *Research in Education*, 69(1), 27–35. DOI: 10.7227/RIE.69.3

Yoon, J., & Bauman, S. (2014). Teachers: A critical but overlooked component of bullying prevention and intervention. *Theory into Practice*, 53(4), 308–314. DOI: 10.1080/00405841.2014.947226

Yoon, J., Sulkowski, M. L., & Bauman, S. A. (2016). Teachers' responses to bullying incidents: Effects of teacher characteristics and contexts. *Journal of School Violence*, 15(1), 91–113. DOI: 10.1080/15388220.2014.963592

Younan, B. (2019). A systematic review of bullying definitions: How definition and format affect study outcome. *Journal of Aggression, Conflict and Peace Research*, 11(2), 109–115. DOI: 10.1108/JACPR-02-2018-0347

Young, J., Ne'eman, A., & Gelser, S. (2012). *Bullying and Students with Disabilities: A Briefing Paper from the National Council on Disability*. National Council on Disability.

Yudin, B. M. (2019). *Keeping students with disabilities safe from bullying*. StopBullying.gov. Retrieved April 22, 2024, from https://www.stopbullying.gov/blog/2013/08/23/keeping-students-disabilities-safe- bullying

Zablotsky, B., Bradshaw, C. P., Anderson, C. M., & Law, P. (2014). Risk factors for bullying among children with autism spectrum disorders. *Autism*, 18(4), 419–427. DOI: 10.1177/1362361313477920 PMID: 23901152

Zablotsky, B., Bradshaw, C. P., Anderson, C., & Law, P. A. (2013). The association between bullying and the psychological functioning of children with autism spectrum disorders. *Journal of developmental and behavioral pediatrics. Journal of Developmental and Behavioral Pediatrics*, 34(1), 1–8. DOI: 10.1097/DBP.0b013e31827a7c3a PMID: 23275052

Zahid, S., & Fatima, S. (2023, November 27). *Encountering Stigma in Special Education Research - Ideas*. Ideas. Retrieved September 15, 2024, from https://ideasdev.org/the-fieldwork-diaries/encountering-stigma-in-special-education-research/

Zhang, H., & Chen, C. (2023). "They just want us to exist as a trash can": Parents of children with autism spectrum disorder and their perspectives to school-based bullying victimization. *Contemporary School Psychology*, 27(1), 8–18.

Zhao, Q. (2023). Relationship between parenting styles and school bullying behaviour among adolescents. *SHS Web of Conferences*. DOI: 10.1051/shsconf/202318002030

Zhou, Z., Tang, H., Tian, Y., Wei, H., Zhang, F., & Morrison, C. M. (2013). Cyberbullying and its risk factors among Chinese high school students. *School Psychology International*, 34(6), 630–647. DOI: 10.1177/0143034313479692

Zych, I., Farrington, D. P., Llorent, V. J., & Ttofi, M. M. (2017). School bullying in different countries: Prevalence, risk factors, and short-term outcomes. *SpringerBriefs in Psychology*, 5–22. DOI: 10.1007/978-3-319-53028-4_2

Zych, I., Ortega-Ruiz, R., & Del Rey, R. (2015). Scientific research on bullying and cyberbullying: Where have we been and where are we going. *Aggression and Violent Behavior*, 24, 188–198. DOI: 10.1016/j.avb.2015.05.015

About the Contributors

Sohni Siddiqui has completed her Ph.D. at the Department of Educational Psychology, Technische Universität Berlin, dedicates her research to the professional development of educators, with a particular focus on addressing challenges related to antisocial bullying and cyberbullying within educational environments. Her diverse research portfolio extends to inclusive education, technology integration in education, sustainability in higher education, gender discrimination in educational settings, and parenting practices, all with notable achievements. Additionally, she has contributed as an external reviewer for numerous esteemed international journals and currently serves as a Guest Associate Editor for Frontiers in Education. With a track record of successfully completing and publishing over 30 research studies in reputable international journals, Siddiqui has established herself as a proficient and accomplished researcher.

Mahwish Kamaran holds a PhD in Education (Special Education/Inclusive Education) from Iqra University. After completing her M.Phil. and Ph.D. research based on children with disabilities and promoting inclusive educational practices. She came up with a Praxis Inclusive Education Model which she will implement to promote inclusive educational practices. She has been conducting professional development workshops for teachers. She has presented her research papers at many international and national conferences. She has published many research papers in international journals. Also, she is an author of a book chapter. She is a part of research projects including NRPU's project. Other areas of interest are curriculum development, qualitative research, thematic analysis, bullying and cyberbullying.. Currently Editor at "Frontiers in Education".

***

Anastasia Alevriadou is Professor of Psychology of Special Education at the Aristotle University of Thessaloniki– Greece. She has published more than 150 articles in Greek and international journals, 5 books and 6 chapters in American books on these issues, and many conference proceedings. She has also participated in many European and International conferences. She is a member of many Greeks and International Associations of Psychology and Special Education. Fulbright Scholar in psychology/special education in 2019, Nisonger Center of Developmental Disabilities, OSU, USA. Visiting Professor in USA, Czech Republic and Cyprus.

Julianna Casella is a Ph.D. candidate in Counseling Psychology and School Psychology at the University at Buffalo. She is also a research assistant at the Alberti Center for Bullying Abuse Prevention. She is currently completing her pre-doctoral internship at the University of Maryland with the National Center for School Mental Health. She earned a bachelor's degree in biology and psychology with a minor in writing from Stony Brook University. She is interested in school crisis prevention and intervention, with an emphasis on promoting positive school climates for all students.

Vasiliki Folia earned her graduate degree from the Department of Psychology at Aristotle University of Thessaloniki and holds a master's degree in Cognitive Neuroscience from Radboud University, The Netherlands. Her PhD, completed at Karolinska Institutet, Department of Clinical Cognitive Neuroscience, Sweden, focused on Implicit Learning of Artificial Grammars/Syntax via neuroimaging and neurophysiological methods (fMRI, EEG and rTMS). Following her doctoral studies, Dr. Folia taught at the Amsterdam University of Applied Sciences (AUAS), as an Assistant Pofessor from 2009 to 2012; and as an Associate Professor from 2013 to 2018. She also served as a Research Chair from 2016 to 2018. She joined the Department of Psychology in Aristotle University in 2021. Her primary research interests lie in the field of neuropsychology of language, both in healthy and clinical populations. Specifically, her work revolves around investigating neural language mechanisms, serial language processing, implicit learning and other cognitive functions that contribute to syntactic and linguistic ability. To achieve these objectives, she employs a combination of behavioral/neuropsychological, neurophysiological, and neuroimaging methods.

Marie Gomez Goff is an Assistant Professor in the Department of Teaching and Learning at Southeastern Louisiana University in Hammond, Louisiana. In addition to teaching undergraduate- and graduate-level courses in the areas of special education, early intervention, early childhood education, and educational leadership, Dr. Goff also currently serves as an academic advisor and mentor for aspiring teacher candidates.

Afroditi Malisiova is an EFL teacher and a Ph.D. candidate in the Department of Psychology at Aristotle University of Thessaloniki, Greece. She holds a degree in English Language and Literature from the Aristotle University of Thessaloniki, a Master's degree in Teaching English as a Foreign Language (TEFL) from the Hellenic Open University, and a Master of Science in Educational Psychology from the University of Neapolis, Pafos. Since 2005, she has been working as an English language teacher in both the private and state sectors of Greek primary and secondary schools. Her research interests lie in the fields of teaching English as a foreign language, cognitive psychology, special education, and intercultural education.

Afaf Manzoor a gold medalist, is a social scientist with 20 years of teaching, research, and leadership skills. She is the first female Pakistani to complete a Post-Doctorate in Inclusion and Special Needs at the University College London, UK, awarded by the Punjab Higher Education Commission, Pakistan. At present, she is serving as an Assistant Professor at the Division of Education, University of Lahore. Dr. Afaf is an inclusion advisor, international speaker, special needs consultant. She is also one of Pakistan's top proponents of the inclusive education movement especially for disabilities. She is a well- known and experienced educationist, who also serves as principal and co-principal investigator for various research projects at National and international levels. She has presented proposals, research designs, and implementation of evidence-based investigations, data analyses, report preparation, and consultation and coordination with regulatory authorities. She practiced excellent skills in leading, organizing and managing study participant recruitment and retention to achieve project goals. She is a unique individual in Pakistan who began her journey as a special education teacher and rose to the top of her profession as HET (Higher Education Teacher). Propelling her passion, she worked as administrator in the districts of Lahore, Sheikhupura, and Kasur and revitalized many schools. Her transformational leadership in the field laid foundations for her elevated impact at university level, where she designed various courses and scheme of studies for teacher education programs with a focus on revamping teacher education and preparation of future teachers for the inclusion of diverse learners. Recognized for her exceptional contributions, she received numerous accolades and holds esteemed potions such as Chairperson Disability Inclusion Council, Pakistan Health Parliament; Associate of Center for Inclusive Education at University College London.; Board of Directors, Comparative Education Society of Asia CESA. Her extensive international engagements, including several research publications in HEC & International recognized journals, 35+ research presentation and keynote sessions underscore her commitment to global educational advancement. Dr. Manzoor is also practicing as Consultant Special Needs and Disabilities Rehabilitation. Through this platform she is trying to put her research into practice and to serve community by delivering various assessment, intervention and rehabilitation protocols. Her journey is full of success stories of life transformations for persons with disabilities and their families. Additional to above, she possesses excellent skills for speaking on TV shows, Podcast and other social media platforms. Her multiple appearance on TV has added her public recognition where she spreads awareness and reach out public on various topics related to education, health, carrier and job planning, disabilities, life transition and rehabilitation. She can also be reached through LinkedIn, YouTube, Research-Gate, Academia and Google Scholar @ Afaf Manzoor

Amanda B. Nickerson, Ph.D., NCSP is a professor of school psychology and director of the Alberti Center for Bullying Abuse Prevention at the University at Buffalo, the State University of New York. Her research focuses on school crisis prevention and intervention, violence and bullying prevention, and building social-emotional strengths of youth.

Asimenia Papoulidi holds a PhD in Developmental Psychology from Panteion University of Social and Political Sciences. She holds a bachelor's degree in Psychology from the same university, as well as a degree in Communication from the Open University of the UK. Additionally, she holds a master's degree in Child and Adolescent Mental Health from University College London (Institute of Child Health) and has been trained in the Child and Adolescent Mental Health Service at Great Ormond Street Hospital (NHS Trust-UK). Currently, she is a postdoctoral researcher at the Department of Social Work at the University of West Attica. She is teaching psychology courses at the University of West Attica and the Hellenic Open University as Collaborating Teaching Staff. She also works as a School Psychologist in Primary Education. She has participated in national and international funded research programs (Horizon), in collaboration with other universities in Greece and abroad. Her scientific and research work has been published in Greek and international scientific journals and books, and she has performed oral presentations at scientific conferences.

Hannah Rapp, PhD, is a Postdoctoral Research Associate at the Alberti Center for Bullying Abuse Prevention which is located at the State University of New York at Buffalo. Her research centers on bullying abuse among individuals with learning disorders and developmental disabilities, and social and emotional learning. In her free time, she enjoys playing ultimate frisbee, eating ice cream, and spending quality time with friends and family.

Thanos Touloupis is an Assistant Professor in "Educational Psychology" at the Department of Primary Education of the University of the Aegean. He has graduated from the Department of Primary Education of the University of Thessaly, while he has followed Master's, Doctoral and Postdoctoral studies at the Department of Psychology of the Aristotle University of Thessaloniki (Section of Developmental and School Psychology). He has worked as a Laboratory Teaching Staff (E.D.I.P.) in "Educational Psychology" at the Department of Psychology of the University of Western Macedonia, and as a contractual Lecturer/Academic Scholar at Higher Educational Institutions in both Greece and Cyprus. Furthermore, he has many years of teaching experience in Primary Schools of Mainstream and Special Education. His research interests focus on problematic online behavior of school and university student populations with and without special educational needs, on socio-emotional and academic factors associated with this behavior, as well as on sexually inclusive education. Additionally, he is interested in the interdisciplinary implementation of related prevention programs in the school community. His scientific work has been published and presented in international and Greek scientific journals and conferences respectively.

Index

A

Acceptance 11, 22, 30, 47, 99, 101, 141, 168, 170, 174, 180, 186, 193, 199, 200, 201, 208, 219, 225, 238, 253, 255, 258, 267, 269, 279, 280, 282, 283, 284, 286, 290, 291, 292, 293, 294, 295, 297, 301, 302
Adolescence 16, 28, 30, 39, 57, 60, 87, 90, 97, 121, 147, 149, 206, 207, 210, 241, 252, 271, 275, 298, 300
Adolescent Health 55, 151, 216, 246, 274
Antibullying Intervention 32, 60, 123, 181, 231, 246
Anxiety 1, 2, 3, 4, 5, 6, 7, 8, 12, 13, 14, 16, 17, 18, 21, 22, 24, 25, 26, 40, 46, 47, 49, 66, 67, 70, 71, 72, 73, 74, 76, 77, 78, 79, 82, 83, 84, 87, 88, 90, 91, 94, 131, 138, 177, 191, 211, 217, 218, 219, 220, 239, 241, 244, 246, 256, 264, 282, 298
Attention Deficit Hyperactivity Disorder 65, 66, 67, 70, 72, 85, 91, 189, 219, 220
Autism 2, 5, 6, 7, 12, 19, 22, 32, 33, 41, 42, 44, 55, 57, 58, 65, 66, 67, 68, 70, 71, 72, 73, 76, 78, 79, 82, 85, 87, 88, 89, 90, 91, 92, 117, 127, 129, 132, 144, 145, 146, 147, 148, 149, 150, 151, 152, 153, 154, 167, 168, 189, 207, 210, 212, 219, 226, 238, 239, 240, 242, 245, 246, 247, 253, 254, 277, 296, 298, 299, 301, 302
Autism Spectrum Disorder 2, 5, 6, 19, 22, 32, 41, 44, 55, 57, 58, 65, 66, 70, 71, 72, 73, 79, 85, 87, 88, 89, 90, 91, 127, 129, 147, 150, 152, 153, 154, 168, 189, 219, 226, 239, 240, 245, 246, 254, 296, 298, 301, 302

B

Bully 27, 28, 31, 39, 40, 46, 48, 53, 56, 60, 74, 76, 88, 93, 94, 95, 98, 99, 108, 112, 115, 117, 126, 131, 133, 135, 136, 137, 139, 144, 147, 149, 153, 170, 173, 205, 206, 212, 216, 226, 238, 245, 247, 251, 252, 257, 262, 277, 281, 285, 294, 295
Bullying 1, 2, 3, 4, 5, 6, 7, 8, 9, 10, 11, 12, 13, 14, 15, 16, 18, 19, 20, 21, 22, 23, 24, 25, 26, 27, 28, 29, 30, 31, 32, 33, 35, 36, 37, 38, 39, 40, 41, 42, 43, 44, 45, 46, 47, 48, 49, 50, 51, 52, 53, 54, 55, 56, 57, 58, 59, 60, 61, 62, 63, 65, 66, 67, 68, 69, 70, 71, 72, 73, 74, 75, 76, 77, 78, 79, 81, 82, 83, 84, 85, 86, 87, 88, 89, 90, 91, 92, 93, 94, 95, 96, 97, 98, 99, 100, 101, 102, 103, 104, 105, 106, 107, 108, 109, 110, 111, 112, 113, 114, 115, 116, 117, 118, 119, 120, 121, 122, 123, 124, 125, 126, 127, 128, 129, 130, 131, 132, 133, 134, 135, 136, 137, 138, 139, 140, 141, 142, 143, 144, 145, 146, 147, 148, 149, 150, 151, 152, 153, 154, 155, 156, 157, 158, 159, 164, 167, 169, 170, 171, 172, 173, 176, 177, 178, 180, 181, 182, 183, 185, 186, 187, 188, 189, 190, 191, 192, 193, 194, 195, 196, 197, 198, 199, 200, 202, 203, 205, 206, 207, 208, 209, 210, 211, 212, 213, 215, 216, 217, 218, 219, 220, 221, 222, 223, 224, 225, 226, 227, 228, 229, 230, 231, 232, 233, 234, 235, 236, 237, 238, 239, 240, 241, 242, 243, 244, 245, 246, 247, 249, 250, 251, 252, 253, 254, 255, 256, 257, 258, 259, 260, 261, 262, 265, 266, 267, 268, 269, 270, 271, 272, 273, 274, 275, 276, 277, 278, 295, 296, 297, 298, 299, 300, 301, 302
Bullying Prevention 28, 31, 52, 56, 90, 102, 106, 113, 116, 121, 122, 124, 125, 127, 134, 135, 136, 137, 140, 143, 145, 149, 150, 151, 181, 183, 186, 196, 202, 203, 209, 210, 211, 217, 218, 221, 231, 234, 235, 236, 237, 240, 241, 244, 258, 259, 261, 267, 269, 273, 299

Bullying Victimization 9, 29, 32, 41, 42, 43, 52, 55, 58, 71, 75, 77, 81, 82, 83, 84, 87, 89, 91, 125, 126, 127, 128, 129, 130, 133, 134, 136, 139, 141, 142, 143, 146, 147, 148, 150, 154, 172, 176, 198, 219, 223, 236, 240, 241, 242, 243, 246, 247, 254, 272, 300

C

Case Study 4, 7, 12, 13, 22, 24, 27, 30, 117, 155, 158, 159, 160, 162
Children 2, 6, 9, 10, 14, 19, 23, 28, 29, 31, 32, 33, 35, 36, 37, 38, 39, 40, 41, 42, 43, 44, 45, 46, 47, 48, 49, 50, 51, 52, 53, 54, 55, 56, 57, 58, 59, 60, 61, 62, 68, 70, 73, 74, 76, 77, 78, 79, 83, 87, 88, 90, 91, 92, 93, 94, 95, 96, 97, 98, 99, 100, 101, 102, 103, 104, 105, 106, 107, 108, 109, 110, 111, 112, 113, 114, 115, 116, 117, 119, 120, 123, 124, 125, 126, 127, 128, 129, 130, 131, 132, 133, 134, 135, 136, 137, 138, 140, 141, 142, 143, 144, 145, 146, 147, 148, 149, 150, 151, 152, 153, 154, 155, 156, 157, 158, 159, 160, 162, 163, 164, 165, 166, 167, 168, 169, 170, 171, 172, 173, 174, 175, 176, 177, 178, 180, 181, 182, 202, 205, 207, 208, 209, 210, 211, 212, 218, 219, 222, 224, 226, 230, 231, 232, 234, 236, 237, 238, 240, 241, 242, 243, 245, 246, 247, 249, 250, 251, 252, 253, 254, 255, 256, 257, 261, 262, 266, 268, 269, 271, 272, 273, 274, 275, 276, 278, 280, 281, 295, 296, 297, 299, 300, 301
Children with Learning Disabilities 115, 157, 158, 164, 165, 169, 171
Children with Special Needs 29, 35, 36, 37, 38, 39, 40, 41, 42, 43, 44, 45, 46, 47, 48, 49, 50, 53, 56, 61, 93, 94, 95, 96, 97, 98, 99, 101, 102, 103, 104, 105, 106, 107, 108, 109, 110, 111, 112, 113, 114, 115, 119, 124, 163, 164, 165, 167, 168, 169, 170, 175, 182, 207, 218, 231, 236, 237, 241

Cognitive Functions 3, 4, 11, 18, 25, 26
Collaboration 21, 23, 24, 125, 127, 142, 143, 160, 196, 197, 198, 199, 200, 201, 202, 203, 208, 222, 239, 250, 251, 257, 261, 266
Comparative Study 29, 279, 302
Counseling 21, 22, 112, 122, 134, 195, 222, 250, 258, 259, 260, 261, 262, 263, 264, 265, 266, 267, 268, 269, 270, 272, 273, 274, 277
Counselor 22, 106, 108, 228, 259, 260, 263, 264, 265, 268, 270, 274
Cyberbully 285, 286, 288, 289, 290, 291, 292, 294
Cyber-Victim 285, 286, 288, 289, 290, 291, 292, 294

D

Depression 1, 2, 7, 8, 12, 13, 18, 21, 22, 25, 26, 40, 46, 47, 49, 66, 67, 71, 72, 73, 75, 77, 78, 79, 83, 84, 87, 88, 97, 105, 133, 191, 217, 218, 219, 239, 240, 244, 245, 256, 257, 276, 298
Disability 19, 31, 36, 38, 39, 41, 42, 43, 44, 45, 50, 52, 53, 54, 59, 62, 63, 66, 70, 72, 87, 90, 94, 97, 126, 127, 129, 134, 136, 137, 138, 139, 141, 143, 144, 145, 146, 147, 148, 150, 151, 152, 153, 156, 164, 167, 170, 176, 178, 182, 187, 188, 189, 192, 201, 205, 206, 208, 210, 211, 212, 213, 219, 225, 237, 238, 243, 244, 247, 254, 255, 275, 296
Disability Harassment 187, 188, 212, 213

E

Education 2, 3, 4, 6, 10, 12, 14, 19, 20, 27, 28, 29, 31, 37, 39, 40, 41, 44, 45, 47, 48, 49, 50, 51, 52, 53, 54, 55, 56, 57, 58, 59, 60, 61, 62, 63, 66, 74, 88, 93, 95, 100, 101, 102, 103, 106, 110, 111, 113, 115, 116, 117, 119, 120, 121, 122, 123, 124, 126, 127, 128, 129, 134, 135, 136, 137, 140, 141, 143, 144, 145, 146, 147, 148, 149,

151, 152, 153, 154, 155, 156, 157, 158, 159, 160, 162, 163, 167, 168, 169, 170, 172, 174, 176, 177, 178, 179, 180, 181, 182, 186, 187, 188, 191, 192, 194, 195, 197, 198, 205, 206, 209, 210, 211, 212, 215, 216, 217, 220, 221, 222, 224, 225, 226, 227, 238, 239, 240, 241, 242, 244, 245, 246, 247, 250, 253, 254, 258, 268, 269, 270, 272, 273, 275, 276, 277, 278, 280, 281, 285, 292, 294, 297, 299, 300, 302

Educators 26, 37, 39, 45, 48, 51, 60, 101, 104, 111, 128, 129, 155, 156, 158, 169, 171, 183, 185, 186, 190, 193, 195, 197, 198, 199, 200, 203, 209, 220, 249, 250, 253, 258, 260, 261, 266, 267

Elementary Schools 120, 179, 188, 280, 284

Emotional Distress 2, 6, 8, 9, 12, 13, 15, 16, 18, 26, 95, 186, 190

F

Fear of Missing Out 279, 280, 286, 296, 298, 299, 300, 301, 302

Forms of Bullying 38, 96, 185, 186, 188, 189, 190, 198, 203, 262

H

High Functioning Autistic Spectrum Disorder 280

I

Inclusion 21, 22, 30, 53, 55, 68, 80, 86, 93, 98, 99, 100, 114, 123, 125, 127, 141, 144, 148, 151, 155, 156, 157, 158, 159, 160, 164, 172, 173, 174, 176, 178, 179, 182, 183, 190, 196, 205, 208, 209, 211, 215, 217, 220, 222, 223, 224, 225, 226, 227, 238, 239, 240, 244, 246, 251, 254, 255, 257, 266, 267, 273, 277

Interventions 1, 3, 4, 7, 12, 13, 19, 20, 21, 24, 25, 26, 27, 28, 30, 48, 50, 51, 55, 57, 67, 86, 93, 95, 96, 97, 98, 102, 106, 110, 111, 112, 113, 114, 115, 118, 123, 124, 125, 126, 127, 128, 129, 132, 139, 141, 142, 143, 144, 145, 146, 151, 185, 198, 199, 203, 206, 218, 239, 241, 246, 249, 250, 251, 253, 256, 257, 258, 259, 261, 262, 274

L

Learning Disabilities 1, 2, 10, 13, 29, 41, 55, 72, 79, 88, 94, 115, 139, 155, 156, 157, 158, 159, 164, 165, 168, 169, 171, 179, 182, 189, 209, 216, 219, 220, 225, 243, 244, 246, 253, 269, 274, 278

Literature Review 1, 20, 29, 37, 80, 89, 129, 157, 173, 178, 186, 241, 242, 243, 249, 283

M

Mental Health 1, 2, 8, 9, 11, 13, 14, 15, 18, 26, 30, 32, 39, 45, 46, 52, 55, 58, 60, 66, 67, 86, 92, 94, 95, 112, 116, 117, 122, 149, 151, 191, 206, 239, 253, 256, 270, 298

N

Neurodiversity 65, 66, 67, 68

P

Pakistan 1, 32, 35, 36, 37, 38, 42, 43, 44, 45, 46, 47, 48, 49, 50, 52, 53, 56, 57, 58, 59, 60, 61, 62, 93, 94, 97, 98, 99, 100, 101, 102, 103, 104, 110, 111, 112, 114, 115, 116, 118, 119, 120, 121, 122, 123, 155, 157, 162, 163, 172, 173, 174, 177, 178, 179, 180, 181, 182, 246

Parent 30, 71, 77, 78, 83, 84, 87, 113, 126, 127, 129, 130, 131, 134, 135, 136, 137, 140, 142, 143, 144, 145, 148, 149, 152, 153, 170, 202, 224, 240, 243

Pedagogical Practices 155, 156, 157, 158, 159, 160, 162, 164, 173

Peer Bullying 29, 38, 53, 55, 57, 215, 216,

217, 218, 219, 220, 221, 222, 223, 224, 225, 226, 227, 228, 229, 230, 232, 233, 234, 235, 236, 237, 239, 241, 244, 272
Peer Support 9, 11, 15, 17, 21, 22, 26, 51, 113, 115, 117, 172, 181, 183, 196, 200, 201, 203, 240, 258, 259, 282, 283, 297
Perceived Peer Acceptance 279, 280, 282, 283, 284, 286, 290, 291, 292, 293, 294, 295, 301
Perpetrator 40, 88, 199, 262
Prevention and Intervention Strategies 215, 235, 237, 273

S

School Avoidance 2, 7, 16, 18, 26, 40
School-Based Intervention 121, 233, 244
School Bullying 42, 52, 53, 55, 57, 58, 61, 62, 63, 68, 70, 71, 73, 74, 75, 76, 77, 78, 86, 87, 88, 89, 91, 92, 117, 119, 121, 122, 123, 128, 133, 136, 137, 149, 177, 181, 186, 211, 243, 250, 251, 252, 256, 257, 259, 269, 270, 271, 272, 275, 276, 278, 301
School Climate and Culture 192, 194
School Violence 43, 53, 58, 62, 119, 124, 149, 207, 209, 241, 242, 243, 273
Self-Esteem 8, 9, 10, 11, 12, 13, 14, 18, 24, 26, 41, 44, 48, 66, 71, 77, 78, 83, 87, 94, 105, 127, 132, 190, 191, 200, 217, 218, 219, 228, 236, 239, 255, 256, 257
Social and Cultural Factors 35
Social Isolation 7, 9, 10, 11, 12, 13, 17, 46, 85, 96, 141, 226, 286, 297
Special Educational Needs 27, 28, 29, 31, 35, 37, 42, 44, 45, 46, 47, 50, 51, 54, 70, 82, 92, 117, 123, 147, 150, 156, 159, 160, 162, 167, 168, 175, 176, 237, 249, 251, 253, 268, 269, 270, 271, 272, 275, 285, 295, 300
Students 1, 2, 3, 4, 5, 6, 7, 8, 9, 10, 11, 12, 13, 14, 15, 16, 17, 18, 19, 20, 21, 22, 23, 24, 25, 26, 27, 28, 29, 31, 32, 36, 39, 40, 41, 42, 43, 44, 45, 46, 48, 49, 50, 53, 56, 57, 58, 59, 61, 62, 63, 65, 66, 70, 72, 81, 82, 84, 85, 86, 88, 91, 92, 94, 95, 96, 98, 99, 100, 105, 106, 107, 108, 109, 112, 113, 114, 115, 116, 117, 118, 120, 123, 127, 128, 133, 134, 135, 138, 139, 142, 143, 144, 145, 146, 147, 148, 149, 150, 151, 152, 153, 154, 155, 156, 158, 159, 160, 164, 166, 167, 168, 169, 170, 171, 172, 173, 174, 176, 178, 179, 182, 183, 185, 186, 187, 188, 189, 190, 191, 192, 193, 194, 195, 196, 197, 198, 199, 200, 201, 202, 203, 205, 206, 207, 208, 210, 211, 212, 213, 215, 216, 217, 218, 219, 220, 221, 222, 223, 224, 225, 226, 227, 228, 229, 230, 231, 232, 233, 234, 235, 236, 237, 238, 239, 240, 241, 242, 244, 245, 246, 247, 249, 250, 251, 252, 253, 254, 255, 256, 257, 258, 259, 260, 261, 262, 263, 264, 265, 266, 267, 268, 269, 270, 271, 272, 273, 274, 275, 276, 278, 279, 280, 281, 282, 283, 284, 285, 286, 287, 288, 289, 290, 291, 292, 293, 294, 295, 296, 297, 298, 300
Students with Disabilities 2, 27, 31, 32, 44, 45, 53, 58, 59, 94, 114, 116, 117, 127, 128, 138, 139, 143, 144, 146, 147, 148, 149, 151, 153, 154, 156, 164, 167, 169, 172, 178, 186, 189, 192, 193, 194, 195, 198, 205, 206, 208, 210, 211, 213, 239, 240, 242, 247, 270, 274, 275, 276
Students with Special Needs 16, 57, 95, 98, 99, 112, 113, 171, 176, 185, 186, 187, 188, 189, 190, 191, 192, 193, 194, 195, 196, 197, 198, 200, 201, 203, 205, 215, 216, 217, 218, 219, 220, 221, 222, 223, 224, 225, 226, 227, 229, 230, 235, 236, 237, 272
Student-teacher relationship 20, 252, 261, 272

V

Victim 27, 28, 31, 39, 40, 74, 76, 83, 84, 85, 88, 105, 108, 117, 130, 137, 144, 176, 187, 191, 199, 206, 216, 235, 238,

262, 280, 281, 285, 286, 288, 289, 290, 291, 292, 294, 295, 298